Mastering Corporate Tax

Carolina Academic Press Mastering Series
Russell Weaver, Series Editor

Mastering Administrative Law
William R. Andersen

Mastering Adoption Law and Policy
Cynthia Hawkins DeBose

Mastering Alternative Dispute Resolution
Kelly M. Feeley, James A. Sheehan

Mastering American Indian Law
Angelique Wambdi EagleWoman, Stacy L. Leeds

Mastering Appellate Advocacy and Process, Revised Printing
Donna C. Looper, George W. Kuney

Mastering Art Law
Herbert Lazerow

Mastering Bankruptcy
George W. Kuney

Mastering Civil Procedure, Third Edition
David Charles Hricik

Mastering Constitutional Law, Second Edition
John C. Knechtle, Christopher J. Roederer

Mastering Contract Law
Irma S. Russell, Barbara K. Bucholtz

Mastering Corporate Tax, Second Edition
Gail Levin Richmond, Reginald Mombrun, Felicia Branch

Mastering Corporations and Other Business Entities, Second Edition
Lee Harris

Mastering Criminal Law, Second Edition
Ellen S. Podgor, Peter J. Henning, Neil P. Cohen

Mastering Criminal Procedure, Volume 1: The Investigative Stage, Second Edition
Peter J. Henning, Andrew Taslitz, Margaret L. Paris, Cynthia E. Jones, Ellen S. Podgor

Mastering Criminal Procedure, Volume 2: The Adjudicatory Stage, Second Edition
Peter J. Henning, Andrew Taslitz, Margaret L. Paris, Cynthia E. Jones, Ellen S. Podgor

Mastering Elder Law, Second Edition
Ralph C. Brashier

Mastering Employment Discrimination Law
Paul M. Secunda, Jeffrey M. Hirsch

Mastering Evidence
Ronald W. Eades

Mastering Family Law
Janet Leach Richards

Mastering Income Tax
Christopher M. Pietruszkiewicz, Gail Levin Richmond

Mastering Intellectual Property
George W. Kuney, Donna C. Looper

Mastering Labor Law
Paul M. Secunda, Anne Marie Lofaso, Joseph E. Slater, Jeffrey M. Hirsch

Mastering Legal Analysis and Communication
David T. Ritchie

Mastering Legal Analysis and Drafting
George W. Kuney, Donna C. Looper

Mastering Negotiable Instruments (UCC Articles 3 and 4) and Other Payment Systems, Second Edition
Michael D. Floyd

Mastering Negotiation
Michael R. Fowler

Mastering Partnership Taxation
Stuart Lazar

Mastering Products Liability
Ronald W. Eades

Mastering Professional Responsibility, Second Edition
Grace M. Giesel

Mastering Property Law, Revised Printing
Darryl C. Wilson, Cynthia Hawkins DeBose

Mastering Secured Transactions: UCC Article 9, Second Edition
Richard H. Nowka

Mastering Statutory Interpretation, Second Edition
Linda D. Jellum

Mastering Tort Law, Second Edition
Russell L. Weaver, Edward C. Martin, Andrew R. Klein, Paul J. Zwier, II, John H. Bauman

Mastering Trademark and Unfair Competition Law
Lars S. Smith, Llewellyn Joseph Gibbons

Mastering Trusts and Estates
Gail Levin Richmond, Don Castleman

Mastering Corporate Tax

SECOND EDITION

Gail Levin Richmond
Nova Southeastern University College of Law

Reginald Mombrun
North Carolina Central University School of Law

Felicia Branch
Attorney at Law

Carolina Academic Press
Durham, North Carolina

Library of Congress Cataloging-in-Publication

Names: Richmond, Gail Levin, author. | Mombrun, Reginald, author. | Branch, Felicia, author.
Title: Mastering corporate tax / Gail Levin Richmond, Reginald Mombrun, and Felicia Branch.
Description: Second edition. | Durham, North Carolina : Carolina Academic Press, [2017] | Series: Carolina Academic Press Mastering Series | Includes bibliographical references and index.
Identifiers: LCCN 2017044273 | ISBN 9781531008024 (alk. paper)
Subjects: LCSH: Corporations--Taxation--Law and legislation--United States. | Corporate reorganizations--Law and legislation--United States. | Income tax--Law and legislation--United States. | Dividends--United States. | Corporation law--United States.
Classification: LCC KF6464 .M664 2017 | DDC 343.7305/267--dc23
LC record available at https://lccn.loc.gov/2017044273

Carolina Academic Press, LLC
700 Kent Street
Durham, North Carolina 27701
Telephone (919) 489-7486
Fax (919) 493-5668
www.cap-press.com

Printed in the United States of America

Contents

Series Editor's Foreword

The Carolina Academic Press Mastering Series is designed to provide you with a tool that will enable you to easily and efficiently "master" the substance and content of law school courses. Throughout the series, the focus is on quality writing that makes legal concepts understandable. As a result, the series is designed to be easy to read and is not unduly cluttered with footnotes or cites to secondary sources.

In order to facilitate student mastery of topics, the Mastering Series includes a number of pedagogical features designed to improve learning and retention. At the beginning of each chapter, you will find a "Roadmap" that tells you about the chapter and provides you with a sense of the material that you will cover. A "Checkpoint" at the end of each chapter encourages you to stop and review the key concepts, reiterating what you have learned. Throughout the book, key terms are explained and emphasized. Finally, a "Master Checklist" at the end of each book reinforces what you have learned and helps you identify any areas that need review or further study.

We hope that you will enjoy studying with, and learning from, the Mastering Series.

Russell L. Weaver
Professor of Law & Distinguished University Scholar
University of Louisville, Louis D. Brandeis School of Law

Preface

This book covers tax aspects of a corporation's life. It begins with topics that are relevant to multiple transactions. These include types of corporations, situations in which the normal capital-ordinary gain and loss provisions do not apply, and doctrines that may be invoked to change a transaction's outcome.

The next chapters cover the C corporation's taxable income and E&P, funding through stock and securities, and transfers to a controlled corporation. Additional chapters discuss distributions through dividends, redemptions, liquidations, and reorganizations. Later chapters focus on taxable transfers of stock or assets, controlled corporations, affiliated groups, consolidated returns, and tax attributes. The final chapter considers S corporations and their shareholders.

Examples throughout this book illustrate the concepts discussed. References to examples in the regulations are also included.

Several Code and regulations sections were amended since this book's first edition, and more changes are likely. Congress is currently considering changes to both individual and corporate taxes. New tax rates are probable; changes in the treatment of dividends or other aspects of double taxation may also occur. In studying corporate tax, focus on the concepts and you will be able to navigate through future amendments to the Code or regulations.

Gail Levin Richmond
Reginald Mombrun
Felicia Branch
August 2017

Mastering Corporate Tax

Chapter 1

Introduction

Roadmap

- Overview of coverage
- Policies and doctrines
- Forms of doing business
- Status as a corporation for taxation
- Taxation of entity income
- Categorizing corporations
- Sales or exchanges between related persons
- References
- Executive Order 13789

A. Overview of Coverage

Federal taxes apply to individuals, trusts, estates, corporations, and other business entities. Because the reach of federal taxation is so wide, law schools are unlikely to offer a survey course that covers the entire field. Most schools begin with a course covering income taxation of individuals. Separate courses cover such topics as estates and gifts, trusts, foreign-source income, tax-exempt entities, corporations, and other business entities. As its title indicates, this book focuses on one of those topics: corporate tax.

You might assume that a book covering corporate tax limits itself to the federal tax rules covering formally incorporated entities. While this book covers those rules, that is not its only focus. For example, an unincorporated business may voluntarily subject itself to tax rules governing corporations. Alternatively, as is true for publicly traded partnerships, it may be forced to use those rules. In addition, there is no single set of tax rules covering corporations. Different rules may apply based on the type of income the corporation earns, whether it is widely or closely held, or other relevant factors.

The corporate income tax is one part of the overall tax system. It applies to both small corporations owned by a single shareholder and to publicly traded corporations whose shareholders include individuals, other corporations, and tax-exempt pension funds and charities. Although corporations of all sizes have a profit motive in common, their economic circumstances—such as access to capital, geographic reach, and percentage of stock owned by key employees—vary significantly. Not surprisingly, many Code sections include exceptions based on such factors as gross receipts or concentration of stock ownership. Others focus on the type of activity involved, such as personal services or farming.

This book focuses on business entities that are taxed as corporations. Coverage includes topics you might encounter in a corporate tax course. This chapter introduces the topic, various judicial or regulatory doctrines, and characteristics, such as related taxpayers, that are relevant in several chapters. Other chapters cover methods for funding corporations; tax consequences of transferring property to the entity; computing the entity's taxable income and earnings & profits (E&P); redemptions; reorganizations; liquidations; carryover of tax attributes; taxable transfers of corporate assets; and affiliated corporations and consolidated returns. The book concludes with a chapter covering S corporations.

B. Policies and Doctrines

The Code includes provisions designed to encourage particular activities or to prevent abuse; these add to the Code's complexity. As you work through transactions, pay close attention to the Code language. A transaction that does not comply with statutory requirements is unlikely to yield the desired tax benefits. As you consider proposed transactions, you should consider whether they follow not only the statutory language, but also its purpose.

Before enacting tax legislation, Congress considers many factors. In addition to raising revenue, these include promoting or discouraging certain types of business activity, responding to the tax climate in other countries, and appropriately distributing tax burdens based on income or wealth. Congress also considers taxpayer actions. It frequently enacts new provisions, or amends existing ones, in response to transactions that it considers abusive.

Even if a transaction follows the language of any relevant statute, the IRS might attack it based on a perceived abuse. For example, it might claim that the transaction's form does not reflect its substance, that the transaction lacked a business purpose or had no economic substance other than tax benefits, or that the transaction's steps should be collapsed and some of them ignored. These concepts, which are not limited to corporate tax, are discussed below. Other concepts, particularly continuity of business enterprise and continuity of interest, are discussed in later chapters.

1. Substance over Form

In particularly egregious cases, the IRS may ask a court to tax a transaction's substance rather than its form. For example, a corporation might regularly reduce its taxable income to zero by paying bonuses to its sole shareholder-primary employee. The corporation reports the bonus as a deductible salary, but it is arguably a nondeductible dividend. In *Menard, Inc. v. Commissioner*, 560 F.3d 620 (7th Cir. 2009), the government unsuccessfully asserted that a $17.5 million bonus paid to Mr. Menard was a dividend rather than deductible compensation. Although his compensation exceeded amounts received by his counterparts at larger, publicly traded corporations, Menard, Inc., enjoyed a higher rate of return, which the court believed was attributable to his efforts. Its opinion took note of his "workaholic, micromanaging ways" and rejected the possibility that he was "in substance though not in form, [merely] clipping coupons." 560 F.3d at 627.

There are limits to the use of this doctrine. In February 2017, the Sixth Circuit rejected the IRS's substance over form analysis to limit tax benefits that involved DISC income ultimately received by Roth IRA accounts. The transactions establishing the DISC and its corporate parent met the letter of the Code, but the IRS argued that they were designed to avoid the limit on contributions to IRAs. The court held that Congress had enacted the relevant provisions as a means of reducing taxes. "By congressional design, DISCs are all form and no substance, making it inappropriate to tag Summa Holdings with a substance-over-form complaint with respect to its use of DISCs." *Summa Holdings, Inc. v. Commissioner*, 848 F.3d 779, 786 (6th Cir. 2017), *rev'g* T.C. Memo 2015-119.

The taxpayer, not the government, is responsible for a transaction's form. Not surprisingly, courts are less likely to let a taxpayer invoke the substance over form doctrine to change the transaction's tax consequences.

2. Business Purpose and Economic Substance

The concept of business purpose underlies many Code sections. For example, § 162 allows a deduction for ordinary and necessary expenses paid or incurred in carrying on a trade or business. The business purpose for these expenses is generally obvious. They support continuing business operations. Changes in a corporation's structure, such as may occur in a reorganization, are usually undertaken to benefit the business. But that is not always the case.

A Supreme Court decision that is frequently cited for the business purpose doctrine is *Gregory v. Helvering*, 293 U.S. 465 (1935). *Gregory* involved a purported corporate reorganization that, if upheld, would have let Mrs. Gregory transform dividend income into long-term capital gain. Although the Court agreed that taxpayers have a legal right to decrease their taxes, it disregarded the transaction in this case. The Court noted, "When subdivision (B) speaks of a transfer of assets by one corporation to another, it means a transfer made 'in pursuance of a plan of reorganization' . . . of corporate business; and not a transfer of assets by one corporation to another in pursuance of a plan having no relation to the business of either, as plainly is the case here." 293 U.S. at 469.

The IRS can assert the economic substance doctrine if it believes that a transaction has no economic benefit other than the tax savings. Congress codified the economic substance doctrine in § 7701(o). The codified doctrine applies to disallow income tax benefits if the transaction does not have economic substance or lacks a business purpose. I.R.C. § 7701(o)(5)(A). Section 7701(o) was enacted as part of the Affordable Care Act, which President Trump indicated will be repealed and replaced. At this point, it is impossible to predict whether it will remain in the Code. If it is repealed, the doctrine—which was judicially recognized before it was added to the Code—may survive. In that situation, some courts might approve a transaction only if it has economic substance other than tax benefits and has a business purpose. Other courts might approve a transaction that satisfies only one of those tests.

3. Step Transaction

If there were no income tax, taxpayers would structure transactions as simply as possible. They would limit the number of steps involved to reduce such nontax transaction costs as attorney and broker fees. The stakes may change when the income tax is factored in. Two or more successive steps, each with "desirable" tax consequences, might have the same outcome as a single step with "undesirable" tax consequences. If the IRS believes that the separate steps were part of a single transaction, it may ask a court to ignore the intermediate steps.

Multiple steps may indicate that the step transaction doctrine should apply, but there may be nontax reasons for the structure used. In deciding whether to apply the doctrine, courts generally rely on one of three tests: end result; mutual interdependence; or binding commitment.

The end result test applies if separate transactions appear to be components of a single plan and each step was taken for the purpose of reaching the specific result. This test focuses on the end result. The mutual interdependence test focuses on the interdependence of the steps taken. It applies if the steps were so dependent on each other that none would be taken unless each was taken. The binding commitment test applies if the IRS can establish that there was a binding commitment to take each step. Proving a binding commitment generally requires the existence of a written document or other convincing evidence.

C. Forms of Doing Business

Individuals forming a business can select from several options. Traditionally, business owners selected from sole proprietorships, partnerships, and C corporations. More recent forms include limited liability companies (LLCs) and S corporations. In selecting the appropriate entity, owners are influenced by both tax and nontax consequences. Examples of the latter include obtaining limited liability for business debts, increasing access to capital by issuing marketable ownership interests, and providing for centralized management. This section focuses on selecting an appropriate form of ownership and becoming subject to taxation as a corporation.

A commonly cited definition of trade or business focuses on the taxpayer's activities: "the taxpayer must be involved in the activity with continuity and regularity and . . . the taxpayer's primary purpose for engaging in the activity must be for income or profit." *Commissioner v. Groetzinger*, 480 U.S. 23, 35 (1987). Mere ownership or management of property is not enough to constitute a trade or business. *Higgins v. Commissioner*, 312 U.S. 212 (1941).

If an entity, through employee-owners or through employees who are not owners, is engaged in a trade or business, it may be taxed as a sole proprietorship, as a partnership, or as a corporation. There are many benefits to incorporating a business, including limited liability and the ability to raise funds by simply selling shares in the corporation. Other business forms such as limited partnerships also provide limited liability for the limited partners, but they encumber the general partners with unlimited liability. The LLC allows both limited liability and avoidance of the double tax regime associated with C corporations. Despite the potential double tax, owners might choose the corporate form because it is more familiar or because state law requires that form for a particular business activity.

Because an entity must be a corporation, or treated as one, to be subject to tax provisions governing corporations, we begin with that determination. We then consider various corporate categories. As that discussion indicates, there is no "one-size-fits-all" treatment. Relevant classifications include number of shareholders, concentration of ownership, amount of capital, and type of income. To add to the confusion, some terms—such as small business—have different definitions and different tax consequences in different contexts.

D. Status as a Corporation for Taxation

As indicated in the preceding section, the corporate form is one option for conducting business. This section indicates how an entity becomes subject to tax as a corporation. Discussion in later chapters assumes the entity is subject to tax as a corporation.

1. Entities with Mandatory Corporate Tax Status

Section 7701(a)(3) indicates that the term "corporation" includes associations, joint-stock companies, and insurance companies, but it does not actually define the term "corporation." Reg. § 301.7701-2(b)(1) lists several entities that are taxed as corporations: "A business entity organized under a Federal or State statute, or under a statute of a federally recognized Indian tribe, if the statute describes or refers to the entity as incorporated or as a corporation, body corporate, or body politic." In other words, if the entity is organized as a corporation under the relevant law, it is a corporation for tax purposes.

Even if the entity is not organized as a corporation, it may be treated as one. The regulations repeat much of the Code language by including associations, joint-stock companies and joint-stock associations, insurance companies, and certain banking and other domestic and foreign entities. Reg. § 301.7701-2(b)(2)–(9). If § 7701(a)(3) and its regulations classify the entity as a corporation, it is generally taxed as either a C corporation or (if it qualifies and elects) an S corporation.

With one major exception, an entity that is a publicly traded partnership is taxed as a corporation. I.R.C. § 7704. A publicly traded partnership is a partnership whose interests are traded on an established securities market (or are readily tradable in a secondary market). Corporate tax status is not mandatory if at least 90% of the partnership's gross income is from certain passive sources (such as dividends, interest, and real property rents). I.R.C. § 7704(c)–(d).

You may encounter the term "per se corporation" in your coursework or in practice. A per se corporation is simply an entity for which the Code or regulations mandate taxation as a corporation.

2. Entities That Elect Corporate Tax Status

a. Historical Context

Business entities have an important common feature: a profit motive. Unless organized as a sole proprietorship or a single-member LLC, they also have more than one owner. A corporation has four additional characteristics: separation of ownership and management; freely transferrable ownership interests; limited liability of shareholders for corporate debt; and potentially unlimited life. Sole proprietorships and general partnerships lack some or all of those characteristics.

The entities' tax consequences reflect the differences between a corporation on the one hand and unincorporated entities on the other. A sole proprietor includes the entity's net income on his personal tax return; each partner does likewise for her share of partnership income. The entity itself is not separately subject to federal income tax. Corporations pay tax on their taxable income even if they distribute it to shareholders as dividends. Shareholders report corporate income on their own returns only if they receive a dividend distribution.

Over time, governments authorized the formation of "hybrid" entities that have some, but not all, of the traditional corporate characteristics. These new entities include limited partnerships, limited liability partnerships (LLP), and limited liability companies (LLC). Each provides limited liability for at least some of the entity's owners and allows centralization of management. Under previous regulations reflecting the decisions in *Morrissey v. Commissioner*, 296 U.S. 344 (1935), and *United States v. Kintner*, 216 F.2d 418 (9th Cir. 1954), the IRS taxed hybrid entities as corporations if they had at least three of the four corporate characteristics. During this period, corporate tax status was not elective. If the entity's owners desired corporate tax status, they structured it to have at least three corporate characteristics. If not, they structured it with no more than two such characteristics.

b. Check-the-Box Regulations

Regulations issued in 1996 adopted the check-the-box regime that is currently in effect. An unincorporated entity (other than a publicly traded partnership) can now select between taxation as a corporation and taxation as a pass-through entity. To select corporate tax status, it simply checks the box on the appropriate form. The entity uses Form 8832 to elect classification as a corporation or to change its election. If it wants to be taxed as an S corporation instead of as a C corporation, it uses Form 2553.

Unincorporated single-member entities are referred to as disregarded entities (and sometimes, colloquially, as tax nothings) if they do not check the box. They are referred to as disregarded entities because they are not separate from their owner for income tax purposes, not because they are ignored for tax purposes. An unincorporated entity with more than one owner is taxed as a partnership if it does not check the box. Reg. § 301.7701-3(b)(1)(i). One exception applies. Disregarded entities are treated as separate entities for purposes of federal employment taxes. Reg. § 301.7701-2(c)(2)(iv).

The election (or failure to make an election) does not permanently bind a taxpayer. An eligible entity that did not make the election and was initially taxed as a disregarded entity or partnership may later elect to be taxed as a corporation. An entity that initially elected to be taxed as a corporation may later rescind that election.

The regulations do not allow unlimited changes in classification. Generally, the entity cannot change its classification for at least 60 months. The Commissioner can allow an earlier change if more than 50% of the entity's ownership interests are owned by persons who had no ownership interest when the prior election was made or became effective. Reg. § 301.7701-3(c)(1)(iv).

Two challenges to the validity of the check-the-box regulations were unsuccessful. *McNamee v. Department of the Treasury*, 488 F.3d 100 (2d Cir. 2007); *Litriello v. United States*, 484 F.3d 372 (6th Cir. 2007), *cert. denied*, 552 U.S. 1186 (2008).

E. Taxation of Entity Income

1. Who Is Taxed on an Entity's Income?

Generally, shareholders do not pay tax on C corporation profits unless they receive a dividend distribution. The corporation is a separate taxpaying entity with its own rate structure. It files a Form 1120 and pays tax on its taxable income. Although shareholders report dividends as gross income, the corporation cannot deduct paying those dividends. Thus, the corporation's income is potentially taxed at two levels—to the corporation that earns it and to the shareholders that receive distributions of that income.

Sole proprietorships and partnerships operate as conduits. Their owners pay tax on entity profits (and may be able to deduct entity losses) even if they do not receive distributions. In effect, a partnership is treated as the aggregate of its owners, and a sole proprietorship is treated as an extension of its owner. A partnership files a Form 1065. Each partner receives a Schedule K-1, which indicates how to report her share of income and deductions. A sole proprietorship files a Schedule C, which is part of the owner's Form 1040.

As discussed above, unincorporated businesses can make a check-the-box election and be taxed as if they were corporations. Corporations, on the other hand, cannot make an election to be taxed as partnerships or proprietorships. For that reason, owners may choose to form their entity as an LLC and not elect to be taxed as a corporation. They obtain limited liability and other benefits associated with corporations and the single tax on profits associated with partnerships and sole proprietorships. In the early years, when they might expect the entity to operate at a loss, they can deduct their share of that loss on their own tax returns.

2. Avoiding Double Tax on Corporate Earnings

Corporations and their shareholders might try to avoid the double tax on corporate earnings. If they are eligible, they can elect S corporation status. That status generally results in a single level of tax, imposed at the shareholder level. Because there are restrictions on the number of shareholders and permissible types of shareholders, an S election will not be available to every corporation.

The corporation might try to reduce its taxable income by paying salaries and bonuses to shareholder-employees, but that method has potential drawbacks. First, some shareholders may not be employees. Second, the IRS may challenge the salaries as being unreasonable. I.R.C. § 162(a)(1). Third, salaries and bonuses are subject to employment taxes; these include Social Security, Medicare, and unemployment taxes. I.R.C. §§ 3101, 3111, 3301. Fourth, at least under current law, the maximum tax rate imposed on dividends is lower than that imposed on salary income. I.R.C. § 1(a)–(d), (h)–(i).

Corporations can raise funds by borrowing rather than by issuing stock. Because interest payments are deductible, a closely held corporation might be capitalized with large amounts of debt owed to shareholders instead of primarily with equity investments. This is less likely to occur in a publicly traded corporation; its lenders are less likely to be shareholders who will willingly forgo payment of principal and interest. Section 385 lists factors to consider in deciding whether a debt instrument should be classified as equity.

Corporations might also retain earnings rather than distributing them to shareholders. If the corporation needs additional funding for expansion or other business purposes, retaining earnings may be less costly than borrowing from a bank or issuing bonds. If the corporation prospers, its shareholders' stock should increase in value. A shareholder who sells his stock at a profit reports capital gain. If it is long-term capital gain, it is taxed at a lower rate than salary or interest (and, at least historically, at a lower rate than dividends). But if the corporation accumulates income to avoid shareholder-level tax, the government may assert liability for the accumulated earnings tax.

Although individuals, estates, and trusts invest directly in stock, many shares—particularly of publicly traded companies—are held by tax-exempt entities (such as universities and museums) or in IRAs, 401(k)s, and other retirement accounts. Tax-exempt entities do not pay tax on receiving dividends. Beneficiaries of retirement accounts do not pay tax until they withdraw funds from the account. If the retirement account is a so-called Roth account, they may never pay income tax on those funds. If the entity is tax-exempt, or the retirement funds are in a Roth account, double taxation is not a factor. If the retirement funds are not in a Roth account, the tax is deferred until the beneficiary withdraws funds. But because they are withdrawn as retirement distributions rather than received as dividends, the amounts withdrawn do not qualify for the lower tax rate on dividends. Retirees thus make a tradeoff between lower rates applied immediately and tax deferral while the funds remain invested.

F. Categorizing Corporations

1. Relevant Internal Revenue Code Subchapter

Corporations and unincorporated entities taxed as corporations are generally classified as C corporations because rules governing their formation, distributions, reorganization, and liquidation appear in Subchapter C of United States Code title 26 (Internal Revenue Code), Subtitle A (Income Taxes), Chapter 1 (Normal Taxes and Surtaxes). An elective tax regime for qualifying smaller corporations is covered in Subchapter S of that same chapter. Not surprisingly, these entities are referred to as S corporations. Although there is a separate Subchapter S, many provisions governing C corporations also apply to S corporations.

C and S are not the only possible subchapters. Some corporations are categorized by industry for tax purposes. These entities and subchapters are: Exempt Organizations (Subchapter F); Banking Institutions (Subchapter H); Natural Resources (Subchapter I); Insurance Companies (Subchapter L); Regulated Investment Companies and Real Estate Investment Trusts (Subchapter M); and Cooperatives and Their Patrons (Subchapter T).

Even if another subchapter applies to it, an entity may also be covered by provisions in Subchapter C. Although this book covers only Subchapters

C and S, your practice may involve entities that are subject to industry-specific subchapters.

2. Closely Held or Widely Held

A corporation may have only one shareholder, or it may have millions of shareholders. The former is clearly a closely held entity; the latter is widely held. But these distinctions are not based on the Code. The Code does look to the number of shareholders in several instances, most notably whether a corporation can be an S corporation or whether it is a personal service corporation or a personal holding company. In other instances, such as ability to use the cash method of accounting, the corporation's gross receipts may be relevant. This book indicates when the number of shareholders or other size-related characteristics are relevant to tax consequences.

3. Small Business Corporations

Several Code sections refer to "small business," but the Code does not use a common definition for this status. Three common uses involve S corporations, gains on disposition of so-called small business stock, and losses on disposition of such stock. Each provision defines small business differently.

a. S Corporations

An S corporation generally pays no income tax. Instead, its shareholders report the corporation's income, losses, deductions, and credits on their own tax returns. S corporation status is elective, and it is available only if the corporation qualifies as a small business corporation as defined in § 1361(b). An S corporation is limited to 100 shareholders, with exceptions for family groups. Certain shareholders, such as other corporations and nonresident aliens, are not allowed, and the corporation cannot have more than one class of stock outstanding. The tax treatment of S corporations and their shareholders is discussed further in the last chapter.

b. Section 1202

If a shareholder realizes a gain on a sale or exchange of stock, the gain is generally gross income and usually qualifies as a capital gain. If the stock is § 1202 qualified small business stock held for more than five years, and acquired after enactment of the Creating Small Business Jobs Act of 2010, the shareholder may be able to exclude the entire realized gain. I.R.C. § 1202(a)(4).

Section 1202 limits the excludible gain to the greater of two amounts. The first amount is $10 million reduced by exclusions taken with respect to that corporation's stock in prior years. The second amount is 10 times the aggregate adjusted bases of the corporation's qualified small business stock the taxpayer disposed of during the year. The $10 million amount is halved for married taxpayers who file separate returns. I.R.C. § 1202(b). These limitations apply per issuer, not per taxpayer.

Stock is qualified small business stock for this purpose if it was issued by a qualified small business after the effective date of the Revenue Reconciliation Act of 1993. The shareholder realizing the gain must generally have acquired the stock when it was issued, directly or through an underwriter. The shareholder must have done so in exchange for money or other property (not including stock) or as compensation for services. I.R.C. § 1202(c)(1).

To be a qualified small business for this purpose, the corporation must meet three conditions. First, its aggregate gross assets could not exceed $50 million at any time after the enactment of the Revenue Act of 1993 and before the stock was issued. Second, its assets immediately after the stock was issued could not exceed $50 million. Third, it must agree to file any reports to the government and its shareholders that the IRS determines are necessary to effectuate the purposes of § 1202. The aggregate gross assets test looks to the corporation's basis for its non-cash assets. Its basis for contributed assets is deemed to be their fair market value on the date of contribution if the corporation took the shareholder's basis. If the corporation is a member of a parent-subsidiary controlled group, all group members are aggregated in determining the aggregate gross assets. I.R.C. § 1202(d)(3).

Two conditions must be met during substantially all of the shareholder's holding period. The corporation must have been a C corporation and it must have met an active business requirement or have qualified as a specialized small business investment company. I.R.C. § 1202(c)(2). The corporation meets the active business requirement if, during the taxpayer's holding period, it uses at least 80% of the value of its assets in a qualified trade or business and it is an eligible corporation. The term "qualified trade or business" is defined in the negative. Businesses that render personal services in a variety of fields cannot qualify. Banking, insurance, financing, leasing, investing, farming, mineral production or extraction, and lodging and restaurant businesses are also precluded. A corporation is an eligible corporation if it is a domestic corporation and is not a DISC or former DISC, a corporation that has a § 936 election in effect, or a real estate investment trust, regulated investment company, REMIC, or cooperative. I.R.C. § 1202(e).

c. Section 1045

Section 1045 lets shareholders elect to postpone recognizing gains realized from sales of qualified small business stock. Nonrecognition is available to shareholders other than corporations. It uses the § 1202(c) definition of qualified small business stock, but it has a shorter required holding period than that imposed by § 1202. A shareholder qualifies if he has held his stock for more than six months. Only gain that is not ordinary gain qualifies for nonrecognition.

A shareholder recognizes gain only to the extent he does not reinvest his amount realized in shares of qualified small business stock. He has a 60-day period in which to reinvest.

His cost basis for the new shares is reduced by the gain he did not recognize on selling the original shares. If he does not purchase shares in a single transaction, the basis reduction is applied to the new shares in their order of purchase.

The shareholder can add the holding period of the old stock to that of his new stock for purposes of the capital gain and loss provisions. He cannot add that holding period for purposes of qualifying the new stock for § 1045 nonrecognition.

d. Section 1244

Assuming she does not sell to a related person, a shareholder who realizes a loss on selling her stock can deduct a loss on a transaction entered into for profit. I.R.C. § 165(c)(2). The deductible loss is normally a capital loss. When § 1244 applies, at least part of her loss is a fully deductible ordinary loss. The § 1211(b) limits on deducting capital losses do not apply. Only individuals and partnerships can use this provision.

Section 1244 imposes limits on the amount of ordinary loss a shareholder can deduct. Losses exceeding those limits retain their status as capital losses. The maximum amount covered by § 1244 is $100,000 on a joint return and $50,000 on any other individual return. I.R.C. § 1244(b). The maximum applies per year. A shareholder does not increase the limit by selling stock in more than one corporation in the same year.

Although the loss is generally computed the normal way, there are two exceptions. First, the shareholder's basis for the stock may reflect the basis of property she transferred in exchange for that stock. If that property's basis exceeded its value when it was transferred, her basis for purposes of § 1244 is reduced by that excess. Second, the shareholder's basis for the stock may reflect a later contribution she made to the corporation's capital. That increase in basis is ignored in computing the amount eligible for ordinary loss treatment. I.R.C. § 1244(d)(1).

Section 1244 applies to stock that meets four requirements. The issuing corporation must be a domestic corporation. The corporation must have been a small business corporation when the stock was issued. The stock must have been issued in exchange for money or other property (not including stock or securities). During the five taxable years ending before the date the shareholder sustained the loss, the corporation must have derived more than 50% of its gross receipts from sources other than royalties, rents, dividends, interests, annuities, and sales or exchanges of stock and securities. The gross receipts test is applied to aggregate gross receipts, not to receipts in each year separately. I.R.C. § 1244(c)(1). Section 1244(c)(2) relaxes these requirements for corporations with a less than five-year existence and for corporations that sustained a net loss for the period. In addition, it counts only gain rather than gross receipts for corporate sales of stock or securities.

A corporation is a small business corporation when the shareholder acquired his stock if it had received no more than $1 million in money and property for stock, as contributions to capital, and as paid-in surplus. Property counts for this purpose using the corporation's basis for gain, reduced by any liability to which the property is subject or assumed by the corporation when it acquired the property. I.R.C. § 1244(c)(3).

4. Personal Service Corporations

A corporation may be engaged in manufacturing, selling, performing personal services such as accounting, or some combination of these. Corporations that manufacture or sell goods earn income from using corporate assets (capital) rather than from relying primarily on the services of their shareholders or other employees.

Several Code sections refer to personal service corporations, often referring to other sections for a definition. The referring section might use the definition to which it refers or it might add one or more modifiers. If the entity's status as a personal service corporation affects the outcome of a problem, be sure to use the correct definition.

Section 269A(a) is a starting point for this term. It applies when a personal service corporation performs substantially all its services for one other entity and the principal purpose for forming or using the personal service corporation is avoidance or evasion of federal income tax by its employee-owners. In that situation, the IRS has the power to reallocate income, deductions, credits, exclusions, and other allowances between the corporation and its employee-owners.

The definition of personal service corporation covers any corporation that has the performance of personal services as its principal activity if such services are substantially performed by employee-owners. An employee is an employee-owner if she owns more than 10% of the corporation's outstanding stock on any day during the year. In determining her stock ownership, we look to both actual and constructive ownership. Constructive ownership uses the § 318 attribution rules, with modifications designed to increase the likelihood that an individual is an employee-owner.

In the next chapter, we encounter personal service corporations in two other settings: the corporation's options for selecting a taxable year and its ability to use the cash method of accounting.

5. Controlled Corporations

Some tax benefits depend on one or more shareholders being in control or attaining control of a corporation. These include § 351, which allows transferors to avoid recognition of gain on transfers of property if they are in control of the corporation immediately after the transfer. Similarly, several reorganizations described in § 368 require control as a condition of nonrecognition. Nonrecognition also applies to liquidations of controlled subsidiaries. I.R.C. § 332.

Control may also be important in determining if a group of corporations is sufficiently related for purposes of filing consolidated returns or for sharing certain tax benefits on a group basis rather than allowing each corporation to take the full benefit.

Finally, several provisions limit tax benefits on transactions between related persons. Some of these, such as § 1239, use the term "control." Others, such as § 267, use an ownership test but do not formally require control.

Because each provision has a different purpose, they do not use the same definition of control. Discussion of each topic includes an indication of the relevant control requirements.

6. Domestic or Foreign Corporations

Even before the 2016 presidential election, there were many attacks on the way the United States taxed domestic corporations. Critics focused on nominal rates, claiming they were too high, even though many corporations paid much lower effective rates after subtracting deductions and credits. In addition, the tax base was broader than that taxed in other countries because the United States taxed the corporation's foreign source income. Because other countries imposed lower nominal rates or taxed only income earned in the country, many U.S. corporations shifted their country of incorporation elsewhere by undergoing a corporate inversion.

The term corporate inversion refers to the process by which a U.S. corporation combines with a foreign entity in such a way that the latter is deemed the surviving corporation. That process results in converting the U.S. corporation into a foreign corporation and reducing or eliminating its exposure to U.S. taxation. Anti-inversion provisions in the Code are likely to be covered in international tax courses.

President Trump has indicated a desire to reduce corporate tax rates and take other steps to make the U.S. tax regime friendlier to corporations. In addition to those proposed carrots, he has also indicated he would impose tariffs or other penalties on companies that moved operations abroad and then sent products back to the United States. Changes in various aspects of corporate taxation are likely to occur in 2017 or 2018.

Some foreign entities may be classified one way for U.S. tax purposes and another way in their country of incorporation. Or they may realize gains that are exempt from U.S. taxation from transactions with related U.S. taxpayers that can deduct losses from those transactions. If a U.S. corporation that dealt with a related foreign entity could deduct a payment that went untaxed in the other country, it would receive a benefit that was arguably not in accord with economic reality. Not surprisingly, various Code or regulations provisions seek to prevent this type of situation. As is true for many anti-abuse provisions, these rules also add to complexity. Although this book mentions some of these provisions, its focus remains on domestic corporations.

G. Sales or Exchanges Between Related Persons

When a corporation is owned by relatively few shareholders, relationships between them matter. This book addresses situations involving shareholders who are related to each other by blood or marriage, parent-subsidiary corporate relationships, and affiliated groups of corporations. But relationships may be irrelevant in other situations, assuming of course that the substance of a transaction mirrors its form. When relationships are relevant to the outcome, the text and examples indicate the parties' relationship to each other. If relationships are not mentioned, you should assume that the parties are not related or that a relationship alone would not change the outcome.

Although general rules may not apply to certain transactions between related persons, the Code does not provide a single definition of that term. Taxpayers that are related persons for purposes of one section may be unrelated for purposes of other sections. When dealing with these provisions, read them carefully. Note whether shareholders and corporations are related based on the amount of stock owned, the value of stock owned, voting power, or some combination of factors. Determine if preferred stock is included or excluded from those computations. Study any attribution rules to determine if the taxpayer has constructive ownership of stock owned by family members or by entities in which he has an interest.

Provisions involving related persons appear throughout this book. Topics include whether a shareholder treats a distribution as a sale or exchange or as a dividend, whether gain or loss is recognized, and basis for property received. Those topics are based on provisions governing relationships between the corporation and its shareholders. Two relevant provisions are not so limited, and you may have encountered them in your initial tax course. Section 267(a)(1) disallows losses on sales or exchanges between related persons, while § 1239 treats a gain as ordinary instead of as capital gain or § 1231 gain if a related transferee can depreciate the property. We must consider these provisions when working through a problem involving gain or loss.

1. Section 267(a)(1)

Section 267(a)(1) disallows a deduction for a loss on a sale or exchange of property between related persons. It applies even if the property is sold at fair market value. Two types of relationships are relevant: (1) relationships between members of a family; and (2) relationships between owners (or beneficiaries) and entities or between two entities with common owners. I.R.C. § 267(b). Although there are 12 owner-entity and entity-entity relationships, this discussion focuses on those between owners and corporations and between corporations with sufficient common ownership.

An individual and a corporation are related persons if the individual owns (directly or indirectly) more than 50% of the corporation's stock value. I.R.C. § 267(b)(2). Two corporations are related persons if they are members of the same controlled group. I.R.C. § 267(b)(3). The definition of control is based on the definition in § 1563 but uses a more than 50% ownership test. I.R.C. § 267(f). Two S corporations are related to each other if the same persons own more than 50% of the stock value of each. I.R.C. § 267(b)(11). An S corporation and a C corporation are related if the same persons own more than 50% of the stock value of each. I.R.C. § 267(b)(12).

Constructive ownership provisions attribute stock owned by one person to a related person. Shareholders, partners, and beneficiaries are treated as owning a proportionate amount of the stock owned by a corporation, partnership, trust, or estate. Individuals are treated as owning stock owned by their family members: brothers, sisters, spouse, ancestors, and lineal descendants. There is no limit to how remote an ancestor or lineal descendant can be. Nieces, nephews, aunts, uncles, and cousins are not relatives for this purpose unless a sale to one of them is indirectly a sale to a listed family member. If an individual owns stock in a corporation, he is treated as owning any stock owned by his partner. This rule does not apply if he owns stock only because of family attribution. Finally, stock that a person constructively owns by attribution from a corporation, partnership, trust, or estate can be reattributed to another related person. I.R.C. § 267(c)(1)–(5).

Section 267 applies even if the parties have no actual relationship to each other. Constructive ownership alone is sufficient.

> **Example 1-1.** Fred sold investment property to ABC Corporation for an amount equal to its fair market value. Fred's children owned all the ABC stock. If Fred sustained a $14,000 loss on selling the property, he could not deduct it. He constructively owns more than 50% of the value of the ABC stock. The result would be the same if ABC sold loss property to Fred; ABC could not deduct the loss.

If the loss disallowance rule applies, the purchaser may later benefit from the seller's disallowed loss. The purchaser takes a cost basis for the property but also is "credited" for the seller's disallowed loss. The purchaser can reduce any gain realized on a subsequent sale by the amount of the previously disallowed loss. I.R.C. § 267(d). This benefit is not available if the purchaser realizes a loss on the later sale.

> **Example 1-2.** If ABC Corporation later sells the property for a gain of $20,000, it will be taxed on only $6,000 of that gain. If it instead sells the property for a $2,000 loss, it cannot deduct more than $2,000. Section 267 does not allow it to increase its loss by any of the related person's previously disallowed loss.

Section 267 does not disallow every loss between related persons. It does not apply to a distributing corporation or a distributee that realizes an otherwise-deductible loss on a distribution made in a complete liquidation. I.R.C. § 267(a)(1). Losses realized on sales or exchanges within a controlled group are deferred until the property is transferred outside the group and loss would be recognized under consolidated return principles. I.R.C. § 267(f)(2). Section 267 does not apply to transfers covered by § 1041—transfers between spouses or between former spouses if incident to a divorce. I.R.C. § 267(g). Reg. § 1.267(d)-1(c)(2) provides that it does not apply if the loss is not allowable because of the § 1091 wash sale provisions. Those provisions apply to taxpayers who realize a loss on selling stock or securities and who acquire substantially identical stock or securities within 30 days before or after the sale.

2. Section 1239

If a closely held corporation redeems the stock of a controlling shareholder, as might occur if control is being transferred from parent to child, § 1239 might apply. It might also apply if a controlling shareholder transfers appreciated property to a corporation in a nonrecognition transfer covered by § 351 and receives money or other property in addition to stock.

Section 1239 treats recognized gain as ordinary gain, rather than as capital gain, if the related transferee can depreciate the property. A corporation and its shareholder are related persons for this purpose if the shareholder is deemed to own more than 50% of the value of the corporation's outstanding stock. The § 267 constructive ownership rules apply for this purpose, but with one exception: a taxpayer is not treated as owning stock owned by his partner. I.R.C. § 1239(b)–(c).

This section applies even if the property was not depreciable in the seller's hands. For example, a shareholder who sells a vacation home to her wholly owned corporation cannot report the gain attributable to the building as capital if the corporation will use the property as an office, thus making it depreciable property in the hands of the corporation. Gain attributable to the nondepreciable land can qualify as capital gain.

Section 1239 also applies to property the corporation transfers to a controlling shareholder. For example, it could transfer a building that it no longer needs to a shareholder who will use it as a rental property. Although corporate capital gains are not currently taxed at a lower rate, failure to qualify a gain as capital may still matter. Because a corporation can deduct capital losses only against capital gains, the conversion of potential capital gain into ordinary income may result in disallowing an otherwise deductible capital loss for that year.

H. References

1. References to Authority

Unless a citation indicates otherwise, references in this book to the Code are to the Internal Revenue Code of 1986, as amended. If a section enacted as part of the 1954 Code retains the same section number in the 1986 Code, as is generally the case, this book does not cite to it as a 1954 Code section. The same is true for Treasury regulations interpreting the Code.

A textual reference to a section number, such as Section 267 or § 267, is to a Code section number. A citation to the Code is to I.R.C. §. A textual reference or citation that begins with either Reg., Prop. Reg., or Temp. Reg. is to a final, proposed, or temporary regulation section number. Textual references or citations to other administrative pronouncements indicate their status as revenue rulings, revenue procedures, or notices.

2. References to Taxpayers

Examples refer to individual taxpayers by first names or by relationships (e.g., Father). They refer to entities by initials or by an entity name that indicates the entity's status for purposes of the relevant provisions. Thus, when one corporation is acquiring another corporation's stock, the example may refer to them as Acquiring and Target.

3. References to the Government

This book refers to the Internal Revenue Service (IRS) when indicating actions taken by the IRS. It also refers to the IRS when discussing documents drafted by IRS personnel but issued by the Treasury Department (regulations) and tax controversies initiated by the IRS but litigated by Justice Department attorneys (decisions by District Courts, Court of Federal Claims, Courts of Appeals, and Supreme Court).

I. Executive Order 13789

On April 21, 2017, President Trump issued Executive Order 13789, which applies to significant tax regulations issued on or after January 1, 2016. The Treasury Department is charged with reviewing those regulations and identifying those that fall into any of three categories. The first category covers regulations that impose an undue financial burden on taxpayers. The second category covers regulations that add undue complexity to the tax laws. The third category covers regulations that exceed the IRS's statutory authority. The review is not limited to regulations identified as significant pursuant to Executive Order 12866, as amended.

Several proposed, temporary, and final regulations related to Code sections discussed in this book were issued during the relevant period. These include regulations issued for §§ 305, 337, 351, 355, 358, 362, 368, and 385. When the review is completed, these regulations might be withdrawn or amended; they might also continue as currently issued. Some of them have been named in IRS notices discussed later in this book.

Checkpoints

- Business owners can select from several forms, including sole proprietorship, various forms of partnership, C corporation, S corporation, and limited liability company.
- Some unincorporated entities are treated as corporations for tax purposes by provisions in the Code or regulations despite being unincorporated for state law purposes.
- The check-the-box regulations allow some unincorporated entities to decide whether to be taxed as a corporation or to instead be treated as a partnership or a disregarded entity.
- Although certain corporations, such as insurance companies, are subject to their own tax regimes, most actual or per se corporations are covered by provisions in Subchapter C or S of Internal Revenue Code Subtitle A, Chapter 1.
- Owners of entities that are not taxed as C corporations are taxed on undistributed profits.
- Because dividends paid by a C corporation are not deductible, both the corporation and its shareholders are taxed on distributed corporate profits.
- To reduce the double tax burden, shareholders of a closely held corporation may increase their salaries and bonuses or capitalize the corporation with debt instead of stock.
- Transactions that do not follow statutory language are likely to fail a government challenge.
- Even transactions that follow statutory language may be ignored if a court finds they do not comport with congressional purpose. Doctrines such as substance over form, business purpose, step transaction, and economic substance may be invoked.
- A corporation's status as a small business corporation, personal service corporation, or controlled corporation may be relevant in applying certain Code provisions.
- A domestic corporation with no more than 100 permissible shareholders who hold only one class of stock may elect S status.
- Individuals who are citizens or residents of the United States, certain trusts, and certain estates may hold shares in an S corporation.
- Shareholders of other types of small business corporation may be allowed to exclude gains from selling their stock or to treat losses as ordinary losses rather than as capital losses. The relevant sections define small business corporation differently.
- Personal service corporations and their employee-owners may lose tax benefits when they are formed or used for the principal purpose of avoiding or

evading tax on their employee-owners. The IRS can reallocate income, deductions, and credits between the corporation and the employee-owners.

- A personal service corporation is a corporation that has the performance of personal services as its principal activity if such services are substantially performed by employee-owners.
- Transactions between related persons may be scrutinized more closely than other transactions. The definition of related person is not the same in all contexts.
- Some Code sections apply even though the Code sections governing the transactions do not directly refer to them. Sections 267(a)(1) and 1239 are examples of such provisions.
- Different Code sections may define a term in the same way, or they may define it differently.

Chapter 2

Taxation of C Corporations

Roadmap

- Gross income and exclusions
- Deductions and credits
- Accounting methods
- Taxable year
- Capital gains and losses
- Tax rates
- Other corporate taxes
- Earnings and profits
- Shareholders' gross income

A. Chapter Overview

Determining that an entity is treated as a corporation for tax purposes is a first step. The second step is to determine the tax consequences of each event in the entity's life. Corporate tax consequences fall into two broad categories, which often overlap: events related to the corporation's relationship to its investors and events related to its operations. The first category includes formation of the corporation, distributions in redemption or liquidation, and corporate reorganizations. These rules are described in Subchapter C, which runs from § 301 through § 385. Many corporate tax courses focus on those events rather than on operating income. This book follows that path after the brief discussion of operating income in this chapter.

This chapter discusses determining a corporation's income, deductions, accounting methods, taxable year, rates, and similar items. These tax consequences are not part of Subchapter C. In fact, many of them also apply to individuals. That should not surprise you, as the owners and managers of corporations have the same general concerns as do individuals. Should a receipt be reported as gross income? Is an outlay deductible or not? What accounting methods are available? Is the appropriate accounting period a calendar year or a fiscal year? What rates apply to taxable income? Do any credits apply? What about additional taxes? Although the computations are identical for many items, there are both major and minor differences.

In addition to computing taxable income, C corporations must track their earnings and profits (E&P). Distributions to shareholders are taxable as dividends only to the extent the corporation has E&P. This chapter addresses differences between the taxable income and E&P computations.

In working with a corporate income tax issue, keep these five concepts in mind. First, the Code follows a structure. Although there are exceptions, Code sections involving gross income are grouped together, followed by sections involving deductions. The same is true for most sections covering accounting methods, appropriate taxable year, nonrecognition, and capital gain and loss. Second, the Code may group sections by whether they apply to both individuals and corporations or to only one of those groups. Code sections covering deductions follow this format. Third, no matter where a Code section appears, its opening language may indicate if it applies to corporations. Fourth, even if the opening language is silent, limitations on the section's application may appear later in the section. Fifth, limitations may apply to all corporations, only to C or S corporations, or only to certain types of corporations, such as farming corporations. Careful reading of statutory language is critical.

> **Example 2-1.** ABC Corporation made a charitable gift of inventory that it held for sale to customers. ABC paid $1,000 for the inventory, and it was worth $1,250 at the time of the donation. Generally, § 170(e)(1)(A) would reduce the $1,250 gift by the $250 gain that was not eligible for long-term capital gain treatment, leaving ABC with a potential $1,000 deduction. However, § 170(e)(3) provides an alternate computation that may result in a higher charitable gift. That computation is available only to C corporations.

An unknown factor is important. President Trump and several members of Congress have indicated their desire to reduce corporate tax rates and perhaps to increase some deductions, while decreasing others. The final rate structure and other changes are likely to be determined sometime in 2017 or 2018.

B. Gross Income and Exclusions

1. General Rule

Section 61, which defines gross income, applies to both individuals and corporations. The Code sections that flesh it out, by adding, limiting, or precluding exclusions, also generally apply to all taxpayers. Some by their nature are limited to individuals. For example, a corporation does not receive alimony or damages for personal physical injury. Others could be relevant to corporations, but the Code makes them inapplicable. For example, C corporations cannot use the exclusion for a discharge of qualified real property business indebtedness. I.R.C. § 108(a)(1)(D). They also cannot exclude gain from the sale of "qualified small business" stock. Individuals can exclude 100% of such gain if the stock is held for more than five years. I.R.C. § 1202.

2. Contributions to Capital

One exclusion section applies only to corporations. Section 118 excludes contributions to capital from the corporation's gross income. That exclusion is generally not available for amounts paid to the corporation to aid construction or for amounts provided by a customer or potential customer. I.R.C. § 118(b). The regulations list two types of qualifying payments. First, if the corporation needs additional funds, voluntary pro rata contributions by existing shareholders qualify. Second, payments from governments or civic groups can qualify if they are made to induce the corporation to locate in their community or to expand its operations. Reg. § 1.118-1. The regulation indicates that a payment is not a contribution to capital if it is made in "consideration for goods or services rendered" or if it is a subsidy the corporation receives in exchange for limiting its production.

Although § 118 is an exclusion section, it does not permanently shield the corporation from tax on the value of what it receives. This is particularly true for contributions from a non-shareholder. In that case, § 362(c) applies. The corporation takes a basis of zero for property other than money it receives. If the corporation receives money, it reduces the basis of corporate property by the amount of the money received. The reduction is first applied to any property the corporation acquires with that money during the 12 months after receiving it. If that reduction is less than the amount of the money, the corporation reduces its basis for other property it owns at the end of the 12 months.

Example 2-2. City X transferred land worth $100,000 to DEF Corporation as an excludible contribution to capital. Its basis for the land is zero. Because it has a zero basis, DEF will report the amount it receives as gross income when it sells the land.

Example 2-3. City Y transferred $100,000 to GHI Corporation as an excludible contribution to capital. One month later, GHI purchased land for $125,000, using the funds it received from Y and other funds. GHI's basis for the land is $25,000. Although it paid $125,000 for the land, it must reduce that cost by the $100,000 contribution to capital.

If the corporation receives a contribution to capital from a shareholder, it takes the shareholder's basis, increased by any gain the shareholder recognizes. I.R.C. § 362(a)(2). If, however, the shareholder is not acting for reasons associated with his shareholder role, the corporation takes the same zero basis that applies to contributions from non-shareholders.

C. Deductions and Credits

Section 63, which defines taxable income, applies to both individuals and corporations. There are two major differences. Only individuals can take a standard deduction and deductions for personal exemptions. I.R.C. § 63(b). Because corporations "itemize" all their deductions, the § 62 computation of adjusted gross income does not apply to them.

Other deductions fall into one of three categories: deductions available to both individuals and corporations; deductions available only to individuals; and deductions available only to corporations. Although the headings in the Code refer to all three categories as "itemized deductions," that terminology is potentially confusing. Most individual taxpayers use the term "itemized" to refer to deductions available only if they do not take the standard deduction. The Code headings, on the other hand, use the term to indicate a list of deductible "items." To avoid confusion, this discussion omits the term "itemized" when referring to these categories.

In addition to categories of deductible items, the Code also lists items that are not deductible or that are subject to deduction limitations. Several of those items apply only to corporations or apply differently to corporations and individuals.

1. Deductions Available to Individuals and Corporations

The discussion in this section highlights differences between the corporate and individual rules for deductions available to both groups. Some differences should not be surprising. For example, § 163(h), which disallows a deduction for "personal interest," does not apply to corporations.

Section 170(b)(1) limits an individual's charitable contributions deduction based on modified adjusted gross income (AGI). A C corporation has a deduction ceiling equal to 10% of its taxable income. For this purpose, taxable income is computed before considering the charitable contributions deduction (thus avoiding a circular computation). In determining taxable income for this purpose, the corporation also ignores the dividends received deduction, the deduction related to income from domestic production activities, net operating loss carrybacks to the deduction year, and capital loss carrybacks to the deduction year. I.R.C. § 170(b)(2).

Section 165(c), which specifies which property losses an individual may deduct, does not apply to corporations. Neither does § 166(d), dealing with nonbusiness bad debts. A corporation's bad debt losses are not subject to the capital loss rules unless they are evidenced by a security, and a corporation can deduct partially worthless bad debts. Section 183, covering activities not engaged in for profit, applies to individuals and S corporations but not to C corporations.

2. Deductions Available Only to Individuals

Sections 212 through 223 list deductions available only to individuals. The deductions listed are for expenses for the production or collection of income; medical expenses; alimony paid; interest and property taxes paid by cooperative housing corporation tenant-stockholders; moving expenses; retirement savings contributions; Archer medical savings accounts; interest on education loans; qualified education expenses (not effective after 2016 unless reenacted); and contributions to health savings accounts. You should not be surprised if Congress amends or repeals some of these provisions or adds others.

Although these Code sections apply only to individuals, C corporations can deduct some of these items under other Code sections. For example, a corporation can deduct its outlays for employee medical, educational, or moving expenses, or contributions to pension plans, as ordinary and necessary business expenses if they are reasonable compensation for services rendered. I.R.C. § 162(a)(1). It can also rely on § 162 to justify deducting expenses to produce non-operating income.

3. Deductions Available Only to Corporations

Sections 243 through 249 list three types of deductions available only to corporations: organizational expenditures; dividends received; and premium paid on repurchasing corporate debt that is convertible into stock.

a. Organizational Expenditures

1. Qualifying Outlays

Organizational expenditures are outlays that meet each of three tests. They must be: (1) incident to the corporation's creation; (2) chargeable to capital account rather than being expenses; and (3) outlays that would have been subject to amortization over the corporation's life if the corporation had been formed for a limited term. I.R.C. § 248(b). The current version of the regulations does not disqualify outlays incurred after the taxable year in which the corporation began business. Reg. § 1.248-1. A pre-2008 version disqualified such outlays.

The regulations provide examples of items that meet these tests and of items that do not meet them. Qualifying items include legal services incident to the organization of the corporation, such as drafting the charter and bylaws and the terms of the original stock certificates; accounting services; expenses related to organizational meetings of directors or stockholders; and fees paid to the state of incorporation. Reg. § 1.248-1(b)(2). Items that do not qualify include costs of selling stock or other securities and costs connected with the transfer of assets to the corporation. Reg. § 1.248-1(b)(3). Costs connected with asset transfers are added to the asset's basis as a cost of acquisition.

Note the distinction above with respect to the corporation's stock. Outlays for setting the terms, such as par value, qualify as organizational expenditures. Outlays related to selling the stock, such as commissions and printing costs, do not.

2. Beginning the Corporation's Business

Determining when a corporation begins business is important because the corporation cannot take this deduction until that taxable year. The regulations indicate that this is a question of fact, to be decided based on the circumstances. Merely coming into existence by obtaining a corporate charter is not the same as beginning business. Although starting operations indicates that the business has begun, earlier activities, such as acquiring operating assets, may be sufficient. Reg. § 1.248-1(d).

3. Deducting Organizational Expenditures

After determining which items qualify as organizational expenditures, the corporation must decide whether to elect the deduction. If it does not make the election, the corporation cannot deduct any of its organizational expenditures until it ceases operations. Although the language of § 248 implies that the corporation must affirmatively make the election, the regulations apply a different rule. The corporation is deemed to have made the election unless it elects to capitalize those outlays. Reg. § 1.248-1(c).

A corporation that takes advantage of § 248 can immediately deduct up to $5,000 of organizational expenditures and amortize any remaining expenditures over a 180-month period. That period begins in the month that the corporation begins business. I.R.C. § 248(a)(1)–(2).

> **Example 2-4.** JKL Corporation incurred organizational expenditures of $4,000 in September 2016. JKL began business in October 2016 and reports on a calendar year. It could deduct all $4,000 on its 2016 tax return.

> **Example 2-5.** JKL Corporation instead incurred organizational expenditures of $7,000 in September 2016. JKL could deduct $5,000 on its 2016 tax return. It could also deduct part of the remaining $2,000 on that return. Because JKL began business in October, when there were three months left in the taxable year, it could deduct 3/180 of the remaining $2,000 on its 2016 tax return. It would deduct the remaining 177/180 over the next 177 months.

A dollar-for-dollar phase-out reduces the corporation's ability to deduct the first $5,000 of expenditures if organizational expenditures exceed $50,000. If, for example, a corporation spends exactly $50,000 on organizational expenditures, it can deduct the first $5,000 and amortize the remaining $45,000 over 180 months. Because of the dollar-for-dollar reduction, the corporation cannot take an immediate deduction if its outlays equal or exceed $55,000. I.R.C. § 248(a)(1).

> **Example 2-6.** MNO Corporation incurred organizational expenditures of $52,000 in September 2016. It began business in October 2016 and reports on a calendar year. MNO could deduct $3,000 plus 3/180 of $49,000 on its 2016 tax return. Because its outlays exceeded $50,000 by $2,000, it lost the immediate deduction for $2,000 of its outlays. It did not permanently lose the ability to deduct that $2,000; instead, it amortizes that amount over the 180-month period.

> **Example 2-7.** MNO Corporation instead incurred organizational expenditures of $58,000 in September 2016. It can deduct 3/180 of $58,000 on its 2016 tax return. Because its outlays exceeded $50,000 by at least $5,000, it completely lost the immediate deduction.

4. Distinction Between Sections 248 and 195

Section 248 applies to expenditures for organizing a corporation. It is available in addition to any deduction allowed by § 195 for start-up expenditures. Start-up expenditures are deductible irrespective of the entity's form—sole proprietorship, corporation, or partnership. They are costs incurred for investigating and creating an active trade or business. Section 195 also has $5,000 first-year, $50,000 outlay phase-out, and 180-month amortization rules. The deduction is taken in the year in which the active trade or business begins; amortization in that year begins in the month in which the business begins.

b. Dividends Received and Premium on Repurchasing Debt

The § 243 dividends received deduction reduces the corporate tax burden on dividends that a C corporation receives from other corporations. The § 249 provisions relating to repurchasing the corporation's debt limit the deduction the corporation might otherwise take on repurchasing debt that was convertible into stock.

4. Nondeductible Items

Sections 262 through 280H disallow, limit, or defer certain otherwise deductible items. Several of these sections apply to both individuals and corporations. These include provisions related to capital expenditures, life insurance premiums, expenses to produce tax-exempt income, and travel and entertainment expenses. One provision in this group, § 280A, applies to individuals and S corporations but not to C corporations. It limits deductions for business or rental use of a dwelling unit that is used as a residence.

Several sections apply only to corporations. Sections 269 (acquisitions made to evade or avoid income tax), 269A (personal service corporations formed or availed of to avoid or evade income tax), 269B (stapled entities), and 279 (interest on certain subordinated indebtedness incurred to acquire stock or assets of another corporation) relate to potential abuse situations. Section 280G applies to parachute payments that are contingent on a change in ownership or effective control of a corporation or ownership of a substantial portion of its assets. Section 280H relates to the deduction for amounts paid to employee-owners of personal service corporations.

If a corporation sells loss property to a shareholder, or vice versa, the loss is not deductible if the buyer and seller are related persons. I.R.C. § 267(a)(1). These rules, which also apply to related individuals and related corporations, are discussed in Chapter 1.

5. Section 291 Preference Items

Section 291 reduces the corporation's tax benefits from certain items. These include gains from selling § 1250 property, percentage depletion of iron ore and coal, and amortization deductions for pollution control facilities.

6. Credits

As is true for individuals, corporations may qualify for certain dollar-for-dollar reductions in their tax liability. Some credits are available only to individuals; others are available to both individuals and corporations. Some credits, because of the nature of the activity (e.g., mining) are effectively limited to corporations. Credits are found in § 21 through § 54AA. Congress regularly adds new credits and extends the sunset date of credits that would otherwise expire.

D. Accounting Methods

1. In General

The two primary accounting methods are cash receipts and disbursements and accrual. Taxpayers can usually adopt either method so long as the method selected clearly reflects income. I.R.C. § 446(a)–(c).

Certain C corporations cannot use the cash receipts and disbursements method. These include farming corporations described in § 447 and other corporations listed in § 448(a). The § 448 limitation applies to most non-farming corporations with average gross receipts exceeding $5 million. Average gross receipts are computed over a three-year period. I.R.C. § 448(c).

A qualified personal service corporation is not subject to § 448 and can use the cash receipts and disbursements method even if it fails the gross receipts test. To be a qualified personal service corporation, the entity must meet tests related to activities and ownership. Substantially all its activities must involve performing health, law, engineering, architecture, accounting, actuarial science, performing arts, or consulting services. Substantially all its stock value must be held directly (or indirectly through certain entities) by employees performing those services, retired employees, and estates of deceased or retired employees. Stock owned by a person who received it by reason of an employee or deceased employee's death is also counted, but only for the two years following that death. I.R.C. § 448(d)(2).

2. Related Taxpayers

In addition to cash versus accrual rules, matching rules apply to accrual-method corporations making payments to related persons who report on the cash method. If, for example, an accrual-method corporation paid its unrelated cash-method employee on January 2, 2017, for work done in December

2016, the employer could deduct those wages on its 2016 tax return because all events necessary to fix the obligation had occurred and the employee had performed the services. It would not matter that the cash-method employee reported no income until 2017. If, however, the corporation and employee are related persons, the corporation's deduction is postponed until the year in which the employee reports the income. I.R.C. § 267(a)(2).

In determining if a corporation is related to its employee, landlord, or other payee, we consider actual and constructive ownership of the corporation's stock. The § 267 attribution rules that apply to losses on sales between related persons also apply in this context.

> **Example 2-8.** PQR Corporation, an accrual-method taxpayer, paid its December 2016 rent in January 2017. PQR's landlord used the cash method, and her two children owned all the PQR shares. Because its landlord constructively owned more than 50% of the value of its stock, PQR could not deduct the rent on its 2016 tax return. It took the deduction in 2017, when the landlord reported the rental income.

3. At-Risk and Passive Activity Limitations

Individuals may have to postpone loss deductions attributable to activities for which they are not deemed at-risk or that are considered passive activities. I.R.C. §§ 465, 469. Both sections provide for carrying disallowed losses over for deduction in future years.

These rules also apply to certain types of C corporations. A C corporation is subject to the at-risk and passive activity limitations if, at any time during the last half of the taxable year, more than 50% of its stock value is held by five or fewer individuals. Both direct and indirect ownership are considered in determining if the corporation satisfies the test. I.R.C. §§ 465(a)(1)(B), 469(a)(2)(B), 469(j)(1), 542(a)(2). A C corporation is also subject to the passive activity rules if it is a personal service corporation. I.R.C. § 469(a)(2)(C). A personal service corporation is defined for this purpose as a corporation whose principal activity is the performance of personal services, and the services are substantially performed by employee-owners. Those individuals must own more than 10% of the corporation's stock value. I.R.C. §§ 269A(b), 469(j)(2).

Discussion throughout this book ignores the possible application of the at-risk and passive activity rules. These rules may be relevant in practice, particularly for closely held corporations.

E. Taxable Year

Section 441 generally authorizes using a calendar year or a fiscal year. Because individuals almost always use a calendar year, a calendar year is simple for corporate officers to understand. Despite the calendar year's simplicity, many corporations adopt a fiscal year ending on the last day of a month other than December. The fiscal year may better correspond to the end of the company's operating cycle—for example, a fireworks company might do almost all its business in June and July and close its books on July 31. Another perceived advantage of the fiscal year relates to income deferral by shareholders who are employees. If the corporation can take a deduction on a tax return that is due before the employee-owner must file and report the income, the fiscal year provides a benefit. The benefit may be increased further if the corporation takes deductions on the accrual method but postpones payments to the cash-method taxpayer.

The Code limits a closely held corporation's ability to adopt a fiscal year. A personal service corporation must use a calendar year as its required year unless it establishes a business purpose for using a fiscal year. Deferral of income to shareholders is not a business purpose. I.R.C. § 441(i)(1). The definition of personal service corporation tracks the definition described above in the discussion of passive activity losses. The corporation must meet both the type of services and performance by employee-owner requirements. I.R.C. §§ 269A(b), 441(i)(2).

Section 444 lets personal service corporations and S corporations use a fiscal year without establishing a business purpose—but only if the deferral period is three months or less. The deferral period begins on the first day of the year being elected. It ends on what would be the last day of the "required taxable year" that ends within the desired fiscal year. That ending date would generally be December 31 because the required year would generally be a calendar year.

Example 2-9. STU Corporation is a personal service corporation. Because its normal business cycle ends in June, it can establish a valid business reason for adopting a fiscal year ending June 30. It can elect a June 30 fiscal year under § 441(i).

Example 2-10. If STU does not have a valid business reason for adopting a fiscal year, the calendar year would be its required year. It can instead elect a fiscal year ending September 30 (three-month deferral from October 1 to December 31); October 31 (two-month deferral); or November 30 (one-month deferral). Temp. Reg. § 1.444-1T(b)(4)(ii).

Section 280H imposes deduction limits on personal service corporations that adopt a § 444 fiscal year. These limits do not apply to personal service corporations that establish a valid business purpose for the fiscal year. Section 280H applies to amounts the corporation pays an employee-owner that are includible in the recipient's gross income. There are two exceptions: it does not apply to gains from the sale or exchange of property between the corporation and the employee-owner or to dividends. If the corporation does not distribute at least a minimum amount during the deferral period, it is subject to a maximum deduction limit for the year. It can carry disallowed amounts over to the next taxable year.

F. Capital Gains and Losses

1. Tax Rate Applied to Net Capital Gains

If an individual has a "net capital gain," the tax rates applied to that gain are lower than the rates applied to ordinary taxable income. The rules in effect at the end of 2016 even included a 0% rate applied to the gains of taxpayers in the lowest rate brackets. I.R.C. § 1(h). Section 1201(a) technically limits the top rate on a corporation's net capital gains to 35%. However, that limitation applies only if the corporation would otherwise be subject to a higher tax rate. Because the top corporate tax rate was exactly 35% at the end of 2016, no separate rate for net capital gains applied.

2. Limitations on Deducting Net Capital Losses

Both individuals and corporations can deduct capital losses up to the amount of their capital gains. I.R.C. § 1211(a)–(b). Individuals can deduct up to $3,000 of additional capital losses against ordinary income. C Corporations cannot offset capital losses against ordinary income.

Both individuals and C corporations can carry nondeductible net losses to other taxable years and use them to offset capital gains (and, for individuals, up to $3,000 of ordinary income) in those years. An individual can carry excess losses forward indefinitely; only her death extinguishes the potential carryover. Losses carried forward by an individual keep their character as short-term or long-term. I.R.C. § 1212(b). With exceptions for foreign expropriation losses, corporations can carry excess losses back three years and forward up to five years. Losses carried over by a corporation are treated as short-term capital losses. I.R.C. § 1212(a).

Example 2-11. In 2015, VWX Corporation reported net long-term capital gain of $50,000, net short-term capital gain of $15,000, and ordinary taxable income of $500,000. In 2016, it reported net long-term capital loss of $20,000 and ordinary taxable income of $500,000. Although VWX could not deduct the $20,000 long-term loss on its 2016 tax return, it could amend its 2015 return and deduct that loss against the capital gains it reported in 2015. Because corporate excess capital losses are treated as short-term, the $20,000 that VWX carried to 2015 was first applied to wipe out the $15,000 short-term gain; the remaining $5,000 reduced the long-term gain. This distinction would have been important if the corporate rate structure changed and lower rates applied to a corporation's long-term capital gains.

3. Other Capital Gain and Loss Limitations

If a corporation sells property to a shareholder, or vice versa, at an arm's-length price, the gain or loss is generally treated the same as a sale to a stranger. Section 1239 is an exception. It converts the seller's gain from capital (or § 1231) to ordinary if the related buyer could depreciate the property. Corporations cannot treat a loss on the sale of stock in a § 1244 "small business corporation" as ordinary. Individuals can do so, subject to the relevant dollar limits.

C corporations cannot use the § 1237 safe harbor, which can prevent subdivided realty from being treated as property held for sale to customers. Individuals and S corporations can take advantage of this safe harbor.

G. Tax Rates

Section 11(b)(1) provides four rates:

Rate	Taxable Income
15%	Amounts up to $50,000
25%	Amounts exceeding $50,000 but not exceeding $75,000
34%	Amounts exceeding $75,000 but not exceeding $10 million
35%	Amounts exceeding $10 million

Unlike the rates applied to individuals, the rates applied to corporations are not adjusted annually to reflect inflation. This section was last amended in 1993.

The corporate tax rates are graduated; they increase as taxable income increases. When a corporation's taxable income increases to the next rate bracket, the higher rate applies only to the income in the next bracket. For example, if a corporation has taxable income of $100,000, its income tax is 15% of $50,000, plus 25% of $25,000, plus 34% of $25,000—a total of $22,250. The rate on additional taxable income would be 34% until taxable income exceeded $10,000,000.

There are two exceptions to the tax rate computations. One exception applies to qualified personal service corporations. Those corporations are taxed at a flat 35% on all their taxable income. I.R.C. § 11(b)(2). The definition of qualified personal service corporation is the same as that used in determining which corporations can use the cash method of accounting.

The other exception applies to corporations with taxable income exceeding $100,000 and to corporations with taxable income exceeding $15 million. Although these exceptions are expressed as increases in the tax itself, they are effectively increases in the marginal rates applied to higher-income corporations. These effective rate increases do not, however, entitle an affected corporation to use the 35% rate limit for net capital gains. I.R.C. § 1201(a).

When a corporation's taxable income exceeds $100,000, it computes its tax using the rates above and then adds an additional amount. The additional amount is the lesser of 5% of taxable income greater than $100,000 or $11,750. Because $11,750 is 5% of $235,000, this increase is fully phased in when the corporation's taxable income reaches $335,000. If a corporation's taxable income exceeds $100,000 but does not exceed $335,000, its marginal rate on amounts exceeding $100,000 is 39% instead of 34%. The effective marginal rate drops back to 34% for taxable income exceeding $335,000.

A second effective rate increase occurs when taxable income exceeds $15 million. The tax increase for amounts exceeding that amount is the lesser of 3% of the excess or $100,000. Because $100,000 is 3% of $3,333,333, this increase is fully phased in when the corporation's taxable income exceeds $18,333,333. If a corporation's taxable income exceeds $15 million but does not exceed $18,333,333, its marginal rate on amounts exceeding $15 million is 38% instead of 35%. The effective marginal rate drops back to 35% for taxable income exceeding $18,333,333.

In late April 2017, President Trump released a brief outline of his tax proposals. Those include reducing the top corporate tax rate to 15%, applying only three individual tax rates (15%, 25%, and 35%) instead of seven, significantly increasing the standard deduction, and eliminating most personal deductions, the corporate alternative minimum tax, and the estate tax. Congressional consideration of these and other proposals is expected in 2017.

H. Other Corporate Taxes

C corporations are subject to the alternative minimum tax (AMT) that applies to individuals. In addition, some C corporations may also be subject to the accumulated earnings tax or the personal holding company tax.

1. Alternative Minimum Tax

In addition to computing their taxable income and income tax as discussed earlier in this chapter, corporations also do a separate computation to determine if they are subject to the AMT. The corporation pays whichever tax is higher. Although the AMT is not designed to penalize any specific behavior, it limits an affected taxpayer's ability to take full advantage of certain otherwise allowable tax benefits.

To compute its tentative AMT, the corporation first computes alternative minimum taxable income (AMTI). To do so, it recomputes taxable income by considering adjustments and preferences. I.R.C. §§ 56, 57, 58. Some items apply to all taxpayers, some only to individuals, and some only to corporations.

The corporation then reduces its AMTI by a $40,000 exemption, multiplies the remaining amount by a flat 20%, and subtracts its AMTI foreign tax credit. I.R.C. § 55(b)(1)(B), (d)(2). The exemption phases out at a rate of 25% for each dollar that AMTI exceeds $150,000. I.R.C. § 55(d)(3)(A). It is fully phased out when AMTI reaches $310,000.

Corporations are exempt from the AMT if their average annual gross receipts are $7,500,000 or less in every preceding three-taxable-year period. If a corporation meets this test, its tentative minimum tax for the year is zero. It is also zero in the corporation's first taxable year. The gross receipts test is $5 million or less during the first three-taxable-year period. I.R.C. § 55(e).

The AMT requires taxpayers to compute taxable income under two separate regimes. Some of the adjustment items are permanent; others are timing differences that reverse over time. Not surprisingly, the AMT has been criticized for increasing compliance costs. The potential revenue loss has thus far prevented its elimination, but repeal is part of the plan President Trump outlined in late April 2017.

2. Accumulated Earnings and Personal Holding Company Taxes

Some C corporations are also subject to one of the two taxes prescribed in Subchapter G, Corporations Used to Avoid Income Tax on Shareholders. The accumulated earnings tax and the personal holding company tax are imposed in addition to the regular income tax or AMT. I.R.C. §§ 531 (accumulated earnings tax), 541 (personal holding company tax). Each is imposed at a flat rate of 20%.

Both taxes originated when individual income tax rates on all types of income, and particularly on dividends, were significantly higher than they are today. Both were designed to limit shareholders' ability to reduce their taxes by: (1) avoiding the double tax on corporate earnings; (2) transforming profits attributable to retained earnings into capital gains on selling the stock; or (3) avoiding all income tax by holding corporate stock until death, at which time the § 1014 basis rules could eliminate all untaxed appreciation.

a. Accumulated Earnings Tax

The accumulated earnings tax applies to the accumulated taxable income of any corporation formed or availed of to avoid the income tax with respect to its shareholders (or the shareholders of any other corporation). I.R.C. § 532(a). The tax does not apply unless there is both "accumulated taxable income" and the specified purpose.

To determine its accumulated taxable income, a corporation adjusts its taxable income to more accurately reflect its ability to pay dividends to shareholders. This computation is analogous to the earnings and profits (E&P) computation discussed later in this chapter. For example, the corporation's federal income tax is not deductible in computing taxable income, but it does reduce the resources available for distributing profits to shareholders. On the other hand, the dividends received deduction does not reduce the corporation's resources and is added back in computing accumulated taxable income. The following items are treated differently for purposes of the accumulated earnings tax: federal income tax; charitable contributions; dividends received; net operating losses; and capital gains, capital losses, and capital loss carryovers. I.R.C. § 535(b).

If the corporation pays dividends, it deducts them in computing accumulated taxable income. I.R.C. § 535(a). For this purpose, dividends include amounts the corporation paid and additional amounts that common shareholders consent to report as dividends ("consent dividends"). I.R.C. §§ 561(a)(1)–(2), 565. Consent dividends are treated as if they were distributed to the shareholder and then transferred back to the corporation as a contribution to capital.

In computing its accumulated taxable income, the corporation can deduct earnings retained for the reasonable needs of the business. Corporations are generally entitled to retain a minimum of $250,000 over and above their E&P at the close of the preceding taxable year; that amount is reduced to $150,000 for corporations whose principal function is the performance of health, law, engineering, architecture, accounting, actuarial science, performing arts, or consulting services. I.R.C. § 535(c). Although referred to as the accumulated earnings *credit*, it is a *deduction* in computing accumulated taxable income.

Section 533 provides that accumulating earnings beyond the reasonable needs of the business is determinative of the purpose to avoid a shareholder-level income tax. The corporation must prove to the contrary by the preponderance of the evidence. The reasonable needs of the business include both current needs and reasonably anticipated needs. The computation also includes amounts the corporation will need to redeem stock from a shareholder who has died, to redeem stock from certain private foundations, and to pay reasonably anticipated product liability losses. I.R.C. § 537. In discussing reasonable needs of the business, the regulations refer to "the amount that a prudent businessman would consider appropriate for the present business purposes and for the reasonably anticipated future needs." Reg. § 1.537-1(a). The regulations list the following examples: bona fide expansion of business or replacement of plant; acquiring a business through purchasing stock or assets; retiring bona fide business indebtedness; providing working capital for the business; providing for investments or loans to suppliers or customers if necessary to maintain the business; and providing for payment of reasonably anticipated product liability losses. Reg. § 1.537-2(b).

Although this tax is most likely to be assessed against closely held corporations, § 532(c) provides that it applies without regard to the number of shareholders. Keep in mind, however, that the tax applies only if there is an excessive accumulation that was made to avoid shareholder-level tax. For example, in *Technalysis Corp. v. Commissioner*, 101 T.C. 397 (1993), the court found that a publicly traded company had excessive accumulations but that the accumulations were not made for the shareholders' benefit. Notwithstanding the double tax on corporate earnings, the current tax treatment of dividends—individual tax rate of 0%, 15%, or 20%—probably reduces the likelihood of litigation over improper accumulations. If tax rates imposed on dividends return to the rates imposed on salary, interest, and rent, corporations may need to be more careful in documenting the rationale for earnings accumulations.

b. Personal Holding Company Tax

Corporations that are classified as personal holding companies are taxed on their undistributed personal holding company income. I.R.C. § 541. The paragraphs below discuss both definitions. This discussion omits numerous special rules involved in the computations described below and provisions related to foreign corporations.

A corporation is a personal holding company if at least 60% of its adjusted ordinary gross income is personal holding company income and more than 50% of its stock value is owned—at any time during the last half of the taxable year—by five or fewer individuals. I.R.C. § 542(a). Section 542(c) exempts several types of corporations (including banks and life insurance companies) from personal holding company status.

In determining if a corporation meets the 60% of adjusted ordinary gross income test, § 543(b)(1) defines ordinary gross income as gross income other than gains from the sale or exchange of capital assets or § 1231 assets. It makes certain adjustments with respect to rents, mineral royalties, and interest in computing adjusted ordinary gross income. If 60% of that sum is attributable to dividends, interest, certain mineral and copyright royalties, rents, use of corporate property by a shareholder, personal service contracts, and income from a trust or estate, the corporation meets the 60% test. I.R.C. § 543(a)–(b). For example, a corporation that has $100,000 of gross income from sales and $70,000 from dividends does not meet the 60% test. Although its dividend income is more than 60% of its sales income, it is only 41% of its total adjusted ordinary gross income.

In determining whether five or fewer individuals own more than 50% of the corporation's stock value, § 542(a)(2) indicates that ownership can be direct or indirect and that it can include beneficial ownership ("ownership by or for"). Actual ownership is not required. Individuals are deemed to constructively own certain stock owned by corporations, partnerships, estates, and trusts in which they have ownership or beneficial interests; stock owned by certain family members and by partners; and stock subject to a purchase option. I.R.C. § 544.

The tax is applied only to undistributed personal holding company income. Undistributed personal holding company income is computed by adjusting taxable income by items that decrease or increase a corporation's available cash. These include reductions for federal income taxes and charitable contributions, increases for any dividends received deduction and certain net operating loss carryovers, and special computations for capital gains and for depreciation and other expenses related to property for which the corporation receives rental income. I.R.C. § 545(b). The corporation can deduct dividends paid during the taxable year and consent dividends (described above in the discussion of the accumulated earnings tax). I.R.C. §§ 545(a), 561(a)(1)–(2). Section 561(a)(3) also allows a deduction for certain dividends paid during the two preceding taxable years. That computation is described in § 564. Finally, § 547 provides for a deduction for deficiency dividends. These are amounts paid in a later year after a judicial determination, closing agreement, or other agreement between the taxpayer and IRS establishes that there is a personal holding company tax deficiency. The corporation has 90 days in which to make these dividend payments and 120 days in which to claim the deduction.

I. Earnings and Profits

The discussion below focuses on the concept of earnings and profits (E&P) and items that affect it. Later chapters cover the difference between current and accumulated E&P and the allocation of E&P to corporate distributions.

Accounting net income, taxable income, and E&P are all measures of corporate income. They treat many items the same way; they differ markedly for other items. That is not surprising, as each has a different function. Accounting net income provides information that investors and creditors can use to judge a corporation's solvency, efficiency, and profitability. Code sections defining taxable income measure a corporation's ability to pay income tax; they also provide incentives (or disincentives) for particular activities, such as investing in machinery and equipment. We use E&P to measure a corporation's ability to pay a taxable dividend.

The computation of E&P begins with § 312 and its regulations. Although that section indicates how several items affect E&P, it does not list every relevant item. It does not even define the term E&P.

1. Accounting Methods and Timing

A corporation generally uses the same accounting method for computing E&P that it uses for computing taxable income. Reg. § 1.312-6(a). For most C corporations, that will be the accrual method. I.R.C. § 448.

Although the corporation uses the same general accounting method for both taxable income and E&P, the accounting rules differ for several items. Those differences reflect the different purposes for the two computations. For example, income tax depreciation is computed using short useful lives and, for property other than real estate, accelerated methods. Tangible personal property may be fully deductible in the year in which it is placed in service. I.R.C. §§ 168,

179. Depreciation is deducted more slowly for E&P purposes. I.R.C. § 312(k). Because depreciation reduces the asset's basis, the corporation has one adjusted basis for income tax purposes and a different one for E&P purposes. Gain or loss reported for each purpose reflects the basis used for that purpose.

Corporations can use last-in, first-out (LIFO) inventory accounting in computing taxable income. LIFO generally results in lower taxable income than would be reported using first-in, first-out (FIFO). That is because taxpayers using LIFO treat their most recent inventory purchases, which are usually costlier than older items, as the first items sold. That results in a lower gross profit than using FIFO. For E&P purposes, the corporation adjusts its inventory accounting to reflect the FIFO method. I.R.C. § 312(n)(4).

Other accounting differences involve accounting for long-term contracts and for installment sales. Corporations that report long-term contracts for income tax purposes using the completed contract method report income sooner—by using the percentage of completion method—when computing E&P. I.R.C. § 312(n)(6). In addition, corporations that use the installment method to report taxable gain on deferred payment sales report their gain in the year of sale when computing E&P. I.R.C. § 312(n)(5).

If a corporation's deductions exceed its gross income, it can deduct the resulting net operating loss on tax returns for other years. I.R.C. § 172. When computing E&P, the corporation reduces its E&P by the net loss in the year in which it is sustained. That is the year in which the corporation's financial resources are reduced.

2. Income and Deductions

Income items that increase a corporation's financial ability to pay dividends are included in E&P even though they are excluded from gross income. Reg. § 1.312-6(b). These items include interest received with respect to state and local bonds and proceeds of a life insurance policy. Even if the corporation received no income other than these items, and thus had no taxable income, it would still have E&P. Distributions from those E&P would be taxable to its shareholders.

The § 108 exclusion for income from discharge of indebtedness applies in computing E&P to the extent that the taxpayer takes a § 1017 basis reduction for its property. I.R.C. § 312(l). The basis reduction will give rise to a larger gain (or a smaller loss) realized when the property is later sold. Instead of taking a basis reduction, the corporation may reduce other tax attributes as provided in § 108(b).

Items that are deductible in computing taxable income are not deductible in computing E&P if they do not reduce the corporation's financial ability to pay dividends. The § 243 dividends received deduction is an example of this type of item. Conversely, items that are not deductible in computing taxable income may reduce E&P if they reduce the corporation's financial ability to pay dividends. The federal income tax is an example of this type of item. Another example is a loss that was realized but was disallowed by § 267 because the corporation sold property to a related taxpayer. That loss is allowed in computing E&P. Reg. § 1.312-7(b)(1). Other items covered by this rule are charitable contributions and net capital losses. Those items are subject to income tax limitations that do not apply in computing E&P.

J. Shareholders' Gross Income

Shareholders of C corporations do not report gross income merely because the corporation has taxable income, E&P, or both. Shareholders report gross income only when they receive a distribution or agree to a consent dividend.

Because shareholders who receive dividends are taxed on earnings that were already taxed at the corporate level, Congress often considers methods for reducing the double tax burden. The current method, a lower tax rate on dividends received by individuals and a deduction for dividends received by corporations, is not the only possibility. Other options include letting the corporation deduct the dividends it pays or reducing the tax rate on dividends to zero for all shareholders. Do not be surprised if Congress revisits integrating corporate and shareholder taxation sometime in 2017 or 2018.

Checkpoints

- Many of the rules governing individuals apply, often with modifications, to C corporations. These rules apply to gross income, deductions, accounting methods, taxable year, capital gains and losses, credits, and the alternative minimum tax. The tax rates applied to C corporations are different from those applied to individuals.
- In some instances, C corporations are subject to different rules based on their gross receipts, ownership concentration, or status as a personal service corporation.
- The accumulated earnings tax and personal holding company tax apply to C corporations. They do not apply to S corporations because their owners are taxed on undistributed income.

- A corporation's E&P account reflects its ability to pay taxable dividends. The E&P computation includes some items that are excluded from gross income and subtracts some items that are not deductible in computing taxable income. There are also timing differences between the two computations for items such as depreciation.
- C corporation shareholders generally report no gross income until they receive a dividend distribution.

Chapter 3

Funding Corporations

Roadmap

- Debt
- Equity
- Section 385
- Securities

A. Chapter Overview

All business entities need funds and can look to various sources for meeting those needs. Funding needs range from paying creditors and employees to acquiring machinery and equipment. Funding sources can be categorized in two overlapping ways: short-term funding versus long-term funding and creditor funding (debt) versus owner funding (equity).

Short-term funding generally involves amounts that will be repaid within one year. This type of funding is generally attributable to borrowing. The debt may be represented by an account payable, a note payable, or the current year's installment on a bond or mortgage obligation. Unpaid salaries, rent, interest, and taxes are also forms of short-term debt.

A corporation can obtain long-term funding by issuing preferred or common stock in exchange for money or other property. Both are equity interests. Alternatively, it can raise funds by issuing debt payable more than a year after its issue.

The individuals involved in forming the corporation determine its initial capital structure. As the corporation's funding needs increase over time, its management must assess available funding sources. Sources that were appropriate at the corporation's formation may not be the best sources several years later. Both tax and nontax factors are relevant to these decisions, and courts generally defer to the business judgment of those managing the entity.

This chapter covers tax and nontax characteristics of debt and equity funding. It also considers instruments that have characteristics of both debt and equity.

B. Debt

1. Nontax Characteristics

If a corporation issues a debt instrument, either a note or a bond, the instrument is likely to include both a fixed payment date (lump sum or installments) for the loan principal and an appropriate interest rate. The interest represents rent for the use of the lender's money. Even less-formal debt, such as accounts payable and credit card debt, is likely to include a payment due date and involve the payment of interest.

Debt may also include a security interest, such as a mortgage. If the borrower defaults, the creditor can take the secured property. If a corporation is in financial distress, creditors' rights are affected by a variety of factors. These include statutory rules giving some creditors preference over others, the terms of any security interest, and the terms of the debt instrument itself. For example, some debt may by its terms be subordinated to the rights of other creditors.

> **Example 3-1.** ABC Corporation applied to Lender for a loan. Because ABC was only modestly profitable, Lender refused to make the loan unless ABC's existing creditor, Financier, agreed to subordinate its rights to those of Lender. If Financier agrees, Lender will have priority for repayment if ABC cannot repay both loans.

Because debt must be repaid, the corporation may have less flexibility in using funds for operations. The corporation must pay interest on its debt on a regular basis and must repay the debt when it comes due. If it cannot repay its debt or refinance it, its shareholders may lose control of the corporation in a bankruptcy proceeding.

One advantage of debt, from the shareholders' perspective, relates to control. If the shareholders want to retain control of the corporation, they may prefer to issue debt—which generally has no voting rights—rather than additional shares of stock. Although lenders do not generally have voting rights, some debt instruments may provide for such rights if the corporation defaults on the loan.

Another advantage of debt, at least for a successful corporation, relates to its fixed rights. If the corporation can earn a higher rate of return on borrowed funds than it pays in interest, the difference benefits the shareholders. If, on the other hand, the corporation earns a lower rate of return, the shortfall reduces the value of its shareholders' equity.

> **Example 3-2.** DEF Corporation borrowed funds to finance a new factory. DEF agreed to repay the debt plus 7% interest. DEF earned a

12% rate of return from the new factory's operations. Even after paying 7% interest and installments of principal, DEF had a positive cash flow, which increased the value of its shareholders' equity.

2. Tax Consequences

a. *Corporate Debtor*

A corporate debtor can usually deduct interest it pays on its debt. I.R.C. § 163(a). Although repayment of principal for debt used to acquire an asset is not deductible, the asset's basis includes the amount borrowed. *Crane v. Commissioner*, 331 U.S. 1, 11 (1947).

The corporation generally reports no gross income on borrowing. Because it is subject to an obligation to repay the debt, borrowing does not increase its income. If it does not fully repay the debt, the corporation may have income from discharge of indebtedness. Its ultimate tax consequences depend on whether it is bankrupt, insolvent, or eligible for one of the other § 108 gross income deferral provisions.

A corporation does not have to be in financial distress to have debt discharge income. Market conditions may allow it to repurchase its debt for less than the amount it originally borrowed. In that case, it has income from discharge of indebtedness. *United States v. Kirby Lumber Co.*, 284 U.S. 1 (1931).

> **Example 3-3.** GHI borrowed $1 million by issuing 200 10-year bonds. Each bond paid 5% annual interest and had a $5,000 face value. Two years later, market interest rates increased to 7%. Because lenders could buy bonds from other issuers and earn 7%, the value of GHI bonds declined below their face value. DEF paid $3,800 to purchase one of its bonds on the open market. DEF has $1,200 debt discharge income with respect to that bond.

b. *Creditor*

A creditor reports interest accrued or received as gross income. I.R.C. § 61(a)(4). The creditor does not report gross income when the debt is repaid because that is merely a return of the amount borrowed.

If the debt is not repaid, the creditor may take a tax deduction for any unrecovered basis, which is generally the amount still outstanding. The character of that deduction depends on how the debt is classified and, for some debts, whether the creditor was itself a corporation.

If the debt was not evidenced by a security, and the creditor is a corporation, the bad debt is deductible as an ordinary loss. If the creditor is not a corporation, the loss is either a business or nonbusiness bad debt. A bad debt is a business bad debt if the loan was made or acquired in connection with the creditor's trade or business, or if the loss was incurred in the creditor's trade or business. I.R.C. § 166(d)(2). If neither condition is met, the loss is from a nonbusiness bad debt. A loss from a business bad debt is an ordinary loss; in appropriate circumstances, the creditor can take a deduction for partial worthlessness. I.R.C. § 166(a). A loss from a nonbusiness bad debt is treated as a short-term capital loss; the creditor cannot take a deduction until the debt is totally worthless. I.R.C. § 166(d). Similar treatment is available to a guarantor who is called upon to pay any of a corporation's debt. Reg. § 1.166-9.

The worthless security rules take precedence over the bad debt rules if the corporate debt is a security. I.R.C. § 166(e). If the debt was evidenced by a security, and the security is a capital asset, the creditor's loss is treated as a loss from the sale or exchange of a capital asset on the last day of the year. Corporate bonds, debentures, and notes are securities for this purpose if they are issued with interest coupons or in registered form. I.R.C. § 165(g). The loss will be disallowed entirely for obligations that are not in registered form if they are covered by the § 163(f) registration-required provisions.

C. Equity

1. Nontax Characteristics

Shareholders are the corporation's owners. They vote for its board of directors, who in turn set corporate policy. Shares of corporate stock do not bear repayment dates and they do not guarantee that the shareholder will receive distributions of corporate profits (dividends). Because a corporation's creditors must be repaid before shareholders receive liquidation proceeds, the shareholders of a bankrupt corporation risk recovering none of their original investment. But because a creditor's rights are generally fixed, the shareholders may benefit, as described in Example 3-2, from profits attributable to borrowed funds.

a. Potential Equity Interests

A person who has an equity interest in the corporation is a shareholder. His equity interest may be identical to that of every other shareholder or it may differ significantly. In the former situation, the corporation has issued only one class of stock, voting common. In the latter situation, it may have issued a variety of equity interests. These include nonvoting common, nonvoting preferred, voting preferred, and convertible preferred. The corporation may have issued rights to acquire stock, which ripen into equity interests if the holder exercises those rights. It may also have issued debt instruments that are convertible into shares of stock upon the happening of specified events or on a specified date.

b. Preferred Stock

Preferred stock generally has fixed dividend and liquidation rights. Its voting rights are generally limited to matters affecting the preferred stock. The interests of preferred shareholders are subordinated to those of creditors, but they have priority over the interests of the common shareholders.

Because preferred shares are equity interests, preferred shareholders are not guaranteed they will receive their fixed dividend each year. If the corporation performs poorly, the directors may decide not to declare a dividend. But the preferred shareholders are entitled to receive their dividends before the corporation pays dividends to the common shareholders. Their stock is preferred because it has a preference with respect to distributions of corporate earnings, not because investors prefer it to common.

The corporation does not increase the preferred shareholders' dividends to reflect successful operations. Participating preferred shares are an exception to that rule. They provide for preferred shares to receive not only the fixed dividend but also to share in amounts paid common shareholders when specified conditions are met.

c. Common Stock

1. Return on Investment

Common shareholders are the residual owners. They receive dividend payments only after the corporation makes any required payments to creditors and distributes dividends to preferred shareholders. The common dividend payment is not a fixed amount. Common shareholders may receive large dividends if the corporation is successful and much smaller amounts (or even no dividends) if it is not. Even if the corporation is successful, it may distribute relatively small dividends. The directors may decide the corporation would be best served if they retained the profits to fund future corporate growth.

A shareholder's potential return on investment is not limited to the receipt of dividends. At some point, he might dispose of his stock. The corporation might redeem that stock, or the shareholder might sell his stock to another person. The buyer might be an existing shareholder, but that is not required unless the stock is subject to an agreement that gives another shareholder a right of first refusal or some other buy-sell agreement is in effect.

Stock dispositions can occur in other settings. The corporation might sell its assets and liquidate, in which case shareholders receive funds remaining after the corporation satisfies its debt. The corporation might be acquired by another corporation. In that situation, shareholders might receive equity interests in the other corporation, or they might receive money or other property. Because preferred shareholders' rights are generally limited by the terms of the stock, they are unlikely to receive much more than their purchase price on disposing of their stock. Common shareholders, on the other hand, are the residual owners. If the corporation is successful, they may receive significantly more than their investment when they dispose of their stock. If, on the other hand, it performs poorly, they may receive little or nothing.

2. Voting Rights

Common shareholders are generally the only shareholders who can elect the corporation's directors. The significance of voting rights usually reflects the corporation's status as closely held or widely held. Most individuals who own stock in publicly traded corporations own only a minimal percentage of the entity's stock. They do not have enough voting power to affect corporate policy. Shareholders of closely held corporations, on the other hand, may be able to control the corporation if they own enough shares to elect its governing board.

If the controlling shareholders decide to transfer shares to the next generation or to trusted employees, they may initially take steps to preserve their controlling interest. They can do so by exchanging some of their voting shares for nonvoting shares and transferring the latter shares to the new shareholders. They do not recognize gain on exchanging solely shares of the same class—common for common or preferred for preferred. I.R.C. § 1036(a). Alternatively, they can make the transfer contingent on the recipients' agreeing to place their shares in a voting trust or agreeing to give the transferors an irrevocable proxy.

2. Tax Consequences

a. Corporate Issuer

The corporation cannot deduct amounts it pays as dividends on its stock or amounts it pays to repurchase the stock. Neither of those outlays constitutes a business expense.

The corporation does not report gross income when it issues stock in exchange for money or other property. I.R.C. § 1032. If the corporation received assets in exchange for its stock, or purchased assets with the funds received from selling stock, it acquires a basis for those assets. If the acquisition event was part of the corporation's formation, it generally carries over the basis its shareholders had for the property. I.R.C. § 362(a). If it instead purchased the property, it takes a cost basis.

Because the corporation has no obligation to repurchase its stock, it does not report gross income if it reacquires the stock for less than the issue price or if it goes bankrupt and cannot return its shareholders' investment. The corporation does not report gain or loss if it reissues shares it previously repurchased for an amount other than the original repurchase price.

b. Shareholder

The rules discussed here are subject to the exceptions discussed in chapters covering redemptions, liquidations, and reorganizations. Shareholders report any dividends received as gross income. I.R.C. § 61(a)(7). The tax rate currently applied to dividends received by individuals ranges from 0% to 20%. I.R.C. § 1(h). That rate may be significantly lower than the rate applied to a shareholder's other taxable income. Unless it is repealed, high-income shareholders may be subject to a 3.8% additional tax on net investment income, including dividends. I.R.C. § 1411. Investment income escapes the employment taxes imposed on compensation for services. If the shareholder is itself a corporation, it may qualify for the § 243 dividends received deduction.

The shareholder reports no gross income on purchasing the corporation's stock with money. If he instead transfers property, his tax consequences depend on whether the transfer is described in § 351. If it is, he does not recognize gain or loss or may recognize only part of his gain. His basis for the stock is the same as his basis for the property transferred (increased by any gain he recognized). I.R.C. § 358(a)(1). If he instead transfers the property in a taxable transaction, his basis for the stock received is its fair market value. If he receives stock in exchange for performing services, he reports gross income (and takes a basis for the stock) equal to the value of the stock received.

If the shareholder realizes a profit on selling the stock to a third party, the gain is gross income and eligible for capital gain treatment. If the stock is § 1202 qualified small business stock held for more than five years, and acquired after enactment of the Creating Small Business Jobs Act of 2010, the shareholder excludes the entire realized gain. I.R.C. § 1202(a)(4).

Shareholders who realize a loss on selling their stock can deduct that loss as a § 165(c)(2) loss on a transaction entered into for profit. They cannot deduct their loss if they sell to a related party. I.R.C. § 267(a)(1). The deductible loss is normally a capital loss; it is long-term or short-term depending on the seller's holding period. When § 1244 applies, the loss becomes ordinary. Those losses are fully deductible even if the seller realized no capital gains that year.

If the stock becomes worthless, the loss is covered by the § 165(g) worthless security rules. If the shareholder sells the stock back to the corporation, the redemption may give rise to taxable gain, deductible loss, or a taxable dividend.

c. *Nonqualified Preferred Stock*

For corporate law purposes, preferred stock is either voting or nonvoting, participating or nonparticipating, and subordinated or not subordinated to other preferred stock. For various corporate tax purposes, Congress classifies some preferred stock as nonqualified preferred stock. Stock so classified may be barred from otherwise available tax benefits. For example, a person who transfers property to a controlled corporation in exchange for its stock cannot receive nonrecognition treatment if the stock is nonqualified preferred stock. I.R.C. § 351(g). Similar treatment applies to nonqualified preferred stock received in reorganizations and corporate separations. I.R.C. §§ 354(a)(2)(C), 355(a)(3)(D). Each provision uses the definition of nonqualified preferred stock found in § 351(g)(2). That definition is discussed in the next chapter.

D. Section 385

1. Hybrid Debt

A corporation might issue an instrument that has both debt and equity characteristics. Convertible bonds are an example of a hybrid instrument. If the bondholder does not exercise the conversion right, the corporation pays the required rate of interest and redeems the bonds at the contractual amount on their due date or earlier date of redemption. If the bondholder exercises the conversion right, she becomes a shareholder. Her return, if any, will come from dividends and proceeds from disposing of her interest.

The controlling shareholders in a closely held corporation might acquire convertible debt instead of more shares because of the perceived tax advantages debt carries. The corporation can deduct interest payments, and the bondholder is unlikely to report gain (or dividend income) when the bond is repaid. Even if the debt is evidenced by a written promise to pay and bears interest, we might wonder if it is true debt if it is owned only by the corporation's shareholders. Would they force the corporation to make interest payments if that might impede the entity's operations and reduce the value of their investment?

Even if the debt is not convertible, we might question its status if the creditors are also the corporation's controlling shareholders. As with convertible debt, they may be seeking the tax benefits of debt when we doubt they would enforce its provisions as would a third-party creditor.

In these situations, we might ask how to treat the debt instrument. Should it be treated as debt until it is converted into equity? Or should it be treated as equity from the beginning? If it is treated as debt until conversion occurs, the corporation can deduct pre-conversion interest payments. If it is treated as equity from the time it is issued, the corporation cannot deduct interest payments. Section 385 is a statutory attempt at categorizing hybrid instruments.

2. Relevant Factors

When Congress enacted § 385 in 1969, it authorized the Treasury Department to issue regulations that are necessary or appropriate to determine whether an interest in a corporation is stock, indebtedness, or part stock and part indebtedness. I.R.C. § 385(a). Section 385(b) lists five factors that the regulations can indicate will be considered. This list is neither exclusive nor mandatory. The regulations can list other factors and can omit factors included in § 385(b). The five factors are:

- Is there a written unconditional promise to pay on demand or on a specified date a sum certain in money in exchange for an adequate consideration in money or money's worth, and to pay a fixed rate of interest?
- Is there subordination to or preference over any indebtedness of the corporation?
- What is the corporation's ratio of debt to equity?
- Is the interest convertible into the corporation's stock?
- What is the relationship between holdings of stock and holdings of the interest in question?

These factors provide useful guidance. For example, answering the first question in the affirmative indicates a debt-like instrument. Debt requires repayment; equity does not. The second question looks to either subordination or preference. Subordination to another interest may indicate equity, because shareholders receive no liquidation proceeds until creditors have been paid. Conversely, preference over other interests may indicate debt. The third question relates to the corporation's overall capital structure. Although there is no single debt-to-equity ratio that is the "right" ratio, similar companies tend to have similar, industry-specific ratios. If a company's debt-to-equity ratio is significantly higher than the industry norm, it is possible that some purported debt instruments are equity interests. Obviously, if an interest is convertible into stock, that interest is more equity-like than a debt interest that lacks the conversion feature. Finally, if the shareholders hold the interest in the same ratio as their stockholdings, they are not as likely to enforce its terms as an independent creditor would be. Payment to shareholders with respect to either stock or the interest in question will be pro rata to their stockholdings.

3. Classification by the Issuing Corporation

The government is not bound by the issuer's classification of an interest in the corporation. The issuer and holders of the interest are bound by this classification. I.R.C. § 385(c)(1). Although the time for determining the issuer's classification is the time of issue, the binding effect also applies to subsequent holders. Section 385(c)(2) provides a means by which a holder may avoid being bound by the issuer's classification. That option requires the holder to disclose the inconsistent treatment on a tax return.

4. Significance for S Corporations

We consider the requirements for S corporation status in the final chapter. One requirement relates to stock issued by the corporation. The corporation cannot have more than one class of stock outstanding. It can have more than one type of the same class, such as voting common and nonvoting common. If § 385 results in a purported debt instrument being treated as a second class of stock, the corporation will not qualify for S corporation status. A safe harbor applies to straight debt in the S corporation context. I.R.C. § 1361(c)(5); Reg. § 1.1361-1(l)(5).

5. Regulations

Regulations issued in October 2016 and amended in January 2017 focus on corporations and partnerships that issue purported indebtedness to related corporations and partnerships. The preamble to the regulations indicates that they do not apply to foreign issuers and S corporations. The preamble also includes the following language: "The section 385 regulations are intended to apply to related-party transactions undertaken by large corporate taxpayers that are responsible for a majority of corporate business activity and that have organizational structures that include subsidiaries or affiliated groups. These businesses represent about 0.1 percent of all corporations . . . but are responsible for about 65 percent of all corporate interest deductions and 54 percent of corporate net income." 81 Fed. Reg. 72941 (2016).

The regulations require that the parties be able to provide appropriate documentation of loan-type features. These include an unconditional and binding obligation to pay interest and principal on fixed dates. They also require that the creditor's rights be superior to those of a shareholder, that there be a reasonable expectation that the borrower has the ability to repay the debt, and that there are actions that are evidence of the debtor-creditor relationship. Reg. § 1.385-2(c)(2). Additional regulations recharacterize purported debt as equity if the loan does not result in new investment in the issuer's operations. Reg. § 1.385-3.

In Notice 2017-36, 2017-33 I.R.B. 208, the IRS announced a 12-month delay in the application of the documentation provisions. Notice 2017-38, 2017-30 I.R.B. 147, included these regulations in a group that will either be reformed or withdrawn to mitigate their burden on taxpayers. These regulations were identified as significant regulations requiring additional review pursuant to Executive Order 13789.

E. Securities

An instrument's status as a security varies depending on the context. As noted earlier in this chapter, losses on worthless securities are treated as losses from the sale or exchange of a capital asset on the last day of the year. I.R.C. § 165(g). That section defines security as a share of stock, a right to subscribe for or receive a share of stock, or a bond, debenture, note, or certificate, or other evidence of indebtedness. The debt instrument must be issued by a corporation or a government and must have interest coupons or be in registered form. I.R.C. § 165(g)(2).

That definition applies only for purposes of § 165(g). The § 368 reorganization provisions discussed in later chapters differentiate between stock and securities but do not define either term. In determining the tax consequences of a reorganization, we treat nonqualified preferred stock as neither stock nor securities. I.R.C. § 356(e). Section 7701(a)(7) defines stock to include shares in an association, joint-stock company, or insurance company but provides no other information. Section 7701(a) does not define securities. Reg. § 1.354-1(e) provides that, for purposes of § 354, the term "securities" includes rights to acquire stock. It does not indicate any characteristics of a security that is not a right to acquire stock.

Checkpoints

- A corporation can issue both debt and equity to finance its capital needs.
- Debt generally involves a fixed obligation to repay and bears interest. Creditors' rights are superior to those of shareholders.
- Shareholders do not have a right to dividends or to repayment of their investments. Preferred shareholders generally have limited rights to share in corporate earnings and assets, but they are entitled to payment ahead of common shareholders.
- The corporation can deduct interest payments and the creditor reports them as gross income. If the debt is not repaid, the corporation has debt discharge income, subject to any exceptions in § 108. The creditor's deduction depends on whether the creditor is a corporation or other taxpayer, whether the debt is a business bad debt or a nonbusiness bad debt, and whether the debt is evidenced by a security. Both nonbusiness bad debts and losses from worthless securities are capital losses.
- The corporation cannot deduct dividend payments but the shareholder reports them as gross income. Gain with respect to the stock will be fully taxed, generally as capital gain, unless the sale qualifies for the § 1202 exclusion. Loss with respect to the stock may be capital or ordinary depending on whether the stock is covered by § 1244. A redemption may be treated as a dividend or a sale, depending on the extent to which it changes the shareholder's relationship to the corporation.
- The distinction between stock and indebtedness is blurred when a corporation issues debt that can be converted into stock or issues debt that is held only by shareholders.
- Section 385 lists factors the IRS can consider in issuing regulations categorizing an interest in the corporation as stock or indebtedness.
- A corporation and the holders of a hybrid interest are generally bound by its classification. The government is not bound.

Chapter 4

Transfers to a Corporation

Roadmap

- Section 351
- Shareholder's tax consequences
- Corporation's tax consequences
- Transfers to an investment company
- Overlap with other Code sections
- Post-incorporation funding
- Miscellaneous procedural matters

A. Chapter Overview

The potential shareholders may incorporate a business before beginning operations. Alternatively, they may begin operations as a partnership or LLC and incorporate later. They may incorporate for tax or nontax advantages or for some combination of those advantages.

Because a corporation is an entity separate from its owners, incorporation involves more than drafting articles of incorporation and bylaws, submitting them to the proper state official, and paying any necessary fees. The corporation must acquire assets that it will use in conducting its operations. It can acquire those assets directly from its incorporators, it can purchase them from third parties with funds acquired from those incorporators or from third parties, or it can rent assets from its incorporators or third parties. Whether they provide money or other property, the incorporators will generally receive shares of stock, debt instruments, or some combination of shares and debt instruments.

If the incorporators transfer property other than money in exchange for corporate stock or other consideration, the transfer is a sale or other disposition on which they compute realized gain or loss. The same is true for subsequent transfers. I.R.C. § 1001. After computing realized gain or loss, they determine how much of that gain or loss is recognized, their basis for any shares or other consideration they receive, and when their holding period begins. The corporation makes the same determinations with respect to its receipt of money or other property.

If the transfers are covered by § 351, the shareholders do not recognize gain or they recognize less than their total gain realized. This chapter focuses on § 351 and the tax consequences for the shareholders and the corporation to which they transfer property.

B. Section 351

Although § 1001(c) provides a general rule—that realized gains and losses are recognized—it is subject to exceptions elsewhere in the Code. Section 351 is one such exception. Section 351(a) provides that "No gain or loss shall be recognized if property is transferred to a corporation by one or more persons solely in exchange for stock in such corporation and immediately after the exchange such person or persons are in control (as defined in § 368(c)) of the corporation." This provision has four general requirements: (1) there must be a transfer of property to a corporation; (2) by a person or persons; (3) who receive only stock in the exchange; and (4) who must control the corporation immediately after the transfer. Section 351 may apply when the corporation is formed; it may also apply to subsequent transfers.

Section 351 reflects a congressional policy of encouraging (or at least not discouraging) incorporation of existing businesses. An incorporation generally involves a mere change to the business form. Requiring gain recognition would have a chilling effect on such incorporations.

Although transfers that reflect mere changes in form may justify nonrecognition, other transfers may not merit such treatment. For example, instead of incorporating a business, the taxpayers might transfer assets to an existing corporation in exchange for shares in that corporation. They may receive a significant interest in that corporation, but they may—if it is a publicly traded corporation—receive only an insignificant percentage of the corporation's stock. Alternatively, instead of incorporating an existing business or a potential business, a group of investors might diversify their individually owned assets by transferring them to a newly formed corporation. These situations do not reflect the purpose behind § 351—allowing nonrecognition when there is a mere change in form. As discussed later in this chapter, it does not apply in either situation.

Section 351 primarily applies to incorporations of relatively small entities or transfers to controlled subsidiaries. Most stock transfers involve sales by existing shareholders. Unless the corporation is closely held, in which case it likely has placed restrictions on transfers, those transfers occur in a secondary market. Even in the primary market (sale of stock by the corporation), most stock transfers do not involve § 351 but instead involve cash sales. The person transferring cash to a corporation has no realized gain or loss. The purchase of stock is no different from the purchase of any other asset.

1. Transfer of Property to a Corporation

a. Property

A broad definition of property applies. Even though a taxpayer who transfers only money to the corporation does not realize any gain or loss, money is treated as property. Rev. Rul. 69-357, 1969-1 C.B. 101. This makes sense, as a business needs funds for working capital, to meet short-term expenses, and to purchase assets. Tangible assets, such as land, buildings, and machinery, are property. Intangibles, such as promissory notes, trade secrets, goodwill, and industrial know-how also qualify. Section 351 does not require that each person transfer the same type of property.

Some types of consideration are not treated as property. Nonqualifying items are services, indebtedness of the transferee corporation not evidenced by a security, and interest on indebtedness of the transferee corporation that accrued after the beginning of the transferor's holding period for the debt. I.R.C. § 351(d). The reason for these exceptions is to ensure that § 351 is used for changes in the form of a business or for providing additional funds for an ongoing business. Thus, a service provider cannot avoid tax on receiving stock in exchange for services rendered. A creditor cannot avoid tax on receiving stock in exchange for unpaid interest. A person who transfers both items that qualify as property and items that do not reports income only on the latter items. The transfer of property may still qualify for nonrecognition if the other § 351 requirements are met.

b. Transfer

A transfer generally entails the passing of title from one person to another. It also generally entails the passing of every property right to the other person. In some instances, the transferor may want to retain some rights to the property transferred. Those rights may have value even after the remaining rights are transferred. For example, granting another person a *nonexclusive* right to use a patent does not make the patent unusable by the patent holder. The IRS has ruled that a transfer entails the transfer of all the substantial rights in the property. It requires the transfer of an unqualified, exclusive right in perpetuity to use an item of property. Rev. Rul. 64-56, 1964-1 C.B. 133. It has also ruled that it will not treat the right to use a patent as property for § 351 purposes. Rev. Rul. 69-156, 1969-1 C.B. 101. Note that at least one court has held that a nonexclusive transfer of a patent can qualify for § 351 purposes even though the transferor did not transfer all the rights under the patent. *E.I. Du Pont de Nemours & Co. v. United States*, 471 F.2d 1211 (Ct. Cl. 1973).

c. *Transferee Corporation*

Section 351(a) requires that property be transferred to a corporation of which the transferors are in control after the transfer. In most cases, the transferee corporation is easily identifiable. It is the corporation that receives the property. In some cases, it is not so clear. The examples below involve situations that appear similar but that have different tax consequences.

> **Example 4-1.** ABC Corporation merged into Subsidiary Corporation, a subsidiary of Parent Corporation. Amy, the sole shareholder of ABC, received 50% of Parent's stock. As part of the same transaction, Barry transferred land to Parent in exchange for 30% of Parent's stock. Although Amy and Barry were in control of Parent after these transfers, § 351 did not apply. Some of the property for which control of Parent was received was transferred to Subsidiary rather than to Parent.

> **Example 4-2.** DEF Corporation merged into Parent Corporation. Arlene, the sole shareholder of DEF, received 50% of Parent's stock. As part of the same transaction, Bill transferred land to Parent in exchange for 30% of Parent's stock. Parent then transferred the DEF assets to its subsidiary, Subsidiary Corporation.

The second transaction qualified even though it had the same outcome as the first transaction. Rev. Rul. 84-44, 1984-1 C.B. 105, holds that the first transaction cannot qualify because the assets of ABC were not transferred to Parent. In the second transaction, the assets were transferred to Parent, which remained the transferee corporation even though it dropped the assets down to Subsidiary. The drop-down is permitted by § 368(a)(2)(C), a reorganization provision. Rev. Rul. 84-44 would not prevent qualification under § 351.

A transfer can take many forms. It may be a direct transfer from the owner of the property to the corporation. It may also be a merger transaction or other reorganization. This means that different rules may apply to the transaction, and parties to the transaction may have their tax consequences determined by different Code sections. The Code sometimes provides priority rules for overlap situations, and other times it does not. When no priority rule applies, tax consequences can be derived from more than one Code section. The examples above illustrate how Code sections can sometimes overlap in their coverage. In both examples, § 368 applied to the merger. Assuming the requirements of that section are met, the parties qualify for nonrecognition treatment even if § 351 does not apply to the transaction. In the second example, both sections apply to the merger portion of the transaction, and tax consequences flow from both sections. This may have negative consequences because § 357(c), which does not normally apply to mergers, would apply because of § 351.

2. Transfer by Person or Persons

Section 351 applies to transfers by one or more persons. If the transfers are simultaneous, they are considered together. If they are not simultaneous, the outcome may depend on whether they are treated as parts of a single plan.

> **Example 4-3.** On the same day, Ilene and Jack each transferred appreciated property to newly formed MNO Corporation in exchange for all its stock. Ilene and Jack both qualify for § 351.

> **Example 4-4.** Kate transferred appreciated property to PQR Corporation in exchange for all its stock (900 shares). Larry later transferred appreciated property to PQR and received 100 shares of its stock. After this transfer, Kate and Larry owned all the PQR stock: Kate owned 90%; Larry owned 10%. Kate qualifies for § 351 even if Larry's transfer is not considered along with hers. Larry qualifies only if the two transfers are considered together.

3. Transfer Solely in Exchange for Stock

a. General Rule

A transferor must receive no consideration other than stock to be covered by § 351(a). Two types of transferor are not covered even if they act simultaneously with other transferors. A transferor who receives both stock and other consideration recognizes gain but not loss with respect to the property she transfers to the corporation. Section 351(b) applies to her. A transferor who receives only a debt instrument or some other consideration that is not stock recognizes both gain and loss unless another Code section changes the outcome.

b. Receipt of Preferred Stock

Section 351(a) does not specify whether the shares received must be common or must have voting rights. Section 351(g) is relevant if a transferor receives preferred stock. It provides that nonqualified preferred stock is not treated as stock for purposes of § 351(a). If the transferor receives common stock and nonqualified preferred stock (or receives nonqualified preferred stock and other preferred stock), § 351(b) might still apply. If the only shares he receives are nonqualified preferred stock, he does not qualify for nonrecognition.

Because only *nonqualified* preferred stock is ineligible, the inquiry into tax consequences involves two determinations: whether the stock received is preferred and, if it is, whether it is nonqualified preferred stock. Section 351(g)(3)(A) defines preferred stock as stock with two characteristics. It is limited and preferred as to dividends, and it does not participate in corporate growth to any significant extent. Stock is not treated as participating in corporate growth to any significant extent unless there is a real and meaningful likelihood of the shareholder's participating in the corporation's earnings and growth. Even if the stock has a participating feature, the shareholder must have a real and meaningful likelihood of receiving dividends in excess of any stated preference to avoid having the stock treated as preferred for purposes of § 351(g).

Section 351(g)(2)(A) makes preferred stock nonqualified if it has any of four characteristics:

(1) the shareholder has the right to require the issuer or a related person to redeem or purchase the stock;
(2) the issuer or a related person is required to redeem or purchase the stock;
(3) the issuer or related person has the right to redeem or purchase the stock, and as of the issue date, it is more likely than not that the right will be exercised; or
(4) the dividend rate varies in whole or in part (directly or indirectly) with reference to interest rates, commodity prices, or other similar indices.

The listed characteristics indicate that Congress intended to limit nonrecognition to situations in which the transferor's investment is tied to the corporation's success. If the transferor receives common stock, the stock's value is tied to the success or failure of the corporation. That is less likely with preferred stock, particularly if it has limited dividend and liquidation rights. But even with those limits, it is not nonqualified unless it also has one of the four characteristics listed.

Example 4-5. As part of a group of transferors, Mary transferred appreciated property to STU Corporation in exchange for STU preferred stock. Mary had the right to require STU to redeem the stock at any time. The preferred stock is nonqualified preferred stock. Mary recognized gain on the property she transferred to STU.

Section 351(g)(2)(B) limits the application of the first three characteristics listed above. They apply only if the right or obligation to redeem or purchase is exercisable within 20 years after the stock is issued. Even if the right or obligation may apply within that period, these characteristics are ignored if the right or obligation is subject to a contingency that makes the likelihood of the redemption or purchase remote.

Example 4-6. As part of a group of transferors, Nick transferred appreciated property to VWX Corporation in exchange for VWX preferred stock. Nick had the right to require VWX to redeem the stock after 25 years. The stock is not nonqualified preferred stock.

Stock is not nonqualified preferred stock if the right or obligation to redeem or purchase the stock may be exercised only upon the holder's death, disability, or mental incompetence. I.R.C. § 351(g)(2)(C)(i)(I). But the stock is nonqualified preferred stock if any stock in the corporation is readily tradable on an established securities market or if the transaction's purpose is to make the stock readily tradable on an established securities market. I.R.C. § 351(g)(2)(C)(ii).

Example 4-7. If Nick also had the right to require purchase of his stock at any time after he became disabled, the stock is not nonqualified preferred stock.

Stock is also not nonqualified preferred stock if the holder is an employee who received it as reasonable compensation, and the right or obligation could be exercised only upon her separation from service from the issuer or a related person. I.R.C. § 351(g)(2)(C)(i)(II).

Exercise of the right to redeem or purchase the stock in situations described in § 351(g)(2)(C)(i) presumably is made for nontax reasons. Hence, when the stock was obtained, it evidenced a long-term investment in the corporation.

4. Control of the Corporation Immediately After the Transfer

a. Control

Section 351 applies only if the transferor(s) control the corporation immediately after the transfer. Control, which is defined in § 368(c), has two 80% requirements. The transferor(s) must own stock possessing at least 80% of the corporation's total combined voting power and at least 80% of the total number of shares of all other classes of stock. The inclusion of both requirements limits taxpayers' ability to qualify unless they have significant voting *and* economic interests in the corporation. In interpreting the statutory language, the IRS has applied the second requirement on a class-by-class basis. Rev. Rul. 59-259, 1959-2 C.B. 115.

b. Immediately After the Transfer

Section 351(a) requires that the transferor(s) have control of the corporation immediately after the transfer. It does not require them to acquire control *in* the transfer. Transfers as part of the original incorporation and later transfers can both qualify.

> **Example 4-8.** Olivia and Patrick each transferred property to newly incorporated ABC Corporation. They each received half of ABC's common stock. ABC has no other class of stock. Section 351(a) applies to these transfers.

> **Example 4-9.** Two years later, when ABC needed additional funds, Olivia and Patrick again transferred property to it. They each received half of ABC's newly issued nonvoting common stock. Section 351(a) applies to these transfers. As ABC's only shareholders, Olivia and Patrick satisfy the control requirement.

One or more taxpayers in a control group might later dispose of stock. If "immediately after" looks only to a single point in time, that disposition should not prevent the application of § 351. But in appropriate situations, the IRS can argue that the disposition was part of a plan to qualify an otherwise disqualified transfer. The step transaction doctrine may play a role in determining whether a transferor has control immediately after the transfer. If, before entering into the transaction, the transferor agreed to transfer the stock to a third party, perhaps one who provided only services, the step transaction doctrine might cause the transaction to fail. The transferor would be treated as having never received control of the transferee corporation.

Although the IRS normally invokes the step transaction doctrine, taxpayers may do so if they perceive benefit in doing so. For example, in *Culligan Water Conditioning of Tri-Cities, Inc. v. United States*, 567 F.2d 867 (9th Cir. 1978), the taxpayer argued for application of the step transaction doctrine. If the corporation could take a fair market value basis instead of the transferor's lower basis for the property acquired, it could take larger depreciation deductions. The court rejected the taxpayer's argument. Its decision echoed that reached in *American Bantam Car Co. v. Commissioner*, 11 T.C. 397 (1948).

In at least one ruling, the IRS applied the immediately after requirement somewhat more leniently. Rev. Rul. 2003-51, 2003-1 C.B. 938. It treated transfers by two corporations, each of which operated a particular type of business in common, as separate § 351 transfers. The second corporation (X) operated that business in a wholly owned subsidiary; the first corporation (W) operated the business directly. W transferred the business to a newly created subsidiary (Z) in exchange for 100% of Z's stock. Pursuant to a binding commitment, W then transferred all the Z stock to X's subsidiary (Y) in exchange for 40% of Y's stock. X transferred money to Y in exchange for additional shares of Y stock. Y transferred that money and its own business assets to Z. In the end, Z was a wholly owned subsidiary of Y, using the business assets formerly used by W and Y, W owned 40% of Y's stock, and X owned the remaining 60%. Note that W and X could have combined the separate businesses directly if W had transferred the business assets to Y instead of to Z while X transferred additional money to Y.

c. *Nonsimultaneous Transfers*

Because transferors need not transfer property simultaneously, the requirement that they control the corporation immediately after the transfer does not apply literally. Instead, the "immediately after" language is generally interpreted as requiring that control be achieved as part of the transaction. If multiple transferors want to qualify their transfers, it is prudent for them to reduce their agreement to writing and indicate that any agreement is pursuant to a plan to obtain control of the transferor corporation.

> **Example 4-10.** Arnold, Betty, and Carl transferred property and money to ABC Corporation, and each received one-third of ABC's stock. Arnold transferred his property in January. Betty transferred money in May. Carl transferred property in November. If they did not have a written agreement, they risked an IRS claim that the transfers were unconnected. If the IRS challenge succeeded, only Arnold's transfer would qualify. As 100% shareholder in January, he met the control requirement. Because Betty transferred money, she does not care if § 351 applies. Carl would recognize gain or loss on his transfer.

d. *Transfers Made to Qualify Others*

As noted earlier in this chapter, services are not property. The value of services as compared to the value of property transferred affects whether the transfer is covered by § 351. If service providers receive 20% or less of the corporation's stock, other transferors can qualify for nonrecognition. Only the service providers report gross income, in this situation as compensation for services rendered. If service providers receive more than 20% of the corporation's stock, none of the transfers would qualify because the persons who transferred property would not be in control of the corporation immediately after the transfer. They would recognize gain or loss, as appropriate, on any property they transferred in exchange for the corporation's stock.

> **Example 4-11.** Alexis and Bob transferred property of equal value in exchange for 80% of ABC Corporation stock. As part of the same transaction, Alexis also received 20% of ABC stock for services rendered to the corporation. Both transfers of property qualify for nonrecognition because the persons who transferred property were in control of the transferee corporation. Alexis is taxed on the value of the stock she received for her services.

> **Example 4-12.** If Alexis instead received all her ABC stock for services rendered, none of the transfers qualifies. Bob, who transferred property, was not in control of the corporation immediately after the transfer. All transfers by Alexis and Bob were taxable events.

The parties cannot change the result by having the service provider also transfer a small amount of property. Thus, if Alexis transferred $100 and services worth $20,000, Bob's transfer in Example 4-12 would not qualify even though Alexis did transfer property and the two property transferors were in control immediately after the transfers. Reg. § 1.351-1(a)(1)(ii) applies if the property transferred is of relatively small value in comparison to the value of stock the transferor receives in exchange for services and the primary purpose for transferring it is to qualify another person for § 351. It also applies if the property transferred is of relatively small value in comparison to the value of stock the transferor already owns and the primary purpose for transferring it is to qualify another person.

> **Example 4-13.** Beth wanted to invest in DEF Corporation by transferring appreciated property to it in exchange for 5% of the DEF stock. She did not want to recognize her gain. Arthur owned 100% of the DEF stock and wanted to facilitate Beth's investment. When Beth made her transfer, Arthur transferred $200 to DEF in exchange for one share of its stock. Beth's transfer does not qualify for nonrecognition. Arthur's primary purpose in transferring the minimal amount of money was to qualify Beth's transfer.

The regulation illustrates the need for transactions to reflect the statute's language and its spirit. The IRS long ago indicated it would not give an advance ruling that an existing shareholder qualifies as part of the group unless he conveys property worth at least 10% of the value of the stock he already owns. Rev. Proc. 77-37, 1977-2 C.B. 568. Rev. Proc. 2017-3, 2017-1 I.R.B. 130, provides that the Service currently limits its § 351 rulings to transactions involving significant issues.

e. Disproportionate Transfers

The regulations provide for reconstituting the transfers if one or more persons receives an interest that is disproportionate to the value of property transferred. A transfer covered by this rule will have both the tax consequences associated with a proportionate transfer and the tax consequences associated with the deemed transfer from one shareholder to another. The deemed transfer might be treated as a gift, as compensation, or as satisfying an obligation. Reg. § 1.351-1(b)(1).

C. Shareholder's Tax Consequences

1. Transferors to Consider

If a transfer qualifies under § 351(a), the transferor recognizes no gain or loss. Each transferor is considered separately for this purpose. It is possible that one transferor will be covered by § 351(a) because she transferred only property and received only stock in the controlled corporation. Another transferor may be covered by § 351(b) because he received both stock and other consideration in exchange for transferring property. A third transferor may not be covered by § 351 at all. She may have rendered services in exchange for all her stock, or she may have received only nonqualified preferred stock or debt instruments in exchange for her property. A fourth transferor may not care whether § 351 applies because he transferred only money in exchange for his stock.

2. Tax Consequences to Consider

Transferors consider the following tax consequences after transferring money or other property, or rendering services, to a corporation. First, did the transferor realize gain or loss with respect to any property transferred? Second, to what extent is that gain or loss recognized? Third, if there is a loss and § 351 does not apply, does any other Code section disallow the loss deduction? Fourth, what basis do the transferors take for the stock or other consideration they receive from the corporation? Fifth, what holding period do they take? The discussion in this section addresses those questions. It assumes that none of the transferors is a dealer in stock or securities who might have to clearly identify the stock received as investment property under § 1236(a) to ensure that it is a capital asset. It also assumes that persons who receive stock in exchange for services report gross income that year. That will not necessarily be the case if the stock is subject to a substantial risk of forfeiture. I.R.C. § 83.

3. Transfers Covered by Section 351(a)

a. Transfer of One Item in Exchange for One Class of Stock

The best place to begin in determining tax consequences is with transfers that are covered only by § 351(a). In those situations, the transferors realize a gain or loss on transferring money or other property to the corporation solely in exchange for its stock. They have control immediately after the exchange, and they make no disposition that leads the IRS to question whether they had a plan to divest themselves of control. In this first situation, we will assume that some taxpayers transferred money and the others transferred unencumbered land they held for investment.

Several Code sections apply to this situation. Section 1001(a) computes their realized gain or loss as the difference between the basis of the property they transfer and the amount of money and fair market value of any other property they receive. Section 351(a) provides that they do not recognize any realized gain or loss. Section 358(a)(1) provides that their basis for the stock they receive is the basis they had for the property they transferred to the corporation. None of the adjustments provided in that section apply in this situation. The stock they receive is a capital asset because none of the exceptions provided in § 1221 applies. Because its basis is computed with reference to the basis they had for their property, their holding period for the stock includes their holding period for that property if the property they transferred was a capital asset or a § 1231 asset. I.R.C. § 1223(1). The holding period for stock received in exchange for money begins when the taxpayer receives the stock; that taxpayer takes a cost basis.

The basis rules preserve the shareholder's unrecognized gain or loss by building it into his basis for the shares received. He can recognize the gain or loss when he sells the stock unless another provision prevents recognition.

> **Example 4-14.** Alan, Barbara, Calvin, and Debra formed XYZ Corporation and became its only shareholders. They transferred the following items to XYZ solely in exchange for 1500 shares of XYZ common stock. Alan transferred $25,000 in exchange for 100 shares. Barbara transferred $75,000 in exchange for 300 shares. Calvin trans-

ferred land he had acquired 10 years ago, with a basis of $10,000 and now worth $100,000, for 400 shares. Debra transferred land she had acquired six years ago, with a basis of $240,000 and now worth $175,000, for 700 shares.

Alan and Barbara made purchases. Because they transferred only money, their results do not depend on § 351 applying. They are important to Calvin and Debra because they acquired more than 20% of the XYZ shares. If neither was part of the group, Calvin and Debra would not qualify; together they did not acquire at least 80% of the XYZ stock. Alan's basis for his stock is $25,000; Barbara's basis for her stock is $75,000. The stock is a capital asset; their holding period begins when they acquire the stock.

Calvin and Debra have similar tax consequences because each exchanged property and received only XYZ stock. Calvin realized a $90,000 gain on transferring his land to XYZ. None of that gain is recognized. Calvin's basis for his XYZ shares is the same as his basis for his land, $10,000. The stock is a capital asset. His holding period includes the 10 years he owned his land because the land was a capital asset and his basis for the stock is the same as his basis for the land. Debra realized a $65,000 loss on transferring her land to XYZ. None of that loss is recognized. Debra's basis for her XYZ shares is the same as her basis for her land, $240,000. The stock is a capital asset. Her holding period includes the six years she owned her land.

Because she had a loss, Debra may have preferred that § 351(a) not apply to her transfer. Because that provision is mandatory rather than elective, she cannot avoid its reach if her transfer is part of the transactions to which the parties agreed. If XYZ did not need Debra's land, she might have instead sold the land to a third party and transferred money to XYZ. In that case, she could have deducted her loss. Alternatively, if Debra made her transfer later and was not part of the original plan, she could also have deducted her loss. Section 267 would not have disallowed her loss because she and XYZ were not related persons; Debra did not own more than 50% of the value of XYZ's stock. Because Debra's land was a capital asset, her annual loss deduction would be subject to the § 1211(b) limits.

b. Transfer of One Item in Exchange for More Than One Class of Stock

A transferor might receive both voting common stock and nonvoting common stock in exchange for the property transferred. Or he might receive both common stock and preferred stock that is not nonqualified preferred stock and thus can be received without gain or loss recognition. In those situations, he allocates his basis for the shares received between the different classes of stock. The allocation reflects the total value of each class of stock he receives. Reg. § 1.358-2(b)(2).

> **Example 4-15.** Alan, Barbara, Calvin, and Debra each instead received 100 shares of XYZ voting common stock worth $25,000. In addition, Barbara received 120 shares of nonvoting common stock worth $50,000; Calvin received 180 shares of nonvoting common stock worth $75,000; and Debra received 360 shares of nonvoting common stock worth $150,000.

Because they received two different classes of stock, Barbara, Calvin, and Debra allocate the basis computed in Example 4-14, between the voting and nonvoting shares.

Barbara received voting shares worth $25,000 and nonvoting shares worth $50,000. The voting shares represent 1/3 of what she received; the nonvoting shares represent 2/3 of what she received. Barbara allocates the $75,000 she transferred in those ratios. Her basis for her 100 voting shares is $25,000 (1/3 * $75,000); her basis per share is $250. Her basis for her 120 nonvoting shares is $50,000 (2/3 * $75,000); her basis per share is $416.67.

Calvin received voting shares worth $25,000 and nonvoting shares worth $75,000. The voting shares represent 1/4 of what he received; the nonvoting shares represent 3/4 of what he received. Calvin allocates his $10,000 basis for the land he transferred in those ratios. His basis for his 100 voting shares is $2,500 (1/4 * $10,000); his basis per share is $25. His basis for his 180 nonvoting shares is $7,500 (3/4 * $10,000); his basis per share is $41.67.

Debra received voting shares worth $25,000 and nonvoting shares worth $150,000. The voting shares represent 1/7 of what she received; the nonvoting shares represent 6/7 of what she received. She allocates her $240,000 basis for the land she transferred in those ratios. Her basis for her 100 voting shares is $34,285.71 (1/7 * $240,000); her basis per share is $342.86. Her basis for her 360 nonvoting shares is $205,714.29 (6/7 * $240,000); her basis per share is $571.43.

c. Transfer of More Than One Item in Exchange for Stock

In the last two examples, each shareholder transferred only one item to the corporation. If a shareholder transfers more than one item of property, we compute his tax consequences separately for each item transferred.

> **Example 4-16.** Calvin instead transferred two pieces of land, with a combined value of $100,000 in exchange for 400 shares of XYZ voting common stock. He acquired Blackacre for $4,000 eight years ago; it is currently worth $40,000. He acquired Whiteacre six months ago

for $42,000; it is currently worth $60,000. Because he received only stock in exchange for his property, Calvin did not recognize any of his realized gain on Blackacre or Whiteacre. Because Blackacre represents 40% of the value Calvin transferred to XYZ, 160 of his XYZ shares (40%) take his basis and holding period for Blackacre. His other 240 XYZ shares (60%) take his basis and holding period for Whiteacre. If either Blackacre or Whiteacre was not a capital asset or § 1231 asset in Calvin's hands, his holding period for the stock he received for that land would instead start when he received it.

4. Transfers Covered by Section 351(b)

a. Gain or Loss Recognized

Section 351(b) applies to a shareholder who received both stock and money or other property in exchange for transferring property to the corporation. If he transferred appreciated property, he recognizes at least part of his gain. If he transferred loss property, he cannot recognize any of his loss.

The amount of gain recognized is the lesser of the actual gain realized or the value of consideration other than stock received. If some of the property transferred was gain property and other property transferred was loss property, the IRS treats each item separately in determining the transferor's tax consequences. Rev. Rul. 68-55, 1968-1 C.B. 140. In other words, a transferor who has an overall loss may still have recognized gain. Prop. Reg. § 1.351-2(b) includes an example of these computations.

Example 4-17. Amanda transferred property worth $300 to GHI Corporation in exchange for 80% of its stock and other consideration. Amanda's basis for that property was $100. She received $50, nonqualified preferred stock worth $60, and common stock worth $190. Although she realized a gain of $200, she recognizes only $110 of that gain. The $110 value of the money and nonqualified preferred stock she received was less than her $200 realized gain.

Example 4-18. Bob transferred two pieces of land to JKL Corporation in exchange for all its stock (worth $150) and $50. Bob had a basis of $78 for Greenacre, which was worth $120. He had a basis of $300 for Blueacre, which was worth $80. Although Bob's loss on Blueacre exceeded his gain on Greenacre, Bob must recognize part of his gain. Because Greenacre was worth 60% of the total value transferred ($120/$200), he allocates 60% of the stock and 60% of the money to the amount realized for Greenacre. His amount realized for

Greenacre is thus stock worth $90 and $30 of cash. His gain realized is $42, the difference between his $120 amount realized and his $78 basis. His gain recognized is limited to the $30 cash he received.

b. Basis and Holding Period

The transferor allocates the basis of his property among the shares of stock he receives. Those shares take his holding period for the property transferred, assuming it was a capital asset or a § 1231 asset. He takes a fair market value basis for any nonqualified preferred stock or other property received. His holding period for those items begins when he receives them.

When the shareholder receives property other than stock ("boot"), the § 358(a) basis computation covers property he can receive without recognizing gain. It also covers any other property (except money) he receives.

1. Shareholder Receives Money

The basis computation for property that qualifies for nonrecognition begins with the shareholder's basis for the property he transferred. He subtracts three items: the value of any property (other than money) he receives; the amount of money he receives; and any loss he recognized on the exchange. He adds two items: any amount treated as a dividend; and any gain (other than the amount treated as a dividend) he recognized on the exchange. I.R.C. § 358(a)(1).

Example 4-19. Alec transferred property worth $300 to newly created MNO Corporation in exchange for all its stock (worth $160) and $140. Alec's basis for that property was $100. Alec recognized $140 of his $200 gain. His basis for the MNO stock is $100. His starting point in computing basis was his $100 basis for the property he transferred. He reduced that by the $140 he received and increased it by the $140 gain he recognized. The computation involved only those three amounts because Alec received no property other than money, had no loss to recognize, and—because MNO was newly formed—could not have received a dividend.

The result above might lead you to believe that the shareholder's basis for his stock always equals his basis for the property he transfers. That is the result in many situations, but it is not always the case. The shareholder's basis for his stock should reflect the difference between its value and any gain or loss he did not recognize on the transfer. In Example 4-19, Alec had unrecognized gain of $60. If he sold his stock for its $160 value, he would realize and recognize a $60 gain.

Example 4-20. Alec instead received all the MNO stock (worth $95) and $205. Alec recognized all $200 of his gain because he received at least that much money. His basis for the MNO stock is $95. His starting point in computing basis was his $100 basis for the property he transferred. He reduced that by the $205 he received and increased it by the $200 gain he recognized. Because Alec already recognized all his gain, the $95 basis we computed for his stock is equal to its value.

Example 4-21. Alec instead had a basis for his property of $318 in Example 4-20. Alec recognized none of his $18 loss even though he received money. His basis for the MNO stock is $113. His starting point in computing basis was his $318 basis for the property he transferred. He reduced that by the $205 he received. If Alec sells this stock for its $95 value, he will realize and recognize an $18 loss.

Because we compute the shareholder's basis for his stock with reference to his basis for the property transferred, his holding period for the stock includes his holding period for that property unless the property transferred was not a capital asset or § 1231 asset. I.R.C. § 1223(1).

2. *Shareholder Receives Other Property*

The shareholder might receive only property other than money, or she might receive both other property and money, in addition to receiving stock. As was true in the preceding discussion, her basis for what she receives is the difference between its value and her unrecognized gain or loss. That difference is reflected in her basis for the shares rather than in her basis for the other property because only the shares constitute nonrecognition property. The other property takes a fair market value basis rather than a substituted basis. I.R.C. § 358(a)(2).

Example 4-22. Joan transferred property worth $500 to PQR Corporation in exchange for all its stock (worth $300) and a PQR bond worth $200. Joan's basis for that property was $80. Joan recognized $200 of her $420 gain. Her basis for the PQR stock is $80. Her starting point in computing basis was her $80 basis for the property she transferred. She reduced that by the $200 value of the bond she received and increased it by the $200 gain she recognized. She takes a $200 basis for the PQR bond. If she sold the PQR stock for its $300 value, she would realize and recognize the $220 gain she did not recognize on the original transfer.

Because we compute Joan's basis for her stock with reference to her basis for the property transferred, her holding period for the stock includes her holding period for that property unless the property transferred was not a capital asset or § 1231 asset. I.R.C. § 1223(1). Her holding period for the bond begins when she acquires it.

Keep in mind that nonqualified preferred stock is treated as other property for purposes of these basis rules. It takes a fair market value basis and a holding period that begins when the shareholder receives it.

c. Dividend Language

Section 358(a)(1) increases basis by any amount treated as a dividend. This aspect of the basis computation may seem surprising with respect to transfers to form a corporation. After all, a newly formed corporation has no earnings with which to pay a dividend. In working with § 358, keep these facts in mind. First, it applies not only to § 351 exchanges but also to Code provisions involving corporate reorganizations and separations. Those exchanges may involve distributions that are treated as dividends. Second, § 351 is not limited to the initial incorporation. It can apply to transfers to an existing corporation if the later transferors meet the control requirement. It is possible that the exchange will resemble a dividend distribution and be treated like one.

> **Example 4-23.** Ben owns 100% of the stock of STU corporation, which has been in existence for 10 years. This year, he transferred property to STU in exchange for additional stock and $400. The IRS might successfully argue that some or all of the $400 was a distribution of STU's E&P rather than a transfer in exchange for Ben's property. If so, Ben would report an appropriate amount of dividend income.

5. Assumption of Liabilities

a. General Rule

You should not be surprised that property may be mortgaged or subject to other debts. If a person transfers that property to the corporation in exchange for its stock, it is likely that the corporation will agree to pay the debt. It could formally assume the debt or it could take the property subject to the debt. In either case, the shareholder is relieved of paying the debt and receives less stock than he would if he transferred unencumbered property. Debt relief is thus a component of the transferor's amount realized.

When encumbered property is transferred in exchange for any type of consideration, the transferor's amount realized includes the debt the other party assumes or agrees to pay. Reg. § 1.1001-2(a). Unless a nonrecognition provision applies, the transferor recognizes any gain realized on the transfer. Section 357(a) is the nonrecognition provision that applies to debt assumed in a transfer that would otherwise satisfy the requirements of § 351(a). It provides that assumption of liability in a § 351 transaction is not treated as money or other property. When this general rule applies, debt assumption does not cause gain recognition. This rule makes sense. The taxpayer does not realize an economic windfall when the property is transferred because he still owns the property subject to the debt, albeit indirectly, in his role as a shareholder.

> **Example 4-24.** Albert owned property worth $500,000, for which he had a basis of $320,000. The property was subject to a $100,000 debt. Albert transferred the property to ABC Corporation in exchange for all the ABC stock, which was then worth $400,000. ABC also assumed the $100,000 debt encumbering that property. Albert realized a $180,000 gain. Because the debt assumption was not treated as money or other property, Albert recognized none of his gain.

These transactions may involve recourse or nonrecourse debt. Recourse debt generally means that the creditor can satisfy the debt by looking to the debtor's other property in addition to looking to the encumbered property; the debtor is personally liable for recourse debt. If a liability is nonrecourse, the creditor can only look to the encumbered property for repayment. If a liability is recourse, it is treated as assumed by the transferee if, based on the facts and circumstances, the transferee has agreed to satisfy it and is expected to satisfy it. It does not matter whether the transferor is relieved of liability. Nonrecourse liability is treated as assumed by the transferee with respect to any asset subject to that liability. I.R.C. § 357(d)(1). The amount of nonrecourse liability deemed assumed is reduced if the transferor owns other assets that are subject to that same debt and has both agreed to, and is expected to, satisfy that debt. If the value of those other assets is less than the amount of the debt, the lower value is the reduction. I.R.C. § 357(d)(2).

b. Exceptions

1. Tax Avoidance Motive

The transferor treats the debt assumption as money if the principal purpose of the transfer is to avoid federal income tax or is not a bona fide business purpose. I.R.C. § 357(b)(1). A tax advantage or purpose may coexist with a business purpose. The motive for the transaction is judged based on the nature of the liability and the circumstances surrounding the arrangements for its assumption. If the taxpayer has the burden of proving that the debt assumption should not be treated as money, he must do so by the clear preponderance of the evidence. I.R.C. § 357(b)(2).

If § 357(b) applies, we treat all debts assumed as money. This rule taints even debts that did not involve a tax avoidance purpose. Reg. § 1.357-1(c).

> **Example 4-25.** Belinda owned appreciated property worth $500,000 subject to a purchase money mortgage of $100,000. She planned to transfer the property to DEF Corporation in exchange for a controlling stock interest. Belinda wanted to receive $60,000 from DEF but did not want to pay tax on receiving boot. Before making the transfer, she borrowed $60,000 from a bank, using her equity in the property as security. DEF took her property subject to both loans and issued stock worth $340,000 to Belinda. Section 357(b) treats both the original $100,000 loan and the new $60,000 loan as money or other property. Belinda recognizes the lesser of her actual gain realized or $160,000.

2. Liabilities That Exceed Basis

The transferor recognizes gain if the liabilities assumed exceed his basis for the assets he transferred. The excess is gain recognized; its character depends on whether the property transferred was a capital asset or another type of asset. I.R.C. § 357(c). Determination of basis is made on an aggregate basis and not asset by asset. A taxpayer can thus avoid, or at least limit, the effect of this provision by transferring additional property or money. Some courts have even allowed taxpayers to transfer their own IOUs to the corporation. *Lessinger v. Commissioner*, 872 F.2d 519 (2d Cir. 1989); *Peracchi v. Commissioner*, 143 F.3d 487 (9th Cir. 1998). Those decisions cited Rev. Rul. 68-629, 1968-2 C.B. 154, but ruled for the taxpayers.

> **Example 4-26.** Carl transferred two pieces of property to GHI Corporation in exchange for all its stock. He had a basis of $100,000 in Blackacre, which was worth $500,000 and was subject to a $120,000 mortgage. He had a basis of $250,000 in Whiteacre, which was worth $300,000. Although GHI assumed Carl's mortgage, he recognized no gain. The mortgage exceeded his basis for Blackacre but it did not exceed his combined bases for Blackacre and Whiteacre.

Two other provisions in § 357(c) are important. First, § 357(b) governs transactions covered by both it and § 357(c). I.R.C. § 357(c)(2)(A). Second, § 357(c) ignores liabilities that give rise to a deduction unless they result in the creation of (or increase in) the basis of any property. I.R.C. § 357(c)(3).

c. Basis and Holding Period

Even if debt assumption does not result in gain recognition, it affects the transferor's basis for the stock she receives. Because I.R.C. § 358(d) treats a liability assumption as money received by the transferor, the assumption reduces the transferor's basis for that stock. She will realize a larger gain (or smaller loss) if she later sells that stock.

Example 4-27. Dorothy transferred property worth $180,000 to JKL Corporation in exchange for all its stock. Dorothy's basis for the property was $100,000. The property was encumbered by a $25,000 purchase money mortgage, which JKL assumed. Dorothy's basis for her JKL stock is $75,000. That is her $100,000 original basis for the property transferred reduced by the $25,000 debt assumption.

Example 4-28. If Dorothy's property had been encumbered by a $125,000 mortgage, she would have recognized gain of $25,000. That is the amount by which the liability exceeded her basis. Her basis for the stock she received would be zero. That is her original $100,000 basis reduced by the $125,000 debt assumption, and increased by the $25,000 gain recognized.

Section 358(d) contains an exception for liabilities that give rise to a deduction covered by § 357(c)(3). The transferor received no tax benefit from those liabilities. Instead, the corporation that assumed them will take the deduction. It would be unfair to reduce the transferor's basis by those amounts.

Example 4-29. Edward transferred property worth $160,000 to MNO Corporation in exchange for all its stock. Edward's basis for the property was $100,000. In addition to transferring its stock, MNO agreed to pay the $8,000 property tax due with respect to the property. Because MNO can deduct the property tax, the $8,000 liability is not treated as money. Edward's basis for the stock he received is his $100,000 basis for the property he transferred to MNO.

In the situations described above, the shareholder computes his basis for his stock with reference to his basis for the property he transferred. If that property was a capital asset or a § 1231 asset, his holding period for the stock includes his holding period for the property transferred. I.R.C. § 1223(1).

D. Corporation's Tax Consequences

1. Gain or Loss Recognized

A corporation recognizes no gain or loss on the receipt of property in exchange for its stock. I.R.C. § 1032. This section applies whether or not the shareholder qualifies for nonrecognition on the transaction.

Section 1032 applies only if the corporation transfers its stock. If it also transfers other property, part of the property it receives is for consideration other than its own stock. If that other property is money, the corporation does not realize gain or loss. But if it transfers property other than money, § 351(f) applies the § 311 rules: the corporation recognizes gain but not loss.

> **Example 4-30.** Flora transferred land to PQR Corporation in exchange for 40% of PQR's stock and equipment worth $100. Greg transferred money to PQR in exchange for 40% of PQR's stock. PQR had a basis for the equipment of $25. PQR realized and recognized a gain of $75 on transferring the equipment to Flora. If PQR's basis for the equipment had instead been $110, it would have realized a loss of $10. It would not recognize that loss.

2. Basis

a. General Rule

The corporation's basis for property received is the same as the transferor's basis, increased by gain, if any, recognized by the transferor. I.R.C. § 362(a)(1). Although the transferee corporation had no basis for the stock it transferred, it nevertheless acquires a basis for the property received.

> **Example 4-31.** Harry transferred property worth $150 to STU Corporation in a § 351 transaction. His basis for that property was $100. Harry received only STU common stock worth $150 and recognized none of his $50 realized gain. STU's basis for the property is $100.

> **Example 4-32.** If Harry instead received stock worth $145 and $5, he recognized $5 of his $50 realized gain. STU's basis for the property is $105. That represents Harry's basis, increased by the gain he recognized.

Section 362(d) limits the corporation's basis increase for gain recognized. If the gain recognized is attributable to the corporation's assumption of a liability, the basis cannot exceed the property's value.

Example 4-33. Ilana transferred property worth $150 to VWX Corporation in a § 351 transaction. Her basis for that property was $100. Ilana received VWX common stock worth $100, and VWX also assumed a $52 liability encumbering the property. Ilana realized and recognized a $52 gain. VWX's basis for the property is $150, not $152, because its basis cannot exceed the property's value.

Because the corporation can increase its basis to reflect at least some of the shareholder's recognized gain, the gain avoids being taxed twice—first, when the shareholder transfers the property to the corporation and second, when the corporation eventually sells it.

b. Loss Limitation Provisions

If the property transferred is worth less than the shareholder's basis, both the shareholder and the corporation have unrecognized potential losses. Reflecting Congress' continuing concerns regarding loss transactions, § 362(e) limits the potential loss duplication benefits associated with these transfers.

Section 362(e)(1) limits the importation of "built-in losses." It applies to transfers from non-U.S. persons to domestic corporations. A loss importation occurs if the aggregate adjusted bases of property transferred exceed the aggregate value of that property. Property transferred in a § 351 transaction is covered by § 362(e)(1) if gains or losses on such property are not subject to federal income tax in the hands of the transferor immediately before the transfer but are subject to federal income tax in the hands of the transferee immediately after the transfer. When this provision applies, the corporation's basis for the property is its fair market value and not the transferor's higher basis.

Example 4-34. In a § 351 transaction, ABC Domestic Corporation acquired an item of property worth $80 from DEF Foreign Corporation. DEF was not subject to federal income tax. If DEF's basis for that property was $100, ABC's basis is limited to $80.

Section 362(e)(2) limits the transfer of built-in losses. It applies even though the transferor is subject to federal income tax. It alters the general § 362 basis rules to prevent the deduction of built-in losses at both the shareholder and corporate levels. If the aggregate adjusted bases of property transferred to the corporation exceeds its value, the corporation's basis cannot exceed the property's value. The corporation allocates the reduction to each property based on its share of the built-in loss. I.R.C. § 362(e)(2)(B). Instead of reducing the corporation's basis for the property, the transferor shareholder and transferee corporation can instead elect to reduce the transferor's stock basis. I.R.C. § 362(e)(2)(C). This election may benefit shareholders who do not intend to sell their stock relatively soon. It may allow the acquired corporation to take advantage of higher depreciation deductions or to recognize a loss on selling property. Reg. § 1.362-4(h) provides several examples of transfers subject to § 362(e)(2).

3. Holding Period

If the corporation computes its basis with reference to the transferor's basis, its holding period includes the transferor's holding period. I.R.C. § 1223(2).

E. Transfers to an Investment Company

Section 351(e) prevents transfers to an investment company from qualifying. Those transfers do not involve the structure of an operating business. Instead, they are an indirect means of diversifying the transferors' investments. Section 351(e)(1) provides an extensive list of property counted in determining whether an entity is an investment company. In addition to including stock or securities, it treats certain other assets (including money, interests in precious metals, and interests in publicly traded partnerships) as stock or securities.

Reg. § 1.351-1(c)(1) treats a transfer as made to an investment company if it meets two conditions. First, the transfer results, directly or indirectly, in diversification of the transferors' interests. Second, the transferee is either a regulated investment company (RIC), a real estate investment trust (REIT), or a corporation more than 80% of the value of whose assets (excluding money and nonconvertible debt obligations) are held for investment and are readily marketable stocks or securities, or interests in RICs or REITs. RICs and REITs have certain tax advantages, including avoiding double taxation of corporate profits.

Diversification requires that two or more persons transfer nonidentical assets to a corporation. Reg. § 1.351-1(c)(5). Obviously, if there is only one transferor, or if the transferors transfer identical property, diversification does not occur. There is also no diversification if a transferor or transferors transfer assets that are already diversified. Reg. § 1.351-1(c)(6). Even if transfers result in diversifying the transferors' assets, § 351 may still apply if the transferee corporation is not a RIC, a REIT, or a corporation that meets the 80% test described in the preceding paragraph. Transferors that make transfers to an operating company and do not use such transfers as a ruse to diversify their investments are unlikely to run afoul of § 351(e)(1).

Example 4-35. Jake has owned GHI Corporation stock for 20 years. The stock is highly appreciated but subject to value fluctuations. His investment in GHI constitutes 60% of his total investments. To balance his portfolio, Jake organized a swap fund. He and several other individuals transferred their shares in different companies to JKL Corporation in exchange for all its stock. Jake and his fellow transferors have made transfers to an investment company and must recognize their gains and losses.

F. Overlap with Other Code Sections

Section 351 overlaps with §§ 368 and 304, both of which are discussed in other chapters. A transaction may qualify both as a § 351 transfer and as a § 368 reorganization because one corporation merges into a second corporation simultaneously with other persons transferring property to the second corporation. When this occurs, the taxpayers may be subject to tax consequences under both sections. This may benefit a transferor who is trying to qualify under § 351 if he cannot take advantage of the reorganization provisions. If a transaction is described in both §§ 351 and 304, § 304(b) provides that § 304 takes priority. Instead of enjoying § 351 nonrecognition, the transferors may be treated as receiving a dividend taxable under § 301.

More than one Code section applies if the transaction is described in each section and neither section indicates that one of them takes priority. One section may have more rigorous requirements than the other. For example, the regulations under the reorganization provisions include business purpose, continuity of interest, and continuity of business enterprise requirements. Those requirements don't appear to directly apply to § 351 transactions. With respect to business purpose, the IRS has attempted to impose such a requirement in the § 351 context, and some courts have been receptive to that position. Rev. Rul. 55-36, 1955-1 C.B. 340; *West Coast Marketing Corp. v. Commissioner*, 46 T.C. 32 (1966) (transfer to controlled corporation was intermediate step before purported reorganization). Nevertheless, it is not clear whether a business purpose in addition to merely wanting to incorporate is needed. With respect to the continuity of interest and continuity of business enterprise requirements, the § 351 regulations do not impose such requirements. This is not surprising, given that § 351 generally requires only that the transferor(s) of property control the corporation immediately following the transfer(s).

G. Post-Incorporation Funding

The corporation may be able to fund its operations using the assets it received when it incorporated, plus any post-incorporation profits it retains. But that will not always be the case. If the corporation needs additional funds, it may issue more stock—either to existing shareholders or to new shareholders; it may issue debt instruments to existing shareholders, existing creditors, or new creditors; or it may receive a contribution to capital without the need to issue stock. Each of these actions has tax consequences.

Transfers of stock in exchange for additional property do not qualify for § 351 nonrecognition unless the transferor(s) are in control immediately after the transfer. Thus, transfers by some—but not all—of the current shareholders may be insufficient. This matters only to those shareholders who transfer property other than money. Shareholders who transfer money do not benefit from § 351.

Debt instruments have certain perceived advantages. The corporation can deduct interest payments, and shareholders do not report repayments of principal as dividends. But if debt instruments are held in the same proportions as stock, the shareholder-creditors risk an IRS challenge to the instruments' status as debt. If the debt is treated as a second class of stock, the corporation cannot make (or maintain) an S corporation election. Funding sources are discussed further in the preceding chapter.

H. Miscellaneous Procedural Matters

The regulations impose certain reporting requirements on the transferor(s) and the transferee corporation. Reg. § 1.351-3. The corporation may also qualify for several elections. These include selecting an accounting method and electing S corporation status.

Checkpoints

- No gain or loss is recognized on the transfer of property solely for stock of a corporation if the transferor(s) control(s) the corporation immediately after the transfer.
- Immediately after the transfer, the transferor(s) must control the corporation within the meaning of § 368(c).
- Corporations do not recognize gain or loss on issuing stock for property or services even if the transaction is not covered by § 351.

- The shareholder's basis and holding period for the property transferred generally carry over to the stock she receives. The corporation generally takes the shareholder's basis and holding period for the property transferred to it.
- The shareholder recognizes gain, but not loss, if he also receives boot. His basis computation for stock received takes both recognized gain and boot into account.
- The shareholder does not treat debt assumption as boot for purposes of gain recognition unless the primary purpose for the assumption is tax avoidance or a non-business purpose or unless the debt exceeds basis. The shareholder does treat debt assumption as boot in computing his basis for the shares.
- Section 362(e) might limit the corporation's basis when it receives property that has a built-in loss.
- Almost anything transferred to the corporation qualifies as property. Services do not qualify as property.
- The IRS holds that the transferor must transfer an unqualified, exclusive right to the property. This can be a problem for transfers of rights to patents.
- The property must be transferred to the controlled corporation. A subsequent drop-down of assets does not disqualify the initial transfer.
- The transferor(s) must receive either common or preferred stock of the transferee corporation. Nonqualified preferred stock is not eligible for nonrecognition.
- Transfers to investment companies do not qualify for § 351 treatment. The regulations generally treat transfers that result in diversification of the transferor's interest as transfers to an investment company.

Chapter 5

Dividend Distributions

Roadmap

- Dividend defined
- Amount distributed and amount of dividend
- Distributing corporation's tax consequences
- Shareholder's tax consequences
- Nontaxable distributions of stock or rights
- Taxable distributions of stock or rights
- Allocating E&P to distributions

A. Chapter Overview

If a corporation transfers money or other property, its tax consequences—and those of the recipient—depend on how the transfer is classified. The payment might be compensation for services, rent for use of property, interest on a loan, or a distribution with respect to the corporation's stock. This chapter covers one type of distribution with respect to the corporation's stock: a dividend distribution. Later chapters cover redemption, reorganization, and liquidation distributions.

This chapter considers several topics related to dividends. These include the relevant definitions, the corporation's tax consequences, the shareholder's tax consequences, and the effect on the corporation's earnings and profits (E&P). The form the distribution takes—money, other property, or additional shares of the corporation's own stock—affects those tax consequences.

B. Dividend Defined

Section 316(a) defines a dividend as a distribution of property by a corporation to its shareholders out of its current or accumulated E&P. This definition has three elements: the distribution must be to shareholders; it must be of property; and it must be from current or accumulated E&P. Unless the corporation makes a distribution that meets these tests—or is treated as making one—its shareholders do not have dividend income. Distributions of stock that are not treated as distributions of property are generally subject to rules discussed later in this chapter.

1. Distributions to Shareholders

Although § 316(a) says "to a shareholder," that term is both broader and narrower than it might appear. That is because the transfer to the shareholder must be *with respect to its stock* and not for some other reason. The "with respect to" language appears in § 301(a), which governs the tax consequences of dividends.

Shareholders may have additional relationships to the corporations in which they own stock. They may, for example, also be employees, landlords, or creditors. Whenever a dual relationship exists—particularly in a closely held corporation—we must determine the reason for the transfer to ascertain its tax consequences. For example, transfers to shareholder-employees might be salary, or they might be dividend distributions.

> **Example 5-1.** ABC Corporation paid Mark a reasonable salary for services rendered. Mark owns less than 1% of ABC's stock and is unrelated to the corporation's other shareholders and employees. The salary payment is not a distribution. Mark received it in his status as an employee, not in his status as a shareholder.

> **Example 5-2.** DEF Corporation paid Nina—its only shareholder—a salary that exceeded a reasonable amount for services rendered. Some of the payment is probably a distribution to Nina with respect to her DEF stock.

Correctly classifying the distribution is important because the corporation cannot deduct dividends but can deduct salaries, interest, and rent. Classification also affects the recipient's tax consequences. Examples in the remainder of this chapter treat the distributions as made with respect to the shareholder's stock.

In appropriate cases, payments to a non-shareholder may be treated as distributions to a shareholder. For example, the corporation might pay an unreasonably high salary to an employee who is its sole shareholder's child. At least part of that salary could be treated as an indirect distribution to the shareholder-parent.

2. Distributions of Property

Section 317(a) defines the term "property" to mean money, securities, and any other property. It also adds an exception to that rule: shares of stock in the corporation making the distribution are not property. Rights to acquire such shares are also not property. In addition to money, property thus includes tangible real and personal property (such as land or machinery) and intangible property (such as copyrights). Although the term does not include the distributing corporation's own stock, it does include its obligations.

> **Example 5-3.** GHI Corporation distributed three items to its common shareholders pro rata based on their stock ownership: money, additional GHI common shares, and shares of XYZ Corporation. GHI had purchased the XYZ shares as an investment; the two corporations are not related to each other. The money and XYZ shares are property. The GHI shares are not property.

Although a corporation's own stock is not generally treated as property, there are exceptions. Section G discusses situations in which we treat a distribution of the corporation's stock as a distribution of property.

3. Distributions from E&P

Two facts are relevant. First, E&P is not the same as either accounting income or taxable income. A corporation that sustains a net loss for either of those purposes may still have E&P. Second, a corporation may have current E&P or accumulated E&P. Although it often has both, a distribution can be a dividend even if the corporation has only current E&P or only accumulated E&P.

C. Amount Distributed and Amount of Dividend

The amount distributed depends on the type of property distributed. If the corporation distributes money, it is the amount of money. If the corporation distributes other property, it is the fair market value of that property. I.R.C. § 301(b)(1). We determine value on the date the corporation distributes the property. I.R.C. § 301(b)(3). The value when the corporation declares the distribution is irrelevant.

> **Example 5-4.** JKL Corporation distributed property worth $4 million to its shareholders. JKL purchased the property for $3 million several years ago. It was worth $3.8 million on the day JKL announced the distribution. The amount distributed is $4 million.

We reduce the amount otherwise treated as a distribution by any corporate liability that the shareholder assumes in connection with the distribution. We also reduce the amount of the distribution by any liability that the property was subject to both before and after the distribution. We do so even if the shareholder does not actually assume the liability. I.R.C. § 301(b)(2). For example, the shareholder may take the property subject to a mortgage.

One exception applies. The amount of the distribution is not reduced below zero even if the liability exceeds the property's value.

> **Example 5-5.** MNO Corporation distributed property worth $10,000 (subject to a $4,000 liability). Its shareholders took the property subject to the liability. The amount distributed is $6,000. If the liability had been $11,000, the amount distributed would have been zero, not negative $1,000.

If the amount distributed does not exceed the corporation's E&P, it is a dividend. If the amount distributed exceeds the corporation's E&P, the excess amount is not a dividend.

> **Example 5-6.** PQR Corporation distributed $1 million to its shareholders with respect to their stock. If PQR had only $900,000 of E&P, only $900,000 of the distribution is a dividend.

D. Distributing Corporation's Tax Consequences

1. Income Tax Consequences

A corporation cannot deduct distributions to shareholders as expenses. This rule applies to distributions of money and to distributions of property other than money. It applies even if the corporation must recognize gain on distributing appreciated property.

Distributions of property other than money can have tax consequences. The distributing corporation computes realized gain or loss by comparing the basis of the property distributed to its value. If appreciated property is subject to a liability, the value used in this computation cannot be less than the amount of the liability. I.R.C. § 311(b)(2), which is based on § 336(b).

> **Example 5-7.** STU Corporation distributed land worth $100,000 (subject to a $90,000 liability). If STU had a basis of $82,000 for the land, it realized a gain of $18,000. If the land had instead been subject to a $103,000 liability, STU realized a gain of $21,000.

Any gain realized is recognized and included in the distributing corporation's gross income. I.R.C. § 311(b)(1). Because the flush language of that provision treats the corporation as if it sold the property to its shareholders, the gain retains its character as capital or ordinary.

If the property distributed is worth less than its basis, the corporation realizes a nondeductible loss. I.R.C. § 311(a). In this situation, the corporation would achieve a better tax result by selling the property to an unrelated person, deducting the loss, and distributing the sales proceeds to its shareholders. That route is unavailable if there is a reason a shareholder must receive that item.

Anti-abuse rules apply if the corporation distributes a partnership or trust interest. Section 311(b)(3) authorizes the Treasury Department to issue regulations to prevent the corporation from reducing its overall gain on the distribution if loss property had been contributed to the partnership or trust for the principal purpose of recognizing the loss. No temporary or final regulations had been issued by the end of July 2017.

2. Effect on E&P

If the corporation distributes money, it reduces its E&P by the amount of money distributed. If it distributes a corporate liability, it reduces its E&P by the principal amount of the obligation (or its issue price if the obligation has original issue discount). I.R.C. § 312(a)(1)–(2). If it distributes any other property, it reduces E&P by the property's adjusted basis unless the property was appreciated. I.R.C. § 312(a)(3). If the property was appreciated, the corporation increases its E&P by the difference between the property's value and its basis; it then reduces its E&P by the property's fair market value. I.R.C. § 312(b).

The corporation's E&P reduction is adjusted to reflect any liabilities that the property is subject to or that the shareholders assume. I.R.C. § 312(c). If the corporation's E&P basis differs from its income tax basis, it uses the E&P basis in computing its E&P reduction when it distributes property. I.R.C. § 312(b)(flush language).

> **Example 5-8.** VWX Corporation distributed land worth $100,000 (subject to a $60,000 mortgage). Its basis for the land was $15,000. VWX increases its E&P by its $85,000 gain. It reduces its E&P by $40,000, the value of the property offset by the debt. VWX also reduces its E&P by any income tax it pays on its $85,000 gain.

Example 5-8 has the same effect on E&P as a sale to a third party, followed by a distribution of money to the shareholders. If VWX sold the land, it would report gain of $85,000. Presumably the buyer would have assumed the $60,000 mortgage and given VWX $40,000, which VWX would distribute to its shareholders. VWX would have increased its E&P by the $85,000 gain, reduced its E&P by the $40,000 distribution, and reduced its E&P by any income tax on the $85,000 gain.

Section 312(a) provides for reducing E&P "to the extent thereof." A distribution of money or other property cannot reduce E&P below zero.

E. Shareholder's Tax Consequences

1. Gross Income

A shareholder who receives a distribution of money or other property that is covered by E&P reports the amount distributed as gross income. I.R.C. § 301(c)(1). For this purpose, we use the § 301(b) definition of amount distributed: the amount of money and the fair market value of property other than money (minus any obligations assumed or to which the property is subject).

If the distribution exceeds the available E&P, the excess distribution reduces the shareholder's basis for her stock. I.R.C. § 301(c)(2). In most situations, once basis is reduced to zero, she reports any additional amount as gain from the sale of the stock. If the corporation has a history that predates the income tax, any amount representing a pre-March 1, 1913, increase in value is exempt from tax. I.R.C. § 301(c)(3).

> **Example 5-9.** YZ Corporation had E&P of $4,000. It distributed $2,500 to Alan, its only shareholder, with respect to his stock. Alan has dividend income of $2,500. The result would be the same if YZ instead distributed property worth $2,500.

> **Example 5-10.** ABC Corporation had E&P of $6,000. It distributed $7,500 to Beth, its only shareholder, with respect to her stock. Before the distribution, Beth had a basis of $10,000 for her stock. Beth has dividend income of $6,000. She reduces her stock basis by the $1,500 portion of the distribution that was not a dividend. Her stock basis is now $8,500.

> **Example 5-11.** DEF Corporation had E&P of $8,000. It distributed $12,500 to Carl, its only shareholder, with respect to his stock. Before the distribution, Carl had a basis of $1,000 for his stock. Carl has dividend income of $8,000. The remaining $4,500 is not a dividend. Carl reduces his stock basis to zero. If DEF does not have a pre-March 1, 1913, history, Carl also reports a $3,500 gain with respect to his stock. It does not matter that he still owns the stock.

2. Dividends Received Deduction

Because a corporation cannot deduct paying a dividend as an expense, distributions from one corporation to a second corporation may be taxed twice. If the second corporation then distributed its profits to its own shareholders, they would also be taxed. Successive rounds of income tax would reduce the amounts available for the "ultimate" shareholders. Recognizing this problem, Congress enacted the dividends received deduction, which applies to dividends received by shareholders that are corporations.

The dividends received deduction is computed as a percentage of the dividend received. As a rule, the deduction is 70% of the dividend. I.R.C. § 243(a)(1). The deduction is 80% of the dividend if the recipient corporation owns at least 20% of the payor's stock value and voting power. I.R.C. § 243(c). The deduction is 100% if the payor is a small business investment corporation or if the payor and payee corporations are part of an affiliated group. I.R.C. § 243(a)(2)–(3).

> **Example 5-12.** GHI Corporation owns 4% of the stock of JKL Corporation. If JKL pays a dividend of $1 per share, GHI reports the $1 per share as gross income; it deducts 70 cents per share in computing its taxable income.

Section 246 limits a corporation's ability to purchase stock, hold it long enough to receive a dividend eligible for the dividends received deduction, and then sell it. To qualify for the deduction, the corporate shareholder must hold the stock more than 45 days during the 91-day period that begins 45 days before the stock's ex-dividend date. I.R.C. § 246(c)(1). The ex-dividend date is the date on which entitlement to the dividend is determined. Additional rules apply to certain dividends from foreign corporations, dividends on preferred stock, and dividends on debt-financed portfolio stock. I.R.C. §§ 245, 246(c)(2), 246A.

Section 1059 applies when a corporation receives an extraordinary dividend and has not held the stock for at least two years on the date the dividend is announced. A dividend generally is considered extraordinary if it exceeds 5% of the corporation's basis for preferred stock and 10% of its basis for other stock. A corporation that does not meet the two-year holding period requirement must reduce its basis for the stock by the amount of the dividends received deduction. If that amount exceeds its basis for the stock, the corporate shareholder treats the excess as gain from the sale of the stock.

3. Relevant Tax Rate

Most dividends received by individuals qualify for a lower tax rate. Instead of the rates imposed by § 1(a)–(d) (as modified by § 1(i)), dividends are taxed at the rates applied to net capital gain. I.R.C. § 1(h)(11). Taxing the dividend at a lower rate is not the same as excluding part of the dividend from gross income and adjusted gross income. For example, the full amount of the dividend is used in computing phase-outs for tax benefits (e.g., the medical expense deduction) that decline as AGI increases. In addition, a taxpayer who elects to use the lower tax rate cannot use the dividend income in computing net investment income. I.R.C. § 163(d)(4)(B). This rule affects taxpayers who are subject to the § 163(d) limitation on deducting investment interest expense. In addition, because dividends are investment income, they may be subject to the 3.8% tax on net investment income imposed by § 1411.

Although no special tax rate applies to dividends received by shareholders that are themselves corporations, the dividends received deduction effectively reduces the tax rate. For example, if a corporation that would normally be taxed at 35% receives a dividend, it can deduct at least 70% of that dividend. Because the 35% tax rate is applied to no more than 30% of the dividend received, the corporation's maximum effective rate is 10.5%.

4. Basis and Holding Period

The shareholder's basis for any property received is its fair market value. I.R.C. § 301(d). He does not reduce that basis by the amount of any debt to which the property is subject. The shareholder starts a new holding period; he does not tack on the corporation's holding period for the property.

A distribution of money or other property usually does not affect the shareholder's basis for the stock. There are two exceptions, both of which are discussed earlier in this section. First, the shareholder's basis for the stock is reduced (but not below zero) by any portion of the distribution that is not covered by E&P. Second, a corporation that receives an extraordinary dividend may have to reduce its stock basis by the amount of its dividends received deduction.

F. Nontaxable Distributions of Stock or Rights

As a rule, a corporation that distributes its own stock (or rights to acquire that stock) is not distributing *property*. I.R.C. § 317(a). Most distributions that non-lawyers refer to as stock dividends are not § 301 dividends and are not included in the recipient shareholder's gross income.

After corporations began using such distributions to facilitate tax-free ownership shifts, Congress responded with exceptions to the rule that a corporation's own stock was not property. If one of these exceptions applies, the tax consequences for both the recipient shareholder and the corporation follow those associated with a property distribution. Even shareholders who did not receive the stock may have those tax consequences.

1. Exclusion from Shareholder's Gross Income

Section 305(a) provides that a shareholder's gross income does not include a distribution of the corporation's own stock that is made with respect to that stock. It reflects the Supreme Court's opinion in *Eisner v. Macomber*, 252 U.S. 189 (1920). That case involved the Revenue Act of 1916, which included a distribution of the corporation's stock in the shareholder's gross income. In holding that that the distribution did not result in gross income, the Court noted that the distribution merely reconfigured the taxpayer's existing investment (and that of the other shareholders). It did not transfer any corporate assets to the shareholders. The opinion indicated that the corporation's reduction of its surplus account was "no more than a book adjustment." 252 U.S. 210.

Instead of distributing shares of stock, the corporation could distribute rights to acquire such stock. This distribution is treated the same as a distribution of the corporation's stock. I.R.C. § 305(d).

Section 305(a) applies only if the corporation distributes its own stock, not that of another corporation. Likewise, it applies only if the distribution is made with respect to the shareholder's stock. For example, a shareholder-employee who receives stock as a year-end bonus does not exclude the value of that stock from gross income. The payment is compensation for services.

2. Basis and Holding Period

a. *General Rule*

Although stock received in a distribution covered by § 305(a) does not result in gross income, it does receive a basis. The shareholder allocates her basis for the original stock between the original stock and the newly distributed stock. I.R.C. § 307(a). The allocation is based on the fair market value of each block of stock on the distribution date. Reg. § 1.307-1(a).

If both blocks of stock are identical, as happens if the corporation has only one class of stock, the basis is allocated based on the number of shares in each block. If the corporation has more than one class of stock outstanding, each block's value must be determined. That determination is easier if the corporation is publicly traded than if it is closely held.

Example 5-13. MNO Corporation has 1,000 shares of voting common stock outstanding. Ed owns 10 of those shares, for which he paid $220 ($22/share). If MNO distributes one share of identical voting common stock for each 10 shares owned, Ed receives one share. He reports no gross income, and he allocates his $220 total basis equally among his 11 shares ($20/share).

Example 5-14. PQR Corporation has 1,000 shares of voting common stock outstanding. Fanny owns 10 of those shares, for which she paid $330 ($33/share). If PQR distributes one share of nonvoting common stock for each 10 shares owned, Fanny receives one share. She reports no gross income, and she allocates her $330 total basis between her 10 voting shares and her one nonvoting share. If, for example, the 10 voting shares are each worth $48 and the nonvoting share is worth $15, the total value of her shares is $495. The voting common shares take a total basis of $320 ($480/$495 * $330). The nonvoting common share takes a basis of $10 ($15/$495 * $330).

The shareholder's holding period for the new stock includes his holding period for the old stock. I.R.C. § 1223(4). This rule reflects the fact that the new shares are treated, at least to some extent, as part of the shareholder's original investment in the old shares.

b. Rights to Acquire Stock

Distributions of rights to acquire stock are generally treated the same as distributions of stock. The shareholder reports no gross income on receiving the rights, and he allocates his basis for the shares between those shares and the rights.

Example 5-15. STU Corporation is publicly traded. Gary owns 10 of STU's voting common shares, for which he paid $70 ($7/share). This year STU distributed the right to purchase one share (for $20) for every 10 shares already owned. These rights expire in 10 years. Immediately after the distribution, each STU share was worth $10; each right was worth $25. Based on those values, we allocate Gary's $70 basis as follows: $56 ($100/$125 * $70) to the stock and $14 ($25/$125 * $70) to the right. Gary had no incentive to exercise his right when he received it, because he could purchase the stock for less than $20/share on the open market. The right will be valuable if STU's share price ever exceeds $20.

Example 5-16. After the STU stock value increased to $24, Gary exercised the right to purchase a share for $20. His $34 basis for the new share includes his $14 basis for the right and the additional $20 he paid.

An exception applies to stock rights with a de minimis value on the distribution date. If the value of the rights is less than 15% of the value of the stock that gave rise to the distribution, a default rule applies. The rights take a basis of zero, and the stock retains its full basis, unless the shareholder elects to allocate basis between the stock and the rights. I.R.C. § 307(b). If the shareholder elects to allocate basis, she must do so for all rights distributed at that time with respect to a particular class of stock. Reg. § 1.307-2.

Although the Code provides for allocating basis to stock rights, the regulations allocate basis only if the rights are exercised or sold. Reg. § 1.307-1(a). That limitation prevents a taxpayer from deducting what might otherwise be an artificial loss.

Example 5-17. Assume that STU's stock value declined, and Gary decided not to purchase any more STU stock. If the right lapses before he can sell it, he cannot deduct his $14 loss. The regulations prevent him from allocating any basis to the right in that situation. The $14 basis would remain with Gary's original stock. Instead of a $56 basis for the 10 shares, he will have a $70 basis. Rev. Rul. 74-501, 1974-2 C.B. 98.

Gary did not own enough stock to control corporate policy. His situation is quite different from that of an individual who owns 100% of the corporation's stock. That shareholder has no incentive to exercise rights, as she already owns all the outstanding stock. And if she sells some of the rights, she reduces her control over the corporation. It makes sense that she cannot allocate basis to rights that she neither sells nor exercises. She still has 100% ownership, and she suffers no economic loss when the rights expire.

3. Effect on Issuing Corporation

A distribution of stock or stock rights does not affect the issuing corporation's tax computation. Because the stock or rights distributed are not treated as property, the corporation does not compute gain or loss. There is no effect on its taxable income or on its E&P account. The corporation also has no tax consequences if the shareholder later exercises rights and purchases additional stock. The corporation does not recognize gain or loss on receiving money or other property in exchange for newly issued or previously issued (treasury) stock. I.R.C. § 1032.

G. Taxable Distributions of Stock or Rights

1. Distributions Covered by Section 305(b)

Although distributions of a corporation's own stock are generally tax-free, exceptions to that rule apply. The exceptions cover distributions that let some shareholders receive an increased interest in the corporation while others receive money or other property. The discussion in this section assumes the distribution does not exceed the corporation's E&P.

a. Election to Take Stock or Property

A distribution is treated as if it was made in property if any shareholder can elect to take either stock or property (including money). I.R.C. § 305(b)(1). It does not matter whether a shareholder makes the election before or after the corporation declares the dividend. It does not matter what a shareholder chooses. Both shareholders who receive stock and shareholders who receive money or other property report gross income.

b. Disproportionate Distributions

A distribution is treated as if it was made in property if it results in some shareholders receiving money or other property and others receiving an increased interest in the corporation's assets or E&P. I.R.C. § 305(b)(2). The major difference between this rule and that discussed above involves the triggering mechanism. Section 305(b)(1) applies if shareholders can elect between stock and money or other property. It looks to the option rather than to the result. Because § 305(b)(2) tests the result, it applies even if shareholders had no choice at all. If some shareholders received money while others had their interests increased, both groups report gross income.

> **Example 5-18.** VWX Corporation has two classes of outstanding stock, voting common and nonvoting common. VWX declared a dividend of $5 per share with respect to its nonvoting stock and one new share (worth $5 per share) with respect to its voting stock. After this distribution, shareholders who owned voting stock before the distribution had an increased interest in future corporate earnings because they owned a greater percentage of VWX stock than they did before the distribution. It does not matter if they received voting or nonvoting common stock.

Section 305(b)(2) applies to single distributions and to series of distributions that have the prohibited result. For example, Reg. § 1.305-3(b)(2) applies the rule to a corporation that pays annual cash dividends on one class of stock and quarterly stock dividends on its other class of stock. It focuses on the result, not on whether there was a plan to change shareholders' interest in the corporation. It includes a cut-off date for combining multiple distributions. Section 305(b)(2) does not cover a receipt of money or other property more than 36 months after the receipt of stock, or vice versa, unless the IRS establishes that the distributions were made pursuant to a plan. Reg. § 1.305-3(b)(4).

This provision may apply even if one class of stock is common and the other is preferred. In that situation, the rights of each class are relevant. For example, preferred stock generally has fixed dividend and liquidation rights. Common shareholders do not have fixed rights, as they are the residual owners. Their income and liquidation rights are subordinated to those of the preferred shareholders. If a corporation distributes money or other property to preferred shareholders and stock to common shareholders, the preferred shareholders report gross income; they have received a dividend. The common shareholders' tax consequences depend on whether the distribution changes the relative rights of shareholders in the two classes.

> **Example 5-19.** YZ Corporation has both preferred and common shares outstanding. The preferred has fixed dividend and liquidation rights. YZ distributed money to the preferred shareholders and more common stock to the common shareholders. The preferred shareholders report gross income from dividends. The common shareholders report no gross income. They did not receive property, and the stock they received did not increase their residual interest in the corporation—it was 100% before the distribution and 100% after.

> **Example 5-20.** If YZ had instead distributed preferred stock to the common shareholders, their interest in the corporation would increase and they would report dividend income. They would have received an interest that came ahead of their residual interest unless the preferred stock they receive is subordinated to the existing preferred stock. In that case, even though they receive preferred stock, the common shareholders would still have only a residual interest. Reg. § 1.305-3(e) Example 3.

We apply the § 305(b)(2) tests at the stock level, not at the shareholder level. For example, an individual who owned the same percentage of each class of a corporation's stock might argue that no combination of money and stock distributions would change his interest in the corporation. The regulations indicate that if the interest of a class of stock is changed, the interest of the shareholders is deemed changed. Reg. § 1.305-3(b)(6). Reg. § 1.305-3 also includes rules to use when shares are distributed but then purchased by a related corporation in a § 304 redemption or when the corporation has outstanding stock or debt that is convertible into other stock.

A distribution of money in lieu of fractional shares is likely to be exempt. If, for example, a corporation declared a dividend of one share of stock for every 10 owned, it would probably distribute money rather than a fractional share to any shareholder owning fewer than 10 shares. It would probably distribute shares plus money to any shareholder owning at least 10 shares but whose share ownership is not exactly divisible by 10. Section 305(b)(2) does not apply if the corporation distributed money to avoid the "trouble, expense, and inconvenience" of issuing fractional shares and not to increase other shareholders' interest in the corporation's assets or E&P. A safe harbor applies if the amount of money distributed is 5% or less of the market value of the stock distributed (valued on the date the stock dividend was declared). Reg. § 1.305-3(c).

If a shareholder receives money in lieu of fractional shares and § 305(b)(2) does not apply, the regulations treat the corporation as issuing a fractional share and then redeeming it for money. If the shareholder is a minority shareholder, the transaction probably qualifies as a redemption that is not essentially equivalent to a dividend. In that situation, the shareholder has made a sale or exchange of the fractional share.

c. Distributions of Common and Preferred Stock

If the corporation distributes common stock to some of its common shareholders and preferred stock to others, the first group enjoys an increase in its rights to corporate growth. For this purpose, preferred stock is "stock which, in relation to other classes of stock outstanding, enjoys certain limited rights . . . but does not participate in corporate growth to any significant extent." Reg. § 1.305-5(a). When distributions (including a series of distributions) such as this occur, § 305(b)(3) treats them as distributions of property. In the unlikely case that the preferred shares had dividend and liquidation rights equal to those of the common shares, § 305(b)(3) would not apply. Instead, the general rule of § 305(a) would apply, and the distributions would not be taxable.

d. Distributions on Preferred Stock

Section 305(b)(4) treats a distribution of stock as a distribution of property if it is made with respect to preferred stock. It applies to distributions of common stock and to distributions of additional preferred stock. Because preferred stock generally carries only limited rights as to corporate governance, earnings, and assets, preferred shareholders are not interested in the corporation's long-term growth prospects or in voting control. If they were allowed to receive a tax-free distribution of stock and could assign it some of their original stock's basis, they could convert fully taxable dividends into partially taxed capital gain by selling the new stock.

An exception applies to shareholders who own preferred stock that is convertible into common shares. If the corporation distributes additional common shares or splits its stock, it will adjust the conversion ratio to avoid impairing the preferred shareholders' conversion rights. Although that adjustment is a distribution with respect to preferred stock, it is not treated as a distribution of property.

e. Distributions of Convertible Preferred Stock

If she can convert her preferred shares into common stock, a preferred shareholder can become a common shareholder. The conversion feature gives her the opportunity to share in future growth in the corporation's E&P or assets. Not surprisingly, § 305(b)(5) provides that a distribution of convertible preferred stock is treated as a distribution of property unless the corporation establishes that the distribution will not have that result.

This rule applies even if convertible preferred stock is distributed pro rata to all common shareholders. Although their proportionate rights initially remain the same, there is no guarantee that they all would convert the preferred shares into more common stock. Some of them might convert their preferred shares into more common stock while others might sell the preferred stock (or retain it and receive cash dividends). That situation is comparable to the disproportionate distribution situation described above.

The regulations list factors that indicate whether it is likely that all shareholders will convert their preferred shares. A very short period for exercising the conversion right makes it likely that some shareholders will not convert. In that situation, the distribution is likely to be treated as a dividend. The regulations list other factors used in determining if it is likely that some shareholders will convert the shares and others will not. These factors are the dividend rate, the redemption provisions, the marketability of the convertible stock, and the conversion price. Reg. § 1.305-6(a). Contrasting examples in the regulations describe a 20-year conversion period and dividends that are normal in light of market conditions versus a four-month conversion period and a third-party buyer who has offered to purchase any shares that are not converted. The first situation is treated as a tax-free stock distribution because it is impossible to predict the extent to which shareholders will convert the distributed stock. The second situation is treated as a distribution of property because it is anticipated that some shareholders will convert their shares and others will sell them for cash. Reg. § 1.305-6(b).

f. Transactions Treated as Distributions

A transaction can fall outside § 305(b) and still be treated as a property distribution. Section 305(c) authorizes regulations covering other situations that result in the increase in any shareholder's proportionate interest in the corporation's E&P or assets. These transactions include changes in conversion ratio, changes in redemption price, differences between redemption and issue price, redemptions treated as § 301 distributions, and transactions (including recapitalizations) having a similar effect.

Section 305(c) may apply to shareholders who do not directly receive anything from the corporation. For example, if a corporation redeems stock from one shareholder, the redemption increases the percentage of stock owned by other shareholders. Although they did not directly receive any property, their interest in the corporation's future E&P or assets has increased. Section 305(c) does not apply merely because there was a change in conversion ratio or similar transaction. The transaction must have resulted in an increase in a shareholder's interest in the corporation's E&P or assets.

> **Example 5-21.** Carol and her son Dave each owned 50% of the stock of ABC Corporation. ABC redeemed half of Carol's stock. Carol's actual ownership declined from 50% to 33 1/3%. Dave's actual ownership increased from 50% to 66 2/3%. Because of constructive ownership rules, Carol is treated as owning 100% of the ABC shares before and after the redemption. She must report the redemption proceeds as a property distribution because the redemption does not meet any of the § 302(b) tests described in the next chapter. Dave also has gross income, even though he received no property. The redemption of Carol's stock had the effect of one shareholder (Carol) receiving property and another (Dave) receiving an increased interest in ABC's E&P or assets. If the redemption had met one of the § 302(b) tests, Dave would not have been treated as receiving a property distribution.

The current regulations for § 305(c) are the subject of proposed amendments. Prop. Reg. § 1.305-7 expands on the current regulations and includes many examples.

2. Income Tax Consequences

If a distribution of stock or rights is treated as a distribution of property, the shareholder's tax consequences are the same as if she had received money or other property. Assuming the corporation has adequate E&P, the shareholder reports the value of the stock or rights as gross income. That amount becomes the shareholder's basis for the stock received. The shareholder's holding period for the new stock begins when she receives it.

The corporation that made the distribution also follows the rules for property distributions. It reduces its E&P account, but not below zero, by the value of the distributed stock or rights. Reg. § 1.312-1(d).

H. Allocating E&P to Distributions

The discussion below focuses on two E&P topics related to distributions. First, what is the difference between current E&P and accumulated E&P? Second, how do we allocate current and accumulated E&P to distributions?

When working with E&P, keep three facts in mind. First, distributions to shareholders cannot reduce E&P below zero. Although a corporation can have a deficit in its E&P account, that deficit cannot be created or increased by a distribution. In other words, deficits can be attributable to operating losses; they cannot be attributable to distributions. Second, a corporation might realize gain when it distributes property other than money. The realized gain increases both taxable income and E&P. Third, distributions other than dividends may reduce E&P. For example, the corporation's E&P are reduced by redemptions. I.R.C. § 312(n)(7). In addition, if a corporation undergoes a reorganization or § 355 separation, part of its E&P may be transferred to another corporation. I.R.C. § 312(h). These topics are discussed in later chapters.

1. Current and Accumulated E&P

Section 316(a) defines dividends as distributions of property out of E&P accumulated after February 28, 1913, or out of E&P of the current taxable year. A distribution can be a dividend if the corporation has both current and accumulated E&P, only current E&P, or only accumulated E&P. A distribution cannot be a dividend if the corporation lacks both current and accumulated E&P.

We compute current E&P at year-end. We add any current E&P remaining after distributions to the accumulated E&P brought forward to the next taxable year. In other words, a corporation's accumulated E&P account is the sum of the current E&P for all prior years to the extent those amounts were not reduced by dividend or redemption distributions (or allocated to another corporation in a reorganization or corporate separation).

> **Example 5-22.** On the first day of its 2016 taxable year, DEF Corporation had accumulated E&P of $100,000. It had current E&P of $40,000 for 2016 and paid dividends that year of $10,000. On the first day of its 2017 taxable year, DEF had accumulated E&P of $130,000.

2. Allocation Rules

The shareholder's tax consequences from a distribution are explained earlier in this chapter. The earlier discussion indicated the amount of available E&P or assumed the amount was adequate to cover the distribution. The discussion in this section focuses on how to allocate E&P to distributions. That allocation provides the information needed to determine how much of the distribution is a dividend, a return of the shareholder's stock basis, or a gain.

a. Current E&P

The flush language of § 316(a) provides that a distribution is deemed to come first from the most recently accumulated E&P. In determining whether a distribution is a dividend, we look first to the current E&P.

Three rules apply in determining whether a distribution is a dividend based on current E&P. First, we allocate current E&P to distributions without regard to earnings at a particular point in time during the year. We instead compute current E&P for the entire year for this purpose. Second, we allocate current E&P to all distributions made during the year. It does not matter when the corporation made those distributions. Third, accumulated E&P deficits do not affect the corporation's current E&P. The shareholders of a corporation that had $100,000 of current E&P would have dividend income if they received current-year distributions of $100,000 or less. The result would not change if, for example, the corporation began the year with a deficit in its E&P account. I.R.C. § 316(a)(2); Reg. § 1.316-1(e).

If current E&P exceed the amounts distributed for the year, the distributions are dividends from current E&P. If current E&P are less than the amounts distributed, we allocate current E&P pro rata to each distribution made during the year. Reg. § 1.316-2(b)–(c).

> **Example 5-23.** GHI Corporation had current E&P of $72,000 for its taxable year ending December 31. During the year, it distributed $15,000 on February 15, $20,000 on May 15, $25,000 on August 15,

and $30,000 on November 15. The total distributions ($90,000) exceeded current E&P by $18,000. GHI allocates current E&P to each distribution on a pro rata basis: $72,000/$90,000. Thus, 80% of each distribution is a dividend from current E&P.

Perhaps GHI appeared to be profitable early in the year, leading its directors to increase dividends throughout the year. Although later losses reduced the year's total E&P, that fact is irrelevant.

b. Accumulated E&P

We allocate accumulated E&P to a distribution only if current E&P are insufficient. Current E&P could be insufficient because, as described in Example 5-23, they are less than the total amounts distributed. They could also be insufficient because the corporation sustained an operating loss for the year, leading to negative current E&P.

The rules for allocating accumulated E&P to a distribution differ in two respects from those used in allocating current E&P to a distribution. First, we allocate accumulated E&P to current-year distributions based on when the distribution occurred. We do not allocate accumulated E&P pro rata throughout the year. Second, current deficits in E&P offset accumulated E&P in determining whether a distribution is out of accumulated E&P.

1. Allocation to Current-Year Distributions

The corporation allocates accumulated E&P to current-year distributions when they occur. If the first distribution made during a year exhausts the accumulated E&P, later distributions will not be dividends because the corporation will have neither current nor accumulated E&P. Reg. § 1.316-2(b)–(c).

Example 5-24. JKL Corporation has neither positive nor negative current E&P from operations. It began this taxable year with $100,000 of accumulated E&P. JKL made $10,000 distributions on February 15, May 15, August 15, and November 15. All four distributions are dividends.

Example 5-25. If JKL's accumulated E&P had been only $25,000, the February and May distributions, and one-half of the August distribution, are dividends. The rest of the August distribution and the November distribution are not dividends.

Example 5-26. If JKL had $12,000 of current E&P and $25,000 of accumulated E&P, it would use two allocation methods. First, it would treat $3,000 of each distribution as a dividend out of its $12,000 of current E&P. Second, it would allocate the $25,000 of accumulated E&P in this order: $7,000 each to the first three distributions, and $4,000 to the fourth distribution. The full $10,000 distributed in February, May, and August is a dividend. Only $7,000 of the $10,000 distributed in November is a dividend. Thus, a shareholder who sold stock after the second distribution would report more dividend income than would the purchaser who received the third and fourth distributions.

2. *Effect of Current Deficits*

The computation is more complicated if the corporation has a current E&P deficit. The corporation will have a current deficit only if there is a deficit for the entire year.

Current E&P deficits offset accumulated E&P before the accumulated amounts are applied to distributions. Thus, two dates are critical: when the current E&P deficit occurred and when the distributions were made. If the corporation can determine when the current deficit occurred, it reduces accumulated E&P on that date. If it cannot determine when the current deficit occurred, it allocates the deficit pro rata against accumulated E&P. Reg. § 1.316-2(b). The allocation method affects how much of any distribution is treated as a dividend.

Example 5-27. MNO Corporation began the year with accumulated E&P of $36,000. It sustained a current E&P deficit of $24,000, which it could establish occurred in November. MNO made only one distribution this year. It distributed $15,000 on February 1. Because the deficit did not occur until November, all of its accumulated E&P were available on February 1. The entire $15,000 was a dividend. If MNO had instead made its only distribution on December 1, the $24,000 current deficit would have reduced its accumulated E&P from $36,000 to $12,000. Only $12,000 of the distribution would have been a dividend.

Example 5-28. If MNO could not determine when it sustained its $24,000 current deficit, it allocated that deficit pro rata throughout the year. February 1 occurred one month into the year, so 1/12 of the deficit ($2,000) was applied against accumulated E&P on February 1. If MNO distributed $15,000 on February 1, its accumulated E&P would have been $34,000 ($36,000 minus the $2,000 allocated deficit). All $15,000 was a dividend. If MNO had instead made the distribution on December 1, 11/12 of the current deficit ($22,000) would have reduced its accumulated E&P from $36,000 to $14,000. Only $14,000 of the distribution would have been a dividend.

Examples 5-27 and 5-28 involved a single distribution. Examples 5-29 and 5-30 involve multiple distributions. Because we reduce accumulated E&P by current-year distributions, both distributions and current deficits affect how much of each distribution is a dividend.

Example 5-29. PQR Corporation began the year with accumulated E&P of $39,000 and sustained an $18,000 current E&P deficit in November. It made two $15,000 distributions, one on February 1 and one on December 1. Because the deficit did not occur until November, all $39,000 of PQR's accumulated E&P were available on February 1. The entire $15,000 distributed on February 1 was a dividend. That distribution reduced PQR's accumulated E&P from $39,000 to $24,000. The $18,000 operating deficit sustained in November further reduced the accumulated E&P to $6,000. Only $6,000 of the December distribution was a dividend. The remainder of the December distribution reduced the shareholders' stock basis and—if that basis was exhausted—gave rise to taxable gain.

Example 5-30. If PQR could not determine when it sustained its $18,000 current E&P deficit, it allocated that deficit pro rata throughout the year. Thus, 1/12 ($1,500) was allocated to the period ending on February 1 and reduced PQR's accumulated E&P to $37,500. All $15,000 that it distributed on February 1 was a dividend. That distribution reduced its accumulated E&P to $22,500. By the time PQR made its December 1 distribution, 10 more months had elapsed. As a result, $15,000 (10/12) of the current E&P deficit reduced its accumulated E&P to $7,500. Only $7,500 of the December distribution would have been a dividend.

When PQR could determine that its $18,000 deficit occurred in November, it allocated the entire current deficit to the period before the December 1 distribution. When it was unable to determine when the current deficit occurred, it allocated only 11/12 of it (1/12 before the February 1 distribution and another 10/12 before the December 1 distribution) against accumulated E&P. Because part of the current deficit was allocated to the period *after* the December distribution, the shareholders had a larger December dividend in Example 5-30 than in Example 5-29.

Checkpoints

- A dividend is a distribution of property to a shareholder, made with respect to his stock, out of the corporation's E&P.
- Property includes money, other assets, and debt of the distributing corporation.
- The corporation has taxable gain if it distributes appreciated property. It cannot deduct a loss if it distributes loss property.
- The corporation cannot deduct the amount of the dividend it distributes as an expense.
- A dividend distribution reduces the corporation's E&P, but not below zero. Distributions can offset both current and accumulated E&P.
- The shareholder has gross income from dividends if the corporation has sufficient E&P. An individual shareholder may qualify for the § 1(h) tax rates; a corporate shareholder may take the dividends received deduction.
- The shareholder reduces his stock basis by distributions that exceed E&P. If basis is reduced to zero, the shareholder reports gain even if he does not sell the stock.
- The shareholder takes a fair market value basis for property other than money received.
- Stock in the distributing corporation is generally not property. The shareholder reports no gross income and allocates the basis of the original shares between those shares and the new shares.
- Distributions of stock rights are generally treated the same as distributions of stock. If the stock rights are worth less than 15% of the shares on which they are distributed, they take a zero basis unless the shareholder elects to allocate basis. The regulations provide for allocating basis only to rights that are exercised or sold.
- Some distributions of stock or stock rights are treated as distributions of property and are taxable. The distributions covered by § 305(b) can be used to change shareholders' relative interests in the corporation's E&P or assets. Examples include letting shareholders elect to receive stock or money or distributing stock to some shareholders and money to others. In those situations, the shareholder's basis for the new stock is its fair market value.
- A distribution is a dividend if the corporation has sufficient current E&P, accumulated E&P, or both current and accumulated E&P.
- Current E&P are allocated to distributions pro rata.
- Accumulated E&P are allocated to distributions only if current E&P are insufficient.
- Accumulated E&P are offset by deficits in current E&P and are allocated to distributions in chronological order rather than pro rata.

Chapter 6

Redemption Distributions

Roadmap

- Terminology
- Constructive ownership
- Section 302 redemptions
- Section 303 redemptions
- Section 304 redemptions
- Section 306 dispositions
- Corporation's tax consequences
- Shareholder's tax consequences
- Transfers of control

A. Chapter Overview

The dividends discussed in the preceding chapter and most of the redemptions discussed in this chapter involve the distribution of corporate assets. Despite that commonality, dividends and redemptions generally have different tax consequences. Dividends occur as part of a corporation's ongoing operations. They do not generally change the shareholders' relationship to each other or to the corporation. Redemptions, on the other hand, generally change the shareholders' relationship to each other and to the corporation.

A redemption distribution uses corporate funds to reduce or eliminate at least one shareholder's ownership interest. That usually results in other shareholders enjoying an increased ownership interest. The same ownership shift might be accomplished if some shareholders used their own funds to purchase shares from other shareholders. If the corporation is closely held, the form of the transaction (purchase by the corporation) may not reflect its substance (benefit to continuing shareholders). To prevent abuse, the Code includes constructive ownership rules that apply in determining how both groups of shareholders are taxed.

This chapter considers several topics related to redemptions and to dispositions covered by § 306. These include terminology; constructive ownership; types of redemption; computation of the amount distributed; and tax consequences.

B. Terminology

Section 317 defines the terms "redemption" and "property." A redemption occurs "if the corporation acquires its stock from a shareholder in exchange for property, whether or not the stock so acquired is cancelled, retired, or held as treasury stock." I.R.C. § 317(b). This definition focuses on what the corporation received (its own stock) and what it gave up (property). Property includes money, other property, and obligations issued by the corporation. It does not generally include the corporation's own stock or rights to acquire that stock. I.R.C. § 317(a).

Redemptions are generally treated as distributions in exchange for the corporation's stock or as dividend distributions. For purposes of this chapter, redemptions treated as distributions are referred to as dividend distributions, redemptions treated as dividends, or dividends. Obviously, that nomenclature is overbroad, as it assumes that the corporation has sufficient current or accumulated E&P to cover the distribution. We use it to focus your attention on the likely tax consequences if the redemption is not treated as in exchange for the shareholder's stock. In practice, however, you must determine if a redemption treated as a dividend distribution is covered by E&P.

C. Constructive Ownership

Redemptions usually affect both shareholders whose stock is redeemed and shareholders whose ownership interest is increased. When those shareholders are related to each other, a redemption may not actually reduce the redeemed shareholder's ability to control corporate activity. And because continuing shareholders did not have to use their own funds to acquire the redeemed shareholder's ownership interest, we might question whether the redemption is a constructive dividend to them.

Not surprisingly, the redemptions described in this chapter are subject to specific limitations designed to reduce abuse. The § 318 constructive ownership rules limit related persons' ability to structure a transaction as a redemption when its substance more closely resembles a dividend. When those rules apply, stock owned by one person is treated as owned constructively by another. In other words, ownership is attributed to that other person. Section 318 uses both terms—constructive ownership and attribution. When stock is attributed from one person to another, the second person has constructive ownership.

There are four types of attribution: family attribution; attribution from an entity; attribution to an entity; and option attribution. As discussed below, stock attributed to one constructive owner can sometimes be reattributed to a second constructive owner.

Section 318 applies only to Code sections that expressly incorporate it. I.R.C. § 318(a). Constructive ownership rules that apply in other contexts may use different attribution rules. For example, the definition of family members in § 267(c)(4) is broader than that in § 318(a)(1).

1. Family Attribution

Section 318(a)(1) treats an individual as the constructive owner of any stock owned by a family member. The definition of family member includes only the individual's spouse (unless they are legally separated under a decree of divorce or separate maintenance), children, grandchildren, and parents. It does not include brothers and sisters, aunts and uncles, nieces and nephews, cousins, grandparents, or descendants more remote than grandchildren. Individuals who are adopted are treated the same as individuals who are related by birth.

> **Example 6-1.** Mother incorporated ABC Corporation 30 years ago. She transferred shares over the years to Son and his descendants. The shares are currently owned by Mother (20%), Son (30%), Granddaughter (15%), and Great-Grandson (35%). Stock owned by Son and Granddaughter is attributed to Mother. Stock owned by Great-Grandson is not attributed to her. Mother has actual ownership of 20% of ABC's shares and constructive ownership of 45% of ABC's shares, a total of 65% of ABC's shares.

a. Multiple Attributions

Stock that an individual *actually* owns can be attributed to more than one other family member at the same time. In Example 6-1, Mother constructively owns the stock owned by Son and by Granddaughter because they are her child and grandchild. Son constructively owns the stock owned by Mother (his parent), Granddaughter (his child), and Great-Grandson (his grandchild). Granddaughter constructively owns the stock owned by Son (her parent) and Great-Grandson (her child). Great-Grandson constructively owns the stock owned by Granddaughter (his parent).

b. Reattribution

If an individual *constructively* owns stock because of family attribution, the stock is not reattributed from the constructive owner to another family member. I.R.C. § 318(a)(5)(B). Unless the stock can be directly attributed from the actual owner to the second person, the second person does not constructively own it. In Example 6-1, Son constructively owns stock owned by Great-Grandson (Son's grandson). That stock cannot be reattributed from Son to Mother because stock ownership could not be attributed directly from Great-Grandson to Mother. She is too remote an ancestor.

Although stock ownership that is attributed to one family member cannot be reattributed to a second family member, it can be reattributed to an entity. I.R.C. § 318(a)(5)(A). If, in the example above, Son was a partner in the STU Partnership, STU would be treated as the constructive owner of any ABC Corporation stock that Son actually owned and of any stock that he constructively owned by attribution from Mother, Granddaughter, and Great-Grandson.

Stock can also be reattributed from one family member to another if the first family member constructively owns the stock because of attribution from an entity. I.R.C. § 318(a)(5)(A). If Son was a 10% partner in XYZ Partnership, and XYZ owned all the DEF Corporation stock, Son would constructively own 10% of the DEF shares. Those shares could be reattributed from Son to Mother, Granddaughter, and Great-Grandson to make each of them the constructive owner of 10% of the DEF shares.

c. Family Hostility

Section 318(a)(1) ignores stock held by a spouse when there is a legal separation. It does not provide for taking family hostility into account in any other way. Thus, stock owned by an estranged child is still attributed to the child's parent (and vice versa). Although a few judicial decisions have taken family hostility into account, the IRS does not accept family hostility as a reason for ignoring family attribution. For example, in Rev. Rul. 80-26, 1980-1 C.B. 66, it refused to follow the decision in *Haft Trust v. Commissioner*, 510 F.2d 43 (1st Cir. 1975). Perhaps a court might consider family hostility as part of its facts and circumstances analysis when it decides if a redemption is not essentially equivalent to a dividend.

2. Attribution from an Entity

A person who has an ownership or beneficial interest in an entity is treated as owning stock owned by the entity. The amount of stock constructively owned depends on the type of entity and, in some cases, on the person's percentage of ownership in that entity. The entities covered by this provision are partnerships, estates, trusts, and corporations. I.R.C. § 318(a)(2). Although ownership is attributed from both C and S corporations to their shareholders, the operative attribution rules differ.

a. From Partnerships, Estates, and S Corporations

If a partnership owns stock in a corporation, that stock is attributed to its partners in proportion to their partnership interests. I.R.C. § 318(a)(2)(A). S corporations are treated as partnerships in applying attribution from an entity. I.R.C. § 318(a)(5)(E). This rule applies only for attribution of stock owned by the S corporation. It does not apply to attribution of stock issued by the S corporation.

If an estate owns stock, that stock is attributed to the estate's beneficiaries in proportion to their beneficial interests. I.R.C. § 318(a)(2)(A). A person's status as a beneficiary is determined at the time a redemption occurs. After an estate distributes all the property to which a beneficiary is entitled, and there is only a remote chance that the estate will need to reclaim property to pay debts, that person is no longer a beneficiary. At that time, stock owned by the estate will not be attributed to that person. Reg. § 1.318-3(a).

> **Example 6-2.** When Father died, he owned two assets: 60% of the stock of GHI Corporation (worth $100,000) and $140,000 in a bank account. Father's two children owned the remaining GHI shares (20% each). Father devised his GHI stock to his daughter Cindy and his bank account to his daughter Carol. Carol was to receive an equalizing amount of GHI stock if the stock value at Father's death exceeded the money available after paying debts and estate costs. After paying the estate's debts and other costs, the personal representative distributed the remaining $110,000 to Carol. Because that amount exceeded the value of Father's GHI stock, Carol was not entitled to receive any GHI stock. After Carol received the $110,000, she was no longer a beneficiary and did not constructively own any of the GHI stock held by Father's estate. Cindy is still a beneficiary and constructively owns all the stock held by the estate.

In Example 6-2, Father specifically indicated how his stock was to be distributed. If Father had instead devised a fixed amount of money to Carol and the residue (all remaining assets) to Cindy, Carol would receive her devise before Cindy received anything. That is because general devises such as the devise of money take priority over residuary devises. Carol would be a beneficiary until she received her devise, which could be satisfied in money or in other estate assets. If the estate did not have sufficient money, the personal representative might have been forced to sell the GHI stock or distribute it to Carol. Rules concerning testate and intestate succession are provided by state law. Consult the applicable state probate code when determining if an individual would be considered a beneficiary for purposes of ownership attribution.

b. From Trusts

Trust beneficiaries are treated as constructive owners of stock owned by the trust. Each beneficiary's interest is determined based on his or her actuarial interest in the trust. If an individual is treated as the owner of the trust (or any portion thereof) under the "grantor trust" rules, that individual is treated as the constructive owner of any stock owned by the trust (or portion thereof). I.R.C. § 318(a)(2)(B).

c. From C Corporations

If a C corporation owns stock in another corporation, that stock is attributed to any shareholder who owns at least 50% of the value of the corporation that owns the stock. Attribution is done pro rata based on the value of the stock that the shareholder owns. There is no attribution to a shareholder who owns less than 50% of the value of the stock in the corporation that owns the shares. I.R.C. § 318(a)(2)(C).

Keep two facts in mind in applying this rule. First, value is not the same as number of shares. Because different classes of stock have different rights, a shareholder could own 50% or more of the outstanding shares but own less than 50% of the value of the corporation's stock. Second, stock in a C corporation that is owned at least 50% by an S corporation can be attributed to a shareholder who owns less than 50% of the value of the S corporation's stock. That is because an S corporation is treated as a partnership for purposes of the attribution rules.

d. Multiple Attributions

Stock owned by an entity is attributed to its owners based on their pro rata ownership (or beneficial interest). The constructively owned stock can be reattributed from those owners to members of their families or to other entities in which they have an interest. I.R.C. § 318(a)(5)(A).

> **Example 6-3.** George is a 20% partner in ZZZ Partnership, which owns 100 shares of JKL Corporation stock. George constructively owns 20 shares of the JKL stock. Those shares can be reattributed to

George's son Ted. They can also be reattributed to a trust of which George is the beneficiary.

3. Attribution to an Entity

a. Entities

Attribution to an entity applies to the entities and owners or beneficiaries that were subject to attribution from an entity: partnerships; estates; trusts; and corporations. I.R.C. § 318(a)(3). And as was true for attribution from an entity, S corporations are treated as partnerships for purposes of these rules. I.R.C. § 318(a)(5)(E).

There is a major computational difference between the two types of attribution involving entities. As was indicated in the preceding discussion, attribution from entities to their owners and beneficiaries is proportional to their ownership interests. That is not the case for attribution from owners and beneficiaries to entities. All the stock owned by partners, beneficiaries, grantors of grantor trusts, S corporation shareholders, and shareholders who own at least 50% of a C corporation's stock value is attributed to the entity.

> **Example 6-4.** Hannah owns 60% of the value of MNO Corporation's stock and 40% of the value of PQR Corporation's stock. MNO constructively owns Hannah's PQR shares. Because she owns only 40% of the value of its shares, PQR does not constructively own any of Hannah's MNO shares unless PQR is an S corporation.

If a trust beneficiary owns stock, and the grantor trust rule does not apply, her stock is attributed to the trust unless her interest is a remote contingent interest. If the interest is remote and contingent, none of her stock is attributed to the trust. The definition of "remote" is based on valuation, not on the likelihood that the beneficiary will ever receive any trust property. If the actuarial value of the interest, assuming maximum discretion is exercised in that beneficiary's favor, is 5% or less of the value of the trust property, the interest is remote. I.R.C. § 318(a)(3)(B)(i). This rule applies only to interests that are both remote and contingent. If a beneficiary is entitled to 1% of the trust income every year, her interest is vested. Even if 1% of the income is worth 5% or less of the trust's value, her vested interest is not a remote contingent interest.

b. Multiple Attributions

A person can be an owner or beneficiary of more than one entity. That person's stock ownership can be simultaneously attributed to all those entities.

Example 6-5. Ivan owns 40 shares of STU Corporation. Those shares can be attributed to any estate of which Ivan is a beneficiary, any partnership in which he is a partner, any trust of which he is a beneficiary (assuming his interest is not remote and contingent), any S corporation of which he is a shareholder, and any C corporation in which he owns at least 50% of the stock value. All these entities can be treated as constructive owners of the STU shares at the same time.

c. *Reattribution*

If an entity constructively owns shares because of attribution from an owner, those shares cannot be reattributed from the entity to another owner or beneficiary. I.R.C. § 318(a)(5)(C). For example, the 40 shares that an estate constructively owns because of attribution from its beneficiary Ivan cannot be reattributed from the estate to a different beneficiary. This prohibition is often referred to as the rule against sidewise attribution. If the stock cannot be attributed directly from one owner or beneficiary to another, it cannot be done indirectly through the entity.

4. Option Attribution

If a person has an option to acquire stock, or even an option to acquire an option, that person constructively owns the stock covered by the option. I.R.C. § 318(a)(4). If a person could be a constructive owner because of both option attribution and family attribution, the option attribution rule is the one that applies. I.R.C. § 318(a)(5)(D). When the option rule applies, reattribution from one family member constructive owner to another family member would thus be allowed.

D. Section 302 Redemptions

A redemption covered by § 302(a) is treated as a distribution in exchange for the corporation's stock. Because it is treated as an exchange, the shareholder computes gain or loss on the stock redeemed.

The five redemptions treated as exchanges are described in § 302(b). Each qualifies for exchange treatment because the corporation-shareholder relationship changes enough to justify not treating it as a dividend. Three of these redemptions involve objective criteria. I.R.C. § 302(b)(2)–(4). A fourth, a redemption that is not essentially equivalent to a dividend, involves a facts and circumstances test. I.R.C. § 302(b)(1). This chapter discusses that test last because it is a fallback. If the distribution satisfies one of the objective tests, the parties do not have to establish that the redemption was not essentially equivalent to a dividend. This book ignores the fifth redemption that qualifies for exchange treatment: the redemption of shares by a publicly offered regulated investment company. I.R.C. § 302(b)(5).

If a redemption does not qualify for § 302(a) status, § 302(d) describes its treatment. Section 301 dividend treatment is the default provision unless another Subchapter C provision applies. For example, the redemption may qualify under § 303 and avoid dividend treatment.

1. Substantially Disproportionate Redemption

A redemption that is substantially disproportionate is one that satisfies three mathematical tests based on voting power and stock ownership. The first test looks to absolute ownership; the other two judge the reduction in ownership percentage. I.R.C. § 302(b)(2).

Keep three facts in mind. First, the redemption must satisfy all three tests described below. Second, the corporation will have fewer shares outstanding after the redemption than before. This affects the denominator used in determining the post-redemption ownership percentage. Third, the constructive ownership rules discussed above apply in determining both pre-redemption and post-redemption ownership.

a. Ownership Percentage After the Redemption

Immediately after the redemption, the shareholder must own less than 50% of the total combined voting power of the corporation's stock. I.R.C. § 302(b)(2)(B). This test considers all voting shares, both common and preferred. We ignore nonvoting common and nonvoting preferred stock for purposes of this test.

This test does not require any particular decline in voting power. A shareholder who owns less than 50% of the total combined voting power before the redemption automatically meets this test unless the redemption of additional shareholders occurs as part of the same plan and increases her post-redemption voting power to 50% or more.

> **Example 6-6.** Jane owned 400 of the 1,000 voting shares (40%) of VWX Corporation. VWX redeemed 100 of Jane's shares and did not redeem any other shareholder's stock. Jane is not related to any other shareholder. After the redemption, Jane still owns less than 50% of the VWX voting power (300 of its 900 post-redemption shares).

b. Reduction in Voting Stock Percentage

Immediately after the redemption, the shareholder's voting stock percentage must be less than 80% of what it was immediately before the redemption. I.R.C. § 302(b)(2)(C). The Code describes this computation in terms of a ratio. It compares the ratio of the shareholder's voting stock to the corporation's total voting stock both before and after the redemption. The "after" ratio must be less than 80% of the "before" ratio. Because ratios can be stated as percentages, you can also reach the correct result by comparing before and after ownership percentages. The example in the regulations uses percentages instead of ratios. Reg. § 1.302-3(b).

> **Example 6-7.** ABC Corporation had 500 shares of voting stock outstanding. Ken owned 150 of those shares. It redeemed 100 of Ken's shares and made no other redemptions. Before the redemption, Ken owned 150/500 (30%) of ABC's shares. After the redemption, Ken owned 50/400 (12.5%) of ABC's shares. His ownership after the redemption is only 41.7% of his ownership before the redemption (12.5%/30%).

Because this test looks to voting stock percentage, a shareholder who owned only nonvoting stock cannot meet it.

c. Reduction in Common Stock Percentage

Immediately after the redemption, the shareholder's common stock ownership percentage must also decline by more than 80%. This test considers both voting common and nonvoting common stock. It is based on share value rather than on number of shares. I.R.C. § 302(b)(2)(C)(flush language).

A shareholder who owned only voting preferred stock cannot meet this third test. If the shareholder owned both voting common stock that meets all three tests, and nonvoting preferred stock, the simultaneous redemption of the preferred stock can qualify unless it is § 306 stock. Reg. § 1.302-3(a)(flush language).

d. Multiple Redemptions

If a corporation simultaneously redeems stock from more than one shareholder, each shareholder is tested separately. It is possible that all, some, or none of the redemptions will be substantially disproportionate.

Instead of simultaneous redemptions, a corporation might redeem stock in several, seemingly separate, transactions. The IRS can challenge a redemption that, considered alone, appears to be substantially disproportionate but that actually is not. I.R.C. § 302(b)(2)(D), a statutory step transaction provision, applies to a redemption that is made pursuant to a plan that has as its purpose or effect a series of redemptions. If the result does not satisfy the three tests, the redemption is not substantially disproportionate. The determination of whether a plan exists is based on all the facts and circumstances. Reg. § 1.302-3(a)(flush language).

> **Example 6-8.** DEF Corporation had 100 shares of voting common stock outstanding. Lana, Mel, Nina, Oscar, and Pam each owned 20 shares. DEF redeemed 15 of Lana's shares. That reduced her voting power and common stock percentage from 20/100 (20%) to 5/85 (5.9%). If considered alone, that is substantially disproportionate. Two days later, DEF redeemed Mel, Nina, and Oscar's stock. Lana then owned 5/25 (20%) of GHI's outstanding shares. If the redemption two days later was part of a plan, the redemption of Lana's stock no longer qualifies. Her final stock ownership percentage is the same as her initial stock ownership percentage.

e. *Effect of Constructive Ownership*

The examples above ignored constructive ownership. When constructive ownership rules apply, it is harder for a redemption to satisfy the substantially disproportionate ownership tests.

> **Example 6-9.** GHI Corporation had 500 shares of voting common stock outstanding. Quinn owned 150 of those shares. GHI redeemed 100 of Quinn's shares and made no other redemptions. Quinn is related to only one other GHI shareholder: his daughter Rose owns 150 of the GHI shares. Before the redemption, Quinn's actual and constructive ownership was 300/500 (60%). After the redemption, his actual and constructive ownership was 200/400 (50%). Quinn fails all three tests. He is treated as owning exactly 50% of the corporation's voting power and the ratios of his common stock and voting power immediately after the redemption are 83.3% of what they were before the redemption.

If GHI instead redeemed 140 of Quinn's shares, his actual and constructive ownership declines from 60% (300/500) to 44.4% (160/360). This redemption satisfies all three numerical tests.

2. Complete Termination of the Shareholder's Interest

A complete redemption of the shareholder's stock is treated as a redemption in exchange for that stock. I.R.C. § 302(b)(3). This provision applies no matter what type of stock the shareholder owned—voting common, nonvoting common, voting preferred, or nonvoting preferred. This test is easy to meet if the corporation redeems the stock in exchange for money and if none of the attribution rules apply. The situation is more complicated if constructive ownership rules apply or if the corporation redeems its stock in exchange for a corporate debt obligation.

If the shareholder does not constructively own any stock, § 302(b)(3) requires only the redemption of his stock. It does not require the corporation to retire any debt it owes him, and it does not require that he cease serving as an officer, director, or employee.

a. Constructive Ownership

The § 318 constructive ownership rules apply in determining whether a redemption constitutes a complete termination. The shareholder being redeemed may constructively own stock because of family, entity, or option attribution. Unless we can ignore constructive ownership, a complete redemption of stock owned in a closely held corporation may be impossible.

> **Example 6-10.** Mother owns 50% of the shares of JKL Corporation. Son owns the other 50% of JKL's outstanding shares. Each is treated as owning 100% of the JKL shares (50% through actual ownership and 50% through attribution). If JKL redeems Mother's shares, Son will actually own 100% of its shares. Although Mother no longer actually owns any JKL shares, she will constructively own 100% of the shares because of attribution from Son.

b. Waiving Family Attribution by Family Members

Section 302(c)(2)(A) provides a mechanism for waiving family attribution. If all parties follow its requirements, we ignore family attribution in determining if a redemption is a complete termination.

The first requirement relates to the shareholder whose stock is being redeemed. Immediately after the redemption, that shareholder cannot have any interest in the corporation other than as a creditor. The term "any interest" goes beyond stock ownership. She cannot serve as an officer, director, or employee. I.R.C. § 302(c)(2)(A)(i). Although this rule does not prevent her from being a lessor, vendor, or even an independent contractor with respect to the corporation, there is always a risk that the IRS will assert that the formal relationship is, in substance, one of the prohibited relationships. The risk is particularly high if she is claiming independent contractor status but is performing the same type of services she performed before the redemption.

Because the redeemed shareholder can retain an interest as a creditor, the distinction between debt and equity interests is important. The regulations consider a person a creditor only if his rights "are not greater or broader in scope than necessary for the enforcement of his claim." Reg. § 1.302-4(d). The regulations list as non-creditor factors subordination to the claims of general creditors, principal repayments that are dependent on corporate earnings, and an interest rate that is dependent on corporate earnings.

The second requirement also relates to the shareholder whose stock is being redeemed. She cannot acquire any of the prohibited interests within 10 years following the date of the redemption. This prohibition does not apply to stock she receives by bequest or inheritance. I.R.C. § 302(c)(2)(A)(ii). It does apply to stock received by inter vivos gift. Although it also applies to prohibited non-stock interests (serving as an officer, director, or employee), the Tax Court has allowed the former shareholder's spouse to serve as an employee. The spouse had not been a shareholder. *Hurst v. Commissioner*, 124 T.C. 16 (2005).

The third requirement is procedural. The shareholder being redeemed must file an agreement with the IRS. She must agree to notify the IRS if she acquires a prohibited interest and to retain records that are necessary to determining compliance. I.R.C. § 302(c)(2)(A)(iii). Section 302(c)(2)(A) (flush language) extends the statute of limitations on assessment and collection of the tax and interest that would have been due.

In addition to those three requirements, two 10-year look-back rules may prevent waiver of family attribution. These rules cover certain stock acquisitions during the 10-year period ending on the date of the redemption. The first rule applies if the shareholder being redeemed acquired any of the stock being redeemed from a person whose stock ownership would be attributed to him. I.R.C. § 302(c)(2)(B)(i). Attribution is tested on the date of the redemption, not on the date the stock was acquired.

> **Example 6-11.** Mother and Father each originally owned 50% of the stock of MNO Corporation. Father died four years ago, and Son inherited Father's shares. If MNO redeems Son's shares, he can waive family attribution from Mother. Although Son acquired the stock within the 10-year period ending on the date of the distribution, he acquired it from Father. Because Father is dead on the date of the distribution, there would be no attribution on that date from Father to Son.

The second look-back rule applies if some other person owns stock acquired from the redeemed shareholder and that stock would be attributed to the redeemed shareholder. This rule does not apply if the stock triggering this rule is also redeemed in the same transaction. I.R.C. § 302(c)(2)(B)(ii).

> **Example 6-12.** Mother and Father each owned 50% of the stock of PQR Corporation. Mother transferred half of her shares to Daughter

three years ago. If PQR redeems Mother's shares, Mother cannot waive family attribution unless PQR also redeems Daughter's shares in the same transaction. Mother could waive family attribution if she had instead transferred the shares to Daughter more than 10 years ago.

The two look-back rules do not apply if the stock transfers to or from the redeemed shareholder did not have avoidance of federal income tax as a principal purpose. For example, Mother may have transferred stock to Daughter because she hoped that Daughter would become interested in working in the business. The mere fact that the other person is in a lower income tax bracket is not sufficient to establish the prohibited purpose. Reg. § 1.302-4(g)(2).

c. *Waiving Family Attribution by Entities*

Stock in a closely held corporation is often owned through trusts, partnerships, or other corporations. If a family member dies, an estate may own stock during the estate administration period. Because stock owned by entities is attributed to owners and beneficiaries, and stock owned by owners and beneficiaries is attributed to entities, attribution may prevent a redemption from being a complete termination.

Section 302(c)(2)(C) applies to one of the possible situations that can affect an entity and its owners or beneficiaries. It provides a mechanism for an entity to waive attribution from an individual who is an actual owner to a family member who is not an owner and from that family member to the entity. These rules apply to the entity and any "related person." The individual who is the constructive owner is a related person. I.R.C. § 302(c)(2)(C)(ii)(II). The individual who is the actual owner is not a related person.

It is important to focus on what § 302(c)(2)(C) does and does not allow. It applies to an entity that is having its interest completely terminated. If one of the entity's owners (a shareholder, partner, or beneficiary in a trust or estate) also owns stock in the corporation and will continue to do so, it provides no relief because there is no mechanism for waiving attribution from an actual owner to an entity. The section instead applies if a family member of one of the entity's owners or beneficiaries is a shareholder in the corporation. The entity being redeemed can waive attribution from that family member to its owner or beneficiary and from that person to the entity being redeemed.

Example 6-13. STU Corporation's stock is owned by Father (75%) and the YYY Partnership (25%). Father is a 10% partner in YYY. If STU redeems the stock owned by YYY, the redemption will not qualify as a complete redemption. Father was an actual owner of STU stock.

Because he is a partner in YYY, the partnership will still be treated as owning Father's STU shares.

Example 6-14. VWX Corporation's stock is owned by Mother (75%) and the LLL Partnership (25%). Mother's son Xavier is a 15% partner in LLL. If VWX redeems the stock owned by LLL, the redemption may qualify as a complete redemption. Because Xavier was not an actual owner of VWX stock, family attribution can be waived. If they meet the other requirements for waiver, LLL and Xavier can waive attribution from Mother to Xavier and from Xavier to LLL.

Section 302(c)(2)(C) requires that the entity and each related person meet the three tests discussed above for family attribution: retain no prohibited interest; acquire no prohibited interest (other than by bequest or inheritance) for the next 10 years; and file the agreement. The 10-year look-back rules also apply. Each related person must agree to be jointly and severally liable for the tax and interest if a prohibited interest is acquired.

3. Partial Liquidation

a. *Qualifying Shareholders*

Section 302(b)(4) treats distributions as exchanges if: (1) the shareholder being redeemed is not a corporation and (2) the redemption distribution is in partial liquidation of the corporation. A distribution to noncorporate shareholders can qualify even if corporate shareholders also receive a distribution. Stock owned by a partnership, trust, or estate is treated as owned proportionately by its partners or beneficiaries. I.R.C. § 302(e)(5).

Example 6-15. YZ Corporation's stock is owned 50% by OOO Partnership and 50% by Alicia. Each received a redemption distribution that would be treated as a partial liquidation based on the safe harbor discussed below. OOO has two equal partners: Brian and ABC Corporation. The redemption of Alicia's YZ shares qualified for partial liquidation status. The redemption of half of OOO's YZ shares also qualified because they were treated as owned by Brian. The redemption of the other half of OOO's YZ shares did not qualify for partial liquidation status because they were treated as owned by a corporation (ABC).

b. *Qualifying Redemptions*

Section 302(b)(4) differs from the other three redemptions discussed in this section in one important aspect. Qualification under the other three provisions is tested at the shareholder level. Those tests require a meaningful change in the shareholder's ownership interest. Qualification as a partial liquidation, on the other hand, is determined with reference to the corporation making the redemption.

A redemption must satisfy two tests to be in partial liquidation of the corporation. First, the distribution must not be essentially equivalent to a dividend when tested at the corporate level. Second, the distribution must be pursuant to a plan that is accomplished within the required time limit. I.R.C. § 302(e)(1).

The "not essentially equivalent to a dividend" test can be met by satisfying a statutory safe harbor or based on the facts and circumstances. The statutory safe harbor has two requirements. First, the distribution must be attributable to the corporation's ceasing to conduct a qualified trade or business or must consist of the assets of that business. Second, immediately after the distribution, the corporation must be actively engaged in the conduct of a qualified trade or business. I.R.C. § 302(e)(2). The safe harbor applies only if the corporation had been conducting at least two qualified trades or businesses and continued to conduct at least one qualified activity after the distribution.

An activity is a qualified trade or business if it was actively conducted throughout the five-year period ending with the distribution and was not acquired during that period in a transaction involving gain or loss recognition. I.R.C. § 302(e)(3). This test has two parts. The first part looks to the activity and not to the taxpayers that operated it. The activity must have a five-year or longer life. The second part is relevant only if the corporation acquired the activity less than five years before the redemption. If it did, then the test is not met unless no gain or loss was recognized on the acquisition. This test looks to the acquisition of the activity itself, not to individual assets. For example, the corporation could have purchased a machine for an existing activity. The fact that the machine was purchased in a taxable transaction will not prevent the activity from satisfying the five-year test.

> **Example 6-16.** DEF and GHI Corporations merged in a tax-free transaction three years ago. DEF was the surviving corporation and continued to operate both its own business and the business previously operated by GHI. If both businesses are at least five years old, the safe harbor can apply to a redemption in partial liquidation.

A distribution can fail the safe harbor test for various reasons. The corporation may not have had at least two businesses, a business may not have had a five-year history (or was acquired in a taxable transaction during the preceding five years), or the corporation may not cease to conduct any of its businesses. In those situations, the distribution can qualify as a partial liquidation only if it meets a facts and circumstances test. Regulations issued in 1960 for a predecessor section (§ 346) indicate that a distribution attributable to a genuine corporate contraction can qualify. For example, a distribution of insurance proceeds received after a fire that caused a cessation of part of the business will qualify. Distribution of funds held in a reserve for expansion that did not occur will not qualify. Reg. § 1.346-1(a). Both the safe harbor and the facts and circumstances tests focus on a corporate contraction.

A distribution that qualifies as a partial liquidation must be made pursuant to a plan. The distribution must occur within the taxable year in which the plan was adopted or in the next taxable year. I.R.C. § 302(e)(1)(B). The taxable year is that of the corporation, which might be a fiscal year, not that of the shareholders receiving the distribution.

c. *Pro Rata Redemptions*

The fact that a redemption is made pro rata to all shareholders does not prevent it from qualifying as a partial liquidation. I.R.C. § 302(e)(4). Because partial liquidations are tested at the corporate level, not at the shareholder level, you should not be surprised to see a pro rata redemption. If a pro rata redemption occurs, shareholders do not have to surrender any of their shares. Because a pro rata redemption does not change their proportionate interests in the corporation, surrendering shares would be meaningless.

4. Redemption That Is Not Essentially Equivalent to a Dividend

Section 302(b)(1) covers redemptions that are not essentially equivalent to a dividend. Shareholders can look to it in situations that do not qualify under the objective tests described above. Failure to meet the objective tests is ignored in determining if a distribution is not essentially equivalent to a dividend. I.R.C. § 302(b)(6).

Determining if a distribution is not essentially equivalent to a dividend at the shareholder level involves a consideration of the facts and circumstances. Section 302 provides no definition, and the regulations are relatively limited. The regulations provide that redemptions of nonvoting preferred stock that is limited as to both dividend and liquidation rights can qualify. Reg. § 1.302-2(a). They indicate that pro rata redemptions are unlikely to qualify. They also imply that a pro rata redemption of all the shares of one class of stock might qualify if other classes of stock are owned in different percentages or by different shareholders. Reg. § 1.302-2(b)(1).

A redemption is likely to qualify as not essentially equivalent to a dividend if there is a meaningful reduction in a shareholder's interest. *United States v. Davis*, 397 U.S. 301, 313 (1970). In determining if this test is met, the IRS and courts look to the three rights that shareholders normally enjoy: the right to vote; the right to receive dividend distributions; and the right to receive liquidation distributions. Redemptions that reduce a shareholder (or group of shareholders) from a majority interest to a minority interest involve a meaningful reduction in interest; those shareholders lose effective control of the corporation. The IRS has also approved redemptions by publicly traded corporations that simply reduced a minority shareholder's ownership percentage. Rev. Rul. 76-385, 1976-2 C.B. 92.

Because constructive ownership rules apply, the meaningful reduction in interest test is difficult, but not impossible, to meet if the corporation is closely held. If a corporation is publicly traded, shareholders can sell their shares on a stock exchange at any time and not worry about whether the transaction is a sale or a dividend. But there are situations in which the corporation itself may be the buyer. For example, it may buy back shares because its employees have exercised stock options or because it is trying to increase the price of outstanding shares. It may also pay money in lieu of fractional shares as part of a stock dividend. The IRS is likely to treat those redemption distributions as exchanges rather than as dividends.

5. Redemption That Qualifies Under More Than One Provision

Some redemptions may qualify under more than one paragraph of § 302(b). For example, it might be both substantially disproportionate and made in a partial liquidation. Or it might be both a complete termination and not essentially equivalent to a dividend. This overlap is particularly important for complete terminations because of the requirements for waiving attribution. Section 302(b)(6) provides that if both § 302(b)(3) and any of § 302(b)(1), (2), or (4) apply, the relevant other provision will govern with respect to stock acquisitions during the 10 years following the distribution.

Example 6-17. JKL Corporation's shares are owned equally by Mother, Father, Son, and Daughter. JKL has actively conducted two businesses for the past 15 years; each business had the same value. JKL recently sold one of the businesses and plans to distribute the proceeds to Mother and Father in redemption of their shares. If Mother and Father can waive family attribution, this redemption would be a complete termination. Because the redemption could also qualify as a partial liquidation, Mother and Father are not precluded from acquiring JKL stock or being a JKL officer, director, or employee during the next 10 years.

E. Section 303 Redemptions

If a decedent owned stock in a closely held corporation, the constructive ownership rules might prevent a redemption from qualifying as an exchange. Section 303, which applies to shares included in a decedent's estate, provides an alternative route to exchange treatment. If it applies to a redemption, we can ignore constructive ownership.

Section 303 is particularly valuable for shareholders of closely held corporations. Qualifying stock can be redeemed to provide funds for estate taxes and other estate expenses, and the estate can treat the redemption as an exchange instead of as a dividend. Because the § 1014 basis rules wipe out any unrealized gain from the decedent's ownership period, a redemption has better income tax consequences than does a dividend. A redemption soon after the decedent's death is unlikely to involve redemption proceeds that exceed the estate's basis for the redeemed shares. A dividend, on the other hand, is gross income to the extent the corporation has E&P.

Note that a redemption has better tax consequences than a dividend even if President Trump's proposal to limit the § 1014 basis step-up is enacted. That is because the shareholder can still recover the decedent's basis tax-free.

A formula limits the amount of stock that can qualify for § 303 redemption treatment. In addition, the redeemed shares must satisfy four requirements. A redemption that does not qualify under § 303 because it exceeds the limit or fails to meet a requirement may still qualify for redemption treatment under § 302.

The discussion in this section is general. Working with § 303 requires some familiarity with the federal estate tax and the relevant state probate code. The discussion below assumes the federal estate tax continues in its form as of December 31, 2016.

1. Limit on Qualifying Amount

A qualifying redemption cannot exceed the sum of two amounts. I.R.C. § 303(a)(1)–(2). The first is the amount of federal and state estate, inheritance, legacy, and succession taxes imposed because of the decedent's death, increased by any interest collected on those taxes because of late payment. The discussion below refers to those taxes and interest as "death taxes" because the regulations use that terminology. Reg. § 1.303-2(c)(2), -2(g)(2).

The second amount is the sum of funeral and administration expenses allowed as a § 2053 deduction in computing the federal taxable estate. If there is little or no death tax due because the taxable estate is less than the exemption equivalent or because all federal *and* state death taxes are repealed, this section may still apply if the estate has allowable funeral and administration expenses. Alternatively, Congress could consider repealing § 303 if it repeals the federal estate tax.

2. Requirements

a. Inclusion in Gross Estate

Shares do not qualify unless they are included in the decedent's gross estate. I.R.C. § 303(a). Shares acquired after the decedent's death can qualify if their basis is computed with reference to the basis of shares included in the estate. I.R.C. § 303(c). Later-acquired shares might include shares received as a stock dividend or in a reorganization.

Gross estate is a federal tax concept. It includes property that the decedent owns at death. It also includes property in which the decedent had rights or interests listed in the Code's estate tax provisions. The gross estate is not the same as the state law probate estate, although it may resemble the state law augmented estate used to compute a surviving spouse's elective share. The gross estate is generally larger than the taxable estate because it is computed before various deductions.

b. Stock Value

Section 303 does not apply unless the value of the stock included in the gross estate exceeds 35% of the amount by which the gross estate exceeds deductions allowed by §§ 2053 and 2054 (funeral and administration expenses, claims against the estate, and losses during administration). I.R.C. § 303(b)(2)(A). Those deductions are referred to as allowable deductions in the examples below.

If shares of a single corporation do not satisfy the 35% test, the redemption may still qualify based on the decedent's ownership of stock in other corporations. If the decedent owns more than 20% of the value of the stock in more than one corporation, those corporations can be treated as one for purposes of satisfying the 35% rule. The surviving spouse's interest in stock held as community property, tenants by the entirety, joint tenants, or tenants in common is included for purposes of the 20% rule. I.R.C. § 303(b)(2)(B).

The 35% rule is based on how large a percentage of the estate the shares represent. The 20% rule, on the other hand, is based on how much of a corporation's stock the decedent owned.

> **Example 6-18.** When Robert died, he owned 10% of the shares of MNO Corporation (worth $150,000) and 5% of the shares of PQR Corporation (worth $30,000). Robert's gross estate, minus allowable deductions, was $400,000. The stock he owned in MNO Corporation represented 37.5% of that $400,000; the stock he owned in PQR Corporation represented 7.5% of that $400,000. A redemption of Robert's MNO shares might qualify under § 303; a redemption of his PQR shares would not.

> **Example 6-19.** When Sue died, she owned 22% of the shares of STU Corporation (worth $60,000) and 20% of the shares of VWX Corporation (worth $100,000). Sue's gross estate, minus allowable deductions, was $400,000. The stock Sue owned in STU Corporation represented 15% of that $400,000; the stock she owned in VWX Corporation represented 25% of that $400,000. Because she owned at least 20% of each corporation's outstanding stock, we can aggregate the STU and VWX shares. Their $160,000 total value represented 40% of Sue's gross estate minus allowable deductions. A redemption of shares in either or both corporations might qualify under § 303.

The regulations applying § 303(b)(2) do not reflect the current percentage requirements. Reg. § 1.303-2 was last amended in 1975.

A shareholder may reduce his gross estate by making inter vivos gifts of other property. If the gross estate is smaller, the stock he owns at death is more likely to meet the 35% test. Section 2035(c) includes the amounts transferred in computing the value of the gross estate for purposes of § 303(b) even if they are not part of the gross estate for purposes of computing the estate tax. It applies only to transfers made within three years of death.

> **Example 6-20.** If Robert (Example 6-18), had made inter vivos gifts of $100,000 in the three years ending on his death, his gross estate minus deductions for purposes of § 303, would be $500,000 instead of $400,000. Instead of being 37.5% of $400,000, his MNO shares would be only 30% of $500,000. A redemption of those shares would not qualify.

Section 2035(c) does not apply to transfers the decedent did not have to report for gift tax purposes. I.R.C. § 2035(c)(3). Unlike the gift tax return, which allows an exclusion for present-interest gifts ($14,000 per-donee, per-year in 2017), this exception applies only if the decedent did not have to file a gift tax return for transfers to that donee. Thus, if Robert transferred property only to his spouse during the three-year period, we would not add the $100,000 to his gross estate for purposes of § 303. If he limited his transfers to other persons to $14,000 per year each, we would not add those transfers either. But, if the $100,000 included a transfer of $15,000 to his son in a single year, we would add all $15,000 for purposes of § 303.

c. Burden on Shareholder's Interest in Estate

A third requirement relates to "hardship." The redemption qualifies only to the extent the redeemed shareholder's interest in the estate is reduced by death taxes and by funeral and administration expenses. A binding obligation to contribute to these outlays is treated the same as a direct reduction. I.R.C. § 303(b)(3). If, for example, the decedent devised his shares of stock to one beneficiary and his will provides for charging all death taxes, funeral costs, and administration expenses against devises to other beneficiaries, the redemption can qualify for § 303 only if the other estate property is insufficient to pay those expenses.

> **Example 6-21.** When Tom died, he owned shares of YZ Corporation stock that constituted 40% of the value of his gross estate minus deductions allowed by §§ 2053 and 2054. He devised that stock to his daughter Lisa. He devised the residue of his estate to his brother Bill. Tom's will charged all death taxes, funeral costs, and administration expenses against the residue. If the residue is sufficient to pay those taxes, § 303 does not apply to a redemption of Lisa's stock. If, for example, the residue was $5,000 less than the amount of those charges, up to $5,000 worth of the stock devised to Lisa could qualify.

> **Example 6-22.** Tom's will instead charged all death taxes, funeral costs, and administration expenses 25% against the devise to Lisa and 75% against the residue. A redemption of Lisa's stock could qualify. The amount that qualifies cannot exceed 25% of the death taxes, funeral costs, and administration expenses.

Although death taxes, funeral costs, and administration expenses establish the maximum amount that can qualify, the estate does not have to use the redemption proceeds to pay for those items. Section 303 is not conditioned on the estate being illiquid. Nor is it conditioned on the corporation making the redemption with money; the corporation can instead use other property.

d. Time Period for Redemption

A redemption qualifies only if it occurs after the decedent's death. It must usually be completed no later than 90 days after the end of the period for assessing the estate tax. I.R.C. § 303(b)(1)(A). Redemptions can also qualify if made no later than 60 days after a Tax Court decision regarding the tax becomes final or if made during the period covered by a § 6166 election to pay the estate tax in installments. If a redemption occurs more than four years after the decedent's death, the amount of the redemption that qualifies cannot exceed the lesser of: (1) the unpaid taxes and expenses or (2) the amount of such items paid within the one-year period beginning with that redemption. I.R.C. § 303(b)(4).

> **Example 6-23.** Tara died last year. Her estate owed $500,000 in estate and inheritance taxes and funeral and administration expenses. If the stock included in her gross estate meets the other tests, a redemption of up to $500,000 can qualify for § 303 treatment.

> **Example 6-24.** Ted died five years ago. His estate owed $500,000 in estate and inheritance taxes and funeral and administration expenses. The personal representative of Ted's estate sold assets other than stock and paid all but $50,000 of those costs three years after Ted's death. The personal representative has paid nothing since. Even if Ted's estate still owns qualifying stock, the maximum redemption that can qualify this year is $50,000. If the corporation redeems only $30,000 of the stock this year and redeems $20,000 of stock 14 months later, the maximum qualifying amount is $30,000.

3. Interplay of Section 303 with Other Provisions

If a corporation redeems stock from multiple shareholders, it is possible that some redemptions will qualify under § 303, some under § 302, and some under neither provision. Each shareholder is considered separately. Reg. § 1.303-3. If redemptions that might qualify under § 303 do not occur simultaneously, qualification follows the order in which the distributions occur. Reg. § 1.303-2(g). Later distributions can still be tested for qualification under § 302(a).

F. Section 304 Redemptions

Section 304 applies when stock is purchased by a related corporation rather than redeemed by the corporation that issued it. It denies exchange treatment when the purchase is in substance a dividend rather than a qualifying redemption. It also determines how the E&P of the purchasing corporation and the issuing corporation are applied to these transactions.

1. Related Corporations

Section 304 applies to two types of relationships: brother-sister corporations and parent-subsidiary corporations. If a relationship could be characterized as both brother-sister and parent-subsidiary, the parent-subsidiary rules apply. I.R.C. § 304(a)(1)(flush language).

Both types of relationships are defined based on control. Each uses a modified version of the § 318 attribution rules. The discussion below refers to the corporation making the acquisition as the acquiring corporation; it refers to the corporation whose stock is being acquired as the issuing corporation.

a. Brother-Sister Corporations

A brother-sister relationship exists if two corporations are controlled by the same person or persons. I.R.C. § 304(a)(1)(A). Control can be established based on voting power or stock value. To be in control, one or more persons must own stock that accounts for at least 50% of each corporation's combined voting power *or* at least 50% of each corporation's stock value. I.R.C. § 304(c)(1). The statute's language refers to total combined voting power and to total value of shares of all classes of stock. The IRS has ruled that control based on stock value is determined by the combined value of the corporation's outstanding stock. The controlling shareholder(s) need not own 50% of the value of *each* class of the corporation's stock. Rev. Rul. 89-57, 1989-1 C.B. 90. Control of one corporation can be based on voting power, and control of the other can be based on value. Reg. § 1.304-5(a) defines control using the word "or."

> **Example 6-25.** Allan owns 50% of the value of ABC Corporation stock and 80% of the value of DEF Corporation stock. ABC and DEF are brother-sister corporations. The result would be the same if Allan owned 50% of the value of ABC and 80% of the voting power of DEF.

If a shareholder owns at least 50% of each corporation before the transaction occurs, he has control of each corporation even if his ownership percentage in the issuing corporation declines in the transfer. Even if he does not own 50% of the acquiring corporation before the transfer, he is treated as in control if he acquires control in the transfer. Any stock received is considered in determining control. I.R.C. § 304(c)(2); Reg. § 1.304-5(b).

> **Example 6-26.** Barney owned 65% of the value of Issuer Corporation stock and 45% of the value of Acquiring Corporation stock. He trans-

ferred part of his Issuer shares to Acquiring in exchange for additional Acquiring shares. After the transfer, Barney owned 50% of the Acquiring shares. Issuer and Acquiring are brother-sister corporations.

With two exceptions, the § 318 constructive ownership rules apply in determining if a brother-sister corporation relationship exists. I.R.C. § 304(c)(3). Both exceptions involve entity attribution. For purposes of § 304, stock is attributed from a corporation to a shareholder if the shareholder is treated as owning at least 5% (instead of 50%) of the corporation's stock value. The rule that attribution from a corporation to its shareholders is pro rata based on stock ownership still applies. I.R.C. § 304(c)(3)(B)(i). Stock is attributed from a shareholder to a corporation if the shareholder owns at least 5% of the corporation's stock value. If the shareholder owns at least 50% of the corporation's stock value, all of that shareholder's stock in the other corporation is attributed to the first corporation. If the shareholder owns at least 5% but less than 50% of the value of the corporation's stock, only the percentage of stock owned is attributed. I.R.C. § 304(c)(3)(B)(ii). Attribution is based on stock value, not on voting power, for this purpose.

Example 6-27. Betty owns 50% of the voting power of GHI Corporation stock. Betty's daughter owns 80% of the voting power of JKL Corporation stock. Because of constructive ownership, Betty owns the shares owned by her daughter and vice versa. GHI and JKL are brother-sister corporations.

Two corporations can be brother-sister corporations even if the shareholder owns stock in only one of them if that shareholder owns a controlling interest in a corporation that itself owns 50% or more of the other corporation's voting power or stock value. I.R.C. § 304(c)(1). For example, if Barney owned no shares in Issuer Corporation in Example 6-26 but did own 65% of ABC Corporation, which owned 50% of Issuer's stock, Issuer and Acquiring would be brother-sister corporations after the transfer.

b. Parent-Subsidiary Corporations

Section 304 applies when a subsidiary corporation acquires stock of its parent corporation. A parent-subsidiary relationship exists if the corporation that issued the stock controls the corporation that acquired the stock. I.R.C. § 304(a)(2). The definition of control that applied in determining a brother-sister relationship applies in determining a parent-subsidiary relationship. The parent must own at least 50% of the other corporation's stock value or voting power.

2. Testing for Redemption Status

Section 304 is used in testing whether a transaction qualifies as a § 302 redemption. For example, the shareholder who sold the issuing corporation's stock to the acquiring corporation may be deemed to still own that stock. That may prevent qualification as a substantially disproportionate redemption or a complete termination of interest in the issuing corporation. The same testing rules apply in both brother-sister and parent-subsidiary redemptions.

In applying the § 318 constructive ownership rules for this purpose, attribution to and from corporations does not require 50% ownership. I.R.C. § 304(b)(1). The examples in this section use percentage ownership in making those computations. If you are more comfortable working with numbers, assume that each corporation has 100 outstanding shares.

> **Example 6-28.** Dan owned 60% of the stock value of MNO Corporation and 40% of the stock value of PQR Corporation. Dan sold half of his MNO stock to Ethel. That transaction is treated as a sale.

> **Example 6-29.** Dan instead transferred one-half of his MNO stock to PQR in exchange for additional PQR shares. After the transfer, he owned 70% of the PQR shares. He constructively owned 70% of the 30% of the MNO shares that PQR acquired (21%). Dan's actual and constructive ownership of the MNO stock was 51% after the sale (compared to actual ownership of 60% before the sale). The reduction from 60% to 51% did not qualify as substantially disproportionate.

Section 304 also applies to redemptions covered by § 303. For example, a sale to a subsidiary corporation may be treated as a redemption of the parent whose stock is included in the decedent's estate.

3. Consequences of Failure to Qualify as a Redemption

As discussed above, the purchase by the acquiring corporation is tested for § 302 redemption status based on the shareholder's ownership of the issuing corporation. The tax consequences of failure to qualify vary based on whether the purchase occurs in a brother-sister or parent-subsidiary situation.

If the purchase by a subsidiary of its parent's stock fails to qualify as a redemption, the transaction is treated as a distribution in redemption of the parent's stock. I.R.C. § 304(a)(2). It is treated as a dividend to the extent of E&P.

A different rule applies in the brother-sister setting. The transaction is treated as a distribution in redemption of the acquiring corporation's stock. To the extent the distribution is subject to § 301, its treatment is based on two fictions included in § 304(a)(1). First, the transferor is treated as if he transferred the issuing corporation's stock to the acquiring corporation in exchange for the acquiring corporation's stock in a transaction governed by § 351. Second, the acquiring corporation is deemed to have redeemed its stock from the transferor for whatever property it transferred in exchange for the issuing corporation's stock.

Example 6-30. Gilda owned 60% of the stock of both STU and VWX Corporations. She sold 10% of the STU shares to VWX. After the sale, Gilda was treated as owning 50% of STU through actual ownership and 6% (60% of the 10% now owned by VWX) through constructive ownership. This transaction did not qualify as a § 302 exchange of her STU shares. Gilda is treated as transferring her STU shares to VWX (in exchange for VWX shares) in a § 351 transaction. She is then treated as receiving a redemption distribution from VWX in exchange for the hypothetical VWX shares she was treated as receiving.

We use E&P of both corporations in determining if the distribution is covered by E&P. We use E&P of the acquiring corporation before we use E&P of the issuing corporation. I.R.C. § 304(b)(2). This ordering potentially affects other shareholders of each corporation because it reduces the amount that might be treated as a dividend when the corporations make future distributions.

4. Interplay of Sections 304 and 351

As noted above, § 304(a)(1) (brother-sister transaction) treats the distribution as being from the acquiring corporation by way of a hypothetical § 351 transfer followed by a redemption. That language does not necessarily mean that § 351 applies to the transaction. Section 351 uses the 80% control definition of § 368(c). Section 304, on the other hand, uses a 50% control definition.

Even if the transferor met the § 368(c) requirement, § 304 governs the transfer. Section 304(b)(3)(A) provides that § 304 (and not § 351) applies to the property received in this situation. A limited exception applies to certain liabilities the transferor incurred as part of the stock transfer. I.R.C. § 304(b)(3)(B).

G. Section 306 Dispositions

Preferred stock traditionally has limited dividend and liquidation rights and often has no voting rights. But because there is no fixed obligation to repay, it is treated as stock rather than debt. The corporation could issue it for money at any time. It could also issue it as part of a § 351 transfer to a controlled corporation or as a nontaxable § 305 stock distribution.

Because common shareholders can receive preferred stock without reporting income but do not have to surrender significant corporate rights on selling it to third parties, they may view it as a tool for converting ordinary dividend income into long-term capital gain income. If, for example, a corporation with adequate E&P distributes $100 for each share of stock, each shareholder reports the amount received as gross income. If the corporation instead distributes one share of preferred stock (worth $100) for each share of common stock owned, the shareholders report no gross income. I.R.C. § 305(a). They simply allocate part of the basis for their common stock to the preferred stock. I.R.C. § 307(a). Section 1223(4) tacks the shareholder's holding period for the common to her holding period for the preferred. If § 306 did not apply, she could sell the preferred stock to a third party, offset the sales proceeds by the § 307 basis, and be taxed at long-term capital gains rates on the remaining proceeds. She would continue to own the common stock that provided the important shareholder rights. This is referred to as a "preferred stock bail-out."

Section 306 limits shareholders' ability to use preferred stock to convert potential dividend income into capital gain. Unlike the other transactions covered in this chapter, it applies not only to redemptions by the issuing corporation, or by a corporation related to it, but also to sales to third parties.

1. Section 306 Stock

There are four categories of § 306 stock. First, stock is § 306 stock if it was distributed to the seller as a § 305(a) nontaxable stock dividend (other than a distribution of common stock made with respect to common stock). I.R.C. § 306(c)(1)(A). Stock treated as a dividend because of § 305(b) is not § 306 stock. Second, stock is § 306 stock if the shareholder received it in a reorganization or § 355 transaction, it is not common stock, and his gain or loss was not fully recognized. I.R.C. § 306(c)(1)(B). Stock is not covered by this second category if the effect of the transaction was not substantially the same as the receipt of a stock dividend and the stock was not received in exchange for § 306 stock. Third, preferred stock received in a § 351 transfer is § 306 stock if any part of the consideration received would have been a taxable dividend if received in money instead of the preferred stock. I.R.C. § 306(c)(3). Because of the dividend requirement, the third category involves transfers to a corporation that already has E&P.

The fourth category is stock that has a basis computed with reference to § 306 stock. I.R.C. § 306(c)(1)(C). The class of stock does not matter. A shareholder who transferred § 306 stock in Corporation 1 to Corporation 2 in a § 351 transaction treats the Corporation 2 stock she received as § 306 stock even if it was common stock unless the exception described in Section G.2 applies.

A shareholder who receives § 306 stock as an inter vivos gift, and thus takes the donor's basis under § 1015, must treat the stock as § 306 stock. A shareholder who inherited the stock is not subject to this rule, as he uses a § 1014 fair market value basis instead of the donor's basis. Reg. § 1.306-3(e).

Section 306 also applies to rights to acquire stock. If those rights are later exercised and stock is received, the stock is treated as distributed at the time the rights were distributed. The amount subject to § 306 is the value of the rights at the time they were distributed, not the value of the stock when the rights were exercised. I.R.C. § 306(d).

2. Stock That Is Not Section 306 Stock

Stock is not § 306 stock if no part of a money distribution would have been treated as a dividend. This would occur if the corporation had no E&P when it distributed the stock. I.R.C. § 306(c)(2). In addition, common stock is generally exempt if the shareholder received it in exchange for § 306 stock that had been issued with respect to common stock. For example, if a corporation issued a nontaxable dividend in the form of preferred stock to its common shareholders, that preferred stock would be § 306 stock if the corporation's E&P were sufficient. If a shareholder later exchanged that preferred stock for common stock, the common stock would lose any § 306 taint. This rule applies whether or not the preferred stock included a conversion privilege. But if the common stock can be converted into preferred stock, this exemption from § 306 status does not apply. I.R.C. § 306(e)(1)–(2).

3. Dispositions of Section 306 Stock

a. General Rules

If the corporation redeems § 306 stock, the shareholder treats the amount received as a distribution covered by § 301. I.R.C. § 306(a)(2). The amount received is a dividend to the extent of the corporation's E&P. If the distribution exceeds the E&P, he applies the excess to his stock basis. If his basis is reduced to zero, he treats any remaining amount received as gain from the sale of the stock.

If the stock is disposed of in another manner, say by sale to a third party (or even to another shareholder), the seller's amount realized has three layers. I.R.C. § 306(a)(1)(A)–(B). The first layer is the amount that would have been a dividend if the shareholder had received money instead of the § 306 stock. It is based on the value of the stock when it was distributed. The second layer is the shareholder's basis for the stock. The third layer is any remaining amount of the sales proceeds; this layer is the shareholder's gain with respect to the sale. If the amount allocated to the second layer is less than the shareholder's basis, the shareholder realizes a loss. That loss is not recognized. I.R.C. § 306(a)(1)(C). Section 306(a)(1) treats the first layer as ordinary income, but § 306(a)(1)(D) indicates that it is to be treated as a dividend for purposes of the § 1(h) reduced tax rate on dividend income.

An anti-avoidance rule applies in situations involving a substantial change in the terms and conditions applied to the stock. The amount that would have been treated as a dividend or as the stock's fair market value is the greater of the relevant amount when the distribution occurred or when the change in conditions occurred. I.R.C. § 306(g)(1)–(2). In addition, the exemption from § 306 status because the corporation had no E&P applies only if the corporation had no E&P when the stock was distributed *and* when the change in conditions occurred. I.R.C. § 306(g)(3).

> **Example 6-31.** XY Corporation distributed § 306 stock worth $50 per share with respect to its common stock. It later made a substantial change in the stock's terms and conditions. At that time, the stock was worth $80 per share. If a shareholder sells some of the shares to a third party, the ordinary income component is $80 per share, not $50 per share.

b. Exceptions

Section 306(b) provides several exceptions to the rules discussed above. One exception applies to redemptions. If a redemption would qualify as a § 302(b)(3) complete termination of interest or as a § 302(b)(4) partial liquidation, the amount realized is not treated as a dividend. I.R.C. § 306(b)(1)(B). Instead, it will be the amount realized in computing gain or loss.

A second exception applies to a sale to an unrelated person, using § 318 attribution rules to determine who is a related person. If that sale completely terminates the seller's interest in the corporation, § 306 does not apply. I.R.C. § 306(b)(1)(A). This exception is very narrow. The seller must dispose of her entire stock interest in the corporation. Disposing of only the § 306 stock is not sufficient. Constructive ownership rules apply in determining if she retains any stock interest.

A third exception applies to the redemption of stock when the corporation undergoes a complete liquidation. I.R.C. § 306(b)(2). Also exempted are transactions in which no gain or loss is recognized. I.R.C. § 306(b)(3). For example, the § 306 stock might be exchanged for other stock as part of a corporate merger. In that situation, the new stock is likely to be treated as § 306 stock because of § 306(c)(1)(B). Or the transfer may be to the transferor's former spouse incident to their divorce. The transferor recognizes no gain or loss.

I.R.C. § 1041(a). Because she takes the transferor's basis, the recipient will hold the stock as § 306 stock. § 306(c)(1)(C). A final exception applies if the taxpayer can convince the IRS that the transactions were not in pursuance of a plan that has avoidance of the income tax as a principal purpose. I.R.C. § 306(b)(4).

H. Corporation's Tax Consequences

1. Taxable Income

If the corporation redeems its stock using money, its taxable income is not affected even if the redemption is treated as a sale or exchange. If it redeems its stock using property other than money, it computes gain or loss using the normal rules of § 1001(a): amount realized minus adjusted basis. For this purpose, the fair market value of the property is treated as the amount realized. If the corporation realizes a gain, that gain increases its gross income and its tax liability. It cannot deduct a realized loss. I.R.C. § 311(a)–(b). This rule applies to both redemptions that are treated as dividends and redemptions that are treated as sales or exchanges.

2. E&P

The effect on its E&P varies based on what the corporation distributed and whether the distribution was treated as a dividend or as a sale or exchange.

a. Redemption Treated as a Dividend

If the corporation redeems its own stock using money, it reduces its E&P by the amount of money paid. I.R.C. § 312(a)(1). If a related corporation redeems the issuing corporation's stock, we reduce the acquiring corporation's E&P before reducing the issuing corporation's E&P. I.R.C. § 304(b)(2).

If the corporation distributes its own obligations, it does not report gain or loss. It reduces its E&P by the principal amount of the obligation. If the obligation had original issue discount, the corporation reduces its E&P by the issue price. I.R.C. § 312(a)(2).

If the corporation distributes appreciated property, it increases its E&P by the difference between the property's value and the corporation's adjusted basis. I.R.C. § 312(b). It reduces its E&P by the fair market value of any appreciated property and by the basis of any loss property. I.R.C. § 312(a)(3), (b)(2). Because the corporation reduces its E&P by its *basis* for loss property, the nondeductible loss is taken into account for E&P purposes. If the corporation recognizes gain on distributing appreciated property, it will ultimately reduce its E&P by the resulting increase in income tax.

If a corporation distributes property subject to a liability, the liability reduces the value of the distribution. The same is true for any liability that shareholders assume as part of the distribution. The liability also reduces the amount by which the corporation reduces its E&P. I.R.C. § 312(c).

b. Redemption Treated as an Exchange

The reduction in E&P determined in the preceding discussion is the maximum reduction allowed. The reduction might be smaller if the redemption is treated as an exchange. If, for example, the corporation redeems 25% of its only class of stock, the maximum reduction is 25% of its E&P. It does not matter if that amount is less than the amount of money (or other property) used as consideration. Section 312(n)(7) limits the reduction to an "amount not in excess" of the stock's ratable share of E&P.

Section 312(n)(7) does not indicate how to compute the ratable share if the corporation has more than one class of stock outstanding. It also provides no rules for determining the appropriate reduction if a § 304 transaction qualifies for sale or exchange treatment. Presumably, the reduction will be made to the account of the corporation whose stock is treated as having been redeemed.

c. Sales of Section 306 Stock

If a shareholder disposes of § 306 stock by sale to a third party, part of the proceeds may be treated as ordinary income and qualify for treatment as a dividend for purposes of tax rates. I.R.C. § 306(a)(1), (d). That amount is generally the amount of the sales proceeds that would have been a dividend if the corporation had instead distributed money. Because the disposition is not a redemption, and no corporate funds were used, the issuing corporation does not reduce its E&P. Reg. § 1.306-1(b)(1).

3. Basis of Stock Acquired in a Section 304 Transaction

When a corporation acquires stock of a related corporation in a brother-sister transaction governed by § 304(a)(1), it determines its basis for that stock using the § 362(a) contribution to capital rules. Reg. § 1.304-2(a). The acquiring corporation takes the shareholder's basis, increased by any gain that the shareholder recognizes. Although the shareholder reports dividend income if the transaction fails to qualify as a sale, dividend income is not the same as gain for this purpose.

> **Example 6-32.** Angela owned a controlling interest in both ABC Corporation and DEF Corporation. She sold some of her ABC stock to DEF for its $5,000 value. Her basis for that stock was $1,000. The

transaction did not qualify as a sale. Because there were sufficient E&P, Angela reports $5,000 of dividend income. DEF's basis for the ABC stock is Angela's $1,000 basis. Reg. § 1.304-2(c) Example (1).

Example 6-33. Bob owned a controlling interest in both GHI Corporation and JKL Corporation. He sold some of his GHI stock to JKL for its $5,000 value. His basis for that stock was $1,000. If the transaction qualified as a sale because it was a substantially disproportionate redemption of Bob's interest in GHI, he reports gain of $4,000. JKL's basis for the GHI stock is $5,000. This represents Bob's basis, increased by the gain that he recognized. Reg. § 1.304-2(c) Example (3).

I. Shareholder's Tax Consequences

The general rules in this section apply to redemptions that do not involve § 304 or § 306. Section 304 is covered separately in this section. Section 306 and the shareholder's tax consequences when it applies are discussed in Section G.

1. Redemption Treated as a Distribution with Respect to Stock

a. Gross Income

If the amount received is treated as a distribution with respect to stock, the amount of money and the value of any property received (reduced by any liabilities assumed) is taxed as a dividend to the extent of the corporation's E&P. I.R.C. § 301(c)(1). The dividend distribution qualifies for the reduced tax rate authorized by § 1(h) (individual shareholder) or the § 243 dividends received deduction (corporate shareholder).

b. Basis and Holding Period of Property Received

If the shareholder receives property other than money, her basis for that property is its fair market value. I.R.C. § 301(d). Her holding period begins when she acquires the property.

c. Basis of Stock Retained

If the distribution exceeds the corporation's E&P, we normally apply the excess distribution against the shareholder's basis for her stock. I.R.C. § 301(c)(2). This rule was easy to apply to actual dividends. It is more complicated in the context of redemptions because the shareholder surrenders stock in the exchange.

The regulations transfer the shareholder's basis from the stock that is redeemed to any stock that she retains. If she retains no stock, her basis is transferred to persons whose stock ownership was attributed to her. Reg. § 1.302-2(c).

> **Example 6-34.** Jean owned 80 shares of MNO Corporation, for which she paid $100 a share ($8,000) eight years ago. MNO redeemed 10 of those shares, and the redemption was treated as a distribution taxable as a dividend. Jean's remaining 70 shares now have a basis of $8,000.

Regulations proposed in 2002 would have changed this rule. The shareholder whose stock was redeemed would have been allowed a loss deduction. That deduction would be deferred until the shareholder realized a gain from selling other stock in the corporation or until the facts and circumstances that caused the redemption to be treated as a distribution no longer existed. The Treasury Department withdrew the proposed regulations in 2006 but issued a new deferred loss proposal in 2009. Prop. Reg. § 1.302-5.

2. Redemption Treated as an Exchange

a. Taxable Income

If the amount received is treated as in exchange for the stock, the shareholder compares the amount realized (the amount of money received and value of any other property received, net of obligations assumed) to his basis for the stock redeemed. If he realizes a gain, that gain is gross income and is likely to be capital gain.

If he realizes a loss, § 165(c)(2) would generally authorize a deduction because the stock was acquired in a transaction entered into for profit. Section 267(a)(1) may disallow that deduction if the shareholder and the corporation are related persons. That rule applies if the shareholder owns (actually or constructively) more than 50% of the value of the corporation's stock.

b. Basis and Holding Period

If the shareholder receives property other than money, his basis for that property is its fair market value. His holding period begins when he acquires the property. If the redemption is treated as an exchange, there is no effect on his basis for any stock that he retains.

3. Section 304 Redemption

Keep in mind that § 304 redemptions look to the E&P of two corporations—the acquiring corporation and the issuing corporation—in determining how much of a distribution is a dividend.

If a brother-sister redemption is treated as a dividend, the shareholder adds his basis for the stock that was sold to his basis for the shares in the acquiring corporation. Reg. § 1.304-2(a). This rule applies even though he still owns stock in the issuing corporation. Thus, in Example 6-32 involving Angela, her basis for the ABC Corporation stock that she sold to DEF Corporation was added to her basis for her DEF stock. It was not added to her basis for her remaining ABC stock. Reg. § 1.304-2(c) Example (1). The regulations do not indicate what the result would be if the seller had only constructive ownership of the acquiring corporation's stock. Presumably, the outcome would follow that described in Section I.1.

If a parent-subsidiary redemption is treated as a dividend, the shareholder's basis for the parent stock he sold is added to his basis for his remaining stock in the parent. Reg. § 1.304-3(a).

If the redemption is treated as a sale because it qualifies under either § 302 or § 303, the shareholder computes gain or loss as provided in § 1001(a).

J. Transfers of Control

The context in which a redemption occurs is relevant to how it is treated. This section discusses several situations in which nontax events give rise to redemptions. These events include marital dissolutions, buy-sell agreements, and other transfers of control using corporate funds.

1. Marital Dissolution

a. Background

Spouses may be the sole (or controlling) shareholders of a family business. If the marriage ends in divorce, one spouse (the departing shareholder in this discussion) may cease being involved in the business as a shareholder, employee, or both. The other spouse (the continuing shareholder) could purchase the departing shareholder's stock. Alternatively, the corporation could redeem that stock. The relevant tax consequences reflect the Code sections covering sales, redemptions, and transfers incident to a divorce.

If the departing shareholder sold his stock to an unrelated third party, he would compute gain or loss by comparing the sales price to his basis for the stock. That gain or loss is likely to be capital gain or loss. If the issuing corporation instead redeems his stock, the results should be the same if the sale occurs after the divorce or if it occurs before the divorce and the departing shareholder qualifies to waive family attribution from the continuing shareholder.

If the departing shareholder sold his stock to the continuing shareholder, he would not recognize any gain or loss. I.R.C. § 1041(a). If the stock was appreciated, the departing shareholder would prefer this option. That is not necessarily the best option for the continuing shareholder, who must obtain funds to pay for the stock and who would have to use the departing shareholder's basis. I.R.C. § 1041(b)(2). As is often the case with a family business, the corporation may be the best source of such funds, but any distribution to the continuing shareholder would be taxed as a dividend if the corporation had adequate E&P.

What if the corporation redeemed the departing shareholder's stock and he could treat the redemption as a transfer on behalf of the continuing shareholder? The departing shareholder could take advantage of § 1041 and recognize no gain. But the IRS would then argue that the continuing shareholder had received a constructive dividend because the corporation used its funds to satisfy her obligation to the departing shareholder.

Courts became involved in disputes between the IRS and one or both shareholders because the divorcing shareholders treated these transactions inconsistently. The departing shareholder invoked § 1041. The continuing shareholder claimed that she did not receive a dividend because she did not have a primary and unconditional obligation to purchase the departing spouse's stock. If it did not litigate both parties' tax returns together, the government risked losing both cases. That was the outcome in *Arnes v. United States*, 981 F.2d 456 (9th Cir. 1992), and *Arnes v. Commissioner*, 102 T.C. 522 (1994).

b. Treasury Regulations

Regulations issued in 2003 seek to resolve the tax treatment of these transfers. The IRS will look to the divorce or separation instrument or any other written agreement the parties have made. The transfer is treated as a redemption of the departing shareholder's stock, and not as a constructive dividend to the continuing shareholder, if that document provides that both shareholders intend for the redemption to be treated as a redemption of the departing shareholder's stock and the document supersedes any other document concerning the stock. Reg. § 1.1041-2(c). If the departing shareholder's stock is worth less than his basis, he may prefer having the transaction characterized as a sale. Section 1041 will not apply, but he must satisfy the § 302 requirements discussed in this chapter and avoid § 267(a)(1). That provision disallows deductions for losses on sales or exchanges between related parties. It applies if he owns (actually or constructively) more than 50% of the value of the corporation's stock. Postponing the redemption until after the divorce may avoid § 267(a)(1) if the departing shareholder owns 50% or less of the corporation's stock before the redemption. Stock owned by the continuing spouse will not be attributed to the departing spouse after the divorce occurs.

If there is no such agreement, the IRS looks to applicable state law to determine the tax consequences. If the applicable law does not treat the redemption as a constructive dividend to the continuing shareholder, the IRS treats it as a redemption of the departing shareholder's stock. Reg. § 1.1041-2(a)(1). If the redemption qualifies under § 302(b), the departing shareholder reports gain or loss on that transaction. If it does not qualify, the departing shareholder's tax consequences are governed by the § 301 distribution rules. Reg. § 1.1041-2(b)(1).

If, instead, applicable law would treat the transaction as a constructive dividend to the continuing shareholder, she reports dividend income. The departing shareholder takes advantage of the § 1041 nonrecognition rules. Reg. § 1.1041-2(a)(2), -2(b)(2).

2. Other Transfers of Control

Transfers pursuant to a buy-sell agreement also involve a shift in corporate control. The agreement may cover transfers when a shareholder retires or dies, or it may cover some other event. If, instead, the corporation redeems the stock of the departing shareholder, the continuing shareholder increases his ownership percentage without having to spend his own funds. The tax consequences depend on whether the continuing shareholder is primarily and unconditionally liable to make the purchase. If so, the distribution is treated as a constructive dividend to the continuing shareholder. He can avoid dividend treatment if he merely had a nonbinding option to make the purchase. Rev. Rul. 69-608, 1969-2 C.B. 42, includes examples of the primary and unconditional obligation test.

A transfer of control may also occur if a departing shareholder sells stock to an employee or an outsider who wants to acquire the business. Instead of using her own funds to purchase the stock, the new shareholder may prefer having the corporation redeem some or all of the departing shareholder's stock. If the corporation has excess money or other liquid assets, this use of a "bootstrap acquisition" makes sense economically. The new shareholder attains control at a lower out-of-pocket cost, and the departing shareholder reports the redemption as a sale or exchange. If the purchase and redemption transactions are part of a single plan, it does not matter which occurs first. *Zenz v. Quinlivan*, 213 F.2d 914 (6th Cir. 1954).

When corporate funds are used to shift control, whether in a buy-sell situation or bootstrap acquisition, the continuing or new shareholder has a lower stock basis than he would have if he purchased the stock with his own funds. This is not a problem if the value of the retained funds outweighs the future capital gains tax on selling shares with a lower basis.

Checkpoints

- A redemption involves a corporation acquiring its own stock in exchange for property.
- Redemptions can be treated as exchanges if the shareholder's stock ownership is sufficiently reduced or eliminated or if other statutory events occur.
- In determining whether a redemption is treated as a sale, we consider the shareholder's actual *and* constructive stock ownership.
- Stock is constructively owned because it is owned by certain family members, by an entity in which the redeemed shareholder has an ownership or beneficial interest, or by an owner or beneficiary of an entity whose shares are being redeemed. Stock is also constructively owned by any person who has an option to acquire it.
- In some instances, a constructive owner is treated as the actual owner so that ownership can be reattributed to a third person.
- Family attribution can be waived in limited instances.
- Section 302 redemptions qualify as exchanges if they are not essentially equivalent to a dividend, are substantially disproportionate, are a complete termination of a shareholder's interest, or are a partial liquidation.
- Section 303 redemptions qualify as exchanges if stock included in the decedent's gross estate meets certain tests based on value, death-related expenses, and time periods.
- Section 304 applies if stock in one corporation is acquired by a related corporation and the shareholder has more than a 50% ownership interest in both corporations or if the corporations have a parent-subsidiary relationship. Redemptions can satisfy the requirements of § 302 or § 303 even if they are done through a related corporation.
- When § 306 applies, sales and redemptions of preferred stock may be treated as dividends instead of as exchanges. It applies if the distribution and disposition of preferred stock provide a means for the shareholder to convert fully taxed ordinary income into capital gain without losing rights to future corporate growth.
- The reduction in the corporation's E&P is computed differently for redemptions that are treated as dividends and redemptions that are treated as exchanges.
- If a redemption is not treated as an exchange, it is treated as a dividend (assuming adequate E&P). The shareholder's basis for the redeemed stock may be reallocated to his remaining shares or to a related person.
- Redemptions offer a means for transferring control in a marital dissolution or for accomplishing other ownership shifts. The tax consequences are affected by whether the remaining (or new) shareholders were primarily and unconditionally obligated to acquire the redeemed shares.

Chapter 7

Introduction to Reorganizations

Roadmap

- Types of reorganizations
- General reorganization doctrines
- Terminology
- Reorganizations involving investment companies

A. Chapter Overview

Section 368(a)(1) lists seven types of transactions that qualify as reorganizations for federal income tax purposes. We generally refer to each by the letter preceding its definition. For example, the reorganization described in § 368(a)(1)(A) is an A reorganization, and the reorganization described in § 368(a)(1)(F) is an F reorganization. Some types of reorganization are acquisitive, some are divisive, and some are neither. This chapter introduces the seven types of reorganizations by category. Subsequent chapters describe the reorganizations, and their tax consequences, in more detail. This chapter also describes doctrines and terminology applied to reorganizations.

B. Types of Reorganizations

Reorganizations can be initially classified by type of transaction. A reorganization is either acquisitive, divisive, or neither. An acquisitive reorganization involves one corporation acquiring control of another corporation or acquiring the assets of another corporation. A, B, and C reorganizations are acquisitive; some D reorganizations are also acquisitive. In a divisive reorganization, a corporation transfers some of its assets to another corporation. Many D reorganizations are divisive. E and F reorganizations are neither acquisitive nor divisive. They involve mere changes in form or in capitalization of a single corporation. G reorganizations involve a corporation in a bankruptcy proceeding. A bankruptcy reorganization can be acquisitive or divisive; it might be neither.

C. General Reorganization Doctrines

The form of a transaction is important. A transaction that does not satisfy the statutory requirements does not qualify for reorganization treatment; the Code does not provide for reorganizations that "substantially qualify." Meeting those requirements, while necessary, is only a first step. The transaction must also satisfy requirements in the regulations or imposed judicially.

1. Business Purpose

Ever since *Gregory v. Helvering*, 293 U.S. 465 (1935), courts have required a business purpose for transactions claiming nonrecognition treatment under the reorganization provisions. In *Gregory*, the taxpayer engaged in a business transaction to benefit her interests, using certain corporate structures as mere conduits. The *Gregory* court held that, although the transaction met the form required by the statute, it had no corporate business purpose and, thus, would not be granted nonrecognition status.

The regulations reflect the *Gregory* requirement of a valid business purpose. They provide that the purpose of the reorganization provisions is to permit tax-free readjustments of corporate structure that "are required by business exigencies." Reg. § 1.368-1(b). It is important to document the business purpose of the transaction and to retain any supporting paperwork (corporate minutes, statements of consultants, etc.).

It may sometimes be difficult to distinguish between a shareholder purpose and a corporate business purpose. The IRS is likely to challenge a transaction structured solely for a shareholder purpose. Even so, the transaction may survive this scrutiny because some courts have been more lenient than the IRS, even in the context of a closely held corporation. For example, in *Lewis v. Commissioner*, 176 F.2d 646 (1st Cir. 1949), the court held that it was unrealistic to attempt to distinguish between a corporate business purpose and a shareholder business purpose, particularly with respect to closely held corporations. In *Estate of Parshelsky v. Commissioner*, 34 T.C. 946, 953 (1960), *rev'd and remanded*, 303 F.2d 14 (2d Cir. 1962), the Tax Court held that shareholder business reasons would not support a reorganization under *Gregory*. The

Second Circuit, however, remanded the case with the instruction that a valid shareholder non-tax-avoidance purpose could support a reorganization.

2. Continuity of Interest

The continuity of interest (COI) requirement ensures that a reorganization transaction is a mere readjustment of the structure of the corporations involved. It is designed to prevent transactions that technically meet the reorganization requirements, but are disguised sales, from qualifying for nonrecognition treatment.

The COI requirement was developed through a judicial process originating with *Pinellas Ice & Cold Storage Co. v. Commissioner*, 287 U.S. 462 (1933). *Pinellas* held that the sale of corporate assets to another corporation for money and short-term notes should be taxed even though the transaction met the letter, but not the intent, of the reorganization provisions then in effect. *Pinellas* and other early Supreme Court decisions (such as *Helvering v. Watts*, 296 U.S. 387 (1935)) held that some of the consideration in a reorganization should be a certain amount of stock (at least 38%).

The COI requirement is reflected in Reg. § 1.368-1(e), which was last amended in 2011. The regulation focuses on preserving "a substantial part of the value of the proprietary interests in the target corporation." It is designed to prevent transactions that resemble sales from qualifying as reorganizations. Reg. § 1.368-1(e)(1)(i).

The regulation describes when a proprietary interest in the target corporation is preserved and when it is not preserved. The interest is preserved if it is exchanged for a proprietary interest in the issuing corporation. The issuing corporation is generally the acquiring corporation; in a triangular reorganization, it is the corporation in control of the acquiring corporation. Reg. § 1.368-1(b). The interest is also preserved if the acquiring corporation exchanges it for a direct interest in the target corporation enterprise or if it continues in some other way as a proprietary interest in the target corporation. The proprietary interest is not preserved if the issuing corporation acquires the interest in exchange for consideration other than its stock. It is also not preserved if there is a redemption of the issuing corporation stock that was furnished in exchange for the proprietary interest in the target corporation. The determination of the transaction's substance is made based on the facts and circumstances.

The regulation disregards pre-reorganization dispositions of stock in the target corporation if the new owners are unrelated to the target corporation and the issuing corporation. It also disregards post-reorganization dispositions of stock of the issuing corporation to persons not related to that corporation. A related person is a corporation that is a member of an affiliated group within the meaning of § 1504 or a corporation subject to the § 304(a)(2) parent-subsidiary redemption rules. Reg. § 1.368-1(e)(4).

Reg. § 1.368-1(e) also covers the effect on continuity of contract modifications that preserve continuity of interest and modifications that do not preserve continuity of interest, shareholder elections, contingent adjustments, escrows, anti-dilution clauses, dissenters' rights, and fractional shares. There are numerous examples illustrating its effect.

3. Continuity of Business Enterprise

A corporation that issues its stock for stock or assets of a target corporation must either continue the target's historic business or use a significant portion of the target's assets in a business. In other words, there must be continuity of business enterprise (COBE). Reg. § 1.368-1(d)(1). For example, if the target corporation has more than one line of business, the acquiring corporation must continue a significant line of the target's business.

A facts and circumstances test applies in determining whether a line of business is significant. A facts and circumstances test also applies in determining if the acquiring corporation uses a significant portion of the target's historical business assets. The example below is derived from Example (1) in Reg. § 1.368-1(d)(5).

> **Example 7-1.** Target Corporation conducted three lines of business that were of approximately equal value. On July 1, it sold two of those businesses to an unrelated person. On December 1, it transferred its remaining assets to Acquiring Corporation in exchange solely for Acquiring voting stock. If Acquiring continues Target's remaining business, the COBE requirement is satisfied.

4. Step Transaction

The step transaction doctrine is also relevant. When it applies, the transaction may fail to qualify as a reorganization or may be treated as a different type of reorganization than the taxpayer anticipated.

A classic example involved the merger of a target corporation into the subsidiary of the acquiring corporation followed by the liquidation of the subsidiary corporation into its parent. Rev. Rul. 72-405, 1972-2 C.B. 217. Because the outcome could have been achieved in a more direct route, the IRS collapsed the two steps into a single step, the direct acquisition of the target corporation's assets by the acquiring corporation's parent. The transaction still qualified for nonrecognition because it qualified as a C reorganization. This may not be the case for many transactions, because the "solely for voting stock requirement" in a C reorganization may require a larger amount of stock to be exchanged in the transaction.

The Service has invoked the step transaction doctrine in other rulings. In Rev. Rul. 67-274, 1967-2 C.B. 141, it held that a transaction that failed to qualify as a B reorganization could qualify for tax-free treatment as a C reorganization. It has since amplified that ruling and treated the merger of an acquiring corporation's subsidiary into a target corporation—followed by the merger of the target into the acquiring corporation—as a merger of the target into the acquiring parent corporation. Rev. Rul. 2001-46, 2001-2 C.B. 321. In situations like these, the step transaction doctrine might provide beneficial tax results.

The step transaction doctrine has limits. The IRS cannot apply it to create new steps in the transaction. The doctrine can be applied only to eliminate steps that have no economic significance in the transaction and are undertaken only to achieve a desired tax benefit. To protect themselves against application of the step transaction doctrine, taxpayers should ensure that each step of their transaction has economic substance.

5. Net Value

In 2005, the IRS published proposed regulations that introduced the notion of a net value exchange. Prop. Reg. § 1.368-1(b) required that net value be exchanged in most reorganizations. The proposal, which affected transactions involving insolvent corporations, was aimed at preventing transfers that more closely resemble sales from qualifying as reorganizations. 70 Fed. Reg. 11904 (2005). E and F reorganizations, and D reorganizations that met the requirements of § 354, would not be affected. A D reorganization would be exempted only if the value of property the target corporation transferred to the acquiring corporation exceeded the target's liabilities immediately before the exchange and the value of the acquiring corporation's assets at least equaled the amount of its liabilities immediately after the exchange. Prop. Reg. § 1.368-1(f)(4). The regulations provided several illustrative examples.

Prop. Reg. § 1.368-1(f)(1) required the receipt and surrender of net value in the transaction. If one party to the reorganization assumed a net liability instead of transferring stock, the regulation indicated the transaction resembles a sale. The proposed regulations could have been particularly troublesome in situations involving contingent liabilities. The IRS withdrew them in July 2017. 82 Fed. Reg. 32281 (2017).

The proposed regulations also dealt with situations in which a creditor should be treated as having an ownership (proprietary) interest for purposes of meeting the continuity of interest requirement. That proposal was finalized in 2008. Reg. § 1.368-1(e)(6) provides that a creditor claim can be a proprietary interest if the target corporation is in a title 11 or similar case or if the amount of the target's liabilities exceeds the value of its assets immediately before the reorganization. The regulation provides separate valuation rules for the most senior class of creditors and for "junior" classes of creditors.

The net value proposed regulations were not limited to reorganizations. They would have applied to transactions otherwise governed by §§ 351 and 332.

D. Terminology

1. Party to a Reorganization

Favorable tax consequences may depend on a corporation being a party to a reorganization. The relevant nonrecognition provisions apply only if the stock, securities, or other property are received from a party to the reorganization. Which entities can be parties to a reorganization? Obviously, the corporation or corporations engaged in a reorganization are parties to the reorganization. Section 368(b) provides for other corporations also being treated as parties to a reorganization. Reg. § 1.368-2(f) provides the details regarding the definition of party to a reorganization. The list of qualifying corporations is reproduced below, reformatted to make it easier to read.

- The term *a party to a reorganization* includes a corporation resulting from a reorganization, and both corporations, in a transaction qualifying as a reorganization where one corporation acquires stock or properties of another corporation. If a transaction otherwise qualifies as a reorganization, a corporation remains a party to the reorganization even though stock or assets acquired in the reorganization are transferred in a transaction described in paragraph (k) of this section. If a transaction otherwise qualifies as a reorganization, a corporation shall not cease to be a party to the reorganization solely by reason of the fact that part or all of the assets acquired in the reorganization are transferred to a partnership in which the transferor is a partner if the continuity of business enterprise requirement is satisfied. See § 1.368-1(d) . . . .

- A corporation controlling an acquiring corporation is a party to the reorganization when the stock of such controlling corporation is used in the acquisition of properties.
- Both corporations are parties to the reorganization if, under statutory authority, Corporation A is merged into Corporation B.
- All three of the corporations are parties to the reorganization if, pursuant to statutory authority, Corporations C and D are consolidated into Corporation E.
- Both corporations are parties to the reorganization if Corporation F transfers substantially all its assets to Corporation G in exchange for all or a part of the voting stock of Corporation G.
- All three corporations are parties to the reorganization if Corporation H transfers substantially all its assets to Corporation K in exchange for all or a part of the voting stock of Corporation L, which is in control of Corporation K.
- Both corporations are parties to the reorganization if Corporation M transfers all or part of its assets to Corporation N in exchange for all or a part of the stock and securities of Corporation N, but only if: (1) immediately after such transfer, Corporation M, or one or more of its shareholders (including persons who were shareholders immediately before such transfer), or any combination thereof, is in control of Corporation N, and (2) in pursuance of the plan, the stock and securities of Corporation N are transferred or distributed by Corporation M in a transaction in which gain or loss is not recognized under section 354 or 355, or is recognized only to the extent provided in section 356.
- Both Corporation O and Corporation P, but not Corporation S, are parties to the reorganization if Corporation O acquires stock of Corporation P from Corporation S in exchange solely for a part of the voting stock of Corporation O, if: (1) the stock of Corporation P does not constitute substantially all of the assets of Corporation S, (2) Corporation S is not in control of Corporation O immediately after the acquisition, and (3) Corporation O is in control of Corporation P immediately after the acquisition.

The regulation also indicates that the target corporation in a B reorganization, and the surviving corporation in a reverse triangular merger, remains a party to the reorganization even though its stock or assets are transferred in a transaction described in Reg. § 1.368-2(k). Finally, it provides that the acquiring corporation in a forward triangular merger, triangular B or C reorganization, or a G reorganization using stock of a corporation controlling the acquiring corporation, remains a party even though its stock is transferred in a transaction described in that regulation.

2. Control

B, D, and G reorganizations include requirements related to control. The acquiring corporation must be in control of the acquired corporation immediately after the reorganization. Section 368(c) defines control as ownership of stock possessing 80% of the total combined voting power of all stock entitled to vote and 80% of the total number of shares of all other classes of stock. The 80% requirement is reduced to 50% of voting power or stock value in certain D reorganizations. I.R.C. § 368(a)(2)(H).

3. Substantially All

In its simplest terms, an acquisitive reorganization involves one entity acquiring the assets of, or controlling stock interest in, another entity. An important issue when the reorganization involves acquiring assets relates to the percentage of such assets. Not surprisingly, the acquiring entity may not need—or even want—all the other entity's assets.

Although C reorganizations, acquisitive D reorganizations, and triangular A reorganizations are subject to a "substantially all" requirement, § 368 does not define that term. The IRS previously ruled that this requirement, often referred to as the "sub all" requirement, could be met if the acquiring corporation acquires at least 70% of the target corporation's gross assets or 90% of its net assets (assets minus liabilities). Rev. Proc. 77-37, 1977-2 C.B. 568. Those alternative tests provided some flexibility.

The step transaction doctrine may be relevant in determining whether an acquisition satisfies the sub all requirement. For example, a target corporation may sell or distribute some assets prior to the acquisition. If the step transaction doctrine applies, the assets disposed of could be counted in determining if the acquiring corporation obtained substantially all of the target's assets.

Dispositions do not automatically cause a transaction to fail the sub all requirement. For example, Rev. Rul. 88-48, 1988-1 C.B. 117, permitted the sale of 50% of the target's assets prior to a potential C reorganization because the target transferred the money it received to the acquiring corporation along with its other assets. The sale thus changed only the composition of the target corporation's assets. On the other hand, if the target disposes of assets prior to a potential C reorganization, and the disposition is related to the potential reorganization, the assets disposed of count toward the target's total assets and may cause the transaction to fail. For example, Rev. Proc. 77-37 held that assets of a target corporation used to redeem dissenting shareholders were treated as part of the total assets of the corporation for purposes of the sub all requirement. If the target corporation did not engage in a reorganization, it would have no need to redeem dissenting shareholders.

4. Triangular Reorganization

Although a reorganization may involve a single corporation, or an acquisition of one corporation by a second corporation, a triangular reorganization involves a third corporation. A party to a reorganization might, for example, use its parent's stock rather than its own in effectuating an acquisition.

E. Reorganizations Involving Investment Companies

In Chapter 4, we encountered § 351(e)(1), which prevents taxpayers from using the § 351 nonrecognition rules to diversity their investments. A comparable exception applies to reorganizations other than E reorganizations. I.R.C. § 368(a)(2)(F). Generally, it denies nonrecognition treatment to reorganizations involving investment companies. An exception to this general rule applies for reorganizations involving regulated investment companies, real estate investment trusts, or corporations that meet the diversification requirements of § 368(a)(2)(F)(ii). In other words, corporations that are already well diversified can engage in a qualifying reorganization. Another exception applies if the stock of the investment companies is owned substantially by the same persons in the same proportions. I.R.C. § 368(a)(2)(F)(v). In this situation, the shareholders are not diversifying their holdings. Their investment interests remain the same, albeit in a different form.

> **Example 7-2.** ABC and DEF Corporations are investment companies; each is owned equally by the same four shareholders. More than 25% of each corporation's property is invested in two publicly traded corporations that operate in the same industry. To reduce administrative expenses, the shareholders merge ABC into DEF. The merger can qualify as a reorganization. Each investment company is owned substantially by the same persons. Diversification is not achieved in the transaction because the shareholders' investment interests remain the same following the transaction. The corporations are described in § 368(a)(2)(F)(v).

Checkpoints

- A transaction cannot qualify as a reorganization unless it satisfies the requirements of § 368 and its regulations.
- The regulations may require business purpose, continuity of interest, and continuity of business enterprise.
- Doctrines such as step transaction may apply.
- The Code and regulations use reorganization-specific terminology, such as "party to a reorganization" and "substantially all."
- A, B, C, and some D and G reorganizations are acquisitive.
- Other D and G reorganizations are divisive.
- E and F reorganizations involve a single operating corporation.

Chapter 8

Acquisitive Reorganizations

Roadmap

- A reorganizations
- B reorganizations
- C reorganizations
- Acquisitive D reorganizations
- Acquisitive G reorganizations
- Asset drop-downs and push-ups
- Shareholder's tax consequences
- Security holder's tax consequences
- Acquiring corporation's tax consequences
- Target corporation's tax consequences

A. Chapter Overview

This chapter addresses the requirements for and tax consequences of acquisitive reorganizations. These reorganizations have a common feature—the acquisition by one corporation (or persons in control of that corporation) of the assets or a controlling stock interest in another corporation. Each has different requirements. Because there are several types of acquisitive reorganizations, taxpayers can structure an acquisitive transaction in a manner that best suits their goals. This flexibility has limits; the parties must still comply with the requirements in the relevant Code sections and their regulations.

B. A Reorganizations

1. Introduction

There are two types of A reorganization: statutory mergers and consolidations. I.R.C. § 368(a)(1)(A). A statutory merger involves the transfer of all the assets of one corporation to another pursuant to state, federal, or District of Columbia law. A consolidation involves the combination of two or more corporations into a newly formed corporation. Because neither original corporation survives, consolidation may not be appropriate if one of the corporations has licenses, intellectual property, or goodwill associated with its name.

Example 8-1. ABC Corporation merged into DEF Corporation in a statutory merger pursuant to state law. The ABC shareholders received DEF Corporation stock in exchange for their ABC Corporation stock. DEF received all the ABC assets and assumed all its liabilities. The transaction was an A reorganization.

Example 8-2. ABC Corporation and DEF Corporation instead consolidated to form GHI Corporation. The ABC and DEF shareholders received GHI Corporation stock in exchange for their ABC or DEF Corporation stock. GHI received all the ABC and DEF assets and assumed all those corporations' liabilities. The transaction was an A reorganization.

Of all the reorganizations, the A reorganization offers the most flexibility. Unlike other reorganizations, it does not require that solely voting stock be received in the transaction or that a control requirement be satisfied. Unless the merger is triangular, the sub all requirement does not apply. Its main requirement is that the merger or consolidation be undertaken pursuant to state law. Because the reorganization is pursuant to state statute, there is no need to transfer assets and liabilities individually to the acquiring corporation; the transfer occurs automatically.

Laws governing statutory mergers vary from state to state. Beginning in the 1980s, states started to compete with Delaware to be hospitable for incorporation purposes. As part of this competition, many states amended their merger statutes. Texas, for example, passed legislation permitting statutory mergers in which the merged corporation could survive. It also permitted a target corporation to merge into two or more corporations. The IRS issued Rev. Rul. 2000-5, 2000-1 C.B. 436, in response to these transactions. In that ruling, it outlined its view of the elements of a statutory merger or consolidation. It indicated that mere compliance with a merger statute may not be sufficient, that the continuity of business enterprise and continuity of interest requirements both apply, and that the target corporation must cease to exist. The regulations do not exempt A reorganizations from those requirements. A merger pursuant to state law does not qualify if the transferor corporation retains assets and continues in existence. Reg. § 1.368-2(b)(1)(iii) Example 1.

Mergers carry certain risks. These include the acquisition (by state law) of the target corporation's liabilities. If liabilities are subject to contingencies, the acquiring corporation may find itself exposed to significantly more liabilities than it expected. This danger is significantly reduced now that the merger can be into a disregarded entity. Nevertheless, contingent liabilities may ultimately reduce the value of the merger.

2. Triangular A Reorganizations

Congress enacted the forward and reverse triangular A reorganization provisions to benefit corporations that wanted to obtain control of a target corporation's assets but could not engage directly in merger transactions under state law. Triangular A reorganizations offer other potential advantages. They benefit corporations that want to acquire another corporation's assets but do not necessarily want to assume the other entity's liabilities. They allow acquiring corporations to use a currency (stock of a corporation controlling the acquiring corporation) that the target corporation's shareholders may consider more attractive. They can be accomplished without a vote by the shareholders of the controlling corporation. The target corporation's shareholders and the controlling corporation are typically the only parties to vote on the merger. Triangular mergers also have potential disadvantages, which are discussed below.

a. Forward Triangular Mergers

The forward triangular merger is described in § 368(a)(2)(D). Although the target corporation is merged into the acquiring corporation, the target's shareholders receive stock of a corporation in control of the acquiring corporation. The transaction can qualify even if the controlling or acquiring corporation was formed before the merger, in anticipation of the merger, or after preliminary steps were taken to merge the target corporation into the controlling corporation. Reg. § 1.368-2(b)(2).

> **Example 8-3.** ABC Corporation acquired the assets (and assumed the liabilities) of DEF Corporation in a merger governed by the relevant state law. The DEF shareholders received stock of XYZ Corporation. XYZ currently owns 92% of ABC's only class of stock. The transaction was a forward triangular merger.

Reg. § 1.368-2(b)(2) imposes requirements for qualifying as a forward triangular merger. First, the acquiring corporation must meet the sub all requirement. For purposes of the regulations, that requirement has the same meaning as it has for purposes of C reorganizations. Transfers occurring before or after the merger may cause the transaction to fail the sub all requirement if these transfers are combined under the step transaction doctrine. Second, the merger qualifies only to the extent that it would have qualified as a merger had it been into the controlling corporation. The regulation does not require that the transaction would have been permissible under state law. It would have to have met the federal reorganization requirements (such as business purpose, continuity of business enterprise, and continuity of interest) had the merger been into the controlling corporation. Third, stock of the acquiring corporation cannot be used as consideration. Consideration can include other property, including money or securities of either the acquiring or the controlling corporation or both. Use of other property is permitted only to the extent it does not prevent the merger from satisfying the continuity of interest requirement.

b. Reverse Triangular Mergers

The reverse triangular merger, described in § 368(a)(2)(E), is the opposite of the forward triangular merger. Instead of the target corporation merging into a subsidiary of the controlling corporation, the controlling corporation's subsidiary is merged with and into the target corporation. Thus, the direction of the merger does not determine whether it qualifies as a reorganization.

The reverse triangular merger also has a sub all requirement. In a forward triangular merger, the acquiring corporation must acquire substantially all the assets of the target corporation. In a reverse triangular merger, the surviving corporation must instead "hold" substantially all its own properties *and* the properties of the merged corporation. The meaning of "hold" is addressed in Rev. Rul. 2001-25, 2001-1 C.B. 1291. "Hold" is used in the description of the reverse triangular merger because a surviving corporation cannot be said to have acquired its own properties in a merger. Reg. § 1.368-2(j)(3)(iii) provides rules for applying the sub all requirement.

The shareholders of the surviving corporation must transfer a controlling interest to the parent of the target corporation. They receive voting stock in the parent in exchange. Thus, they become shareholders of the parent, and the surviving target becomes a subsidiary of the parent immediately after the merger. If the surviving target was involved in a title 11 or similar case, and none of its shareholders received any consideration for its stock, the requirement is satisfied if its former creditors received voting stock in the controlling corporation. In exchange, they must transfer debt of the surviving corporation worth at least 80% of the total value of the corporation's debt. I.R.C. § 368(a)(3)(E).

3. Mergers Involving a Disregarded Entity

a. In General

The regulations introduced the concepts of combining entity and combining unit to the merger area. A combining entity is defined as a corporation. A combining unit is defined as a combining entity and all disregarded entities whose assets are treated as owned by the combining entity for federal tax purposes. A statutory merger or consolidation is a transaction: (1) effected pursuant to domestic laws (2) in which all the assets and liabilities of each member of one or more combining units become the assets and liabilities of one or more members of another combining unit, and (3) the combining entity of each transferor unit ceases its separate legal existence for all purposes. This means that all the assets of the merging corporation (including those of its disregarded entities) must be transferred to the acquiring corporation or its disregarded entities. Reg. § 1.368-2(b)(1)(ii).

The regulations go beyond the disregarded entity merger and make changes to prior law. First, they state the federal tax requirements for a statutory merger. In addition to meeting the state's statutory requirements (or those of the District of Columbia), a statutory merger must meet the requirements outlined in the regulations. Second, the regulations remove the "corporation law" requirements of the previous regulations. A statutory merger does not have to be under the state's corporation law so long as it is effected pursuant to the statute or statutes necessary to carry out the merger. Reg. § 1.368-2(b)(1)(ii). This change recognizes that many states now have merger provisions embedded in their limited liability company (LLC) statutes. Finally, and most important, the regulations permit a corporation to merge with and into a disregarded entity. Although such a merger looks like a triangular merger, it is not treated as one because the disregarded entity does not have a separate tax existence. The transaction is not subject to the requirements imposed on triangular mergers.

b. Liabilities of Disregarded Entities

The disregarded entity's liabilities present a possible complication. Once an entity becomes a disregarded entity, its assets, liabilities, and items of income and deduction become those of its owner. The regulations provide that an entity that is otherwise disregarded as separate from its owner will be treated as an entity separate from its owner for purposes of "(1) Federal tax liabilities of the entity with respect to any taxable period for which the entity was not disregarded; (2) Federal tax liabilities of any other entity for which the entity is liable; and (3) Refunds or credits of Federal tax." Reg. § 301.7701-2(c)(2)(iii)

(A). Examples involving tax liabilities of a corporation that was merged into a disregarded entity appear in Reg. § 301.7701-2(c)(2)(iii)(B). As to the issues not addressed by the regulations, it appears that state law would still control.

C. B Reorganizations

1. Introduction

The B reorganization has three major requirements. First, a corporation must acquire stock in another corporation. Second, the acquiring corporation must use only its own voting stock or only voting stock of a corporation that controls it. Third, immediately after the acquisition, the acquiring corporation must have control of the acquired corporation. I.R.C. § 368(a)(1)(B). It does not matter whether the acquiring corporation also controlled the acquired corporation before the acquisition. It also does not matter if the target corporation's shareholders obtain control of the acquiring corporation or if they own only a small percentage of its stock. The control requirement relates to the acquiring corporation being in control of the target corporation. Because voting stock is the only consideration allowed, the B reorganization is the least flexible type of acquisitive reorganization.

> **Example 8-4.** MNO issued MNO voting stock to the shareholders of PQR Corporation in exchange for all their PQR shares. PQR became a subsidiary of MNO. The transaction was a B reorganization.

The acquiring corporation can use its own stock *or* it can use the stock of a corporation that controls it. It cannot use stock of both corporations. Under § 368(c), control is defined as stock possessing 80% of the combined voting power of all stock of the target corporation entitled to vote and 80% of the stock of the target corporation not entitled to vote. If the acquiring corporation uses its parent's stock as consideration, it achieves a triangular B reorganization.

> **Example 8-5.** MNO instead transferred voting stock of its parent (JKL Corporation) to the PQR shareholders; MNO received only 95% of the PQR stock. The shareholders who did not exchange their stock continued to be shareholders of PQR. The transaction was a B reorganization.

The B reorganization has several advantages. One advantage, discussed below, is that it can occur in steps. Another advantage is that the acquiring corporation does not have to assume the target's liabilities. Because the target corporation remains in existence, its liabilities remain with it. A third advantage is that the sub all requirement does not apply. The acquired corporation can eliminate dissenting shareholders by distributing assets to them prior to undergoing a B reorganization. The redemption will not violate the continuity of interest requirement. Reg. § 1.368-1(e)(8) Example 9. After the reorganization occurs, the acquiring corporation can transfer subsidiary assets among its affiliates. Now that the regulations permit mergers with disregarded entities, this advantage should matter less. As noted above, if a taxpayer conducts its business through multiple disregarded entities, it can transfer assets acquired in a merger among those entities without recognizing gain. Those transfers are ignored for tax purposes.

2. Creeping B Reorganizations

An advantage of the B reorganization is that the acquisition can occur in several steps. A creeping B reorganization is permissible because the Code requires only that the acquiring corporation have control of the target corporation immediately after the acquisition.

Reg. § 1.368-2(c) provides an example in which the acquiring corporation purchased 30% of the target corporation's stock in 1939. Sixteen years later, it offered to exchange some of its stock for additional target corporation shares. Over a six-month period, it received another 60% of the target corporation stock. The regulation treats the second acquisition as a B reorganization. This treatment applied to all shares it received during the six-month period, including those received after it reached 80% ownership. It states that so long as an acquiring corporation acquires 80% of the target corporation stock, the exchange of stock in which it acquired control and any exchange thereafter qualify for nonrecognition.

The regulation does not limit the acquisition period to six months. It indicates that a series of acquisitions over a relatively short period, such as 12 months, can qualify.

3. Boot Concerns

Tax lawyers typically advise their clients that no consideration other than voting stock can be exchanged in a B reorganization even if 80% or more of the consideration is voting stock. This has been the IRS's litigating position for many years. In Rev. Rul. 75-123, 1975-1 C.B. 115, it held that the acquisition of 80% of a target corporation's stock in exchange for the acquiring corporation's stock did not qualify as a B reorganization; the acquiring corporation purchased the remaining 20% for cash. Earlier judicial decisions also took this position. *Helvering v. Southwest Consolidated Corp.*, 315 U.S. 194 (1942) (consideration in addition to stock included warrants to acquire stock); *Mills v. Commissioner*, 39 T.C. 393 (1962) (no de minimis rule applicable to "solely"), *rev'd on other grounds*, 331 F.2d 321 (5th Cir. 1964).

The regulation cited in the preceding discussion does not contradict this IRS position. Although the acquiring corporation obtained 30% of the target's stock by purchase, that transaction occurred 16 years before the B reorganization. It was "old and cold." Transactions much closer in time risk an IRS attack under the step transaction doctrine; it could argue that the two types of acquisition were part of an integrated plan. If that argument succeeds, the stock acquisition cannot qualify as a B reorganization.

Target corporation shareholders who do not want to own stock in the acquiring corporation are not required to do so. They can sell their shares to third parties on the open market. They can have their shares redeemed by the target corporation before the reorganization transaction occurs. The source of the consideration is critical. If the acquiring corporation had agreed to reimburse the target corporation, the redemption will be treated as non-stock consideration provided by the acquiring corporation. In that situation, the acquiring corporation's acquisition of control of the target cannot qualify as a B reorganization.

D. C Reorganizations

1. Introduction

The C reorganization involves the acquisition by one corporation of another corporation's assets using voting stock as the consideration. I.R.C. § 368(a)(1)(C). There are three major requirements: (1) the acquisition by the acquiring corporation must be solely for voting stock; (2) the target corporation must transfer substantially all its assets to the acquiring corporation; and (3) the target corporation must distribute the shares of stock it receives and its remaining assets in pursuance of the plan of reorganization. The third requirement is imposed by § 368(a)(2)(G). The acquiring corporation can use its own stock or it can use the stock of a corporation that controls it as the consideration. In determining whether the exchange is solely for stock, we disregard the acquiring corporation's assumption of a target corporation's liability, or the fact that property acquired is subject to a liability.

The acquiring corporation does not have to use its own stock as the consideration. It can instead use the stock of a corporation that is in control of it. In either situation, it must use voting stock and it can use only its own or only the controlling corporation's stock.

The C reorganization is often referred to as a virtual merger because it resembles a merger so closely. When the reorganization is complete, the target corporation's assets have been transferred to the acquiring corporation or distributed. Unlike a merger (in which all the assets and liabilities of the target corporation are automatically transferred to the acquiring corporation), the acquiring corporation in a C reorganization can pick and choose (within the limits of the sub all requirement) which assets and liabilities it wants.

2. Boot Relaxation Rules

The C reorganization's "solely for voting stock" requirement is more relaxed than the B reorganization's requirement. The § 368(a)(2)(B) boot relaxation rules allow the transfer of up to 20% of non-stock consideration. Both money and assumption of liabilities can be used. The major concern involves contingent liabilities that may become due after the transaction and thus cause a change in the consideration exchanged in the transaction. That is because liabilities are taken into consideration in judging whether consideration other than voting stock exceeds 20% of total consideration.

> **Example 8-6.** STU Corporation transferred money and voting stock to VWX Corporation in exchange for all the VWX assets. The money represented 10% of consideration, and the STU voting stock represented 90% of the consideration. VWX used some of the money to pay its liabilities. It then liquidated after distributing the STU stock and the remaining money to its shareholders. The transaction was a C reorganization.

> **Example 8-7.** Shortly after the reorganization, certain of VWX's contingent liabilities came due. STU paid them in an amount equal to 15% of the VWX assets acquired. Because the contingent liability was a VWX liability, STU is treated as transferring an extra 15% cash in the transaction. Because the amount of money or non-qualified property transferred in the transaction exceeded 20% of the total consideration, it was not protected by the boot relaxation rules. The transaction failed to qualify as a C reorganization.

3. The Liquidation Requirement

A transaction does not qualify as a C reorganization unless the target corporation liquidates or distributes its remaining assets, including stock and other consideration received from the acquiring corporation, to its shareholders. I.R.C. § 368(a)(2)(G). The government can waive the distribution requirement but can impose conditions on that waiver. A waiver is likely if the target corporation has a good reason to remain in existence and own a particular asset. For example, it may have to remain in existence to defend a lawsuit or to pay creditors. The IRS may also permit it to remain in existence if it has a valuable franchise that can be retained only if it remains in existence.

4. Creeping C Reorganizations

Prior to promulgation of Reg. § 1.368-2(d)(4), prior ownership of target stock could potentially cause the C reorganization to fail because substantially all the assets of the target corporation would not have been acquired "in" the C reorganization. Thus, if the acquiring corporation held target corporation stock prior to the asset acquisition, that stock was not counted for purposes of determining whether the asset acquisition met the sub all requirement.

The current regulations take a different view. The acquiring corporation's "old and cold" ownership of target stock does not necessarily disqualify the later transaction from being a C reorganization. If the prior acquisition of stock would disqualify the transaction (i.e., the consideration used was something other than the acquiring corporation's stock) and is related to the subsequent acquisition, the transaction will not qualify for C reorganization treatment. A prior acquisition of stock for voting stock of the acquiring corporation would not disqualify the transaction because the exchange in the prior acquisition would have been permissible under § 368(a)(1)(C). Two examples appear in Reg. § 1.368-2(d)(4)(ii).

> **Example 8-8.** ABC Corporation acquired 60% of the stock of DEF Corporation in exchange for ABC voting stock in Year 1. In Year 3, DEF transferred all its assets to ABC in exchange for additional ABC voting stock. Assuming all other requirements are met, the later transaction qualifies as a C reorganization whether or not the two acquisitions are related.

> **Example 8-9.** ABC instead used money as the consideration in Year 1. The mere fact that ABC had a prior ownership in DEF did not disqualify the Year 3 transaction as a C reorganization. If ABC's Year 1 acquisition of DEF stock was related to the Year 3 acquisition of DEF assets, the transaction would not qualify as a C reorganization. Collapsing the two transactions would result in ABC having acquired all the DEF assets for consideration that was 60% money and 40% voting stock.

E. Acquisitive D Reorganizations

1. Introduction

The D reorganization has three major requirements. I.R.C. § 368(a)(1)(D). First, there must be a transfer of assets from one corporation to another. The transfer can be of all the transferor's assets or of part of them. Second, immediately after the transfer, the transferor corporation, one or more of its shareholders, or some combination thereof, must have control of the transferee corporation. Persons who were shareholders of the transferor immediately before the transfer are counted for purposes of determining if the group has control. Third, there must be a distribution of the stock or securities received in the transaction. Because the third requirement is essentially a liquidation requirement, the end result of an acquisitive D reorganization is generally a single corporation.

There are two types of D reorganizations. A reorganization that meets the distribution requirement of § 354 is an acquisitive D reorganization if one corporation acquires substantially all the assets of the transferor corporation and the transferor corporation distributes the stock, securities, and other properties it receives along with any properties it didn't transfer. The distribution must be made to its shareholders pursuant to the plan of reorganization. I.R.C. § 354(b)(1). A D reorganization can be divisive rather than acquisitive if it meets the requirements of § 355. A divisive reorganization occurs when the assets of a single corporation are divided among two or more corporations. We consider divisive reorganizations and § 355 in Chapter 10.

2. The Control Requirement

The transferor corporation, its shareholders, or some combination of thereof must have control of the corporation to which the assets are transferred. The control requirement applies immediately after the transfer of assets. The normal 80% control requirements do not apply to an acquisitive D reorganization. Section 368(a)(2)(H)(i) uses the § 304(c) control requirement: 50% of the total voting power or stock value.

Because D reorganizations do not have a "solely for voting stock" requirement, they appear to offer more flexibility with respect to consideration used than do B or C reorganizations. However, this flexibility is limited by the continuity of interest requirement and the step transaction doctrine. Despite the language requiring control immediately after the transfer of assets, the transaction will not qualify as a D reorganization if control is lost in a later transaction that, under the step transaction doctrine, is part of the reorganization transaction.

3. The Distribution Requirement

Section 354(b)(1) requires that the stock, securities, and other property received, and all other properties of the transferor corporation, be distributed. That requirement might lead us to conclude that the transferor corporation must receive stock in the acquiring corporation in exchange for its assets. That is often the case, but not always. If the same person (or persons) own all the stock of each corporation in identical proportions, there can be an acquisitive D reorganization even if the acquiring corporation uses only non-stock consideration. This type of transfer is referred to as the "all-cash D." The transaction is treated as if a nominal amount of stock was transferred. In determining if ownership is identical, we use a modified version of the § 318 attribution rules and treat an individual and all members of his family as one person. We ignore de minimis variations in identity or proportionality. Reg. § 1.368-2(l)(2).

4. Overlapping Provisions

A C reorganization may resemble an acquisitive D reorganization in the following scenario: a target corporation transfers all its assets to an acquiring corporation in exchange for a controlling stock interest in the acquiring corporation. Following the transfer, target shareholders receive control of the acquiring corporation. In this instance, the transaction could qualify for C reorganization treatment because it is a transfer of substantially all the assets of a target corporation in exchange for voting stock of the acquiring corporation. The transaction could also qualify as a D reorganization because it is a transfer of the assets of a corporation to an acquiring corporation over which the target shareholders end up having control. In an overlap between C and D reorganization status, the D reorganization provisions take precedence. I.R.C. § 368(a)(2)(A). The reorganization's tax consequences flow through its qualification as a D reorganization.

A transaction or series of transactions may also involve other nonrecognition provisions. Rev. Rul. 2015-10, 2015-21 I.R.B. 973, involved a series of transactions among members of a controlled group. The parent (P) transferred its entire interest in an LLC that was taxed as a corporation to its wholly owned subsidiary (S1). S1 transferred the LLC interest to its wholly owned subsidiary (S2). S2 transferred the LLC interest to its wholly owned subsidiary (S3). Because P, S1, and S2 each received additional stock in the relevant subsidiary, those transfers satisfied the formal requirements of § 351. After being acquired by S3, the LLC elected to be treated as a disregarded entity. The IRS ruled that the transfers by P and by S1 were governed by § 351 and that the transfer by S2 to S3 was governed by § 368(a)(1)(D). It treated the transfer to S3, followed by the LLC becoming a disregarded entity, as in substance an acquisitive D reorganization instead of as a § 351 transfer followed by a § 332 liquidation.

F. Acquisitive G Reorganizations

Corporations involved in bankruptcy often reorganize rather than liquidate. Taxing these reorganizations would be contrary to the rehabilitative goals of bankruptcy law. Thus, if a corporation undergoing bankruptcy transfers substantially all its assets in a transaction that, but for the bankruptcy proceedings, would qualify as a D reorganization, the transaction qualifies as a G reorganization. I.R.C. § 368(a)(1)(G).

The D reorganization provisions are a useful guide for addressing G reorganizations, but D and G reorganizations are not identical. One important difference relates to ownership. Unlike the rules governing a D reorganization, the original shareholders in a G reorganization do not have to obtain control of the corporation acquiring the assets in the reorganization. In fact, they are likely to lose their interest in the distressed corporation because creditors and other parties with higher priority may receive all the reorganized corporation's stock.

Section 368(a)(3) provides additional definitions and operating rules. A G reorganization involves cases under title 11 or a receivership, foreclosure, or similar proceeding in a federal or state court. Any party to the reorganization must be under the jurisdiction of the relevant court, and the transfer must be made pursuant to the reorganization plan approved by that court. If a transaction qualifies as both a G reorganization and another type of reorganization, the transaction is treated as a G reorganization. The G reorganization rules also take precedence if the transaction is described in both § 368(a)(1)(G) and either § 332 or § 351.

G. Asset Drop-Downs and Push-Ups

Section 368(a)(2)(C) provides that in A, B, C, and acquisitive G reorganizations, the transaction is not disqualified merely because the acquiring corporation transfers part or all the assets or stock it acquired in the transaction to a corporation that it controls. This provision was enacted to eliminate the remote continuity doctrine of *Groman v. Commissioner*, 302 U.S. 82 (1937), and *Helvering v. Bashford*, 302 U.S. 454 (1938). Under that doctrine, transfers of assets following a reorganization were disqualified from reorganization treatment if the continuity requirements were not met.

It makes sense to allow a drop-down of assets now that the definition of merger includes triangular mergers. A post-merger drop-down of assets resembles a triangular reorganization. In Rev. Rul. 2002-85, 2002-2 C.B. 986, the IRS extended the drop-down rules to acquisitive D reorganizations. Its rationale for the extension was that § 368(a)(2)(C) was permissive and not exclusive or restrictive. In Rev. Rul. 2001-24, 2001-1 C.B. 1290, it extended the drop-down rules to cover a transfer of stock of the subsidiary corporation that acquired the assets of a target corporation in a merger.

There is no specific Code language permitting a push-up of assets after a reorganization. Push-ups of assets have, however, been analogized to drop-downs—that is, as mere transfers of property following acquisitions of such assets.

Drop-downs and push-ups are authorized by the regulations. Reg. § 1.368-2(k)(1)(ii). Reg. § 1.368-2(k)(2) provides several examples of such transfers following A, B, C, and D reorganizations.

H. Shareholder's Tax Consequences

1. Relevance of Type of Reorganization

An acquisitive reorganization involves at least two entities, the acquiring corporation and the target corporation. The acquiring corporation's shareholders are normally "silent partners" in a reorganization (except that they may have voting rights provided by state law or by the corporation's governing instruments). Hence, they generally have no tax consequences in the transaction.

The discussion below covers the tax consequences of the target corporation's shareholders. It begins with reorganizations in which they receive only stock and then considers their tax consequences if they also receive other consideration.

2. Shareholder Receives Only Stock

a. *Gain or Loss Recognized*

We determine if the shareholder realized a gain or loss by comparing her adjusted basis for her stock to the value of the stock she received. I.R.C. § 1001(a). We do this separately for each block of stock she owned. If the reorganization is acquisitive, the shareholder will receive stock of the acquiring corporation or stock of the acquiring corporation's parent.

Example 8-10. Ellen purchased 100 shares of GHI Corporation common stock five years ago for $1,000. JKL Corporation issued voting common stock to GHI in exchange for all the GHI assets in a C reorganization. GHI distributed the JKL stock to its shareholders. Ellen received JKL stock worth $1,400 in exchange for her GHI shares. She realized a $400 gain.

Example 8-11. Fred purchased 100 shares of MNO Corporation voting common stock five years ago for $1,000; he purchased 40 shares of MNO preferred stock for $300 two years ago. PQR Corporation issued voting common stock to MNO and acquired all the MNO assets in an A reorganization. MNO distributed the PQR stock to its shareholders. Fred received PQR stock worth $1,400 in exchange for his MNO common shares and PQR stock worth $280 in exchange for his MNO preferred shares. Fred realizes a gain of $400 on his common shares and a loss of $20 on his preferred shares.

Section 354(a)(1) provides that neither gain nor loss is recognized if the shareholder receives only stock in a corporation that is a party to a reorganization. Generally, it does not matter if the class of stock relinquished differs from the class of stock received. Receipt of nonqualified preferred stock is an exception to this rule. As discussed later in this section, it is treated as other property rather than as stock.

b. Basis and Holding Period

A shareholder's basis for the stock he receives is the same as his basis for the stock he relinquishes. I.R.C. § 358(a)(1). He allocates that basis among the shares he received. I.R.C. § 358(b); Reg. § 1.358-2(a)(2)(i)–(ii). The allocation rules vary based on whether the shareholder received the same number of shares he surrendered, received more shares than he surrendered, or received fewer shares than he surrendered. The general rule allocates the old basis to the new shares. If he received more than one class of shares, the allocation is made based on the terms of the exchange if those terms are economically reasonable. Otherwise, the allocation is based on those shares' relative value. When more shares are surrendered than received, two rules apply. The general rule is to allocate basis in a manner that reflects as much as possible that a share was received for shares of stock acquired on the same date and for the same price. If that is not possible, the allocation must minimize the disparity in the holding periods of the surrendered shares whose basis is allocated to any share received. Reg. § 1.358-2(c) includes numerous examples of its application.

Prop. Reg. § 1.358-2 continues these rules, albeit in a better-organized format. It explicitly states a rule addressed in Reg. § 1.358-2(c) Example 14 for situations in which the shareholder surrendered more shares than he received and the surrendered shares were acquired on different dates or for different prices. After allocating the new shares on a pro rata basis to the old shares, it gives any "excess" shares a segmented basis. Each segment has a basis and holding period computed using the rules in that proposed regulation. Prop. Reg. § 1.358-2(b)(3)(ii), -2(i) Example 13.

> **Example 8-12.** Fred's basis for the PQR shares he received in exchange for his MNO common shares is the $1,000 basis he had for those common shares. His basis for the PQR shares he received in exchange for his MNO preferred shares is the $300 basis he had for those preferred shares.

> **Example 8-13.** If Fred had received both voting and nonvoting PQR common shares in exchange for his MNO common shares, he would allocate his $1,000 basis among the two categories of PQR shares based on their relative values. We would expect the voting common shares would receive a higher per-share basis because they have more rights than the nonvoting shares.

Assuming his original shares were capital assets, the shareholder's holding period for the stock received includes his holding period for those original shares. I.R.C. § 1223(1). Because his holding period for the original shares tacks on to his holding period for the new shares, the new shares qualify for long-term capital asset status sooner than they otherwise would.

3. Shareholder Receives Stock and Other Consideration

The discussion in this section assumes that the acquiring corporation transferred only permissible consideration. It does not assume that target shareholders received only permissible consideration. For example, the acquiring corporation in a C reorganization can use only its own or its parent's voting stock in acquiring substantially all the target corporation's assets. That does not mean that the target corporation's shareholders will receive only voting stock in exchange for their target corporation shares. They might also receive property that the target corporation did not transfer to the acquiring corporation.

a. Gain or Loss Recognized

The basic gain or loss realized computation is unchanged. The shareholder compares his adjusted basis to the value of the consideration he receives. If he receives consideration other than stock in a party to the reorganization, he has received "boot," and § 354 no longer applies. Instead, we compute gain or loss recognition under § 356.

Boot is not limited to money. A shareholder who receives securities in a corporation that is a party to a reorganization and did not previously own securities receives boot. I.R.C. § 354(a)(2)(A)(ii). A shareholder who receives other non-stock property receives boot. A shareholder who receives nonqualified preferred stock receives boot. I.R.C. § 354(a)(2)(C). The receipt of nonqualified preferred stock qualifies for nonrecognition only if it is received in exchange for nonqualified preferred stock. Nonqualified preferred stock is defined in § 351(g)(2) and discussed in Chapter 4.

Warrants, which represent rights to acquire stock, are treated differently from actual shares of stock, but they do not necessarily cause gain recognition. Reg. § 1.356-3(b) generally treats warrants as securities. Because it assigns them a principal amount of zero, a shareholder who receives only warrants or receives both stock and warrants does not recognize gain. Reg. § 1.356-3(c) Example 7. One exception applies. If the warrant gives the holder the right to acquire nonqualified preferred stock, it is not a security unless it is received in exchange for nonqualified preferred stock. Reg. § 1.356-6(a).

When a target corporation shareholder receives boot in the transaction, his recognized gain is the lesser of his realized gain or the amount of boot received. I.R.C. § 356(a)(1). He does not recognize any of his realized loss. I.R.C. § 356(c).

> **Example 8-14.** STU Corporation merged into VWX Corporation. Andrew received VWX common stock worth $65 and VWX securities worth $15 in exchange for his STU stock. Andrew's STU stock was worth $80; his basis was $60. Because Andrew received securities and did not surrender securities, the securities were boot. Andrew recognized $15 of his $20 realized gain.

> **Example 8-15.** Bella received stock in DEF Corporation worth $500 and $60 in exchange for her ABC Corporation stock as part of an A reorganization. Bella's basis for her ABC shares was $700. Bella recognized none of her $140 loss.

b. Character of Recognized Gain

If the shareholder recognizes gain, we must determine whether the gain is capital gain or a dividend. Section 356(a)(2) provides that an exchange that has the effect of a dividend (determined using the § 318(a) attribution rules) is treated as a dividend to the extent of the recipient's ratable share of the corporation's undistributed E&P. Hence, in Example 8-14, if Andrew's ratable share of E&P was $12, he would report a dividend of $12 and a capital gain of $3.

Gain attributable to boot is not automatically treated as a dividend. If the transaction results in a meaningful reduction in shareholder interest, rather than being a pro rata payment, the shareholder may be able to treat the entire gain as capital gain. In *Commissioner v. Clark*, 489 U.S. 726 (1989), the Court examined the transaction as a whole. The sole shareholder of the target corporation, who received both stock and cash, became a .92% shareholder of the acquiring corporation. The Court treated the transaction as a redemption by the acquiring corporation. If he had received only stock in that corporation, he would have owned 1.3% of its stock. Reductions in a minority shareholder's stock interest are generally treated as not essentially equivalent to a dividend.

c. Assigning Consideration

A shareholder who exchanges more than one block of stock may have gain on some shares and loss on others. If he receives boot in addition to shares in the acquiring corporation, we must determine whether to assign a pro rata share of boot to all surrendered shares or only to some of them. If boot was assigned only to shares on which he realized a loss, he would escape reporting dividend income or capital gain on his appreciated shares.

The regulations interpreting § 356 provide allocation rules. First, if the terms of the exchange specify how consideration is allocated, we use those terms so long as they are economically reasonable. If they do not specify an allocation, we allocate consideration pro rata based on the relative value of each share of stock surrendered. Reg. § 1.356-1(b).

> **Example 8-16.** Curt owned 100 shares of GHI Corporation voting common stock. He also owned 100 shares of GHI preferred stock. His preferred stock was not nonqualified preferred stock. He had a basis of $1,000 for his common stock and $400 for his preferred stock. JKL Corporation acquired GHI in an A reorganization. Under the terms of the merger agreement, Curt received 120 shares of JKL common stock, worth $1,200, for his GHI common shares. He received 25 shares of JKL common stock worth $250 and $50 cash for his GHI preferred shares. Assuming the terms of the agreement were economically reasonable, Curt recognizes none of his $200 gain on exchanging his common shares. He recognizes none of his $100 loss on exchanging his preferred shares.

Example 8-17. Assume instead that the agreement did not specify how the consideration was allocated (or that the agreement was not economically reasonable). Because Curt's common shares were worth 80% ($1,200/$1,500) of the total, he is treated as receiving JKL stock worth $1,160 and $40 for those shares. He is treated as receiving JKL stock worth $290 and $10 for his JKL preferred shares. He recognizes a $40 gain with respect to his common shares. That $40 will be treated as either a dividend or as capital gain. He recognizes none of his $100 loss on exchanging his preferred shares.

Prop. Reg. § 1.356-1(b) Example 4 applies § 302 rather than § 356 to the exchange in Example 8-17 and refers to the stock surrendered as Block 1 and Block 2 rather than as Class A and Class B. The proposed regulation was premised on the exchange terms being economically reasonable. It was issued in 2009; it would amend the original regulation, which was last amended in 2006.

d. Section 306 Stock Surrendered

If the shareholder exchanged stock described in § 306 and received other property or money in addition to stock in the acquiring corporation, his results differ from those described earlier in this section. Other consideration allocated to the § 306 stock is treated as a distribution subject to the § 301 dividend rules. I.R.C. § 356(f); Reg. § 1.356-4. The regulation indicates that we use a facts and circumstances test in determining if the other consideration was allocable to the § 306 stock. It also indicates that the other consideration will ordinarily be first assigned to that stock. This regulation has not been amended since 1955.

e. Basis and Holding Period

If the shareholder received other consideration in addition to stock, § 358(a)(1) provides that her basis for the stock she receives is the same as the basis of the stock she exchanged, decreased by the fair market value of property (except money) she received, by the money she received, and by any loss she recognized, and increased by any gain she recognized and any dividend income she reported. If the stock she exchanged was a capital asset, her holding period for the stock she received includes her holding period for the stock she surrendered. I.R.C. § 1223(1).

The shareholder's basis for the other property is its fair market value. I.R.C. § 358(a)(2). She begins a new holding period for that property.

Example 8-18. In Example 8-16, Curt's basis for the 120 shares of JKL common stock he received in exchange for his 100 GHI common shares would be $1,000. His holding period for those shares would include his holding period for his GHI common shares. Curt's basis for the 25 shares of JKL common stock he received in exchange for his 100 GHI preferred shares would be $350. That represents his original $400 basis decreased by the $50 he received. His holding period for those shares would include his holding period for his GHI preferred shares.

Example 8-19. In Example 8-17, Curt's basis for the 120 shares of JKL common stock he received in exchange for his 100 GHI common shares would be $1,000. That represents his original $1,000 basis reduced by the $40 he received and increased by the gain (or dividend) he recognized. His holding period for those shares would include his holding period for his GHI common shares. Curt's basis for the 25 shares of JKL common stock he received in exchange for his 100 GHI preferred shares would be $390. That represents his original $400 basis decreased by the $10 he received. His holding period for those shares would include his holding period for his GHI preferred shares.

If Curt had received other property instead of money, his basis for the other property would be its fair market value. His basis for the JKL stock he received would be the same as computed above.

4. Shareholder Receives No Stock

If the shareholder receives only securities, money, or other property, neither § 354 nor § 356 applies even if the exchange occurs pursuant to a plan of reorganization. The shareholder's transaction is instead tested for redemption or dividend status under the distribution rules discussed in other chapters. Prop. Reg. § 1.354-1(d)(2). This rule applies even if the shareholder also makes a qualifying exchange of some shares of stock.

I. Security Holder's Tax Consequences

A taxpayer may realize a gain or loss on surrendering securities in a party to a reorganization and receiving stock or securities in another party to a reorganization. The determination of gain or loss realized follows the normal § 1001(a) computation: amount realized minus adjusted basis. Sections 354 and 356 govern whether any gain is recognized.

No gain or loss is recognized if the security holder receives only stock. No gain or loss is recognized if the security holder receives only securities and the principal amount of the securities received does not exceed the principal amount of the securities surrendered. No gain or loss is recognized if the security holder receives only stock and securities and the principal amount of the securities received does not exceed the principal amount of the securities surrendered. I.R.C. § 354(a). This rule does not apply to stock or securities received in exchange for interest accrued on the securities exchanged. Gross income includes the value of stock or securities received in exchange for accrued interest. I.R.C. § 354(a)(2)(B).

If the principal amount of the securities received exceeds the principal amount of the securities surrendered, the taxpayer recognizes the lesser of realized gain or the fair market value of the excess principal amount. Gain is also recognized if the security holder receives property other than stock or securities in exchange for his securities. The security holder does not recognize loss. I.R.C. § 356(a), (c), (d); Reg. § 1.356-3.

> **Example 8-20.** PQR Corporation acquired the stock of MNO Corporation solely in exchange for its voting stock. It issued PQR securities with a principal amount of $1,000 in exchange for each outstanding MNO security. Dorothy owned one MNO security, which she had acquired 10 years ago for $800. It had a $1,100 principal amount. Ed owned one MNO security, which he had acquired four years ago for $600. It had a $900 principal amount. MNO and PQR securities were worth $1,000 each when the reorganization occurred. Dorothy recognized none of her $200 gain. The $1,000 principal amount of the PQR security did not exceed the $1,100 principal amount of her MNO security. Ed realized a $400 gain and recognized $100 of it. The $1,000 principal amount of the PQR security exceeded the $900 principal amount of his MNO security by $100.

If the PQR security had been worth less than $1,000, the fair market value of the excess would have been less than $100; Ed's gain would be limited to that lower value. Reg. § 1.356-3(c) Example 5.

The security holder takes a carryover basis and holding period if the nonrecognition rules apply and his security was a capital asset. If they do not apply, his basis for the property he receives is its fair market value and his holding period starts when he receives the property.

J. Acquiring Corporation's Tax Consequences

1. Gain or Loss Recognized

Unlike its shareholders, the acquiring corporation is actively involved in a reorganization. Section 1032 provides that a corporation does not recognize gain or loss if it receives money or property for its stock. The regulations extend this nonrecognition treatment to a subsidiary corporation that uses its parent's stock in forward triangular mergers, triangular B reorganizations, and triangular C reorganizations. Reg. § 1.1032-2(b). The subsidiary qualifies for nonrecognition only with respect to stock of its parent that was acquired for purposes of the reorganization. Any stock of its parent acquired in an unrelated transaction is treated as other property exchanged in the reorganization. Reg. § 1.1032-2(c).

Section 1032 applies only to stock exchanged for property. It does not apply to any property other than its own (or its parent's) stock that the acquiring corporation exchanges as part of the reorganization.

2. Basis and Holding Period

The acquiring corporation takes the transferor's basis for property it receives in the reorganization, increased by any gain that the transferor recognizes. I.R.C. § 362(b).

The basis rules do not work well in every situation. For example, if there is a B reorganization involving widely held corporations, target shareholders may number in the millions. Obtaining basis information from so many target shareholders may be a daunting task. Fortunately, Rev. Proc. 2011-35, 2011-25 I.R.B. 890, issued in response to taxpayer comments solicited in 2004, provides four methodologies taxpayers can use to determine basis: surveys; statistical sampling; estimation from Master Security Files; and estimation from Target Security Position Reports and/or SEC Form 13F filings. If appropriate, the corporation can apply different methods to the same reorganization. Rev. Proc. 2011-35 is not limited to B reorganizations; it is available for use in any transferred basis transaction.

In a triangular transaction, the consideration used is stock in a corporation that controls the acquiring corporation. The target's assets (or stock, in a triangular B reorganization) are transferred to the acquiring corporation. If we do not adjust the controlling corporation's basis for the stock of the acquiring corporation, the controlling corporation will recognize gain when it disposes of that stock.

The regulations prevent such gain recognition. They treat the triangular reorganization as if two steps occurred. First, the controlling corporation acquired the target corporation's assets. Second, the controlling corporation transferred those assets to the acquiring corporation. Because the controlling corporation is treated as directly acquiring the target corporation's assets in a nonrecognition transaction and then transferring the assets to its subsidiary (also in a nonrecognition transaction), the controlling corporation receives a basis for those assets. It transfers that basis to its subsidiary.

Example 8-21. ABC Corporation merged into DEF Corporation, a wholly owned subsidiary of GHI Corporation, in a triangular reorganization. Prior to the merger, GHI had a basis of $10 for its DEF stock; the DEF assets were worth $10. ABC had a basis of $20 for its assets; those assets were worth $20. If GHI did not adjust its basis for DEF stock following the merger, it would recognize a $20 gain when it sold its DEF stock. To prevent this from occurring, Reg. § 1.358-6(c)(1) provides that GHI's $10 basis for its DEF stock is adjusted as if GHI had acquired ABC's assets directly from ABC in a transaction in which GHI's basis for those assets was determined under § 362(b). That would give GHI an aggregate basis of $20 for the ABC assets. GHI is then treated as if it transferred the ABC assets to DEF in a transaction in which GHI's basis for the DEF stock was determined under § 358. GHI's $10 basis for its DEF stock would be increased by its $20 basis for the ABC assets deemed transferred. GHI ends up with a $30 basis for its DEF stock.

The acquiring corporation's holding period for property received is determined under § 1223(2). It includes the transferor's holding period for the property.

3. Target Corporation's Tax Attributes

Under § 381, if a transaction qualifies as a reorganization, the acquiring corporation generally succeeds to certain tax attributes of the target corporation. Section 381(c) lists those attributes, including NOLs and E&P. Because the target corporation continues in existence in a B reorganization, its tax attributes do not transfer to the acquiring corporation.

K. Target Corporation's Tax Consequences

Target corporations are often mere conduits for transferring stock and securities from the acquiring corporation to the target's shareholders and security holders. Although the target corporation often disappears after a reorganization, it may be subject to tax with respect to property it received in the reorganization. The tax consequences depend on what property the target received and what it did with that property.

The target corporation has several potential tax-relevant events: (1) receiving stock, securities, and other property from the acquiring corporation; (2) retaining those items; (3) distributing those items to its shareholders and creditors; and (4) distributing assets it did not receive in the reorganization to its shareholders and creditors.

Section 361(a) provides that the target does not recognize gain or loss on exchanging property solely for stock or securities of another party to the reorganization. Section 361(b) applies if the corporation received both stock or securities and other property or money. Its result depends on what the corporation did with the nonqualifying property. It can avoid recognizing gain by distributing that other property. I.R.C. § 361(b)(1)(A). If the target corporation instead retains the property, it recognizes gain. It recognizes the lesser of its gain realized or the amount of money or other property it retains. I.R.C. § 361(b)(1)(B). In either situation, the target corporation does not recognize loss. I.R.C. § 361(b)(2).

Section 361(c) governs distributions by the target corporation. It can distribute stock or securities received from the acquiring corporation, money or other property received from the acquiring corporation, or property that it did not transfer to the acquiring corporation. The target's tax consequences depend on whether it distributes qualified property or other property.

The target recognizes no gain or loss on distributing qualified property to its shareholders as part of the reorganization. I.R.C. § 361(c)(1). Stock in the acquiring corporation is qualified property. A right to acquire such stock is qualified property. An obligation of the acquiring corporation is qualified property. Stock, rights, and obligations of any other corporation that is a party to the reorganization are also qualified property. I.R.C. § 361(c)(2)(B). Transfers of qualified property to creditors are generally treated the same as distributions to shareholders. I.R.C. § 361(c)(3).

The target recognizes gain on distributing appreciated property that is not qualified property. The amount realized is deemed to be the value of that property. I.R.C. § 361(c)(2)(A). It does not recognize loss on distributing property that is worth less than its basis.

The rules discussed in this section do not apply to target corporations involved in B reorganizations because the target does not exchange either its stock or its assets. It shareholders exchange their stock directly with the acquiring corporation. The target in a B reorganization also retains its tax attributes.

Checkpoints

- A, B, and C reorganizations are acquisitive reorganizations. Some D and G reorganizations are also acquisitive.
- The A reorganization is a statutory merger or consolidation. The B reorganization is an exchange of voting stock of the acquiring corporation solely for stock of the target corporation. The C reorganization is an exchange of substantially all the assets solely for voting stock (but up to 20% boot is permitted). The acquisitive D and G reorganizations involve an exchange of assets for stock.
- The substantially all requirement applies to triangular A, to C, and to acquisitive D reorganizations. The IRS ruling position generally required 90% of the net assets or 70% of the gross assets of the target corporation to be acquired.
- The control requirement applies to B, C, and acquisitive D reorganizations. For B and C reorganizations, control means ownership of stock possessing at least 80% of the total combined voting power of all classes of stock entitled to vote *and* at least 80% of the total number of shares of all other classes of stock of the corporation. For acquisitive D reorganization, the control requirement is lowered to 50% of voting power or stock value.
- Both C and acquisitive D and G reorganizations impose a distribution requirement. The acquired corporation must distribute the assets received in the transaction as well as its other assets. Generally, only one corporation survives.
- Section 368 provides that assets acquired in A, B, C, and G reorganizations can be dropped down to a subsidiary corporation of the acquiring corporation. A revenue ruling permits drop-down of assets in D reorganizations. Regulations permit push-up of assets.
- The target's shareholders recognize no gain or loss on exchanging their stock solely for stock. The target's securities holders recognize no gain or loss on exchanging their securities for stock or securities so long as the principal amount of securities they receive does not exceed the principal amount of the securities they exchange.
- The target recognizes no gain or loss on exchanging its assets for stock or securities. If it receives other property, it does not recognize gain or loss if it distributes that property. If it retains that property, it recognizes gain but not loss.
- The target's basis and other tax attributes carry over to the acquiring corporation in an acquisitive reorganization other than a B reorganization. The target retains its basis and other attributes following a B reorganization.
- Basis and holding period of their old shares carry over to the stock received by the target corporation's shareholders. Basis and holding period of their old securities carry over to the stock or securities received by the target corporation's security holders. Adjustments are made if shareholders or security holders received nonqualified property.

Chapter 9

E and F Reorganizations

Roadmap

- E reorganizations
- F reorganizations
- Tax consequences

A. Chapter Overview

This chapter addresses E and F reorganizations. Unlike acquisitive and divisive reorganizations, E and F reorganizations generally involve only a single corporation. That corporation is recapitalizing (E reorganization) or undergoing a mere change in form (F reorganization). Because only one corporation is involved, the regulations are much shorter than for other types of reorganization. This chapter covers the tax consequences only briefly, as most of them mirror those discussed in the preceding chapter.

B. E Reorganizations

1. Introduction

Section 368(a)(1)(E) treats a recapitalization as a reorganization. The reorganization involves the corporation's capital structure and generally involves a single corporation.

The regulations do not define recapitalization or provide a framework for determining if one exists, but they do provide five examples: (1) discharging a liability represented by bonds by issuing preferred stock to the bondholders; (2) issuing common stock in exchange for a portion of its outstanding preferred stock; (3) issuing preferred stock in exchange for common stock; (4) issuing common stock with no priorities in exchange for preferred stock that had priorities regarding dividends and liquidating distributions; and

(5) issuing other stock in exchange for preferred stock with dividends in arrears. Reg. § 1.368-2(e).

> **Example 9-1.** ABC Corporation has 100 shareholders, none of whom owns more than 20% of its shares. Five of those shareholders also own all of ABC's nonvoting preferred shares. ABC issues additional common stock to those five shareholders in exchange for their preferred stock. This transaction can qualify as an E reorganization.

> **Example 9-2.** DEF Corporation has 100 shareholders, none of whom owns more than 20% of its shares. DEF also owes $500,000 to holders of its bonds. The bondholders agree to exchange their bonds for shares of DEF preferred stock. By retiring this debt, DEF significantly improves its credit rating. This transaction can qualify as an E reorganization.

2. Relevant Doctrines

The continuity of business enterprise and continuity of interest requirements do not apply because there is no target or acquiring corporation. Reg. § 1.368-1(b). The concerns that arise in acquisitive reorganizations are not present in recapitalizations involving a single corporation.

Other doctrines, such as substance over form and step transaction, do apply. A transaction that appears to qualify as an E reorganization may be disqualified if it is part of a larger transaction that would be treated as something other than an E reorganization. The business purpose requirement may also be relevant. Based on the facts, the transaction described in Example 9-2 has a business purpose.

C. F Reorganizations

1. Introduction

A mere change in identity, form, or place of organization of one corporation, however effected, is a reorganization. The "one corporation" language of § 368(a)(1)(F) has been generally recognized as requiring one operating corporation.

The term "mere" is important in this context. If a transaction involves more than a "mere" change, it does not qualify as an F reorganization. It may nevertheless qualify as another type of reorganization. Again, because a single corporation is involved, the continuity of business enterprise and continuity of interest requirements do not apply. Reg. § 1.368-1(b).

Most F reorganizations are effected by the merger of an existing corporation into a newly created shell corporation. The regulations refer to these entities as a transferor corporation and a resulting corporation. Reg. § 1.368-2(m)(1). For example, the reincorporation of a Michigan corporation in Delaware will generally be achieved by creating a Delaware corporation and then merging the Michigan corporation into the Delaware corporation. This transaction is not an A reorganization because it involves only one corporation; the second corporation was created merely to effectuate the change of state. It is an F reorganization because it is a mere change in place of organization.

> **Example 9-3.** GHI Corporation has used the name Gigantic Deals in its advertising for the past 20 years. This year, its shareholders voted to change GHI's official corporate name to Gigantic Deals Corporation. Each GHI shareholder became a Gigantic Deals shareholder; no other change in their relationship to the corporation occurred. The name change is a mere change in identity and qualifies as an F reorganization.

Reg. § 1.368-2(m)(1) lists six requirements for treating the transaction as a mere change. First, all the stock of the resulting corporation must be distributed in exchange for stock of the transferor corporation. Second, the same person or persons must own all the stock of both corporations in identical proportions. It is permissible for one or more shareholders to receive stock having different terms if it is of equivalent value. It is also permissible for one or more shareholders to receive distributions of money or other property from either corporation. Third, the resulting corporation must not hold any property or have any tax attributes immediately before the reorganization. It can hold a de minimis amount of assets (and have tax attributes related to those assets) if the assets are held to facilitate its organization or to maintain its legal existence. Fourth, the transferor corporation must completely liquidate as part of the reorganization. It does not have to dissolve and it can retain a de minimis amount of assets for the purpose of preserving its existence. Fifth, the resulting corporation is the only corporation allowed to hold transferor corporation assets immediately after the reorganization. If another corporation holds any such assets that would result in its assuming the tax attributes listed in § 381(c), the reorganization does not qualify. Sixth, immediately after the reorganization, the resulting corporation cannot hold property acquired from any corporation other than the transferor corporation if such property would result in its assuming the § 381(c) tax attributes.

2. Related Transactions

Reg. § 1.368-2(m)(3)(i)–(iv) applies when an F reorganization is part of one or more related transactions. First, the reorganization can be an F reorganization if a series of related transactions as a group results in a mere change in one corporation. It does not matter that various of the steps involved, if considered alone, would be subject to other provisions; those include §§ 304, 331, 332, and 351. Second, an F reorganization that occurs before, at the same time as, or after other transactions is treated as a mere change even if the resulting corporation has only a transitory existence. The step transaction doctrine can be applied to those other transactions without regard to whether certain steps qualify as an F reorganization. Third, if a shareholder receives money or other property from either the transferor or the resulting corporation, that receipt is treated as part of a separate, unrelated transaction even if it is connected to the reorganization in a formal sense. The shareholder who receives money or other property is subject to the dividend or redemption provisions discussed in the preceding chapter with respect to those items. The stock he receives is covered by the reorganization provisions.

> **Example 9-4.** JKL Corporation had two shareholders: Alvin owned 65% of the stock and Betty owned the remaining 35%. JKL was incorporated in State 1. After its management determined that incorporation in State 2 would be preferable, JKL formed a new corporation, MNO, in State 2. JKL then merged into MNO. Alvin surrendered his JKL stock and received MNO stock in exchange. Betty did not want to continue her stock ownership. She surrendered her JKL stock for money. The merger qualifies as an F reorganization. Betty's exchange of stock for money was a redemption covered by § 302(a). Reg. § 1.368-2(m)(4) Example 2.

The regulation also covers transactions that could have qualified as both F reorganizations and as another type of reorganization. It has two rules. If the potential F reorganization (or a step thereof) qualifies under another reorganization provision, it is not treated as an F reorganization if a corporation that is in control of the resulting corporation is a party to the other reorganization. The § 368(c) definition of control applies. If that first rule does not apply, the reorganization is treated as an F reorganization instead of as an A, C, or D reorganization if it qualifies as both an F and one of those other reorganizations.

D. Tax Consequences

Acquisitive and divisive reorganizations involve at least two entities—the acquiring corporation and the target corporation. E and F reorganizations, on the other hand, involve only one set of shareholders because only one corporation is undergoing a reorganization.

1. Shareholder's Tax Consequences

As discussed in the preceding chapter, the shareholders' tax consequences depend on whether they receive only stock of the corporation undergoing a reorganization, stock and other consideration, or only non-stock consideration. Those rules are discussed in detail in that chapter and are only summarized here.

a. Shareholder Receives Only Stock

A shareholder who receives only new shares of stock in exchange for her original shares does not recognize any of her realized gain or loss. I.R.C. § 354(a)(1). Her basis for the new shares equals her basis for the old shares. I.R.C. § 358(a)(1). If the stock she surrendered was a capital asset, as is likely, her holding period for her new shares includes her holding period for her old shares. I.R.C. § 1223(1).

> **Example 9-5.** Glinda purchased 100 shares of PQR Corporation nonvoting common stock five years ago for $1,000. PQR reorganized this year by changing its capital structure. Glinda received 80 shares of PQR voting common stock worth $1,100 in exchange for her nonvoting common shares. She realized a $100 gain, none of which was recognized. Her basis for her 80 voting common shares is $1,000; her holding period for those shares includes her holding period for the nonvoting common shares she exchanged.

It is possible that the shareholder will receive stock but not relinquish stock she already owns. In that situation, she allocates her basis for the original shares between those shares and the new shares based on their respective fair market values.

A shareholder who exchanges common stock solely for common stock, or preferred stock solely for preferred stock, could also have avoided recognizing gain or loss under § 1036. This section applies to transactions between the shareholder and corporation and to transactions between the shareholder and third parties. It requires no business purpose and applies to non-reorganization transactions. If a shareholder is changing status, however, as in a common for preferred exchange, § 1036 does not apply.

b. Shareholder Receives Stock and Other Consideration

A shareholder who receives both stock and other property in exchange for his original shares recognizes gain. The recognized gain is the lesser of his realized gain or the value of the other property received. I.R.C. § 356(a)(1). The gain might qualify for capital gain treatment. But to the extent it has the effect of a dividend distribution, it is treated as a dividend. The amount treated as a dividend cannot exceed the shareholder's ratable share of the corporation's E&P. I.R.C. § 356(a)(2).

His basis for the stock and other property received is computed using the formula in § 358(a)(1). It begins with his basis for his original stock. We reduce that amount by any money received, by the value of any nonqualifying property received, and by any loss recognized. We increase that amount by any gain recognized and by any amount treated as a dividend. His basis for any nonqualifying property received is its fair market value. I.R.C. § 358(a)(2). Only the stock he receives has a holding period that includes the holding period of the stock he exchanged. I.R.C. § 1223(1).

A shareholder who receives both stock and other property in exchange for his original stock does not recognize loss. I.R.C. § 356(c). His basis and holding period for the stock and other property he receives is computed using the rules covered in the preceding paragraph.

c. Nonqualified Preferred Stock Received

If a shareholder receives nonqualified preferred stock, his tax consequences depend on what he exchanged or whether the corporation is family-owned. Nonqualified preferred stock is described in § 351(g)(2) and discussed in Chapter 4. It is usually treated as other property rather than as stock. It is treated as stock if the shareholder receives it in exchange for nonqualified preferred stock. It is also treated as stock in an E reorganization if the corporation being reorganized qualifies as a family-owned corporation. I.R.C. § 354(a)(2)(C).

The term "family-owned" does not benefit every corporation that has only family members as shareholders. The corporation must qualify under § 447(d)(2)(C)(i) and must do so for an eight-year period. That period begins five years before the date the recapitalization occurs. I.R.C. § 354(a)(2)(C)(ii). Section 447(d)(2)(C)(i) requires that members of a single family own at least 50% of the corporation's total combined voting power and at least 50% of all other classes of stock.

d. Section 306 Stock Surrendered

A shareholder who surrendered stock described in § 306, and received only stock (other than nonqualified preferred stock) in exchange, does not recognize gain or loss. The stock she receives will be § 306 stock. I.R.C. § 306(c)(1)(B). If she receives other property in exchange for her § 306 stock, she reports its value using the § 301 dividend distribution rules. I.R.C. § 356(f).

e. Shareholder Receives No Stock

If the shareholder receives only securities, money, or other property, neither § 354 nor § 356 applies even if the exchange occurs pursuant to a plan of reorganization. The shareholder's transaction is instead tested for redemption or dividend status under the distribution rules discussed in other chapters. Prop. Reg. § 1.354-1(d)(2). This rule applies even if the shareholder also makes a qualifying exchange of some shares of stock.

f. Shareholder's Interest Changes

Although E reorganizations do not generally involve gain recognition, the results may be different if the transaction changes a shareholder's interest. A shareholder who ends up with an increased interest in the corporation's assets or E&P may have reportable dividend income. Reg. § 1.368-2(e)(5) provides for this outcome for an exchange of preferred stock with dividends in arrears for other stock.

2. Security Holder's Tax Consequences

A security holder might receive stock, securities, money, other property, or some combination thereof. As was true for shareholders, the security holder's tax consequences depend on what she receives. The summary below echoes the discussion in the preceding chapter.

A security holder who exchanges her securities and receives only stock recognizes no gain or loss. The same rule applies to a security holder who exchanges her securities and receives only securities with the same or a lower principal amount. I.R.C. § 354(a)(1). Her basis for the new stock or securities equals her basis for the securities she surrendered. I.R.C. § 358(a)(1). If the securities she surrendered were capital assets, her holding period for any stock or securities she received includes her holding period for her old securities. I.R.C. § 1223(1).

As was true for shareholders, a security holder who receives other property in addition to qualifying property recognizes gain. She does not recognize loss. In applying this rule, we treat any excess principal amount of securities received as property for purposes of § 354. A security holder reports gain (but not loss) if the principal amount received exceeds the principal amount surrendered.

The security holder also reports gain (but not loss) if she receives consideration in addition to stock or securities. Nonqualified preferred stock is additional consideration. I.R.C. § 354(a)(2)(C). Any consideration, including stock or securities, received in exchange for accrued interest is also other property. I.R.C. § 354(c)(2)(B).

When determining the security holder's tax consequences, do not automatically assume that every corporate debt is a security. Short-term debt instruments and open account debt obligations are not securities. On the other hand, rights to acquire stock are treated as securities. Reg. § 1.354-1(e).

The security holder receives a carryover basis and holding period only for the stock or securities received that qualify for nonrecognition. Other items received take a fair market value basis and begin a new holding period.

3. Corporation's Tax Consequences

The corporation does not recognize gain or loss on issuing new shares of stock or reissuing previously issued shares. It does not matter if it receives stock or other consideration in exchange for these shares. Nor does it matter if it issues these shares as part of a reorganization. I.R.C. § 1032. Because the reorganization involves a single corporation, its E&P account and other tax attributes generally remain unchanged.

If a corporation's debt is reduced in a reorganization, it might have income from discharge of indebtedness. I.R.C. § 61(a)(12). Exceptions in § 108(a) apply to debtors in a bankruptcy proceeding and insolvent debtors. Section 108(e)(2) excludes any discharged amount that would have given rise to a deduction. Subsections 108(e)(8) and (10) provide rules for determining the extent to which a debt is satisfied if the corporation transfers stock or debt instruments in satisfaction of corporate indebtedness.

One corporate-level concern pertains to § 382. That section is an attempt to limit loss trafficking, and its application is triggered when the ownership of the corporation has changed hands. As a rule, if a "loss corporation" (generally a corporation that has a loss carryover) undergoes an E reorganization resulting in a major change in its ownership structure, it may be subject to the § 382 loss limitation rules.

In addition to providing nonrecognition of gain or loss, F reorganizations escape certain limitations imposed on other reorganizations. This is because the F reorganization poses few risks of tax avoidance. Hence, under Reg.

§ 1.381(b)-1(a)(2), the "acquiring" corporation is treated (for purposes of § 381 attribute carryovers) just as the "transferor" corporation would have been treated if there had been no reorganization. The § 382 limitations on losses would generally not apply because the corporation is treated as remaining in existence. Equity structure shifts defined in § 382(g)(3) do not apply to F reorganizations. The corporation does not have to file a short-year tax return because its taxable year is not closed by the F reorganization.

Checkpoints

- E and the F reorganizations involve a single corporation.
- An E reorganization involves a change in the corporation's ownership structure. None of its assets are acquired; and it does not acquire assets of another corporation.
- An F reorganization involves no change in ownership structure. The ownership structure after the F reorganization must be identical to that of the prior corporation. One or more shareholders may receive money without preventing the transaction from being an F reorganization.
- The step transaction doctrine can apply to an E reorganization.
- The step transaction doctrine has no effect on an F reorganization; an F reorganization is tested separately even if it is part of a larger transaction.
- E and F reorganizations are not subject to the continuity of interest and continuity of business enterprise requirements.
- Shareholders recognize no gain or loss if they receive only stock in exchange for the stock they relinquish. Nonqualified preferred stock may not qualify unless it is received in exchange for nonqualified preferred stock or there is a recapitalization of a family-owned corporation.
- If a shareholder receives consideration other than stock, or in addition to stock, he recognizes gain but not loss. The gain may be taxed as a dividend if it is essentially equivalent to a dividend, as would be the case with a pro rata distribution of nonqualifying property.
- Security holders recognize no gain unless they receive property other than stock or securities in exchange for their securities. If the new security has a principal amount greater than the security surrendered, the excess is treated as other property.
- Security holders do not recognize loss on an exchange in an E or F reorganization even if the principal amounts of the securities received and exchanged differ.
- The corporation does not recognize gain or loss on issuing stock in exchange for stock or other property.

Chapter 10

Divisive Reorganizations; Section 355

Roadmap

- Divisive reorganizations
- Section 355
- Section 355 requirements
- Tax consequences of qualifying distributions
- Taxable divisions

A. Chapter Overview

Chapters 8 and 9 focused on acquisitive reorganizations and reorganizations of a single corporation. This chapter focuses on divisive transactions. Divisive D and G reorganization provisions allow a corporation to transfer assets to another corporation without recognizing gain or loss. To qualify for nonrecognition, however, it must satisfy the distribution requirements imposed by § 355.

Section 355 allows a corporation to separate its assets without gain recognition. It can apply even if the transaction is not part of a reorganization. It applies to the distributing corporation and to its shareholders and security holders. To prevent taxpayers from using it as a device to avoid tax, the Code and regulations include several technical requirements and other limitations.

Qualification under § 355 includes resort to § 356 if the distribution includes nonqualifying property. Section 356 provides for gain, but not loss, recognition with respect to nonqualifying property.

B. Divisive Reorganizations

In a divisive reorganization, a corporation transfers some of its assets to another corporation; in other words, it divides. If the transaction is a divisive

D reorganization, the transferor corporation, its shareholders, or any combination thereof must be in control of the transferee corporation immediately after the transfer. The transferor corporation must distribute stock or securities of the transferee corporation in a transaction that qualifies under § 355. I.R.C. § 368(a)(1)(D). If the transaction is a divisive G reorganization, it must occur in a Title 11 (bankruptcy) or similar case. The transfer must be pursuant to the plan approved by the court. The transferor corporation must distribute stock or securities of the transferee corporation in a transaction that qualifies under § 355. I.R.C. § 368(a)(1)(G), (a)(3)(A)–(B).

There are some important differences between divisive D and divisive G reorganizations. A divisive G reorganization plan must be approved by the court overseeing the bankruptcy. The transferor corporation and its shareholders need not have control of the transferee immediately after the transfer. Because the transferor is in a bankruptcy proceeding, it is likely that its shareholders' equity has been significantly reduced or even eliminated. This chapter does not cover divisive G reorganizations.

C. Section 355

1. Significance

When a corporation distributes property to a shareholder and does not liquidate, the shareholder reports dividend income to the extent the distribution is covered by E&P. I.R.C. § 301(c). If it transfers property to a shareholder in exchange for her stock, her tax consequences depend on whether the transaction qualifies as a redemption (treated as a sale or exchange) or is essentially equivalent to a dividend. In the former situation, she recognizes gain or loss; in the latter, she reports dividend income. I.R.C. §§ 301(c), 302(a). If the corporation liquidates and distributes property to its shareholders, they report gain or loss unless the liquidation involves a controlled subsidiary and its corporate parent. I.R.C. §§ 331, 332. In all these situations, the shareholder is likely to have gross income. If the property distributed is worth more than the corporation's basis for it, the corporation reports its gain as gross income. I.R.C. §§ 311(b) (dividend or redemption), 336(a) (liquidation not described in § 332). Both the corporation and the shareholders to whom it transfers property are potentially taxed in these situations.

If § 355 applies, the results are different. Neither the corporation nor its shareholders report gross income when the property transferred is stock in a corporation controlled by the distributing corporation. Because this is a significant tax benefit, you should not be surprised that the Code and regulations impose significant restrictions on its use.

Do not confuse § 355 with § 305. Section 355 involves distribution of the stock of a subsidiary corporation; § 305 involves distributing the corporation's own stock. Section 355 applies to both the distributing corporation and its shareholders; § 305 applies only to the shareholders.

2. Spin-Offs, Split-Offs, and Split-Ups

There are three basic § 355 transactions, the spin-off, the split-off, and the split-up. They correspond to the three taxable transactions described earlier in this section: dividend; redemption; and liquidation. In a spin-off, the distributing corporation's shareholders end up with stock in both the distributing corporation and the controlled corporation. They receive shares in the controlled corporation even though they do not surrender any of their stock in the distributing corporation. In a split-off, some shareholders end up with stock in the controlled corporation, which they receive in exchange for their stock in the distributing corporation; other shareholders do not surrender their stock and continue as shareholders in the distributing corporation. In a split-up, the distributing corporation divides its assets between two or more controlled corporations, distributes the stock in the controlled corporations to its shareholders, and ceases to exist. The examples below illustrate the mechanics; they assume the transactions meet the requirements addressed later in this chapter.

Example 10-1. ABC Corporation and its wholly owned subsidiary DEF each operated a separate business. ABC distributed the DEF stock to its shareholders pro rata. At that point, DEF was no longer an ABC subsidiary. The ABC shareholders owned all the shares of both ABC and DEF. This transaction was a spin-off.

Example 10-2. ABC Corporation instead distributed the DEF shares to some of its own shareholders (Group 1) in exchange for their ABC shares. At that point, DEF was no longer an ABC subsidiary. Some of the original ABC shareholders (Group 2) still owned ABC shares. The other, now former, ABC shareholders owned all the DEF shares. The transaction was a split-off. The transaction would also be a split-off if ABC transferred the DEF shares in exchange for only part of the shares owned by Group 1, perhaps because Group 1 shareholders owned ABC stock worth more than the value of DEF. In that situation, Group 1 shareholders would own stock in both ABC and DEF. Group 2 shareholders would own stock only in ABC.

Example 10-3. ABC Corporation instead owned all the shares of DEF and GHI Corporations, each of which operated a business. ABC's only assets were its DEF and GHI shares. ABC distributed those shares to its own shareholders in exchange for their stock. ABC corporation ceased to exist. Its former shareholders were now shareholders of DEF and GHI. This transaction was a split-up.

3. Relationship to Divisive Reorganizations

The transactions described above are covered by § 355 even if they are not described in § 368. The reverse is not the case. If a corporation transfers assets to another corporation in a divisive transaction, it must distribute the stock or securities it receives in a transaction covered by § 355. Otherwise it cannot qualify as a divisive reorganization. The transfer of assets, followed by the distribution, is often referred to as a D/355 reorganization.

Example 10-4. JKL Corporation operated two unrelated businesses. It transferred the assets of one of those businesses to a newly created subsidiary, MNO Corporation, in exchange for all its stock. JKL distributed that stock to its shareholders in a transaction described in § 355. This transaction was a D/355 reorganization. If JKL had instead retained the MNO stock, the transaction would be governed by § 351.

Example 10-5. JKL instead transferred the assets of that business to AAA Corporation, an unrelated entity. JKL received 85% of AAA's stock. If JKL retained the AAA stock, § 351 applies to the transaction. If it distributed the AAA stock to its shareholders, it is a D/355 transaction.

D. Section 355 Requirements

Section 355(a)(1) imposes four requirements. The first relates to what can be transferred without tax consequences. There must be a distribution to a shareholder with respect to his stock or to a security holder in exchange for his securities. The stock or securities transferred must be of a corporation that the transferor controlled immediately before the distribution. The transfer must be solely of stock or securities of the controlled corporation. The transferor corporation is the distributing corporation; the other corporation is the controlled corporation.

Second, the transaction must not be principally used as a device to distribute E&P on a tax-free basis. The E&P can be that of the distributing corporation, the controlled corporation, or both corporations. Third, the corporations must meet an active business requirement. Fourth, the distributing corporation must distribute enough of the controlled corporation's stock.

The discussion below describes these and other relevant requirements in more detail. It combines the discussion of the first and fourth requirements before addressing the other requirements.

1. Distribution of Stock or Securities of a Controlled Corporation

a. Property Distributed

Section 355(a)(1)(A) covers distributions to two groups, shareholders and security holders. Any distribution must be made to the shareholders and security holders in their capacity as shareholders or security holders and not as payment for services rendered or for some other reason. The distribution can be pro rata but does not need to be. The distributing corporation can require some or all of its shareholders to relinquish their stock. Because that is not a requirement, the transaction can be a spin-off, a split-off, or a split-up.

As we saw in Chapter 4, nonqualified preferred stock lacks the equity characteristics required for nonrecognition treatment. I.R.C. § 351(g)(2). Nonqualified preferred stock is also disqualified for § 355 purposes; it is not treated as stock or securities unless it is exchanged for nonqualified preferred stock. I.R.C. § 355(a)(3)(D).

The distribution must be of stock or securities in a corporation the distributing corporation controls immediately before the distribution. Control requires ownership of 80% of the voting power and 80% of all other classes of stock. I.R.C. § 368(c).

b. Amount That Must Be Distributed

The distributing corporation must distribute: (1) all the stock and securities it holds in the controlled corporation or (2) an amount of such stock constituting control within the meaning of § 368(c). If it retains any stock or securities in the controlled corporation, it must do so for a valid business purpose. It must establish that the retention is not part of a plan that has tax avoidance as a principal purpose. I.R.C. § 355(a)(1)(D).

If the distributing corporation does not control the other corporation, § 355 does not apply even if it distributed all the stock it owned in the other corporation. The amount of stock that must be distributed and the requirement that the corporation be controlled are separate requirements.

Example 10-6. PQR Corporation distributed to its shareholders all the shares it owned in STU Corporation. The distributed stock represented 85% of STU's only class of stock. This transaction met the distribution requirement. PQR distributed all its STU shares, and STU was a controlled corporation immediately before the distribution. If PQR had owned only 70% of STU's stock, the transaction would not have met the requirement. Although PQR distributed all its STU stock, it did not distribute stock of a controlled corporation. PQR owned less than 80% of the STU stock.

The discussion of tax consequences later in this chapter focuses on when and how the distributing corporation obtained control. Stock acquired in a taxable transaction within five years of the distribution is treated as boot for purposes of gain recognition. I.R.C. § 355(a)(3)(B). Because § 355(a)(3)(B) does not apply to § 355(a)(1)(D), the purchased stock is treated as stock for purposes of determining if the corporation distributed enough stock in the controlled corporation.

Example 10-7. VWX Corporation owned 90% of the stock of YZ Corporation. VWX distributed all its YZ stock in a § 355 transaction. VWX acquired 85% of the YZ stock 10 years ago; it purchased 5% of the YZ stock three years ago. The purchased stock does not jeopardize the distribution requirement.

The restriction imposed by § 355(a)(3)(B) relates only to taxable transactions. Obtaining control shortly before the distribution in a nontaxable transaction is permissible for purposes of both gain recognition and meeting the distribution requirement.

2. Not a Device for Distributing E&P

Section 355 strikes a balance between facilitating transactions that have a business purpose and preventing devices to bail out E&P. Transactions used principally as devices do not qualify for nonrecognition treatment.

Section 355 does not define "device." It provides only that a transaction not be used principally as a device for the distribution of the E&P of either or both corporations. I.R.C. § 355(a)(1)(B). Its only other provision relates to sales of stock or securities after the distribution. A sale or exchange does not necessarily mean the distribution is a device for distributing E&P. A sale or exchange fails the device test if it is made pursuant to an arrangement "negotiated or agreed upon" before the distribution.

Example 10-8. Angus and Bettina own all the shares of ABC Corporation. In addition to its operating assets, ABC holds liquid assets of $100,000 and has substantial E&P. If ABC distributes the liquid assets to Angus and Bettina, they report taxable dividend income.

Example 10-9. If ABC instead transferred the liquid assets to a wholly owned subsidiary, DEF Corporation, and then transferred the DEF stock to Angus and Bettina in a purported § 355 transaction, it would have achieved essentially the same result as a dividend distribution—but Angus and Bettina would not be taxed until they sold their DEF stock or received a distribution from DEF. If they sold their DEF stock, they would have converted ordinary dividend income into potential capital gain. The transfer to DEF, followed by a distribution of its stock, will likely be treated as a device. And, unless DEF had operating assets, it is unlikely it would satisfy the active business requirement.

a. Device Factors

The regulations provide for determining whether a device exists based on all the facts and circumstances. They list several device factors, nondevice factors, and transactions that are ordinarily not considered to have been used as devices; they also provide examples. Reg. § 1.355-2(d)(1)–(5); Prop. Reg. § 1.355-2(d)(1)–(6). These factors and transactions are discussed below.

1. Pro Rata Distribution

The first device factor is a distribution that is pro rata or substantially pro rata to the corporation's shareholders. Pro rata distributions have the greatest potential for avoiding dividend treatment because the shareholders' positions vis-à-vis each other and the corporation do not change following a pro rata distribution.

2. Subsequent Sale or Exchange of Stock

The second device factor is a sale or exchange of stock in either the distributing or controlled corporation following the distribution. The regulations divide this category into subcategories, which have different weights. For example, a prearranged sale or exchange is considered "substantial" evidence of device. A sale or exchange that is not negotiated or agreed upon in advance is merely evidence of device. The evidence of device becomes stronger as the percentage of stock sold increases or the period between the distribution and sale decreases. If the disposition is part of a reorganization that qualifies for nonrecognition, it is not treated as a sale or exchange. The stock received in the reorganization is treated as if it was the stock transferred. A sale or exchange of that stock might be evidence of device.

> **Example 10-10.** Catherine and Devin each owned 50% of the stock of GHI Corporation. GHI owned all the stock of JKL Corporation. GHI distributed its JKL stock to Catherine in exchange for her shares. GHI then merged into MNO Corporation, and Devin received MNO stock in the merger. These transactions should not be treated as a device for the distribution of E&P. All assets remained in corporate form.

A subsequent sale of stock received in a § 355 transaction, although evidence of device, is not necessarily fatal. There may, for example, be a business purpose related to the corporation's employees. In *Pulliam v. Commissioner*, T.C. Memo. 1997-274, a controlled corporation was spun off and 49% of its stock was sold by a shareholder to a key employee. Although the IRS asserted that the prearranged sale was substantial evidence of device, the Tax Court found that the transaction was motivated by the key employee business purpose. The Tax Court distinguished *Pulliam* in *South Tulsa Pathology Laboratory, Inc. v. Commissioner*, 118 T.C. 84 (2002), because state law had precluded a direct sale in *Pulliam*.

3. Nature and Use of Assets

The regulations indicate that the nature, kind, amount, and use of assets by each corporation immediately after the distribution is a relevant factor. There is evidence of device if assets that are not used in an active trade or business are transferred to the controlled corporation or retained by the distributing corporation. Such assets include money and liquid assets that are not related to the reasonable needs of the business. A determination of the strength of this device factor, if present, is made from all the facts and circumstances. Reg. § 1.355-2(d)(2)(iv)(B).

In Rev. Rul. 86-4, 1986-1 C.B. 174, the IRS ruled that a small shift in investment assets will be considered in determining whether device is present. In that ruling, a corporation engaged in the active conduct of two businesses was required to separate them. It transferred one business to a new corporation, along with investment assets not related to the new corporation's business. Although the investment assets represented less than 20% of the new corporation's total assets, the IRS held that the shift in assets should be considered in determining whether device is present.

Rulings regarding the device factor are very fact specific. For example, in Rev. Rul. 78-383, 1978-2 C.B. 142, the IRS permitted a transfer of liquid and movable assets to qualify for tax-free treatment under § 355 because the taxpayer was under imminent threat of nationalization in a foreign country.

A classic business purpose for a distribution is the incompatibility of two or more businesses within a single corporation. If, prior to the separation, one business was functionally related to the other business and the relationship continues following the separation, the transaction may be considered a device. Reg. § 1.355-2(d)(2)(iv)(C) provides that such a situation is evidence of device if one business can be sold without adversely affecting the other.

> **Example 10-11.** PQR Corporation manufactures widgets. Its wholly owned subsidiary, STU Corporation, is engaged solely in selling those widgets. PQR distributed all its STU stock to its shareholders. STU continued to sell PQR's widgets. PQR's business would not have been adversely affected if it sold STU. Because STU continued to engage in the same business activities, it is doubtful there was a good business reason for the spin-off. Under the regulations, this is evidence of device.

Prop. Reg. § 1.355-2(d)(2)(iv), issued in 2016, adds definitions and other requirements. It defines business assets, nonbusiness assets, and total assets. Business assets can include cash and cash equivalents held as working capital or required to meet exigencies or regulatory mandates. It computes a nonbusiness asset percentage based on the corporation's total assets. The larger the nonbusiness asset percentage, the stronger is the evidence of device. Prop. Reg. § 1.355-2(d)(2)(iv)(C)(1). The proposed regulation indicates that differences between the corporations' nonbusiness asset percentages is evidence of device. The strength of that evidence increases as the difference in percentages increases. However, unless other factors apply, this is not evidence of device if: (1) the difference is less than 10 percentage points or (2) the distribution is not pro rata and the difference is attributable to the need to equalize the value of the stock and securities distributed and the stock and securities exchanged by the distributees. Prop. Reg. § 1.355-2(d)(2)(iv)(C)(2).

Prop. Reg. § 1.355-2(d)(5) adds an additional device factor. Separations of nonbusiness assets from business assets are considered to have been principally used as a device even if there are nondevice factors or other nondevice facts and circumstances. This rule would apply if two conditions existed. First, the nonbusiness asset percentage was 66 2/3% or more for either corporation. Second, the corporations' nonbusiness asset percentages fell into any of three relative percentages: (1) either corporation's percentage was at least 66 2/3% but less than 80% and the other corporation's percentage was less than 30%; (2) either corporation's percentage was at least 80% but less than 90% and the other corporation's percentage was less than 40%; or (3) either corporation's percentage was at least 90% and the other corporation's percentage was less than 50%. The proposed regulation would not apply to distributions that would qualify for a dividends received deduction or to transactions not ordinarily considered to be a device.

b. Nondevice Factors

The regulations also discuss three factors that are treated as evidence of nondevice. The presence of any of these factors is evidence that the transaction was not entered into as a device for the distribution of either corporation's E&P. Reg. § 1.355-2(d)(3)(i).

A transaction undertaken for a valid corporate business purpose is evidence of nondevice. Business purpose has significance in two contexts. First, it is an independent requirement imposed by the regulations. Reg. § 1.355-2(b). Second, it is evidence of nondevice. The stronger the evidence of device, the stronger the corporate business purpose must be to counter the device factors. Reg. § 1.355-2(d)(3)(ii). In assessing the strength of the business purpose, the regulation considers the importance of achieving the purpose to the success of the business, the extent to which the transaction is prompted by outside factors beyond the distributing corporation's control, and the immediacy of the conditions prompting the transaction. These factors go to the heart of the business purpose requirement. Prop. Reg. § 1.355-2(d)(3)(ii) indicates that a business purpose that relates to separation of nonbusiness assets from one or more businesses or business assets is not evidence of nondevice unless the business purpose involves an exigency. The exigency must require an investment or other use of the nonbusiness assets in a business of either corporation.

A second evidence of nondevice relates to the corporation's ownership. It applies if the distributing corporation is publicly traded and widely held, and no shareholder directly or indirectly owns more than 5% of any class of its stock. Reg. § 1.355-2(d)(3)(iii). It is unlikely that a corporation with numerous, unrelated shareholders would act in collusion with them, so the potential for device is very low with a publicly traded corporation. The third evidence of nondevice relates to the shareholder receiving the distribution. A distribution to a domestic corporate shareholder entitled to a dividends received deduction is evidence of nondevice. Reg. § 1.355-2(d)(3)(iv). That deduction significantly limits the tax the recipient corporation would pay on receiving a distribution from E&P.

c. Transactions Not Ordinarily Considered Devices

The regulations list three distributions that ordinarily do not present the potential for tax avoidance. As the regulations indicate, "such distributions are ordinarily considered not to have been used principally as a device, notwithstanding the presence of any of the device factors...." Reg. § 1.355-2(d)(5); Prop. Reg. § 1.355-2(d)(6). The first factor relates to the absence of E&P. A distribution of stock in a controlled corporation qualifies if three requirements are met: (1) neither the distributing nor the controlled corporation had accumulated E&P on the first day of its taxable year; (2) neither corporation had current E&P on the date of the distribution; and (3) no distribution of property by the distributing corporation immediately before the separation would require recognition of gain resulting in current E&P for the taxable year of the distribution.

> **Example 10-12.** VWX Corporation, which had no current or accumulated E&P, conducted two businesses. It transferred one of those businesses to newly formed YZ Corporation and distributed the YZ stock it received to its shareholders. Each of the assets VWX transferred to YZ was worth less than VWX's basis for it. Because there were no E&P, this distribution would not be considered a device.

The other two distributions covered by this regulation involve distributions that would be treated as redemptions if § 355 did not apply. The distribution must satisfy the requirements of either § 302(a) (redemptions treated as exchanges) or § 303(a) (redemptions to pay estate taxes and administration expenses). This rule applies on an all-or-nothing basis. The distribution must satisfy that test for each shareholder who receives a distribution.

3. Active Trade or Business

a. General Requirements

The distributing and controlled corporations must each satisfy the active business requirements of § 355(b). I.R.C. § 355(a)(1)(C). This requirement buttresses the no device requirement. Active business assets are less likely than investment assets to be used as devices because moving active assets to a different ownership structure is rarely done without a business purpose. Prop. Reg. § 1.355-9(b) would require that each corporation's five-year business asset percentage be at least 5%.

We consider both corporations for purposes of this requirement, and we consider both pre- and post-distribution activities. The requirement can be satisfied if both the distributing corporation and the controlled corporation are engaged in the active conduct of a trade or business immediately after the distribution. It can also be satisfied if the distributing corporation's only assets, immediately before the distribution, were stock or securities in two or more controlled corporations. Each controlled corporation must be engaged in the active conduct of a trade or business immediately after the distribution. I.R.C. § 355(b)(1).

> **Example 10-13.** ABC Corporation, a holding company not directly engaged in an active trade or business, owned no assets other than the stock of two corporations, DEF Corporation and GHI Corporation, both actively engaged in a trade or business. For valid business reasons, ABC distributed its GHI stock to its shareholders. The active trade or business requirement is satisfied. Immediately before the distribution, ABC had no assets other than stock of controlled corporations that were engaged in an active trade or business immediately after the distribution. Following the distribution, ABC's assets are shares of stock of a controlled corporation engaged in an active trade or business.

Three pre-distribution requirements apply. I.R.C. § 355(b)(2)(B)–(D). The first pre-distribution requirement relates to the history of each active trade or business. The business must have been conducted throughout the five-year period ending on the distribution date. The second pre-distribution requirement applies to the acquisition of that business. If it was acquired in that five-year period, the acquisition transaction cannot have been a taxable transaction. If gain or loss was recognized when the business was acquired, and the acquisition occurred within five years before the distribution date, it does not satisfy the active trade or business requirement. The third pre-distribution requirement relates to acquisition of the corporation conducting the business. It must not have been acquired during the five-year period in a taxable transaction.

A corporation that is less than five years old can still meet these requirements. Section 355(b) looks to the business being conducted for the five years preceding the distribution. If that business has a five-year history and it was acquired in a nontaxable transaction (such as a § 351 transfer), the corporation can satisfy the five-year active business requirement.

The requirement that gain or loss not be recognized does not prevent a corporation from purchasing business assets during the five-year period. The business does not lose its five-year history because, for example, the corporation purchases additional machinery or replaces old machinery with new machinery. The business can add or delete products, increase or decrease capacity, relocate, expand, or make other changes unless the changes are so extensive as to constitute a new or different trade or business. Reg. § 1.355-3(b)(3)(ii), -3(c) Examples 6 & 7.

b. What Constitutes an Active Trade or Business?

Reg. § 1.355-3(b)(2)(i) treats a corporation as engaged in an active trade or business if it meets the requirements and limitations of Reg. § 1.355-3(b)(2)(ii)–(iv). First, a trade or business involves a specific group of activities being carried out by the corporation for the purpose of earning income or profit. The activities included in the group include every operation that forms a part of, or a step in, the process of earning income or profit. The group of activities must include the collection of income and the payment of expenses.

Second, the corporation must itself perform active and substantial management and operational functions. The corporation can satisfy the active trade or business requirement through the activities it performs even though some of its activities are performed by others. Two activities do not constitute the active conduct of a trade or business: (1) the holding, for investment purposes, of stock, securities, land or other property; and (2) the ownership and operation (including leasing) of real or personal property used in a trade or a business, unless the owner performs significant services with respect to the operation and management of the property. Excluding investment companies from active trade or business status prevents taxpayers from bailing out E&P. The restriction on investment companies applies even if the company has a sizable staff of full-time employees. A dealer in securities may, however, be engaged in an active trade or business. The reason for this distinction is that the dealer in securities does not necessarily hold the stock and securities for investment purposes. The dealer is engaged in the business of buying and selling stock and securities.

Although real estate is generally considered a passive asset, ownership of real property does not necessarily preclude active conduct of a trade or business status. If the owner of real property rents the property but provides significant services to its tenants, its activities may constitute an active trade or business. Significant activities would include providing maintenance and repairs, paying for gas, water, electricity, taxes, and insurance, advertising for tenants, and negotiating leases. Reg. § 1.355-3(c) Example 12.

c. Activities Performed by Others

Will a corporation be engaged in an active trade or business if its activities are conducted by employees of a related company? In Rev. Rul. 79-394, 1979-2 C.B. 141, the IRS treated a controlled corporation as engaged in an active trade or business even though its business activities were conducted by employees of related corporations. In the ruling, the controlled corporation reimbursed the other corporation, but, as clarified by Rev. Rul. 80-181,

1980-2 C.B. 121, such reimbursement was not controlling. The active trade or business requirement could still be met even if the controlled corporation did not reimburse the distributing corporation.

Another scenario involves the conduct of an active trade or business by a partnership. In Rev. Rul. 92-17, 1992-1 C.B. 142, the distributing corporation distributed the stock of its only subsidiary corporation, which had been engaged in an active trade or business. The distributing corporation's only remaining asset was a 20% interest as a general partner in a partnership. For more than five years, the distributing corporation's officers had performed active and substantial management functions with respect to the partnership. In addition, they regularly participated in the overall supervision, direction, and control of the partnership's employees in their performance of the partnership's operational functions. The IRS held that the distributing corporation was engaged in an active trade or business immediately following the distribution.

In Rev. Rul. 2002-49, 2002-2 C.B. 288, the IRS extended Rev. Rul. 92-17 to ownership of an interest in an LLC. In the ruling, the distributing corporation owned a 20% interest in an LLC that was taxed as a partnership for federal income tax purposes. The LLC owned several commercial properties, which it periodically refurbished as necessary. The distributing corporation, through its officers, performed active and substantial management functions with respect to the LLC's activities. They also participated in supervising the LLC's employees in their performance of the LLC's operational functions. The ruling held that the distributing corporation met the active trade or business requirement.

In Rev. Rul. 2007-42, 2007-2 C.B. 44, the IRS modified Rev. Rul. 92-17 in the context of another LLC. The later ruling held that the owner of a significant interest in the entity need not itself perform management functions if the entity performs them. If the corporation does not own a significant interest, it must perform active and substantial management functions.

4. Continuity of Interest

Reg. § 1.355-2(c) imposes a continuity of interest requirement. One or more original shareholders must continue to hold an adequate interest in each corporation. They do not have to have the same interest in each corporation. If, for example, a split-off occurred, one group of pre-distribution shareholders may retain an interest in the distributing corporation while another group receives an interest in the controlled corporation. The regulation includes several examples but does not specify a minimum ownership percentage.

5. Business Purpose

Reg. § 1.355-2(b) imposes a business purpose requirement. The principal reason for this requirement is to provide nonrecognition treatment only to distributions that are incident to readjustments of corporate structures required by business exigencies and that effect only readjustments of continuing interests in property under corporate forms. A transaction is carried out for a corporate business purpose if it is motivated in whole or substantial part by a corporate business purpose. Reducing federal taxes is not a valid business purpose. Shareholder purpose is also not a valid business purpose unless it is so coextensive with the corporate business purpose as to preclude any distinction between the two. In such a case, the transaction is carried out for a corporate business purpose.

The transaction must primarily benefit the corporation rather than the shareholders. If the distributing corporation is publicly traded, this is generally not a problem unless it has one or more significant shareholders and the transaction is undertaken to benefit them. If the corporation is closely held, a shareholder business purpose may be acceptable if it would ultimately benefit the corporation. The classic example involves warring shareholder groups: two groups of shareholders whose disputes are harming the corporation's business. Dividing the corporation would benefit both the shareholders and the corporation. Resolving this dispute would be a valid corporate business purpose even though it is coextensive with a shareholder business purpose. For example, in Rev. Rul. 2004-23, 2004-1 C.B. 585, the IRS held that a distribution that was expected to increase the aggregate value of both distributing and controlled corporations satisfied the business purpose requirement even though shareholders would also benefit.

Form is important. The regulation provides that if a corporate business purpose can be achieved through a nontaxable transaction that does not involve distributing the controlled corporation stock, and that is neither impractical nor unduly expensive, the distribution is not made for a corporate business purpose.

> **Example 10-14.** JKL Corporation conducts two businesses. Its directors believe that the two businesses are not compatible and that each business needs to have its own management team. If the IRS determines that JKL could achieve its goals by creating a holding company structure—transferring the businesses to separate corporate subsidiaries run by separate management—it might claim that the transaction lacks a valid business purpose. Reg. § 1.355-2(b)(5) Examples 3 & 4.

E. Tax Consequences of Qualifying Distributions

The tax consequences discussed in this section generally mirror those discussed in Chapter 8. That chapter covers gain and loss issues in more detail. This chapter focuses on tax consequences related to § 355. Section 355 transactions differ in one important respect from transactions discussed in that chapter. Both the shareholders and the distributing corporation are covered by the same Code section when § 355 applies.

1. Shareholder's Tax Consequences

a. General Rule

The shareholder recognizes no gain or loss if the distributing corporation distributes only qualifying stock of the controlled corporation. I.R.C. § 355(a)(1). It does not matter if the distribution is pro rata, if the shareholder surrenders stock in the distributing corporation, or if the distribution is in pursuance of a D reorganization. I.R.C. § 355(a)(2).

> **Example 10-15.** Distributing Corporation distributed all the stock of Controlled Corporation to its shareholders in a transaction that met the requirements of § 355. Amy received 20 Controlled shares in the transaction. She recognized no gain or loss on receiving those shares. It did not matter whether she surrendered any of her Distributing stock.

The shareholder allocates her basis for the distributing corporation's shares she held before the transaction between the controlled corporation shares received in the transaction and any distributing corporation shares retained. I.R.C. § 358(a)(1), (b). The allocation reflects the shares' relative values. Reg. § 1.358-2(a)(2)(iv).

> **Example 10-16.** Ellen had a basis of $100 for her Distributing Corporation shares prior to a § 355 split-off. She exchanged those shares for shares in Controlled Corporation. Following the distribution, Ellen had a basis of $100 for her Controlled shares.

> **Example 10-17.** Fred had a basis of $100 for his Distributing Corporation shares prior to a § 355 spin-off in which he received shares of Controlled Corporation. After the spin-off, Fred owned shares of both Distributing and Controlled. He allocated his $100 basis between the Distributing and Controlled shares based on their relative value. If his retained Distributing shares were worth 80% of the combined

value, his basis for the Distributing shares was $80. His basis for the Controlled shares was $20.

For purposes of computing basis, an actual exchange is not required. The shareholder is treated as if he surrendered the stock he retained in the distributing corporation and then received it back. I.R.C. § 358(c).

A shareholder who acquired stock in the distributing corporation in separate transactions probably owns stock with different bases and holding periods. To the extent possible, he allocates basis to the shares received in a manner that treats each such share as allocable to shares acquired on the same date and for the same price. If that is not possible, the allocation should minimize the disparity in the holding periods of surrendered stock whose basis is allocated to shares received. Reg. § 1.358-2(a)(2)(i); Prop. Reg. § 1.358-2. Chapter 8, Section H, discusses the allocation in the context of an acquisitive reorganization.

If the shareholder held his stock in the distributing corporation as a capital asset, any stock he receives takes a holding period that includes his holding period in that stock. I.R.C. § 1223(1). A shareholder who held § 306 stock will treat stock with a substituted basis as § 306 stock.

b. Stock That Does Not Qualify

Stock acquired by the distributing corporation in a taxable transaction within five years of the distribution is treated as other property and not as stock. I.R.C. § 355(a)(3)(B). Nonqualified preferred stock is treated as other property and not as stock unless it is received in exchange for nonqualified preferred stock. I.R.C. § 355(a)(3)(D). The § 351(g)(2) definition discussed in Chapter 4 applies.

c. Distributing Corporation Retains Stock in the Controlled Corporation

Section 355(a)(1)(D)(ii) permits the distributing corporation to retain some of the controlled corporation stock if it did not do so in pursuance of a plan that has tax avoidance as a principal purpose. Stock retained to pay debts of the controlled corporation or for any other reason approved by the IRS does not adversely affect the transaction's qualification under § 355. If stock is retained for the prohibited purpose, § 355 will not apply.

d. Shareholder Receives Stock and Other Consideration

If the shareholder receives both qualifying stock and other property, § 356 applies instead of § 355. With one exception, his tax consequences resemble those described in Chapter 8, Section H.3. The recognition rules for § 355 transactions differ because that section applies to both exchanges and distributions.

If an exchange occurs, as is likely in a split-off or split-up, the shareholder recognizes gain. Her gain recognized is the lesser of her realized gain or the amount of money and the value of other property received. An appropriate amount of her gain may be treated as a dividend if the exchange has the effect of a dividend distribution. The amount treated as a dividend cannot exceed her ratable share of the corporation's undistributed E&P. The § 318 constructive ownership rules apply in determining if the exchange has the effect of a dividend distribution. I.R.C. § 356(a).

> **Example 10-18.** Carla and her son Don each owned 50% of Distributing Corporation, which held all the stock of Controlled Corporation. For a valid business purpose, Distributing transferred all its Controlled stock to Carla in exchange for her Distributing shares. As part of the transaction, Distributing also distributed $100 to her. The $100 was taxed as a § 301 distribution because Carla constructively owned 100% of Distributing's stock by attribution from Don. I.R.C. § 318(a)(1)(A).

If a distribution occurs, as is likely in a spin-off, the amount of money or other property is treated as a distribution covered by § 301. It is a dividend to the extent of the corporation's E&P; any remaining amount is applied against the shareholder's basis; if basis is exhausted, the shareholder reports any additional amount as gain. I.R.C. § 356(b).

Any money or other property received in exchange for § 306 stock is treated as a distribution covered by § 301. I.R.C. § 356(f).

The shareholder does not recognize loss on either an exchange or a distribution. I.R.C. § 356(c).

> **Example 10-19.** Distributing Corporation owned 80% of Controlled Corporation for 10 years. It acquired the remaining 20% in a taxable transaction four years before the distribution. Distributing distributed all its Controlled stock to its shareholders. Ben received 10 shares of Controlled stock. Because Distributing acquired 20% of the Controlled shares in a taxable transaction, Ben treated two of the 10 shares he received as other property. The result would be the same if Ben had instead received money, nonqualified preferred shares, securities, or some other property.

The shareholder computes his basis for the qualifying stock he receives using the § 358(a)(1) basis rules: the basis of his original stock reduced by any money or other property received or loss recognized and increased by any gain recognized or amount treated as a dividend. His basis for the other property received is its fair market value. I.R.C. § 358(a)(2). His holding period for the qualifying stock includes his holding period for his original stock. I.R.C. § 1223(1). His holding period for the other property begins when he acquires it.

e. *Shareholder Receives No Stock*

If the shareholder receives only securities, money, or other property, § 355 does not apply to her. Her transaction is instead tested for redemption or dividend status under the distribution rules discussed in other chapters. Prop. Reg. § 1.355-1(e)(2). This rule applies even if she also makes a qualifying exchange of some shares of stock.

2. Security Holder's Tax Consequences

If a security holder receives stock or securities that do not exceed the principal amount of any securities surrendered, he recognizes no gain or loss. I.R.C. § 355(a)(1). His basis for the stock or securities received equals his basis for the securities he surrendered. If he receives securities with a principal amount that exceeds the principal amount of the securities he surrendered, the value of the excess principal amount is treated as money or other property. I.R.C. §§ 355(a)(3), 356(d)(2)(C). The security holder recognizes the lesser of his gain realized or the value of the excess principal amount; he does not recognize loss. I.R.C. § 356(b)–(c).

The security holder uses the basis rules used by shareholders and described earlier in this section. If his basis for stock or securities received reflects his basis for securities that he held prior to the § 355 transaction, and those securities were capital assets, his holding period for the stock or securities received includes his holding period for the securities he exchanged. I.R.C. § 1223(1). The only exception is for securities received that have a principal amount that exceeds the principal amount of the securities he exchanged. Because the excess principal amount is other property, that portion of the security received takes a fair market value basis and a new holding period.

A security holder who receives property attributable to accrued interest on a security reports the amount received as gross income. This rule applies even if he receives stock or securities in payment of interest owed him. I.R.C. § 355(a)(3)(C). The stock or securities received take a basis equal to their fair market value. Their holding period begins when they are acquired.

3. Distributing Corporation's Tax Consequences

a. Section 355(c)

The distributing corporation generally recognizes no gain or loss on any distribution of qualified property. The distribution must not be made in pursuance of a plan of reorganization. I.R.C. § 355(c)(1). Property is not qualified unless it is stock or securities in the controlled corporation. I.R.C. § 355(c)(2)(B).

The distributing corporation recognizes gain but not loss on distributing property that is not qualified property. It is treated as if it sold that property to the distributee at its fair market value. I.R.C. § 355(c)(2)(A).

> **Example 10-20.** Distributing Corporation distributed all the stock of Controlled Corporation and other appreciated property. Distributing recognized gain on the distribution of the other property but not on the distribution of the Controlled stock.

The distribution may include property subject to a liability that the shareholder assumes. Alternatively, the shareholder may assume a liability in connection with the distribution. In either case, the distributing corporation cannot treat the value of the property as less than the amount of the liability. I.R.C. § 355(c)(2)(C).

b. Section 355(d)

Section 355(d) is an anti-abuse provision that applies if there is a disqualified distribution. When considering it, focus on two definitions—disqualified distribution and disqualified stock. A distribution is disqualified only if there is sufficient disqualified stock in the distributing corporation or in the controlled corporation and only if the stock was acquired by purchase during the five-year period preceding the distribution. Reg. § 1.355-6 includes extensive discussion, exceptions, and examples, only a few of which are covered in this chapter.

1. Disqualified Stock

Stock in the distributing corporation is disqualified if it was acquired by purchase during the five-year period ending on the date of distribution. I.R.C. § 355(d)(3)(A). Although the term "purchase" can include any acquisition, there are exceptions. I.R.C. § 355(d)(5). One exception involves two characteristics—the taxpayer's basis for the property and the Code section applied to the acquisition. The first basis provision is for property in which the acquirer's basis was computed with reference to the transferor's basis. The second basis provision is for property in which the acquirer uses the § 1014(a) basis rules for property received from a decedent. If the acquiring shareholder used any of these basis provisions, the property was not acquired by purchase. The Code section provisions are §§ 351, 354, 355, and 356. If the property was acquired in a transaction covered by any of these sections, it was not acquired by purchase.

> **Example 10-21.** Amy transferred land and a building to Distributing Corporation four years ago in exchange for 75% of its stock. Boris transferred machinery to Distributing Corporation at the same time in exchange for 25% of its stock. Both transfers were covered by § 351. Distributing Corporation needed funds two years ago and sold stock to Carol. Don inherited Amy's stock in Distributing Corporation when she died last month. Don's acquisition was covered by § 1014(a). Only Carol acquired her stock by purchase.

One exception applies to the above rule. A transferor who acquired stock in a § 351 transaction is treated as acquiring it by purchase if he received it in exchange for money, marketable securities, or debt of the transferor. If, for example, Boris had transferred money to Distributing instead of machinery, he would have acquired his stock by purchase. If he had transferred money and machinery, only the stock he received in exchange for money would be acquired by purchase.

On the other hand, stock acquired in a substituted basis transaction is treated as acquired by purchase if the transferor acquired it by purchase. The acquirer is treated as acquiring it by purchase on the date the transferor acquired it. If, for example, Carol gifted her stock to her daughter Edna, Edna would be treated as acquiring it by purchase two years ago.

Stock in the controlled corporation is disqualified if it was acquired by purchase during the five-year period ending on the date of distribution. I.R.C. § 355(d)(3)(B). The definition of purchase that applies to stock in the distributing corporation applies to stock in the controlled corporation. Stock in the controlled corporation is also disqualified to the extent it is attributable to distributions on disqualified stock of the distributing corporation. Stock in the controlled corporation is also disqualified to the extent it is attributable to distributions on securities of the distributing corporation acquired by purchase during the five-year period ending on the date of the distribution.

Reg. § 1.355-6(b)(2)(iii) provides that stock is not disqualified if the basis acquired by purchase is eliminated. Basis is eliminated when it would no longer be used in computing gain or loss. For example, a parent corporation might liquidate a subsidiary in a § 332 liquidation. If it received stock of that subsidiary's own subsidiary, the parent would take the subsidiary's basis for that stock instead of its original basis for the liquidated subsidiary's stock. Its basis in the subsidiary's stock would have been eliminated. It does not matter if the parent purchased stock in the subsidiary less than five years before the liquidation. Reg. § 1.355-6(b)(3)(vi) Example 7.

2. Disqualified Distribution

A distribution is disqualified if, immediately after the distribution, any person holds disqualified stock in the distributing or controlled corporation that constitutes 50% or more of that corporation's stock. I.R.C. § 355(d)(2). We determine the ownership percentage based on either voting power or stock value. I.R.C. § 355(d)(4).

> **Example 10-22.** Distributing Corporation owned all the stock of Controlled Corporation and other assets. The Distributing stock was worth 52% of the two corporations' combined value. Distributing wanted to dispose of its Controlled stock without recognizing gain. Distributing sold 52% of its own stock to Purchaser. Shortly thereafter, it distributed all its Controlled stock to Purchaser in exchange for Purchaser's 52% stock interest in Distributing. The distribution to Purchaser is a disqualified distribution.

The result above would be the same if Distributing sold its stock to two purchasers. Section 355(d)(7)(B) treats two or more persons as a single person if they act pursuant to a plan or arrangement with respect to acquisitions of stock. If they are related (within the meaning of § 267(b) or § 707(b)(1)), they are treated as one person even if they did not acquire either corporation's stock pursuant to a plan or arrangement. I.R.C. § 355(d)(7)(A).

Section 355(d)(8) applies to indirect ownership, using a modified version of the entity attribution rules in § 318(a)(2). If an entity acquired stock by purchase within the five-year period, its owners and beneficiaries are treated the same way for any of that stock attributed to them. Section 355(d)(8) also applies to securities.

Reg. § 1.355-6(b)(3) allows otherwise disqualified distributions to qualify if they do not violate the purpose of § 355(d). It applies unless the distribution has the effect of increasing a disqualified person's ownership percentage or provides a disqualified person with a purchased basis. Example 10-23 illustrates a transaction that does not violate the purpose of this subsection. It is based on Reg. § 1.355-6(b)(3)(vi) Example 1.

> **Example 10-23.** Frank purchased 60% of the stock of Parent Corporation. Parent owned all the stock of Subsidiary 1 Corporation. Subsidiary 1 owned all the stock of Subsidiary 2. Less than five years after

Frank acquired the Parent stock, Subsidiary 1 distributed all the Subsidiary 2 stock to Parent in a spin-off. Even though Frank is a disqualified person, the distribution did not increase his ownership percentage.

3. Five-Year Period

The five-year period normally begins five years before the distribution date. It can extend even further back if the holder's risk is substantially diminished by options, short sales, special classes of stock, or other devices to reduce risk. The running of the period is suspended during that period. I.R.C. § 355(d)(6).

4. Effect

If § 355(d) applies, the § 355(c) nonrecognition rules do not apply to the distributing corporation. Instead, stock or securities in the controlled corporation are not treated as qualified property. In that case, the distributing corporation recognizes gain on the distribution. It does not recognize loss.

c. Section 355(e)

1. Background

Section 355(e) applies to the type of transaction involved in *Commissioner v. Morris Trust*, 367 F.2d 794 (4th Cir. 1966). That decision allowed a tax-free distribution of a controlled corporation followed by the acquisition of the distributing corporation. Facilitating the disposition of either the distributing or controlled corporation was deemed a valid business purpose.

In *Morris Trust*, the American Commercial Bank (a state-chartered bank) operated an insurance business. Its directors agreed to merge it into the Security National Bank of Greensboro. Because the national bank could not operate an insurance company, American Commercial Bank formed a new corporation (American Commercial Agency, Inc.) and transferred the insurance business to that corporation. American Commercial Bank then distributed the new corporation's shares and a cash dividend to its own shareholders (one of which was the Morris Trust). Following the spin-off, it merged into Security National Bank, which changed its name to North Carolina National Bank. The appellate court held that both the distributing and controlled corporations continued to meet the active business requirement even though the distributing corporation no longer existed as a separate entity.

The *Morris Trust* transaction does not appear to involve undue tax avoidance potential, especially as the merger qualified for nonrecognition treatment. But what if the distribution of the controlled corporation stock was followed by a prearranged stock sale?

2. *Distributions Covered*

Section 355(e) applies to a distribution that is part of a plan pursuant to which one or more persons acquires directly or indirectly stock representing a 50% or greater interest in either the distributing or the controlled corporation. I.R.C. § 355(e)(2). As was the case for § 355(d), we measure the 50% interest by either voting power or stock value. I.R.C. § 355(e)(4)(A).

> **Example 10-24.** Distributing Corporation distributed to its shareholders all its stock in Controlled Corporation. Both corporations had an active trade or business before and after the spin-off, there was a valid business purpose for the transaction, and the transaction was not a device for distributing E&P. Following the spin-off, an unrelated person acquired 60% of one of the corporations. The transaction is covered by § 355(e) if the acquisition was pursuant to a plan.

Section 355(e)(2)(B) presumes the existence of a plan if 50% or more of the stock of either corporation is acquired during a four-year period that begins two years before the date of the distribution. A taxpayer can rebut the presumption by establishing that the acquisition is unconnected to the distribution of the controlled corporation.

The regulations provide that the existence or nonexistence of a plan is determined based on the ultimate facts and circumstances. Reg. § 1.355-7(b)(1). Reg. § 1.355-7 includes numerous exceptions, safe harbors, and examples.

The regulations list certain facts tending to indicate a plan exists when acquisitions follow a distribution. For example, the distributing or controlled corporation and the acquirer may have discussed the acquisition, or a similar acquisition by a different person may occur after the distribution. The weight to be accorded such discussions depends on their nature, extent, and timing.

The regulations also list facts tending to show that a plan does not exist. If there was no discussion between the distributing or controlled corporation and the acquirer, this would tend to indicate that no plan exists. One of the safe harbors applies if an acquisition occurred more than six months after a distribution that was motivated by a corporate business purpose other than a purpose to facilitate the acquisition. In that case, the transaction is deemed not to be a part of a plan covered by § 355(e).

Section 355 is not limited to the actual distributing or controlled corporation. It also applies to predecessors and successors to those corporations. I.R.C. § 355(e)(4)(D). Temp. Reg. § 1.355-8T contains detailed definitions and examples.

3. *Exceptions to Section 355(e)*

Section § 355(e) does not apply if, following the completion of the plan, both corporations are members of a single affiliated group. Because both corporations are part of the same group, the tax-free bailout potential is eliminated. I.R.C. § 355(e)(2)(C). Section 355(e) also does not apply if the transaction is covered by § 355(d). I.R.C. § 355(e)(2)(D). Distributions made in a title 11 proceeding are also exempt. I.R.C. § 355(e)(4)(B).

4. *Effect*

If § 355(e) applies, the § 355(c) nonrecognition rules do not apply to the distributing corporation. Instead, stock or securities in the controlled corporation are not treated as qualified property. In that case, the distributing corporation recognizes gain on the distribution. It does not recognize loss.

d. *Section 355(f)–(h)*

Section 355(f) expands the reach of § 355(e) to transactions involving affiliated groups. Section 355 does not apply to the distribution of stock from one member of an affiliated group to another if the distribution is part of a plan described in § 355(e)(2)(A)(ii).

Section 355(g) applies if two conditions are met. First, after the transaction either the distributing or controlled corporation is a disqualified investment corporation. Second, any person holds, immediately after the transaction, a 50% or greater interest in any disqualified investment corporation and did not hold such an interest in that corporation immediately before the transaction. I.R.C. § 355(g)(1). A distributing or controlled corporation is a "disqualified investment corporation" if the value of its investment assets is 2/3 or more of the value of all its assets. I.R.C. § 355(g)(2). Section 355 does not apply to distributions that are part of transactions covered by § 355(g). Section 355 also does not apply to distributions if either corporation is a real estate investment trust. I.R.C. § 355(h). Limited exceptions apply for certain spin-offs.

e. *Distributions in D/355 Transactions*

If the distributing corporation transfers assets before distributing stock in the controlled corporation, the transfer may qualify as a D reorganization. In that situation, § 361(a) applies to the distributing corporation. It recognizes no gain or loss if it receives stock or securities in another party to the reorganization in exchange for property. It can distribute the stock it receives without gain recognition. I.R.C. § 361(c).

Section 357(c) is relevant if the distributing corporation transfers encumbered property in a D reorganization and then distributes the controlled corporation's stock or securities in a transaction covered by § 355. If the liabilities assumed exceed the total adjusted bases of the property transferred in the exchange, the excess liability amount is treated as gain from the sale or exchange of property. Section 357(c) does not apply to a liability whose payment would give rise to a deduction. It does apply to the extent the incurrence of the liability results in the creation of, or an increase in, the basis of property.

f. Tax Attributes

The treatment of the distributing corporation's E&P depends on whether the distribution was a D/355 transaction. If it was, the distributing corporation's E&P account is divided between it and the controlled corporation based on the value of each corporation's business. Reg. § 1.312-10(a). If the distributing corporation had an E&P deficit, the controlled corporation cannot participate in that deficit. In this sense, the controlled corporation is given a clean slate.

If the controlled corporation was formed and operating prior to the distribution, or was not otherwise part of a D/355 transaction, we determine its E&P under Reg. § 1.312-10(b). We decrease the distributing corporation's E&P by the lesser of: (1) the decrease that would have occurred if the stock had been transferred in the D reorganization; or (2) the amount by which the basis of the controlled corporation's assets (including money) exceeds its liabilities. The controlled corporation's E&P will be the greater of: (1) its E&P prior to the distribution; or (2) the amount of the decrease in the distributing corporation's E&P.

Tax attributes other than E&P generally remain with the distributing corporation. The exceptions provided by § 381, which permit transferring listed tax attributes among corporations in certain transactions, are generally limited to D reorganizations that qualify under § 354. I.R.C. § 381(a)(flush language).

4. Controlled Corporation's Tax Consequences

Controlled corporations are normally passive participants in § 355 transactions. Nevertheless, the controlled corporation does have tax consequences.

If the transaction is a D/355 transaction, the controlled corporation recognizes no gain or loss on receiving the distributing corporation's assets. This transfer qualifies for nonrecognition treatment under § 368(a)(1)(D), and the controlled corporation is a party to the reorganization.

The controlled corporation's basis for its assets held before the transaction does not change. Its basis for assets received from the distributing corporation in a § 351 transaction or a D reorganization is the same as it was in the hands of the distributing corporation, increased by any gain that corporation recognized. I.R.C. § 362. The distributing corporation's E&P are divided between it and the controlled corporation as described in the discussion of the distributing corporation's tax attributes.

F. Taxable Divisions

If the transaction does not meet the § 355 requirements for nonrecognition, it is taxable. Although the distributing corporation and its shareholders recognize gain or loss, § 1032 protects the controlled corporation from taxation to the extent it receives property in exchange for its stock.

The distributing corporation and its shareholders bear most of the burdens from a taxable transaction. The distributing corporation is treated as the seller in a taxable transaction. The controlled corporation's stock is the property being sold.

The distributing corporation's shareholders are taxed on either a § 301 distribution or a § 302(a) redemption. If the transaction is a § 301 distribution and there is adequate E&P, they report the value of the controlled corporation stock they receive as a taxable dividend. If the transaction is instead treated as treated as a redemption, they report taxable gain to the extent the value of what they receive exceeds their basis for their stock. In either case, the basis of the controlled corporation stock they receive is its value.

Section 381 does not provide for transferring tax attributes in a taxable transaction.

Checkpoints

- Spin-offs, split-offs, and split-ups are the major types of § 355 transactions.
- So long as 80% or more of the stock of a controlled corporation is distributed and the other § 355 requirements are met, the transaction qualifies for nonrecognition.
- Congress's main concern in enacting § 355 was preventing taxpayers from using a tax-free distribution as a device for avoiding shareholder-level tax on undistributed E&P.
- Device is determined based on the facts and circumstances of each case. Pro rata distributions, subsequent sales or exchanges of stock, and nonbusiness uses of corporate assets are evidence of device.
- Evidence of nondevice includes the presence of a corporate business purpose, a distribution made by a publicly traded distributing corporation, and a distribution made to a domestic corporation.

- A § 355 transaction that is undertaken for a corporate business purpose will likely qualify for nonrecognition. A corporate business purpose can coexist with a shareholder business purpose so long as the transaction is motivated by the corporate business purpose.
- Either continuing shareholders or former shareholders of the distributing corporation must continue to hold an interest in the controlled corporation. The continuity of business enterprise requirement is subsumed into the active trade or business requirement.
- Both distributing and controlled corporations must be engaged in an active trade or business. A trade or business will be considered active if it involves significant managerial and operational activities.
- Section 355 will not apply to the distributing corporation if 50% or more of the stock of the distributing or controlled corporation was acquired by purchase within the five-year period ending on the distribution date.
- If a distribution is made pursuant to a plan for the acquisition of the stock of the controlled or distributing corporation, § 355 will not apply to the distributing corporation.
- If a transaction qualifies under § 355, no gain or loss will be recognized, the basis of the stock received will generally mirror the basis of the stock exchanged in the transaction, and the shareholder will retain whatever holding period she had in the exchanged stock.
- If a D/355 transaction occurs, the distributing corporation must meet the requirements of §§ 355 and 368(a)(1)(D).

Chapter 11

Liquidations

Roadmap

- Complete liquidation
- Liquidation of subsidiary corporation
- Liquidation of corporation that is not a subsidiary
- Hybrid disposition provisions

A. Chapter Overview

At some point, the corporation may cease operating. Perhaps its business is no longer profitable. Perhaps its shareholder-employees have no identified successors and simply want to invest elsewhere. Perhaps they received an offer they consider too good to ignore.

The events leading to the liquidation may affect how it is carried out. For example, the corporation might sell its assets to a third party and distribute the proceeds to its shareholders. It might instead distribute its assets to its shareholders and let them decide which to sell or retain. It might sell some assets and distribute others (along with the proceeds from those it sold). The corporation, its shareholders, and any purchaser of corporate assets must then determine relevant gain, loss, and basis for acquired assets.

This chapter discusses two types of complete liquidation: a liquidation by a corporation that is a subsidiary of another corporation and a liquidation by a corporation that is not a subsidiary of another corporation.

B. Complete Liquidation

A corporation liquidates for tax purposes when it ceases to be a going concern and its activities are merely for winding up affairs, paying its debts, and distributing any remaining assets to its shareholders. The liquidation is generally accompanied by a formal plan. An informal plan may be found to exist when the shareholders or directors manifest the intent to liquidate.

A complete liquidation differs from the partial liquidation described in the discussion of redemptions. The corporation continues operating after a partial liquidation, albeit with fewer assets. A complete liquidation also differs from the reorganizations discussed in the immediately preceding chapters. Reorganizations involve the transfer of assets (or stock) in exchange for specific types of consideration (usually voting stock), adherence to any required formalities (such as state law merger requirements), or transfer of substantially all the corporation's assets.

C. Liquidation of Subsidiary Corporation

Section 332 applies when a subsidiary corporation distributes property to its parent as part of a complete liquidation. The distribution must satisfy requirements related to control, period for completion, and plan. If it does, neither corporation recognizes gain or loss with respect to assets the subsidiary distributes to its parent.

1. Requirements

a. Control

The parent corporation must own at least 80% of both the voting power and stock value of the corporation being liquidated. The definition in § 1504(a)(2) applies in determining control for this purpose. It excludes certain preferred stock from the definition of stock. The excluded stock has no voting rights; it is limited and preferred as to dividends and does not participate in corporate growth to any significant extent; its redemption and liquidation rights do not exceed the stock's issue rights (other than for a reasonable redemption or liquidation premium); and it is not convertible into other stock.

The corporate parent must own a controlling stock interest from the date of the plan's adoption until the liquidation is complete.

> **Example 11-1.** DEF Corporation has one class of stock outstanding. ABC Corporation owns 79% of the DEF shares. Alice owns the other 21%. ABC does not satisfy the 80% voting power and 80% stock value requirement. The fact that it may have effective control of DEF does not matter.

> **Example 11-2.** JKL Corporation has two classes of stock outstanding. GHI Corporation owns all the JKL voting common stock. Bradley

owns all the JKL nonvoting preferred stock. We ignore Bradley's stock in testing whether GHI meets the voting power and stock value requirements. GHI satisfies the 80% voting power and 80% stock value requirements.

Example 11-3. PQR Corporation has one class of stock outstanding. MNO Corporation initially owned 79% of the PQR shares. Clara owned the remaining 21%. Six months after PQR adopted a plan of liquidation, MNO purchased some of Clara's shares and became an 85% owner. MNO does not satisfy the ownership requirement because it did not own 80% of the PQR stock on the date of the plan's adoption.

Example 11-4. VWX Corporation has one class of stock outstanding. STU Corporation initially owned 85% of the VWX shares. Dennis owned the other 15%. Six months after VWX adopted a plan of liquidation, STU sold one-half of its VWX shares to Ellen. STU does not satisfy the ownership requirement because it did not continue to hold at least 80% of the VWX stock through the date of liquidation. If STU had instead sold no more than 5% of the VWX shares, § 332 could still apply.

b. Period for Completing the Liquidation

Timing requirements apply to the adoption of the plan and the completion of the liquidation. Any distribution must meet one of two alternatives.

The distribution in liquidation must be in complete cancellation or redemption of the liquidating corporation's stock, and the transfer of all its property must occur within one taxable year. Reg. § 1.332-3. If this requirement is met, § 332(b)(2) provides that the shareholder resolution authorizing the distribution is treated as a plan of liquidation even if the resolution fails to specify a completion date. Note that the Code section refers to "the" taxable year, while the regulation refers to "one" taxable year.

Alternatively, the distribution must be one of a series of distributions pursuant to a plan of liquidation. The plan must provide that the transfer of property will be completed within three years from the end of the taxable year in which the first distribution under the plan occurs. I.R.C. § 332(b)(3). If the liquidation is not completed within a single taxable year, the IRS can require the liquidating corporation to post a bond, file a waiver of the statute of limitations, or both. I.R.C. § 332(b)(flush language). This protects the government's right to assess and collect the tax if the liquidation ultimately fails to meet the statute's requirements.

Example 11-5. ABC Corporation has one class of stock outstanding. YZ Corporation owns 85% of the ABC shares. Fred owns the other

15%. In Year 1, ABC adopted a plan of liquidation calling for the distribution of its property no later than three years from the close of the year in which the first distribution occurred. ABC made its first distribution in Year 2. Distributions to YZ qualify so long as all distributions are made by the end of Year 5 and YZ continues to meet the 80% ownership requirement.

Example 11-6. If ABC does not complete the distributions until Year 6, none of the distributions qualifies. Any distributions to YZ in Years 2, 3, 4, and 5 are retroactively disqualified.

Example 11-7. If YZ reduces its ownership below 80% before receiving its final distribution, none of the distributions qualifies even if ABC completes the liquidation by the end of Year 5.

The corporation need not formally dissolve or distribute all its assets to qualify the liquidation. It can retain a nominal amount of assets for the sole purpose of preserving its legal existence. Reg. § 1.332-2(c).

c. Plan of Liquidation

Section 332 requires the adoption of a plan of liquidation. As noted above, a shareholder resolution is treated as a plan if all distributions occur within a single taxable year. Even if the distributions take longer, and satisfy the three-year requirement, the plan need only meet the § 332(b) requirements. A distribution that satisfies these requirements qualifies even if it is not characterized as a distribution or liquidation under the applicable state corporate law. I.R.C. § 332(b)(flush language); Reg. § 1.332-2(d).

2. Liquidating Corporation's Tax Consequences

The liquidating corporation's stock might be 100% owned by a single corporate shareholder. Alternatively, the liquidating corporation may have more than one shareholder, one of which is a corporation that meets the 80% ownership requirements. If the liquidating corporation is indebted to a shareholder, it may distribute property in satisfaction of that debt instead of repaying the debt with money. The identity of the shareholders receiving distributions, and the existence of indebtedness, affect the liquidating corporation's tax consequences.

a. Distributions to 80% Corporate Parent

The liquidating corporation recognizes no gain or loss on distributions to its corporate parent, referred to as the "80-percent distributee." I.R.C. § 337(a). If the liquidating corporation is indebted to the 80-percent distributee on the date of the plan's adoption, transfers of property to satisfy that debt are treated as distributions in the liquidation. I.R.C. § 337(b). The liquidating corporation does not recognize gain or loss on those transfers.

> **Example 11-8.** DEF Corporation owned 90% of the stock (by voting power and value) of GHI Corporation. GHI adopted a plan of liquidation in Year 1 and began winding down its operations. During Year 2, DEF made a loan to GHI so that GHI could pay its rent. If GHI later distributes appreciated property to DEF to repay the loan, GHI recognizes gain on that distribution. The debt to DEF did not exist when the plan of liquidation was adopted.

Exceptions to this general rule apply to distributions to certain tax-exempt distributees, distributions to foreign corporations, and distributions of U.S. real property interests by foreign corporations. Reg. § 1.337-1. Section 337(d) calls for regulations that prevent circumvention of the repeal of the *General Utilities* doctrine through use of any Code or regulation provision or through the use of real estate investment trusts, regulated investment companies, or tax-exempt entities. In June 2016, the IRS issued temporary and proposed regulations carrying out this mandate in the contexts of §§ 337 and 355. Temp. Reg. § 1.337(d)-7T. This regulation was identified in Notice 2017-38, 2017-30 I.R.B. 147, as one that may be modified or withdrawn to reduce regulatory burden.

b. Distributions to Minority Shareholders

Distributions of appreciated property to minority shareholders are generally subject to § 336(a), which provides for gain recognition. The liquidating corporation cannot recognize a loss if the property it distributes to them is worth less than its basis. I.R.C. § 336(d)(3). This section provides less favorable treatment for distributions to minority shareholders in a liquidation described in § 332 than in a liquidation described in § 331. If this rule did not exist, the liquidating corporation might distribute its gain properties to its parent and its loss properties to the minority shareholders, thus avoiding recognition of the gain while being allowed to deduct the loss.

> **Example 11-9.** MNO Corporation has two shareholders. JKL Corporation owns 90% of MNO's stock. Gloria owns the remaining 10%. MNO owns two assets. Asset 1 has a basis of $10,000 and is worth $15,000. Asset 2 has a basis of $160,000 and is worth $135,000. If MNO distributes Asset 1 to Gloria and Asset 2 to JKL, it recognizes $5,000 gain on Asset 1; it recognizes none of its $25,000 loss on Asset 2. Section 336(a) applies to the distribution to Gloria; § 337(a) applies to the distribution to JKL Corporation.

Example 11-10. STU Corporation has two shareholders. PQR Corporation owns 90% of STU's stock. Harold owns the remaining 10%. STU owns two assets. Asset 1 has a basis of $10,000 and is worth $15,000. Asset 2 has a basis of $160,000 and is worth $135,000. If STU distributes Asset 1 and Asset 2 pro rata to PQR and Harold, it recognizes $500 gain on Asset 1 (10% of its gain); it recognizes none of its $25,000 loss on Asset 2. Section 336(a) applies to 10% of Asset 1; § 336(d)(3) applies to 10% of Asset 2; and § 337(a) applies to 90% of each asset.

3. Corporate Parent's Tax Consequences

a. *Gain or Loss Recognized*

The parent corporation recognizes no gain or loss when it receives a distribution with respect to its stock in complete liquidation. I.R.C. § 332(a). This rule applies whether there is a single distribution or a series of distributions. Limited exceptions apply. Section 332(c) applies special rules to distributions from regulated investment companies and real estate investment trusts, and § 332(d) covers distributions by certain domestic holding companies to foreign corporations.

Section 332(a) does not apply to distributions the parent receives in exchange for liabilities owed it by the liquidating corporation. Reg. § 1.332-7. If the indebtedness is satisfied for an amount equal to the parent's basis, there is no gain or loss to recognize. But if the indebtedness is a security issued at a discount or a premium, the parent may realize gain or loss when it receives the obligation's face amount. Although the corporations are related, § 267(a)(1) does not prevent the parent from deducting a loss realized on satisfaction of the indebtedness. This section contains an exception for distributions in complete liquidation. Recognition applies only to the corporate parent. The subsidiary corporation recognizes no gain or loss if it uses property other than money to retire debt existing at the time of the plan's adoption.

If the subsidiary's stock is completely worthless, the parent deducts a loss from a worthless security. I.R.C. § 165(g); Reg. § 1.332-2(b). If § 165(g)(3) applies, the loss is ordinary rather than capital. That provision applies if more than 90% of the subsidiary's aggregate gross receipts for all taxable years came from sources other than royalties, rents, dividends, interest, annuities, and gains from the sale of stock or securities.

b. *Basis and Holding Period for Property Received*

The corporate parent usually takes the distributing corporation's basis for property it receives in the liquidation. I.R.C. § 334(b)(1). This rule applies to property distributed in exchange for the parent's stock or in exchange for any indebtedness to the parent in existence on the date of adoption of the plan of liquidation.

The corporate parent inherits the subsidiary's inside basis for its assets and other tax attributes. Its outside basis for its stock in the subsidiary is eliminated. Depending on which basis is higher (the parent's basis for the stock or the subsidiary's basis for the property), this outcome may result in favorable or unfavorable tax consequences.

> **Example 11-11.** Parent Corporation owned all the stock of Subsidiary Corporation. Parent had a $100,000 basis for its Subsidiary shares. Pursuant to its plan of complete liquidation, Subsidiary distributed property to Parent. Neither corporation recognized any gain or loss on the distribution. The table below illustrates how differences between Subsidiary's basis for the property, Parent's basis for the stock, and the property's value affect tax consequences.

Scenario	Basis for Stock (Parent) or Property (Subsidiary)		Value of the Property	Potential Gain or Loss		Combined or Net Potential Gain or Loss
	Parent	Subsidiary		Parent	Subsidiary	
1	100,000	135,000	130,000	30,000	–5,000	25,000
2	100,000	135,000	115,000	15,000	–20,000	–5,000
3	100,000	135,000	122,000	22,000	–13,000	9,000
4	100,000	60,000	120,000	20,000	60,000	80,000
5	100,000	60,000	92,000	–8,000	32,000	24,000
6	100,000	60,000	60,000	–40,000	0	–40,000

In Scenario 1, Parent and Subsidiary had net gain potential of $25,000. If Parent sells the property, it recognizes Subsidiary's $5,000 loss.

In Scenario 2, Parent and Subsidiary had net loss potential of $5,000. If Parent sells the property, it recognizes Subsidiary's $20,000 loss.

In Scenario 3, Parent and Subsidiary had net gain potential of $9,000. If Parent sells the property, it recognizes Subsidiary's $13,000 loss.

In Scenario 4, Parent and Subsidiary had combined gain potential of $80,000. If Parent sells the property, it recognizes Subsidiary's $60,000 gain.

In Scenario 5, Parent and Subsidiary had net gain potential of $24,000. If Parent sells the property, it recognizes Subsidiary's $32,000 gain.

In Scenario 6, Parent and Subsidiary had combined loss potential of $40,000. If Parent sells the property, it reports neither gain nor loss.

Section 334(b)(1) provides two exceptions to the carryover basis rule. If either applies, the corporation's basis for that property is its fair market value on the date of distribution. I.R.C. § 337(b)(2). The first exception applies if the liquidating corporation recognizes gain or loss with respect to the property distributed. Gain or loss is recognized, for example, if the parent corporation is tax-exempt and won't be using the property in an unrelated business. The second exception limits the importation of built-in losses. It applies if the liquidating corporation is not subject to U.S. income tax, the recipient corporation is subject to U.S. income tax, and the aggregate bases of property described in § 362(e)(1)(B) exceed its aggregate value. Section 362(e)(1)(B) applies to property if gain or loss is not subject to tax while the transferor holds it and is subject to tax while the transferee holds it.

The corporate parent's holding period for property received in the liquidation includes the holding period of the distributing corporation. I.R.C. § 1223(2). That provision applies when a taxpayer's basis for property is computed with reference to another taxpayer's basis. If the distribution is subject to one of the exceptions described in the preceding paragraph, the recipient's holding period does not include the distributing corporation's holding period.

c. E&P and Other Attributes

The corporate parent assumes the liquidating corporation's E&P account. I.R.C. § 381(c)(2); Reg. § 1.312-11(a). If there are minority shareholders, distributions to them result in an appropriate reduction in E&P before the parent assumes the account. Reg. § 1.381(c)(2)-1(c)(2).

If the distributing corporation had a positive E&P balance, it is added to the parent's accumulated E&P but does not affect the parent's current E&P. If the distributing corporation had an E&P deficit, that deficit can offset the parent's post-distribution E&P. The deficit cannot offset the parent's E&P accumulated before the distribution. I.R.C. § 381(c)(2)(B); Reg. § 1.381(c)(2)-1.

The parent corporation also takes over other subsidiary attributes listed in § 381, including net operating loss carryovers, capital loss carryovers, and depreciation methods.

d. Liquidation as Part of a Reorganization

If a subsidiary corporation merges into its corporate parent, the parent might issue its own stock to any of the subsidiary's minority shareholders. In that situation, the parent receives all the subsidiary's assets even though it owns less than all the subsidiary's stock. Section 332(b)(flush language) provides that the receipt of this extra property does not prevent the entire distribution from being covered by § 332. Reg. § 1.332-2(e) includes an example of this type of transaction.

4. Minority Shareholder's Tax Consequences

The tax consequences of minority shareholders are the same as those described in the next section. It does not matter whether they are individuals, corporations, or other entities.

D. Liquidation of Corporation That Is Not a Subsidiary

1. Liquidating Corporation's Tax Consequences

a. Gain or Loss Recognized

The liquidating corporation recognizes gain on a liquidating distribution of property as if such property were sold to the distributee at its fair market value. I.R.C. § 336(a). It recognizes loss unless the limitations described below apply. I.R.C. § 336(d). The liquidating corporation computes gain or loss separately for each asset.

> **Example 11-12.** VWX Corporation owns two assets: land used in its business and stock held for investment. VWX purchased both assets more than one year ago. VWX had a $20,000 basis for the land and a $150,000 basis for the stock. Each was worth $100,000 at the time of VWX's liquidation. After adopting a plan of liquidation, VWX sold both assets and distributed the $200,000 sales proceeds to its shareholders in liquidation. VWX recognized an $80,000 gain on the sale of the land and a $50,000 loss on the sale of the stock. Its gain on selling the land was § 1231 gain. Its loss on selling the stock was a long-term capital loss. The results would have been the same if VWX had instead distributed its assets pro rata to its shareholders.

b. Effect of Liabilities

The corporation might distribute property subject to a liability, or its shareholders might assume a liability in connection with the distribution. In either situation, the property is deemed to have a fair market value at least equal to the amount of the outstanding liability. I.R.C. § 336(b).

> **Example 11-13.** Assume that VWX's land was encumbered by a $120,000 liability. Pursuant to its plan of liquidation, VWX distributed its assets pro rata to its shareholders, and they took the land subject to the debt. The fair market value of the land was deemed to be at least the amount of the $120,000 debt. VWX recognized a gain of

$100,000 on the distribution of the land instead of the $80,000 it recognized in Example 11-12. The tax consequences for distributing the stock are unchanged from that example.

c. *Loss Limitations*

1. Net Capital Loss

Despite the general rule of § 336(a), the corporation may not be able to deduct losses realized on property it distributes in liquidation. Section 1211(a) may limit or completely disallow those losses. It allows a corporation to deduct capital losses only to the extent of its capital gains. Because corporations can carry capital losses backward as well as forward, the corporation may be able to offset a net loss against an earlier net capital gain. I.R.C. § 1212(a).

2. Distributions to a Related Person

Section 267(a)(1) does not ordinarily prevent a corporation from deducting losses on distributions of property to a related person if the distribution is part of a complete liquidation. However, the corporation cannot deduct the loss in two situations: (1) the distribution is not pro rata; or (2) the distribution is of disqualified property.

A shareholder and the corporation are related persons if the shareholder has actual or constructive ownership of more than 50% of the corporation's stock value. The attribution rules in § 267(c) are used to determine constructive ownership. I.R.C. § 336(d)(1)(A).

Example 11-14. Irma owned 30% and Jack owned 70% of YZ Corporation's stock. YZ owned land worth $70,000 (basis of $100,000) and other property worth $30,000 (basis of $22,000). On liquidation, it distributed the land to Jack and the other property to Irma. YZ could not recognize its $30,000 realized loss because the property was not distributed pro rata. It does not matter that Irma received property worth $30,000 on which YZ recognized gain.

Example 11-15. Kate owned 60%, Lewis owned 20%, and Mary owned 20% of ABC Corporation's stock. ABC owned land worth $100,000 (basis of $20,000) and investment stock worth $100,000 (basis of $150,000). ABC also had $50,000 in a bank account. It distributed the stock plus the $50,000 to Kate and divided the land equally between Lewis and Mary. ABC recognized its $80,000 gain on distributing the land. Each shareholder received the appropriate total value, but the distribution was not pro rata with respect to the individual assets. ABC could not deduct the loss on distributing the stock to Kate. She and ABC were related persons and the distribution was not pro rata.

Property is disqualified property if the liquidating corporation acquired it in a § 351 transaction or as a contribution to capital during the five-year period ending on the date of the distribution. Property with a basis that is determined in whole or in part by reference to such property is also disqualified property. I.R.C. § 336(d)(1)(B).

Example 11-16. Ned and Olivia are brother and sister. They each owned 50% of the DEF Corporation stock. Ned and Olivia transferred a parking lot worth $120,000 to DEF as a capital contribution four years before DEF adopted a plan of liquidation. Their combined basis for the parking lot was $150,000. DEF could not deduct the $30,000 loss on the pro rata distribution to its related-party shareholders. Because DEF acquired it within five years of the distribution as a contribution to capital, the parking lot is disqualified property.

Example 11-17. Assume instead that one year after acquiring the parking lot, DEF exchanged it for an office building in a § 1031(a)(1) nonrecognition transaction. Because DEF's basis for the office building is computed with reference to its basis for the parking lot, the office building is disqualified property if DEF distributes it to its related-party shareholders during the five-year period.

3. Property Acquired for Tax Avoidance Purpose

If the liquidating corporation acquires property in a § 351 transaction or as a contribution to capital and a principal purpose of the acquisition is to create a recognizable loss, the corporation must reduce its basis for loss for that property. I.R.C. § 336(d)(2)(A). This is often referred to as an anti-stuffing provision because it might appear that the shareholders were "stuffing" the corporation with potential loss deduction property in anticipation of the liquidation.

Any property acquired by the corporation within the two-year period preceding the adoption of the liquidation plan (or after the plan's adoption) is treated as acquired as part of a plan to recognize loss. I.R.C. § 336(d)(2)(B)(ii). Regulations providing exceptions to this treatment have not yet been issued. It is possible that a taxpayer could convince a court that this provision should not apply if there was a business purpose for acquiring the asset in question and the liquidation was the result of unforeseen circumstances.

If the corporation holds the property until the look-back period expires, it avoids automatic treatment as a plan to recognize the loss. The distribution may still be challenged based on facts and circumstances.

To determine the amount of disallowed loss, the corporation reduces its basis for loss by the built-in loss on the date of contribution. The built-in loss is the excess of the property's basis over its value at that time. I.R.C. § 336(d)(2)(A). Losses attributable to further declines in value are deductible unless the related-person limitations described above apply.

Example 11-18. Patricia owned 80% and Quinn owned 20% of GHI Corporation's stock. Patricia transferred land with an adjusted basis of $100,000 (worth $75,000) in exchange for her stock; Quinn acquired his stock for money. One year after its formation, GHI liquidated and distributed the land to Quinn; it was then worth $60,000. Because GHI realized a loss on distributing the land, it reduced its adjusted basis by the $25,000 built-in loss, taking it from $100,000 to $75,000. GHI could deduct only $15,000 ($75,000—$60,000) of its loss.

Section 336(d)(2) also applies to sales and exchanges that occur in connection with the liquidation. When the sale occurred, the corporation's managers may not have known that the loss should be limited because no plan of liquidation had been adopted. Section 336(d)(2)(C) authorizes regulations letting the corporation recapture the loss as gross income in the year the plan is adopted instead of amending its return for the year the disposition occurs.

Example 11-19. Ruth owned 80% and Sam owned 20% of JKL Corporation's stock. On July 1, Year 1, Ruth transferred $90,000 and land with an adjusted basis of $100,000 (worth $80,000) in exchange for her stock; Sam acquired his stock for money. On January 1, Year 2, JKL adopted a plan of complete liquidation. On February 1, it sold the land to Tammy for $70,000. Because JKL sold the land at a loss in connection with a liquidation within two years of acquiring it, it is presumed that the property was transferred with the prohibited purpose. JKL had to reduce its adjusted basis for loss to from $100,000 to $80,000. It could recognize only a $10,000 loss on its sale to Tammy.

Example 11-20. Tess owned 15% and Umberto owned 85% of MNO Corporation's stock. On July 1, Year 1, Tess contributed land with an adjusted basis of $500,000 (worth $100,000) in exchange for her stock; Umberto acquired his stock for money. On December 1, Year 1, MNO sold the land for $100,000 to Vaughn and recognized a $400,000 loss. On July 1, Year 2, MNO adopted a plan of liquidation. MNO could amend its return for Year 1 and indicate that the built-in $400,000 loss should not have been allowed. If it did not amend its return, it would recapture the loss in Year 2 by adding $400,000 to its gross income.

4. *Effect of Section 362(e)(2)*

Chapter 4 addresses § 362(e)(2). That provision limits the corporation's basis for loss with respect to property received in a § 351 transfer to a controlled corporation. It applies only if the transferor's aggregate adjusted bases for property transferred exceeds the aggregate fair market value of that property. It differs from § 336(d)(2) in this regard; § 336(d)(2) applies to built-in losses on individual items of property even if there is not an aggregate loss. Thus, it is possible that § 336(d)(2) could disallow a loss that would not be disallowed by § 362(e)(2).

d. E&P Account

The corporation's E&P account is extinguished after the liquidation. It does not carry over to its shareholders even if it has shareholders that are corporations.

2. Shareholder's Tax Consequences

a. Gain or Loss Recognized

Section 331(a) treats any amount distributed in complete liquidation as an amount received on the sale or exchange of the stock. The shareholder computes gain or loss realized by comparing the amount distributed to his adjusted basis. I.R.C. § 1001(a). The difference between those amounts is treated as capital gain or loss if, as usual, the stock is a capital asset. The shareholder determines gain or loss separately for each block of stock he owns. Some gains or losses may be long-term capital gains and losses; others may be short-term capital gains and losses. The example in Reg. § 1.331-1(e) involves a shareholder who realized a long-term capital gain and a short-term capital loss.

The shareholder can deduct any realized loss, subject to the limitations of § 1211 if applicable, even if the corporation and shareholder are related persons. I.R.C. § 267(a)(1). If the stock is § 1202 qualified small business stock, an individual shareholder can exclude his realized gain. If the stock is small business stock described in § 1244, at least part of any loss may be ordinary rather than capital. Sections 1202 and 1244 are discussed in Chapter 1.

Shareholders do not have to receive liquidation proceeds in a single transaction. They can instead receive a series of distributions. I.R.C. § 346(a).

b. Basis and Holding Period for Property Received

The shareholder's basis for property received is its fair market value at the time of distribution. I.R.C. § 334(a). Her basis is not decreased by any liabilities she assumes or to which the property is subject. Her holding period does not include the time the corporation held the property.

E. Hybrid Disposition Provisions

Two additional provisions, §§ 336(e) and 338, are addressed in a later chapter. When § 336(e) applies, a parent corporation can elect to treat a sale, exchange, or distribution of the subsidiary's stock as an asset sale rather than as a stock sale and can do so without recognizing gain or loss. Gain or loss is recognized by the subsidiary because the election results in a deemed sale of its assets. Minority shareholders, if any, are not affected by the election. When § 338 applies to the purchase of one corporation's stock by another, the acquired corporation may or must (depending on the transaction) be treated as selling its assets and then repurchasing them. Both Code sections offer corporations the ability to limit the number of taxpayers that report gain attributable to the same assets.

Checkpoints

- In a subsidiary liquidation described in § 332, the subsidiary recognizes no gain or loss on distributions to the corporate parent. It recognizes gain (but not loss) on distributions to minority shareholders.
- The parent corporation recognizes no gain or loss and takes a carryover basis for any property received in the distribution. It also takes over the subsidiary's holding period for the property and assumes the subsidiary's E&P account.
- The parent corporation must own at least 80% of the subsidiary's voting power *and* stock value on the date the liquidation plan is adopted and until it receives the final liquidating distribution.
- If § 332 does not apply, the liquidating corporation recognizes gain or loss on distributions to shareholders in complete liquidation of the corporation. Capital loss limitations apply if the corporation has a net loss on distributing capital assets. Section 336(d) may disallow or limit the corporation's loss on certain distributions to related persons or on sales, exchanges, or distributions of property transferred to it for the purpose of generating a loss. The § 336(d) limitations have look-back periods for determining the property to which they apply.
- If § 332 does not apply, the shareholders recognize gain or loss, which is generally capital rather than ordinary. Their basis for property received in the liquidation is its fair market value at distribution. Their holding period does not include the corporation's holding period for the property.

Chapter 12

Carryover of Tax Attributes

Roadmap

- Section 381
- Section 382
- Section 383
- Section 384

A. Chapter Overview

After it acquires another corporation, the acquiring corporation must determine which of the acquired corporation's tax attributes it can (or must) use. In the appropriate context, the tax attributes covered by § 381 may be as important as a transaction's initial tax consequences. One of the more important tax attributes is a net operating loss (NOL), which can be carried back and forward to shelter otherwise-taxable income. To limit a profitable corporation's ability to acquire a loss corporation primarily (if not solely) for its NOL, Congress enacted the restrictions provided by § 382.

Although this chapter focuses on §§ 381 and 382, two other sections are relevant. Section 383 applies to carryovers of certain credits and of capital losses. Section 384 limits a corporation's ability to offset its losses by gains attributable to another corporation's built-in gains.

The provisions outlined in this chapter apply to liquidations of subsidiary corporations and to reorganizations. They involve terminology that is not covered in other chapters or is covered only in passing.

B. Section 381

Section 381 provides that an acquiring corporation inherits certain attributes that previously belonged to another corporation. It lists those attributes and provides conditions for (and limitations on) their use. In studying this section, focus on the acquisitions it covers, the attributes that the acquiring corporation inherits, and any applicable conditions and limitations.

1. Acquisitions Covered

Section 381 applies to two situations in which one corporation acquires the assets of another corporation: (1) liquidations of controlled subsidiaries covered by § 332; and (2) transfers in connection with A, C, D, F, and G reorganizations if the § 361 nonrecognition rules apply. If the corporation that distributed or transferred its assets had remained in existence, it would have retained its tax attributes. Rather than eliminating the attributes, § 381 transfers them to the acquiring corporation.

Two reorganizations do not involve transfer of attributes from one corporation to another. In a B reorganization, the acquiring corporation acquires the other corporation's stock rather than its assets. Because the acquired corporation remains in existence and continues to own its assets, it retains its attributes. E reorganizations are also excluded because they involve only a change in the corporation's ownership structure; the corporation otherwise remains intact.

As the § 381(a) flush language indicates, some D and G reorganizations are also excluded. Because D and G reorganizations can be divisive in nature, it may not be appropriate to transfer attributes to an acquiring corporation. Section 381 covers only D and G reorganizations that meet the requirements of § 354(b)(1). These are acquisitive D and G reorganizations. The acquiring corporation must acquire substantially all the transferor corporation's assets. The transferor corporation must distribute the acquiring corporation's stock, securities, and other property received (and its own remaining assets, if any) in pursuance of the reorganization plan.

2. Terminology

Section 381 uses two terms to describe corporations: "acquiring corporation" and "distributor or transferor corporation." Although it does not specifically define those terms, we can glean their meaning from the context. Section 381 applies when one corporation acquires the assets of another in the listed liquidations or reorganizations. The acquiring corporation is the corporation that acquires those assets. The distributor corporation is the subsidiary that distributed its assets to the acquiring corporation (its parent) in a § 332 liquidation. The transferor corporation is the corporation that transferred its assets to the acquiring corporation in a reorganization listed in § 381(a).

Reg. § 1.381(a)-1(b)(2)(i) provides additional information regarding the acquiring corporation. First, there can be only a single acquiring corporation. In a liquidation, the parent corporation is the acquiring corporation. In a reorganization, the corporation that directly acquires all the assets of a transferor corporation pursuant to a plan of reorganization is the acquiring corporation. This rule applies even if the transferor corporation's assets are ultimately split among several corporations.

> **Example 12-1.** ABC Corporation acquired all the assets of its subsidiary, DEF Corporation, in a § 332 liquidation. ABC is the acquiring corporation for purposes of attribute carryovers.

> **Example 12-2.** GHI Corporation acquired all the assets of MNO Corporation in a C reorganization. GHI then transferred those assets to a subsidiary, JKL Corporation, pursuant to a plan of reorganization. GHI remains the acquiring corporation even though JKL now owns all the MNO assets. The result would be the same—GHI is the acquiring corporation—if it transferred some of the assets to its subsidiary JKL and the remaining assets to a different subsidiary.

Example 12-2 illustrates a change in the regulation that was finalized in 2014. The regulation previously treated a corporation that ended up with all the assets as the acquiring corporation even if it did not directly receive those assets. The current rule applies to transactions occurring on or after November 14, 2014. Reg. § 1.381(a)-1(e).

A corporation that directly receives assets in a reorganization, and thus is treated as the acquiring corporation, need not use its own stock as consideration for the transfer. A corporation can effectuate a C reorganization using its parent's stock rather than its own stock. The direct recipient, not its parent, is the acquiring corporation. Reg. § 1.381(a)-1(b)(2)(ii) Example 1.

If a corporation that is not the acquiring corporation receives assets, it is not governed by § 381. If it acquires any of the other corporation's attributes, the authority will be a different Code section.

3. Operating Rules

Section 381(b) contains three operating rules that apply to transactions other than F reorganizations. F reorganizations are exempt from all three rules because they involve mere changes in form, name, or place of incorporation. There is no meaningful transfer of assets from one corporation to another.

a. End of Taxable Year

The taxable year of the distributor or transferor corporation ends on the date of the distribution or transfer. I.R.C. § 381(b)(1). It must file a short-year income tax return for the period ending on that date. If it remains in existence, it must file another short-year tax return. That return covers the period beginning on the day following the date of distribution or transfer and ending on the date on which its taxable year would have ended if there had been no distribution or transfer. Reg. § 1.381(b)-1(c).

b. Date of Distribution or Transfer

The date of distribution or transfer is the day on which all the properties of the distributor or transferor corporation that are to be distributed or transferred are distributed or transferred. If the distribution or transfer takes more than one day, the date of distribution or transfer is the day on which the distribution or transfer is completed. I.R.C. § 381(b)(2); Reg. § 1.381(b)-1(b)(1). The two corporations can instead elect to use the date on which substantially all the assets of the distributor or transferor corporation are distributed or transferred and it has ceased all operations other than liquidating activities. Reg. § 1.381(b)-1(b)(2). Both corporations' tax returns must include the statement language provided in Reg. § 1.381(b)-1(b)(3).

Even if the corporations do not make this election, the IRS can treat this day as the date of distribution if distribution of all the assets is unreasonably postponed after the transfer of substantially all the assets and cessation of business. Because the regulations do not define "unreasonably postponed," that determination will be based on the facts and circumstances behind the delay.

A corporation is considered to have distributed or transferred substantially all its assets when it ceases to be a going concern. It can retain assets to pay outstanding debts or preserve its legal existence. The latter retention is important because a corporate charter may have value. Reg. § 1.381(b)-1(b)(2).

c. Acquiring Corporation's NOL and Capital Loss Carrybacks

The acquiring corporation cannot carry back to a taxable year of the distributor or transferor corporation any net operating loss (NOL) or net capital loss for a taxable year ending after the date of distribution or transfer. I.R.C. § 381(b)(3).

> **Example 12-3.** PQR Corporation changed its place of incorporation by merging into newly created STU Corporation and then ceasing to exist. STU now holds all the PQR assets and is responsible for its

liabilities. PQR's shareholders became STU's shareholders. This merger qualified as an F reorganization. In the year following the merger, STU sustained a $100 NOL. Because the transaction was an F reorganization, STU can carry that NOL back to use against PQR's taxable income from a pre-merger year. In this situation, STU is PQR's alter ego.

Example 12-4. VWX Corporation merged into existing YZ Corporation, which assumed all the VWX assets and liabilities. VWX's shareholders received YZ stock. This merger qualified as an A reorganization. In the year following the merger, YZ sustained a $100 NOL. Because the transaction was not an F reorganization, YZ cannot carry that NOL back to use against VWX's taxable income from a pre-merger year.

4. Attributes Covered

Section 381(a) provides that the acquiring corporation takes the distributor or transferor corporation's tax attributes into account as of the close of the day of distribution or transfer. Section 381(c) lists those tax attributes. Each attribute represents a potential tax benefit or detriment or other characteristic that can affect the computation of taxable income. These attributes largely fall into two general types: those that relate to an amount (such as the amount of an NOL) and those that relate to accounting methods.

a. NOL Carryovers

Section 172 provides the NOL computation rules. The NOL has value only to the extent it can offset income of a non-loss year. If a distributor or transferor corporation ceases to exist, its NOL has value only if the acquiring corporation can use it to offset its own income. Although § 381(c)(1) allows the acquiring corporation to use the transferor's NOLs, it imposes limitations on that use. First, losses can be carried only to the acquiring corporation's taxable years that end after the distribution date. Second, in the first such year, a ratio applies to limit the amount of the acquiring corporation's income that can be offset. The numerator of that ratio is the number of days in the acquiring corporation's taxable year occurring after the transfer. The denominator is the total number of days in that taxable year.

Example 12-5. ABC Corporation acquired the assets of DEF Corporation in a C reorganization on April 30, Year 4. ABC's fiscal year ended on May 31, Year 4. DEF had an NOL carryover of $50,000. ABC had taxable income of $300,000 per year in each of Years 1 through

3. ABC cannot use DEF's NOL to offset taxable income for Years 1 through 3 because they ended prior to the transfer.

Example 12-6. ABC Corporation had taxable income of $200,000 in Year 4. There were 31 days in its taxable year after it acquired the DEF assets. Because that represented 8.493% (31/365) of the taxable year, ABC can use the DEF NOL carryover to offset $16,986 (8.493%) of its $200,000 Year 4 income.

It is possible that both the distributor or transferor corporation and the acquiring corporation sustained NOLs. In that case, we compute each corporation's NOLs separately so that loss carrybacks offset only income of the corporation that sustained the loss. Reg. § 1.381(c)(1)-1(a)(2).

The regulations address the sequencing of NOLs, the computation of carryovers and carrybacks when the date of distribution or transfer is not the last day of the acquiring corporation's taxable year, and successive acquiring corporations. There are extensive examples. Reg. § 1.381(c)(1)-1.

b. E&P

The acquiring corporation receives the distributor or transferor corporation's E&P (or E&P deficit) at the close of the date on which the transfer occurs. I.R.C. § 381(c)(2)(A); Reg. § 1.381(c)(2)-1(a). It is possible that both corporations will have positive E&P balances or E&P deficits. Likewise, one corporation may have positive E&P while the other has an E&P deficit. If either corporation has an E&P deficit, that deficit can offset only E&P accumulated after the transfer. I.R.C. § 381(c)(2)(B). A ratio like that discussed for NOL carryovers is used to compute E&P that can be offset in the year of transfer.

c. Capital Loss Carryovers

The rules applied to the distributor or transferor corporation's net capital losses are like those applied to its NOLs. The ratio that limits the carryover to the acquiring corporation's first taxable year ending after the transfer is based on the acquiring corporation's net capital gain income, not on all its income. The capital loss that is carried to this and future years is treated as a short-term capital loss of the acquiring corporation. I.R.C. § 381(c)(3); Reg. § 1.381(c)(3)-1.

d. Accounting Methods and Inventory

The acquiring corporation takes over the distributor or transferor corporation's accounting methods, including those used for inventory. I.R.C. § 381(c)(4)–(5). It is possible that the distributor or transferor corporation's accounting methods, including those for inventory, differ from those used by the acquiring corporation. It is also possible that the acquiring corporation will have received assets from more than one distributor or transferor corporation and that those corporations did not use the same accounting methods. In these situations, the regulations provide the appropriate accounting method rules. Reg. §§ 1.381(c)(4)-1, 1.381(c)(5)-1.

e. Depreciable Property

The acquiring corporation uses the distributor or transferor's depreciation method for property it acquired in the liquidation or reorganization. I.R.C. § 381(c)(6). One exception applies. If the acquiring corporation's basis for the property exceeds the property's basis in the hands of the distributor or transferor corporation, the acquiring corporation depreciates that excess separately. Reg. § 1.381(c)(6)-1(b).

f. Other Attributes

Section 381(c) applies to the following additional attributes: use of the installment method for reporting gain; amortization of premium or discount on bonds issued by the distributor or transferor corporation; treatment of mining development and exploration expenses; deductions for contributions to certain employee benefit plans; recovery of tax benefit items; involuntary conversions; dividend carryovers to personal holding companies; deductions with respect to liabilities that the distributor or transferor corporation could have deducted; deficiency dividends of personal holding companies; percentage depletion covered by § 613(c)(3); excess charitable contributions for the taxable year ending on the date of the distribution or transfer and the four prior taxable years; items related to a distributor or transferor insurance company; deficiency dividends of real estate investment trusts or regulated investment companies; credits covered by §§ 38 and 53; and provisions related to enterprise zones. I.R.C. § 381(c)(8)–(14), (16)–(19), (22)–(26).

C. Section 382

1. Comparison to Section 381

Sections 381 and 382 both limit the deduction for corporate NOLs, but they operate differently. Section 381 is essentially a timing provision. It allows pre-acquisition losses to be carried forward but not backward. Section 382 is an anti-abuse provision that targets "trafficking" in NOLs. It reduces or totally disallows deductions attributable to pre-acquisition losses.

The two sections also have different triggering events. Section 381 is triggered by corporate liquidations or reorganizations. Section 382, on the other hand, focuses on ownership change. Corporate reorganizations can trigger an ownership change but they do not necessarily do so.

2. Terminology

Section 382(a) limits the amount of the taxable income of any "new loss corporation" for any "post-change year" that can be offset by "pre-change losses." The limitation is referred to as the "section 382 limitation." These rules apply when there is an "owner shift" involving a "5-percent shareholder" or an "equity structure shift."

a. Loss Corporations

Section 382(k)(1)–(3) defines loss corporation, old loss corporation, and new loss corporation. A loss corporation is a corporation that is entitled to use an NOL carryover or that has an NOL for the taxable year in which an ownership change occurs. The term also includes any corporation with a "net unrealized built-in loss." A corporation is an old loss corporation if it was a loss corporation before it underwent an ownership change. A corporation is a new loss corporation if it is a loss corporation after an ownership change. A single corporation can be both an old and a new loss corporation.

b. Ownership Change

Section 382(g) determines if there is an ownership change immediately after any owner shift involving a 5-percent shareholder or any equity structure shift. An ownership change occurs if there is a sufficient change in a loss corporation's ownership percentage during a testing period.

The testing period is generally the three-year period ending on the day of any owner shift involving a 5-percent shareholder or an equity structure shift. I.R.C. § 382(i)(1). A 5-percent shareholder is any person who holds 5% or more of the corporation's stock at any time during the testing period. I.R.C. § 382(k)(7).

> **Example 12-7.** On Day 1, Year 1, Loss Corporation was owned by 100 individuals, none of whom owns more than 2% of its stock. If one shareholder purchased stock from another shareholder, the purchaser would end up with no more than 4% of the corporation's stock. Because Loss Corporation does not currently have a 5-percent shareholder, that transaction would not trigger § 382. The result would be the same if a current shareholder sold his stock to a non-shareholder.

Related persons cannot avoid this rule by spreading ownership among themselves in such a way that none of them is a 5-percent shareholder. Section 382(l)(3)(A) provides for using a modified version of the § 318 constructive ownership rules in determining stock ownership.

1. Owner Shift

An ownership change is deemed to occur if, immediately after an owner shift involving a 5-percent shareholder or an equity structure shift, the percentage of the loss corporation's stock owned by one or more 5-percent shareholders has increased by more than 50 percentage points over the lowest percentage of stock of the loss corporation (or any predecessor corporation) such shareholder(s) owned at any time during the testing period. I.R.C. § 382(g)(1).

Example 12-8. Arthur owns 40% and Belinda owns 60% of the stock of Loss Corporation. If Belinda sells her shares to Carl, an owner shift occurs. Carl's ownership increased from 0% to 60%.

Section 382(i) normally begins the testing period three years before the date of the owner shift or equity structure shift. Shorter periods apply when there was a previous owner shift or if the losses were all attributable to a period later than the beginning of the normal testing period.

Example 12-9. On Day 1, Year 1, Loss Corporation is owned by four individuals: Alan, 15%; Beth, 15%; Cam, 25%; and Dee, 45%. On Day 1, Year 2, Alan purchased one-third of Beth's shares. Immediately after that purchase, Alan owned 20% and Beth owned 10%. If no further changes occur, there has been no owner shift and, thus, no ownership change. Alan's ownership increased by only five percentage points.

Example 12-10. If Alan instead purchased all of Beth's shares, he would own 30% and she would own 0%. Although Alan's total ownership is 100% greater than it was in Year 1, no owner shift occurred. An owner shift requires that the ownership percentage increase by more than 50 *percentage points*. Because Alan began with 15% of the Loss Corporation stock, an owner shift would occur only if he ended up with more than 65% of the corporation's stock.

Example 12-11. Assume instead that Alan's ownership percentage began at 15% on Day 1, Year 1; changed to 25% early in Year 2; and changed on the last day of each year to these percentages: Year 4, 60%; Year 5, 66%. Although Alan's ownership increased by more than 50 percentage points, the increase occurred over more than three years. The increase during the testing period (from 25% to 66%) was an increase of only 41 percentage points.

An owner shift can be based on changes in the ownership of more than one 5-percent shareholder. I.R.C. § 382(g)(1). If one shareholder increases ownership from 10 percentage points to 40 percentage points, that would be a 30-percentage-point increase. If two shareholders both increase their ownership in this amount during the testing period, the increase from 20 percentage points to 80 percentage points (60 percentage points) will be an ownership change.

Not every owner shift is tainted. If it were, a loss corporation might be precluded from taking full advantage of an NOL merely because an owner died and devised stock to a family member. Section 382(l)(3)(B) treats the new owner as if he had the old owner's holding period when stock is acquired because of death (§ 1014), inter vivos gift (§ 1015), or divorce (§ 1041(b)(2)). This provision applies even if the recipient's basis is not determined under those sections. For example, if a decedent's personal representative distributes stock instead of money to satisfy a pecuniary devise, the devisee takes a § 1012 cost basis instead of a § 1014 basis; that stock is treated the same way as inherited stock.

2. *Equity Structure Shift*

An equity structure shift is defined as any reorganization except F reorganizations and divisive D and G reorganizations. I.R.C. § 382(g)(3). NOL carryovers are not limited unless the equity structure shift is accompanied by the more than 50 percentage point increase in stock ownership discussed above.

c. Pre-Change Loss and Post-Change Year

A pre-change loss is an NOL carryforward of the old loss corporation to the taxable year that ends with the ownership change or in which the change date occurs. The term also includes any loss the old loss corporation sustains in the taxable year in which the ownership change occurs, but it applies only to the portion of the loss allocable to the period on or before the change date. A post-change year is any taxable year that ends after the change date. I.R.C. § 382(d).

d. Change Date

The change date depends on whether the ownership change was an owner shift or an equity structure shift. If the last component of an ownership change is an owner shift involving a 5-percent shareholder, the change date is the date on which that shift occurs. If the last component is an equity structure shift, the change date is the date of the reorganization. I.R.C. § 382(j).

e. Built-In Gains and Losses

Section 382(h) applies additional limits when an old loss corporation has net unrealized losses. A corporation has a net unrealized loss when the fair market value of its assets immediately before the ownership change is less than its aggregate basis for those assets. If the value exceeds the basis, there is net unrealized gain. The new loss corporation's ability to deduct NOLs is affected adversely as it recognizes unrealized built-in losses; it is affected positively as it recognizes unrealized built-in gains.

3. Operating Rules

Section 382(b) limits NOL carryovers by a formula. When this section applies, the maximum amount of NOL that can be used in a post-change year is the value of the old loss corporation multiplied by the long-term tax-exempt rate. If that limit exceeds the new loss corporation's taxable income for the year, it can add that excess to the following year's limitation.

> **Example 12-12.** GHI Corporation became a new loss corporation on Date 1. It had never earned income for which its NOLs could be used as a carryback. On Date 1, GHI had a value of $100,000 and the long-term tax-exempt rate was 4%. As a new loss corporation, GHI's loss limitation is $4,000.

Section 382(l)(1) prevents taxpayers from increasing the loss corporation's value, and thus increasing the allowable NOL deduction. Capital contributions are ignored if they are made pursuant to a plan a principal purpose of which is to avoid or increase any § 382 limitation. Unless the regulations provide otherwise, contributions within two years of the change date are considered part of such a plan.

Section 382(c) disallows NOL carryovers altogether. It generally applies if the new loss corporation does not continue the business of the old loss corporation throughout the two-year period beginning on the change date.

Section 382 includes exceptions to disallowance. One exception applies to corporations involved in a title 11 (bankruptcy) or similar case. I.R.C. § 382(l)(5). A second exception applies to certain restructuring plans. Section 382(n)(1) provides that the loss limitation will generally not apply if an ownership change is pursuant to a restructuring plan that is required under a loan agreement or a commitment for a line of credit entered into with the Department of the Treasury under the Emergency Economic Stabilization Act of 2008. Losses of such entities will be available notwithstanding an ownership change. This exemption has two exceptions. Section 382(n)(2) makes the limitation applicable to subsequent ownership changes unless those changes are described in § 382(n)(1). Section 382(n)(3) makes § 382(n)(1) inapplicable if, after the ownership change, a single person owns 50% or more of the loss corporation's total combined voting power or of its total stock value. This provision treats related persons as one person in making this computation. It uses the § 267 definition of related persons. It does not apply if the person owning 50% or more is a voluntary employee benefit association.

Section 382 and its regulations contain numerous additional rules. The regulations include several examples.

D. Section 383

Section 383 imposes limitations with respect to excess credits under §§ 39 (unused general business credits) and 53 (credit for prior year minimum tax liability), net capital losses, and foreign tax credits. In general, taxpayers apply the § 382 rules to items covered in this section.

E. Section 384

Sections 382 and 384 complement each other. Section 382 generally prohibits the use of NOLs following the acquisition of loss corporations. Section 384 restricts the use of losses when a loss corporation acquires a gain corporation. If this section did not exist, a gain corporation could easily restructure an acquisition to make the loss corporation the acquiring entity. The effective result would be the unrestricted use of loss corporation NOLs by the gain corporation that had been subsumed under the loss corporation's umbrella.

Section 384(a) applies if a corporation acquires control, directly or indirectly, of another corporation. It also applies if a corporation acquires the assets of another corporation in an A, C, or D reorganization. It applies only if one of the corporations is a gain corporation. A corporation is a gain corporation if it has net unrealized built-in gains. I.R.C. § 384(c)(4). Definitions used in § 382 apply in determining if the corporation has net unrealized built-in gains on the acquisition date. I.R.C. § 384(c)(8). Instead of using the change date, we use the acquisition date in making these determinations.

Section 384 applies during the five-year recognition period following the acquisition date. I.R.C. § 382(h)(7). Section 384(b) provides an exception if the two corporations were part of the same controlled group. It generally defines a controlled group as corporations as to which more than 50% of the stock is commonly owned during the five-year period ending with the acquisition. This period is reduced if one or both corporations had a less than five-year existence.

Example 12-13. Loss Corporation purchased all the stock of Profitable Corporation and did not make an election under § 338. Section 382 does not apply because there was no change in Loss Corporation's ownership. Because § 384 applies, any of Profitable Corporation's recognized built-in gains within the five-year recognition period cannot be used on the corporations' consolidated tax return to shelter Loss Corporation's pre-acquisition losses.

Checkpoints

- Section 381 generally provides that certain tax attributes are not lost in a § 332 liquidation.
- Section 381 also applies to acquisitive reorganizations and F reorganizations.
- When § 381 applies, the taxable year of the transferor or distributor corporation ends on the date of the transfer or distribution.
- The acquiring corporation cannot carry back any NOLs of the acquired corporation when § 381 applies.
- Section 382 severely limits the use of the NOLs of a loss corporation after an ownership change.
- A loss corporation is a corporation that has an NOL carryover or a net built-in loss at the time of the ownership change.
- An ownership change occurs when one or more 5-percent shareholders increase their interest in the corporation by more than 50 percentage points.
- Section 383 applies the § 382 limitations to certain credits and to net capital losses.
- Section 384 imposes limitations when a gain corporation is acquired. In this case, income for any post-acquisition year (to the extent attributable to recognized built-in gains) cannot be offset by any pre-acquisition loss (other than a pre-acquisition loss of the gain corporation). Exceptions apply for corporations that were part of a controlled group.

Chapter 13

Taxable Acquisitions: Sections 338, 336(e), and 1060

Roadmap

- Background
- Section 338
- Section 336(e)
- Section 1060

A. Chapter Overview

Previous chapters focused on corporations that distributed money, other property, or even their own stock to shareholders. If the corporation received no consideration in exchange, the shareholders generally treated the distributions as taxable dividends or as nontaxable stock distributions. The corporation recognized gain, but not loss, if it distributed property other than money or its own stock. If the corporation received back stock in exchange, the transaction might qualify as a redemption, in which case the shareholder reported gain or loss with respect to the stock surrendered. The corporation reported gain, but not loss, if it distributed property other than money. If the exchange did not qualify as a redemption, the tax consequences mirrored those of a taxable dividend. Instead of continuing its operations in their present form, the corporation might engage in a reorganization that qualified for nonrecognition treatment. It might acquire, or be acquired by, another corporation. In either case, the shareholders and corporations involved recognized no gain or loss if the acquiring corporation transferred only consideration permitted by the reorganization provisions.

If a corporation liquidates, the tax consequences depend on whether the liquidation is controlled by § 331 or by § 332, both of which are covered in Chapter 11. That chapter focused on the tax consequences of the liquidation itself rather than on the tax consequences of selling the corporation's operating assets.

This chapter discusses situations in which a corporation sells its business assets as a group (§ 1060), which results in gain or loss recognition by the selling corporation and a fair market value basis for the buyer. Section 1060 is important because it imposes consistency rules on the parties' allocation of the selling price. Because it refers to the allocation rules in § 338, this chapter begins with that section. This chapter also discusses a provision (§ 336(e)) that allows a parent corporation to treat a sale, exchange, or distribution of a subsidiary's stock as an asset sale rather than as a stock sale and not recognize gain or loss. That provision's regulations also refer to § 338 for additional guidance.

When § 338 applies, the parties treat stock purchases as if they were asset acquisitions. The target corporation is treated as if it had purchased its own assets at fair market value. The target corporation's basis for those assets will then equal the acquiring corporation's cost for them. The target corporation may be taxed on the deemed sale of those assets. As discussed below, this section is elective, but some of its provisions are mandatory.

B. Background

Section 338 can be traced to two judicial decisions. *General Utilities & Operating Co. v. Helvering*, 296 U.S. 200 (1935); *Kimbell-Diamond Milling Co. v. Commissioner*, 14 T.C. 74 (1950). Because of the *General Utilities* doctrine, a corporation recognized no gain or loss on making a liquidation distribution to its shareholders. Congress repealed 1954 Code § 336, which codified that doctrine, in 1986. The *Kimbell-Diamond* decision provided that if a corporation acquired the stock of another corporation and liquidated the acquired corporation shortly thereafter, the combined transaction was treated as a direct purchase of the other corporation's assets. The acquiring corporation thus received a cost basis for those assets.

If *General Utilities* and *Kimbell-Diamond* both applied, one corporation could purchase the stock of a second corporation, liquidate it shortly thereafter, and take a fair market value basis for the liquidated corporation's assets. Neither corporation would pay tax on the pre-liquidation difference between the acquired corporation's basis for those assets and their fair market value. Because the *Kimbell-Diamond* doctrine involved the acquiring corporation's intent, taxpayers could claim they lacked the intent to purchase assets if direct purchase treatment did not provide tax advantages. For example, if those assets had a basis greater than their value, the acquiring corporation would prefer taking a carryover basis. To reduce taxpayers' ability to rely on intent, Congress enacted former § 334(b)(2), which provided a bright-line test. If the liquidation of an 80% subsidiary occurred within a specified time after the acquisition, the transaction was treated as an asset purchase. The acquiring corporation took a cost basis for the acquired corporation's assets.

Congress replaced former § 334(b)(2) with § 338 in 1982. This generally resulted in a single level of tax following a § 338 election because the *General Utilities* doctrine provided that the liquidating corporation recognized no gain or loss. Section 338 applied only if the purchasing corporation obtained control of the other corporation.

When Congress repealed the codified *General Utilities* doctrine in 1986, liquidations other than those covered by § 332 became taxable to both the acquired corporation and its shareholders. Not surprisingly, those shareholders might prefer to sell their stock to the purchasing corporation rather than first receiving the target's assets and then selling those assets. A direct sale of stock involved only one transaction and one computation of tax consequences. Receipt of a distribution, followed by a sale of the distributed assets, required two transactions and two computations. The purchasing corporation likely preferred to buy the target's assets rather than its stock if the value of those assets substantially exceeded the target's basis for them.

If § 338 applies, the selling shareholders and the purchasing corporation can both be satisfied. The target's shareholders sell their stock and are taxed accordingly, the target reports gain or loss on its assets even though it hasn't sold them, and it continues operating. The target receives a fair market value basis for its assets. Its basis for those assets thus equals the purchasing corporation's basis for the target's stock.

Section 338 applies to a corporation that acquires a controlling stock interest. It does not benefit the parties if the purchaser is not a corporation or, if it is a corporation, it fails to purchase the required interest. Section 336(e) can fill that gap and provide another means for limiting the number of times gain attributable to the same assets is taxed. It applies to a corporation that sells, exchanges, or distributes stock of a corporation that it controls. It can elect to have the controlled corporation undergo a deemed sale and purchase of its own assets. Although the controlled corporation that is being sold thus has immediate tax consequences, the purchaser's basis for the stock will equal the acquired corporation's new basis for its assets. The selling corporation recognizes no gain or loss on the sale, exchange, or distribution.

Section 1060 serves a different purpose. It prevents parties from treating the sale of a business differently by requiring that the seller and buyer use the same basis and value for the assets transferred. In other words, the seller cannot assign the bulk of the selling price to capital assets while the buyer assigns the bulk of that price to inventory and other short-term items.

C. Section 338

1. Terminology

a. Corporations Involved

Section 338 focuses on a purchasing corporation and a target corporation. A purchasing corporation is a corporation that makes a qualified stock purchase of a target corporation. A target corporation is a corporation whose stock is acquired in a qualified stock purchase. I.R.C. § 338(d)(1)–(2). The target is treated as two corporations because of the election: old target and new target.

b. Qualified Stock Purchase

A qualified stock purchase (QSP) is any transaction or series of transactions in which the acquiring corporation purchases stock representing 80% of the target corporation's voting power and stock value during the 12-month acquisition period. I.R.C. § 338(d)(3).

Section 338(h)(3) broadly defines the term "purchase" as any acquisition, with certain exceptions. An acquisition does not qualify if the purchasing corporation's basis for the stock is determined in whole or in part by reference to the adjusted basis of the stock in the hands of the person from whom acquired or if its basis is determined under § 1014. An acquisition does not qualify if the purchasing corporation acquired it in an exchange described in any of §§ 351, 354, 355, or 356 (or in any transaction in which the entire gain or loss was not recognized). An acquisition does not qualify if the purchasing corporation acquired the stock from a person whose stock ownership would be attributed to it under any provision of § 318(a) other than option attribution.

c. 12-Month Acquisition Period and Date

The acquisition period is the 12-month period beginning with the first acquisition by purchase. The acquisition date with respect to a corporation is the first day on which there is a QSP for that corporation. I.R.C. § 338(h)(1)–(2).

d. Other Relevant Terms

Several other terms, discussed later in this section, are relevant. In applying § 338 to a target corporation's assets, we must differentiate between the "grossed-up basis" of "recently purchased stock" and the "basis" of "nonrecently purchased stock." We must also treat transactions appropriately during a "consistency period."

2. Actual and Deemed Elections

a. Applicable Provisions

Section 338 has two election provisions: a general provision, with election procedures specified in § 338(g), and § 338(h)(10). Two other subsections are also relevant. I.R.C. § 338(e)–(f). Those subsections provide for deemed elections (or non-elections) in situations that might otherwise allow for abuse. The discussion below assumes that the purchasing corporation made a qualified stock purchase and thus is eligible to make an election.

b. Section 338(g) Election

A § 338(g) election is made by the purchasing corporation alone. It must make the election no later than the 15th day of the ninth month beginning after the month in which the acquisition date occurs. The election is irrevocable.

Terminology is important. The "acquisition date" is the date on which the purchasing corporation obtains the requisite ownership. The 12-month acquisition period includes acquisitions by purchase leading up to the purchasing corporation's obtaining 80% ownership.

> **Example 13-1.** Purchasing Corporation made five purchases of Target Corporation's only class of stock: 10% on Date 1, an additional 30% on Date 2, 30% more on Date 3, 20% more on Date 4, and the remaining 10% on Date 5. If all five purchases occurred during a 12-month period, Date 4 is the acquisition date. That is the date on which Purchasing's total purchases equaled at least 80% of Target's voting power and stock value.

c. Section 338(h)(10) Election

A § 338(h)(10) election is available in three situations, two of which appear in the statute. First, the purchasing corporation can make a qualified stock purchase of a target corporation that is a member of a group of corporations that file a consolidated return. That group is referred to as a selling consolidated group. Second, the purchasing corporation can make a qualified stock purchase of a target corporation that is a member of an affiliated group; no consolidated return is required in this situation. Third, as provided for in Reg. § 1.338(h)(10)-1(c)(1), the purchasing corporation can make a qualified stock purchase of an S corporation's stock. Both the purchasing corporation and the selling consolidated group (or the selling affiliate or the S corporation's shareholders) must make the election. Every S corporation shareholder must agree to the election even if some of them do not sell their stock. Reg. § 1.338(h)(10)-1(c)(3).

The step transaction doctrine may apply to separate transactions that are really parts of an integrated transaction. In that situation, the tax consequences are those that would apply to the integrated transaction. The regulations suspend the application of this doctrine when a stock acquisition would be a QSP if viewed independently from subsequent events. For example, a purchasing corporation could make a QSP of a target corporation and later merge or liquidate the target corporation in a transaction that could qualify as a reorganization. If the parties make the election, the transaction is treated as a QSP rather than as a reorganization. Reg. § 1.338(h)(10)-1(c)(2).

The election could be beneficial if the target corporation has substantially appreciated assets (that could lead to greater depreciation deductions) or plans to sell appreciated assets relatively soon. The advantage (or lack thereof) is also influenced by the rate structure in effect when the stock purchase occurs and by any anticipated change in that rate structure.

d. Asset and Stock Consistency Rules

Two provisions limit a corporation's ability to manipulate tax consequences by acquiring some stock or assets outside the 12-month acquisition period. Section 338(e) treats a purchasing corporation as making a § 338 election if it acquires any asset of the target corporation at any time during a "consistency period." That period is the one-year period before the beginning of the 12-month acquisition period for the target, the acquisition period, and the one-year period beginning on the day after the acquisition date. I.R.C. § 338(h)(4).

Section 338(e)(2) provides four exceptions to the deemed election rules: (1) an acquisition of a target asset through a sale made in the ordinary course of the target's trade or business; (2) an acquisition in which the basis of the property is determined in whole or in part with reference to the transferor's basis; (3) an acquisition made before September 1, 1982; and (4) any exception provided under the regulations. The repeal of the *General Utilities* doctrine reduced or eliminated the concerns covered by the consistency rules. The regulations trigger a deemed election only in limited situations. Reg. § 1.338-8.

Section 338(f) provides stock consistency rules for affiliated groups, using an all-or-nothing approach. A purchasing corporation that made a § 338 election for a qualified stock purchase of a target corporation or of a member of an affiliated group with the same common parent (a "target affiliate") is deemed to make the election for subsequent purchases. Conversely, if the purchasing corporation did not make an election when it could have, it cannot make the election for subsequent purchases.

3. Target Corporation's Tax Consequences

a. Gain and Loss Computations

The target corporation is treated as selling all its assets at the close of the acquisition date at fair market value in a single transaction. It is then treated as a new corporation that purchased those same assets as of the beginning of the next day. I.R.C. § 338(a). The target corporation recognizes gain or loss with respect to the assets it "sold."

Because the target corporation does not actually sell its assets, we follow the method for determining gain or loss provided in the regulations. In interpreting the regulations, we follow their emphasis on treating the deemed sale as a real sale.

We compute the target's gain or loss for each asset in accordance with the rules in Reg. § 1.338-6. We compare the aggregate deemed sale price (ADSP) for each asset to the target's basis for that asset. If ADSP is the larger number, the target reports a gain for that asset; if ADSP is the smaller number, the target reports a loss.

The ADSP computation takes two steps. First we compute total ADSP. Then we allocate it to each asset deemed sold. The formula for computing ADSP reflects the actual percentage of the stock that the purchasing corporation acquired. Instead of offsetting the deemed sale price, selling expenses are treated separately. This treatment has significance if the purchasing corporation does not purchase 100% of the target's stock during the 12-month acquisition period.

The computations below relate to computing overall ADSP. We cover allocating ADSP to the individual assets later.

Reg. § 1.338-4(b)(1) defines ADSP as the sum of: (1) the grossed-up amount realized on the sale to the purchasing corporation of the recently purchased target stock and (2) the target corporation's liabilities. Because those liabilities are computed on the day following the deemed asset sale, the target's liabilities can include its tax liability arising from that deemed sale. If the purchasing corporation purchases 100% of the target's stock during the 12-month acquisition period, and the target has no liabilities (including no tax on the deemed sale), the grossed-up amount realized is equal to the purchase price.

Example 13-2. Purchasing Corporation purchased 100% of Target Corporation's stock in a single transaction for $100. Target had no liabilities at the time of the sale. Its unrealized gains and losses were all ordinary and were exactly equal. Target would thus have no income tax liability if it actually sold those assets. The ADSP is $100.

Example 13-3. Target instead had $2 in nontax liabilities, and the deemed sale would give rise to $1 in income tax liability. ADSP is $103.

Section 338 applies to stock acquired during the 12-month acquisition period. That stock is referred to as recently purchased stock. The purchasing corporation may also own other shares on the acquisition date. Those shares are referred to as nonrecently purchased stock. I.R.C. § 338(b)(6). Reg. § 1.338-4(c) computes the grossed-up amount realized in three steps:

(1) Start with the amount realized on the sale to the purchasing corporation of its recently purchased target stock. This amount is determined as if the selling shareholder(s) were required to use old target's accounting methods and characteristics and the installment method was not available. It ignores the selling costs covered by the third part of this computation.

(2) Divide that amount realized by the percentage of target stock (by value, determined on the acquisition date) attributable to that recently purchased target stock.

(3) Subtract the selling costs incurred by the selling shareholders in connection with the sale to the purchasing corporation of its recently purchased target stock. The selling costs are those that reduce the sellers' amount realized on the sale of the stock (e.g., brokerage commissions and any similar costs to sell the stock).

Example 13-4. Target Corporation has two classes of stock outstanding, voting common stock and preferred stock described in § 1504(a)(4) (nonvoting and not participating in corporate growth). On March 1, Year 1, Purchasing Corporation purchased 40% of Target's common stock from Aaron for $500, 20% of Target's common stock from Beth for $225, and 20% of Target's common stock from Charles for $275. On that date, the fair market value of Target's common stock totaled $1,250; the fair market value of its preferred stock totaled $750. Aaron, Beth, and Charles incurred $40, $35, and $25, respectively, of selling costs. Debra continued to own the remaining 20% of Target's common stock. The grossed-up amount realized on the sale to Purchasing of its recently purchased Target stock is calculated as follows: First, we add the amount realized (without regard to selling costs) by Aaron, Beth, and Charles. That amount is $1,000. Second, we determine the percentage of Target stock by value on the acquisition date attributable to that recently purchased stock. That percentage is 50% ($1,000/($1,250+$750)); we express it as .5 in the formula. Third, we subtract the $100 of selling costs. The grossed-up amount realized is $1,900 (($1,000/.5)—$100). Reg. § 1.338-4(c)(2).

b. Basis for Assets Deemed Purchased

Because the target corporation is treated as if it had sold its assets, its post-sale basis for those assets reflects this deemed sale. The regulations provide a method for determining that basis, which is referred to as the adjusted grossed-up basis (AGUB). AGUB is the sum of the following amounts: (1) the grossed-up basis for the purchasing corporation's recently purchased target stock; (2) the purchasing corporation's basis for nonrecently purchased target stock; and (3) the liabilities of new target. Reg. § 1.338-5.

1. Basis Attributable to Stock

To compute the basis allocable to recently purchased stock, multiply the purchasing corporation's basis for that stock by a fraction. The fraction's numerator is 100% minus the percentage of stock in the target corporation attributable to nonrecently purchased stock. The denominator is the percentage of stock in the target corporation attributable to recently purchased stock. Both percentage computations are based on the stock's value. Finally, add the acquisition costs for such stock (brokerage commissions and similar costs). Reg. § 1.338-5(c).

The basis allocable to nonrecently purchased stock is the purchasing corporation's basis unless that corporation makes the election discussed later in this section. The examples below illustrate the basis computation in a situation involving no liabilities.

Example 13-5. Purchasing Corporation purchased 100% of Target Corporation's stock in a single transaction for $200. Because Purchasing acquired all the Target stock within the acquisition period, all that stock is recently purchased stock. The fraction is 100/100. Target's AGUB is the $200 attributable to that recently purchased stock.

Example 13-6. Purchasing Corporation instead purchased 95% of Target Corporation's stock in a single transaction for $190. Five years ago, Purchasing purchased the other 5% of Target's stock for $4. That 5% is worth $10. Only 95% of the Target stock is recently purchased stock. The fraction is 95/95. Target's asset basis attributable to recently purchased stock is $190. Target's asset basis attributable to nonrecently purchased stock is $4. If Purchasing Corporation had acquired only 4% (worth $8) five years ago, and a third party owns the other 1%, the fraction would be 96/95.

2. Election for Nonrecently Purchased Stock

If the purchasing corporation is willing to recognize gain on its nonrecently purchased stock, it can elect a grossed-up basis for assets attributable to that stock. I.R.C. § 338(b)(3); Reg. § 1.338-5(d)(2). The purchasing corporation cannot recognize any loss on such stock. Nor can it offset any losses against gains on such stock. Reg. § 1.338-5(d)(3)(iii).

The corporation is treated as selling the stock on the acquisition date for a "basis amount." That amount is computed by multiplying the grossed-up basis for recently purchased stock by a fraction. The numerator is the percentage of the target's stock value attributable to nonrecently purchased stock. The denominator is 100% minus the numerator percentage. The example below applies the facts in Example 13-6.

Example 13-7. Purchasing Corporation elected to recognize its $6 gain on the 5% of Target's stock that it purchased five years ago. Purchasing's basis for that nonrecently purchased stock is increased to $10. That amount equals the $190 grossed-up basis multiplied by 5/95. Target's basis for its assets also reflects this higher basis. Reg. § 1.338-5(g) Example 1.

3. Redetermination of ADSP and AGUP

The regulations provide for redetermining ADSP and AGUP when appropriate. Reg. §§ 1.338-4(b)(2)(ii), 1.338-5(b)(2)(ii). Redetermination typically occurs when contingent liabilities arise or if there is an increase or decrease in the amount paid for recently purchased stock.

c. Basis Allocation Rules

The basis allocation generally reflects each asset's fair market value, but certain assets (such as money on hand or in a bank) take priority. This result makes sense because, if the target corporation has a bank account containing $100,000, the purchasing corporation would not transfer a higher or lower amount for the account.

The deemed sale is not an asset-by-asset sale; it is the sale of an entire business. While some assets could have been sold separately, assets such as goodwill may have no value outside the business. Because the target corporation is treated as two corporations, both a seller and a buyer, we allocate the ADSP to each asset sold by the old target corporation and allocate the AGUB to each asset purchased by the new target corporation.

Section 338(b)(5) authorizes regulations governing the basis allocation. Reg. § 1.338-6(b) allocates the overall ADSP and AGUB using a seven-class asset ranking order:

Class I: cash and bank accounts other than certificates of deposit;

Class II: certain actively traded personal property and certificates of deposit;

Class III: assets that are marked to market at least annually and debt instruments;

Class IV: inventory assets;

Class V: all assets not assigned to another class;

Class VI: section 197 intangibles other than goodwill and going concern value; and

Class VII: goodwill and going concern value.

If Class I assets exceed AGUB, the new target recognizes ordinary income equal to that excess. The amount assigned to classes I through VI cannot exceed the value of the assets in that class. The amount assigned to each class is allocated within the class based on each asset's relative value. The amount, if any, left after assigning ADSP and AGUB to classes I through VI, is assigned to class VII assets. The regulations provide several examples illustrating the application of these rules.

d. Holding Period and Other Attributes

The target corporation begins a new holding period for its assets. And, because it is treated as a new corporation, its other tax attributes are eliminated.

4. Purchasing Corporation's Tax Consequences

The purchasing corporation computes its basis for the target corporation stock using the normal basis rules. In most cases, its basis is a cost basis. If it makes the § 338(b)(3) election with respect to its nonrecently acquired stock, it recognizes the gain potential in that stock using the stock's value on the acquisition date. It then increases its basis for that stock by the recognized gain.

5. Selling Shareholder's Tax Consequences

The tax consequences of the selling shareholders are affected by their identity. If the target corporation is a C corporation, its shareholders may be a widely dispersed group of individuals and entities. Alternatively, its shareholders may also be corporations in the same affiliated group. It is possible, but not required, that those group members file a consolidated return.

If the target corporation is not part of an affiliated group, the shareholders simply compute gain or loss on their stock as they would for any asset. They recognize any realized gain or loss and likely report the gains and losses as capital gains and losses.

If the target corporation is a member of a consolidated group described in § 338(h)(10), and it recognizes gain or loss on a deemed sale of its assets, group members that sell their stock do not recognize gain or loss on the sale. The same rule applies to members of an affiliated group that includes the target corporation. I.R.C. § 338(h)(10)(A)–(B). Group members do not escape tax consequences, however. The target corporation is deemed to have distributed its assets to members of the selling group immediately after it made the deemed sale of those assets. Group members may report gain or loss on this deemed transfer. Reg. § 1.338(h)(10)-1(d). Reg. § 1.338(h)(10)-1(e) provides numerous examples.

D. Section 336(e)

1. Terminology

Terminology for § 336(e) appears in the regulations. The language used resembles that for § 338 but focuses on the disposition rather than the acquisition.

a. Parties Involved

The regulations focus on a selling corporation (seller), a purchaser, and a target corporation. A seller is a corporation that makes a qualified stock disposition of another corporation. A purchaser is one or more persons that acquire or receive the stock of a corporation in a qualified stock disposition. A target corporation is a corporation whose stock is sold, exchanged, or distributed in a qualified stock disposition. The target is treated as two corporations because of the election: old target and new target. Reg. § 1.336-1(b)(1)–(3). A purchaser does not have to be a corporation.

b. Disposition and Qualified Stock Disposition

A disposition is broadly defined to include sales, exchanges, or distributions of stock. A qualified stock disposition (QSD) is any transaction or series of transactions in which the controlling corporation disposes of stock representing 80% of the target corporation's voting power and stock value during the 12-month disposition period. Reg. § 1.336-1(b)(6)(i). Disposition is broadly defined to include sales, exchanges, or distributions of stock, with certain exceptions. A transaction does not qualify if the transferee's basis for the stock is determined in whole or in part by reference to the adjusted basis of the stock in the hands of the person from whom acquired or if its basis is determined under § 1014. A transaction does not qualify if the transferee acquired it an exchange described in any of §§ 351, 354, 355, or 356 (or in any transaction in which the entire gain or loss was not recognized). A transaction does not qualify if the purchaser acquired the stock from a person whose stock ownership would be attributed to it under any provision of § 318(a) other than option attribution. Reg. § 1.336-1(b)(5), -1(b)(12).

In theory, §§ 336(e) and 338(d)(3) could both apply to a transfer—that is, it could be both a qualified stock purchase and a qualified stock disposition. If so, § 336(e) will generally be inapplicable. Reg. § 1.336-1(b)(6)(ii).

c. 12-Month Disposition Period and Date

The 12-month disposition period is the 12-month period beginning with the first sale, exchange, or distribution of stock included in a qualified stock disposition. Reg. § 1.336-1(b)(7). The disposition date with respect to a corporation is the first day on which there is a QSD with respect to that corporation's stock. Reg. § 1.336-1(b)(8).

d. Aggregate Deemed Asset Disposition Price

In applying § 336(e) to a target corporation's assets, we compute the aggregate deemed asset disposition price (ADADP). The target corporation is deemed to have sold its assets to an unrelated purchaser for that amount. Reg. § 1.336-2(b)(1)(i).

e. Other Relevant Terms

Other terminology used in the § 336 regulations generally mirrors that used in § 338. The regulations thus refer to recently disposed of stock and nonrecently disposed of stock. They allocate the new target's basis for the assets it is deemed to purchase using the § 338 AGUB rules.

2. Tax Consequences

The discussion below covers sales by the seller. The regulations also give examples in which the seller distributes stock rather than selling it or sells some shares and distributes others.

a. Seller Corporation

Section 338 applies to a corporation (the purchasing corporation) that acquires a controlling stock interest. Section 336(e), on the other hand, applies to a corporation (the seller corporation) that sells, exchanges, or distributes stock of a corporation that it controls (the target corporation). The seller corporation can elect to treat the target as having sold its assets to a third party. The target, which will then be referred to as the new target, is treated as reacquiring those assets. The seller corporation recognizes no gain or loss on selling, exchanging, or distributing the target's stock. Examples appear in Reg. § 1.336-2(k).

> **Example 13-8.** Seller Corporation has a basis of $500 for the stock of its wholly owned subsidiary, Target Corporation. Target has a basis of $1,200 for its assets; those assets are currently worth $1,800. Seller will sell its Target stock to Purchaser for $1,800 and will not make a § 336(e) election. Seller realizes and recognizes a $1,300 gain on selling its stock in Target. Target has no tax consequences. If Purchaser qualifies to do so, it can make a § 338 election, in which case Target will be treated as selling and repurchasing its assets.

> **Example 13-9.** Seller Corporation will instead make a § 336(e) election. Seller recognizes none of its $1,300 gain. Instead, Target is treated as two corporations. Old Target is treated as selling all its assets, and it recognizes gain or loss. New Target is treated as purchasing those assets, and thus obtains a basis equal to their value.

The seller need not dispose of 100% of the target corporation's shares. Section 336(e) requires only that the seller dispose of a controlling interest in the target. If the seller disposes of at least 80%, but less than 100%, of the target corporation's shares, it is treated as purchasing the shares it retains at their fair market value on the day after the disposition date. Reg. § 1.336-2(k) Example 2.

b. Minority Shareholder

Because § 336(e) looks to a sale, exchange, or distribution by a controlling seller, it applies even if the old target has minority shareholders. If the minority shareholders sell their old target stock, they recognize gain or loss. If they retain their target stock, they do not report gain or loss; there is no effect on their basis. They are now shareholders of new target. Reg. § 1.336-2(d).

c. Target Corporation

The target corporation recognizes gain or loss on a deemed sale of its assets. It is treated as purchasing those assets in a single transaction from an unrelated party. Its basis for those assets is allocated using the § 338 AGUB rules.

d. Purchaser

The purchaser's basis for the new target stock will initially be the same as the target's post-election basis for its assets.

E. Section 1060

1. Introduction

Taxable acquisitions generally are covered by § 1001. The seller's gain or loss realized is the difference between the amount realized and the adjusted basis for the property sold or exchanged. The purchaser takes a cost basis for the property.

Those rules generally apply when an asset is purchased alone. What if the purchase involves a group of assets representing a trade or business? Sections 336(e) and 338 would not apply because the transaction involves a sale of assets, not stock. Instead, § 1060 might apply. If it does, the allocation rules of § 338(b)(5) apply with respect to both the basis of the assets in the hands of the transferee and gain or loss computed by the transferor.

2. Applicable Asset Acquisition

Section 1060 applies to transactions that meet the definition of an applicable asset acquisition. This definition covers any transfer (whether directly or indirectly) of assets that constitute a trade or business if the transferee's basis is determined by reference to the consideration paid for such assets. I.R.C. § 1060(c). Nonrecognition transactions usually do not fall under § 1060 because the transferee's basis generally carries over from the transferor or from assets the transferee relinquished. Section 1060(c)(3) provides an exception to that rule. The transaction can be an applicable asset acquisition even if some of the assets are transferred in a § 1031 like-kind exchange.

Reg. § 1.1060-1(b)(2)(i) defines trade or business as a group of assets the use of which would constitute an active trade or business under § 355. It also defines a trade or business as a group of assets to which goodwill or going concern value could attach. Reg. § 1.1060-1(b)(1) provides that an applicable asset acquisition is any transfer, whether direct or indirect, of a group of assets if the assets transferred constitute a trade or business in the hands of either the seller or the purchaser. Except for nonrecognition provisions covered by Reg. § 1.1060-1(b)(8), the purchaser's basis for the transferred assets must be determined wholly by reference to the purchaser's consideration.

Section 1060 is not limited to transactions in which gain or loss is recognized. Reg. § 1.1060-1(b)(8) provides that a transfer may be an applicable asset acquisition even if no gain or loss is recognized with respect to a portion of the group of assets transferred. All the assets transferred, including the nonrecognition assets, are considered in determining whether the assets constitute a trade or business.

3. Asset Allocation Rules

Section 1060 provides rules to determine the transferee's basis for assets it receives and gain or loss recognized by the transferor. The § 1060(a) flush language provides for allocating the consideration received in the same manner as amounts are allocated to assets under § 338(b)(5). It also allows the parties to agree on, and be bound by, a written allocation of the consideration or the fair market value of the assets. The IRS is not bound by that agreement. Reg. § 1.1060-1(c)(4). Reg. § 1.1060-1(d) Example 2 illustrates an agreement between the parties and the effect of an IRS redetermination.

Checkpoints

- Section 338 applies by election or deemed election.
- The election is available only if a qualified stock purchase is made. That requires a purchase of 80% or more of the stock of the target corporation within a 12-month period (the acquisition period).
- Gain or loss on the deemed sale is the difference between the aggregate deemed sale price (ADSP) and the target's basis for the assets.
- The basis of the assets deemed purchased is the adjusted grossed-up basis (AGUB) in the assets.
- The § 338(g) election is made by the purchasing corporation. The § 338(h)(10) election is made by both the purchasing corporation and the selling group.
- Under § 338(e), certain asset acquisitions trigger a § 338 election. Under § 338(f), the taxpayer must treat subsequent stock acquisitions of affiliated group members the same way it treated the first such acquisition.
- The gain or loss on the deemed asset sale is determined on an asset-by-asset basis. The regulations provide priority for certain assets.

- A § 336(e) election is available to a corporation that sells, exchanges, or distribute its stock in a target corporation that it controlled. If it makes the election, the target is treated as selling its assets to an unrelated purchaser and then repurchasing those assets at fair market value. The target corporation recognizes gain or losses on its assets. The seller corporation does not recognize gain or loss on the sale, exchange, or distribution of that stock.
- The regulations for § 336(e) reflect much of the rules, with language based on disposition rather than on purchase, used in § 338.
- Section 338 generally governs if both it and § 336(e) could apply to a transfer of a target corporation's stock.
- Section 1060 applies certain allocation rules of § 338 to a purchase that is an applicable asset acquisition (generally a trade or business).

Chapter 14

Controlled and Affiliated Corporations; Consolidated Returns

Roadmap

- Controlled corporations
- Restrictions applied to a controlled group
- Affiliated groups
- Consolidated returns
- Computing consolidated taxable income

A. Chapter Overview

This chapter describes controlled and affiliated corporations. It covers types of controlled corporations. It also covers limitations on controlled and affiliated corporations' ability to act as separate corporations and take advantage of multiple tax benefits. The chapter concludes with a discussion of consolidated returns and the computation of consolidated taxable income.

B. Controlled Corporations

1. In General

Section 1563(a) lists four types of controlled corporate groups: (1) parent-subsidiary controlled group; (2) brother-sister controlled group; (3) combined group; and (4) insurance group. These groups share a common feature: two or more corporations are connected to each other in a structure described in that section. This chapter discusses the first three types of controlled groups.

A single, standalone corporation is not a controlled corporation for this purpose even if it has only one shareholder. Other restrictions may apply to dealings between that shareholder and the corporation. For example, § 267 disallows losses on sales between related persons.

> **Example 14-1.** ABC Corporation has only one shareholder. If that shareholder is an individual, ABC and its shareholder are not part of a controlled group. If that shareholder is another corporation, the two corporations are part of a parent-subsidiary controlled group.

2. Parent-Subsidiary Controlled Group

A parent-subsidiary controlled group exists if one or more chains of corporations are connected through stock ownership and have a common parent. There are two stock ownership tests involved. First, one or more of the corporations must own at least 80% of the total combined voting power of all classes of stock entitled to vote *or* at least 80% of the value of all classes of stock of each corporation other than the common parent. Second, the common parent must own at least 80% of the total combined voting power *or* at least 80% of the stock value of at least one of the other corporations. I.R.C. § 1563(a)(1). Limited constructive ownership rules apply in determining if a parent-subsidiary controlled group exists. I.R.C. § 1563(d)(1). Stock owned by other corporations in the group is ignored in determining if the parent meets the second test. Reg. § 1.1563-1(a)(2)(ii) Example 4.

The test for determining the existence of a controlled group is less stringent than the affiliated group test, which requires 80% ownership of both voting power *and* value.

> **Example 14-2.** ABC Corporation owns 82% of the stock of DEF Corporation. ABC owns 40% and DEF owns 60% of the stock of GHI Corporation. GHI owns 75% of the stock of JKL Corporation. Each corporation has only voting common stock outstanding. ABC, DEF, and GHI form a parent-subsidiary controlled group.

> **Example 14-3.** If GHI owned 80% of the JKL stock, JKL would be part of the parent-subsidiary controlled group. JKL would also be part of the group if GHI owned 75% of its stock and any combination of ABC or DEF owned at least 5% of the remaining JKL stock.

In determining if a parent-subsidiary controlled group exists, we focus on corporate ownership of the stock of other corporations. In Examples 14-2 and 14-3, for example, a parent-subsidiary controlled group exists even if individuals own all the stock of ABC Corporation. If, instead, XYZ Corporation owned at least 80% of the ABC stock, it would be the parent corporation of the controlled group that included XYZ, ABC, DEF, GHI, and—in Example 14-3—JKL.

3. Brother-Sister Controlled Group

The brother-sister controlled group structure also requires at least two corporations. Instead of one or more ownership chains, the structure is parallel. And instead of counting any stock owned in determining control, we count only identical ownership as defined in § 1563(a)(2).

In determining common ownership, we consider only ownership by individuals, trusts, and estates. A group of corporations is a brother-sister controlled group if five or fewer of these shareholders own more than 50% of each corporation's voting power or stock value. Actual and constructive ownership rules apply, using the § 1563(e) attribution rules. For purposes of the brother-sister controlled group determination, we count a shareholder's stock ownership only to the extent it is identical for each corporation.

> **Example 14-4.** Abner and Betty each own 50% of the voting power of both MNO and PQR Corporations. MNO and PQR are a brother-sister controlled group.

> **Example 14-5.** Charles and Dorothy each own 35% of STU Corporation's stock. In addition, Charles owns 60% of VWX Corporation's stock and Dorothy owns 20% of VWX Corporation's stock. STU and VWX have no other shareholders in common. For purposes of common ownership, Charles is deemed to own 35% of each corporation; Dorothy is deemed to own 20% of each. STU and VWX are a brother-sister controlled group because five or fewer shareholders own more than 50% of each corporation's stock. If Dorothy had owned only 10% of the VWX stock, the two corporations would not be a brother-sister controlled group.

4. Combined Group

Section 1563(a)(3) defines a combined group as three or more corporations that meet three requirements. Each corporation must be a member of a group of corporations described in a parent-subsidiary controlled group or a brother-sister controlled group. One of these corporations must be a common parent corporation included in a parent-subsidiary controlled group. That corporation must also be included in a brother-sister controlled group. In other words, members of a combined group include members of a parent-subsidiary controlled group and of a brother-sister controlled group.

The restrictions discussed in this chapter apply to both sets of corporations as a group instead of applying separately to the brother-sister controlled group or parent-subsidiary controlled group. Example 14-6 is based on Reg. § 1.1563-1(a)(4)(ii) Example 1.

> **Example 14-6.** Edward owns 83% of the stock of ABC Corporation and 90% of the stock of DEF Corporation. DEF owns 80% of the stock of GHI Corporation, and GHI owns 90% of the stock of JKL Corporation. Each corporation has only one class of outstanding stock. Considered alone, ABC and DEF are part of a brother-sister controlled group; Edward owns more than 50% of each corporation's stock. Likewise, DEF, GHI, and JKL form a parent-subsidiary controlled group. ABC, DEF, GHI, and JKL together form a combined group.

> **Example 14-7.** The result would be the same even if Edward owned just over 50% of both ABC and DEF. It would also be the same if JKL Corporation did not exist, because DEF and GHI would still be a parent-subsidiary controlled group while ABC and DEF would be a brother-sister controlled group.

C. Restrictions Applied to a Controlled Group

Dividing a business into separate corporations might have advantages for liability or governance purposes, but it is unlikely to yield significant tax benefits because § 1561 subjects the component members of a controlled group to several restrictions.

We determine whether a corporation is a component member on a yearly basis because changes in its ownership may affect its status. A corporation is a component member for a particular year if it is a member of the group as of December 31 and is not an excluded member of the group. December 31 is the testing date even if the corporation uses a fiscal year. The relevant taxable year is the year that includes that December 31. I.R.C. § 1563(b)(1).

A member is excluded if it was a member of the group for less than one-half of the days in that year preceding December 31. A member is also excluded if it is exempt from taxation under § 501(a), a foreign corporation subject to tax under § 881, an insurance company subject to taxation under § 801, or a franchised corporation, as defined in § 1563(f)(4). I.R.C. § 1563(b)(2).

A corporation might still be a component member even if it was not a member of the group on December 31. Section 1563(b)(3) includes in the group any "additional member"—a corporation that: (1) was a member of the controlled group at any time during a calendar year; (2) is not a member of the group on December 31 of that calendar year; (3) is not an excluded corporation; and (4) was a member of the group for at least one-half of the days in that taxable year that preceded December 31.

Section 1561(a) imposes the following restrictions on component members of the group. First, they are limited to total amounts in each taxable income bracket in the tax table in § 11(b)(1) that do not exceed the maximum amount available to a corporation that is not part of a controlled group. Second, they are limited to one $250,000 ($150,000 if any component member is a services corporation described in § 535(c)(2)(B)) amount for purposes of computing the accumulated earnings credit under § 535(c)(2)–(3). Third, they are limited to one $40,000 exemption amount for purposes of computing the alternative minimum tax.

The amounts described above are generally divided equally among the component members of the controlled group unless the members (for the first and third items) or the regulations (for the second item) provide for a different allocation. I.R.C. § 1561(a).

D. Affiliated Groups

1. Membership in Group

Affiliated groups are also defined by ownership. Because a group of corporations cannot file a consolidated return unless it meets the § 1504 affiliation requirements, the discussion here of affiliated corporations and the later discussion of consolidated returns are intertwined.

a. Stock Ownership Requirement

An affiliated group is one or more chains of includible corporations connected through stock ownership with a common parent corporation. The common parent must itself be an includible corporation. I.R.C. § 1504(a)(1)–(2). Any corporation can be included unless it is an ineligible corporation. The common parent must own directly 80% or more of the stock of at least one of the includible corporations. In addition, 80% or more of the stock of each includible corporation must be owned by one or more of the includible corporations. The corporations described in Example 14-3 form an affiliated group.

Section 1504(a)(2) applies the 80% ownership requirement to both voting power *and* stock value. This requirement ensures that taxpayers have a significant economic interest in the corporations with which they are affiliated. In the absence of those tests, corporations could affiliate with other corporations in which they have limited economic exposure. For example, an acquiring corporation could acquire 80% of the voting power of a target corporation but only a small amount of the target corporation's stock value. The corporations could then elect to file their returns on a consolidated basis, offsetting the income of one corporation by the losses of the other. Because both voting power and stock value must meet the 80% tests, the acquiring corporation must make a significant investment in the target corporation. Even if these tests are met, the acquiring corporation is subject to the consolidated return regulations' restrictions on the use of pre-acquisition losses of recently acquired corporations.

Note the difference between how the 80% tests are applied for purposes of establishing a parent-subsidiary controlled group and for establishing an affiliated group. A parent-subsidiary controlled group requires ownership of at least 80% of the total combined voting power *or* at least 80% of the value of all classes of stock of each corporation. I.R.C. § 1563(a)(1).

b. Statutory Definition of Stock

Section 1504(a)(4) defines stock that is considered in the 80% tests discussed above. Preferred stock is not treated as stock if it is not entitled to vote, is limited and preferred as to dividends and does not participate in corporate growth to any significant extent, has redemption and liquidation rights that do not exceed the issue price of such stock, and is not convertible into another class of stock. This definition excludes most types of preferred stock, which generally do not carry governance and corporate growth rights.

Section 1504(a)(5) authorizes regulations implementing the section's purposes. It lists six actions the IRS can take but does not limit it to those actions. First, it can treat warrants, obligations convertible into stock, and other similar interests as stock (and treat stock as not stock). Second, it can treat options to acquire or sell stock as having been exercised. Third, it can provide that the 80% ownership requirements are treated as met if the group, in reliance on a good faith determination of value, treated such requirements as met. Fourth, it can disregard an inadvertent ceasing to meet those requirements caused by changes in relative values of different classes of stock. Fifth, it can provide for ignoring intra-group stock transfers in determining whether a corporation ceases to be a group member. Sixth, it can disregard changes in voting power to the extent they are disproportionate to related changes in value.

c. Regulations

Regulations address the treatment of warrants, options, convertible obligations, or similar interests. Reg. § 1.1504-4(b)(1) provides that options are generally not treated as exercised. The major exception appears in Reg. § 1.1504-4(b)(2)(i), which applies if the option is likely to be exercised and exercise would cause a substantial amount of federal income tax liability to be eliminated. The purpose of these regulations is preventing groups from retaining qualification under § 1504 while divesting their economic interest in a subsidiary. For example, a corporation might want to sell a subsidiary's stock but continue to include the subsidiary in its consolidated returns. If this rule didn't exist, the corporation could accomplish this result by selling options to acquire the subsidiary's stock. Until the purchaser exercised the options, the corporation could include the subsidiary in its consolidated returns and use the subsidiary's losses to shelter other group members' income. By treating the options as having been exercised, the regulations may cause deconsolidation before there is a change in actual stock ownership.

The regulations provide for judging the likelihood of exercise on a measurement date: a date on which an option is issued or transferred or on which the terms of an existing option or the underlying stock are adjusted. There are safe harbor rules under which certain issuances or transfers are not treated as measurement dates. These include transfers by gift, at death, or between spouses or former spouses. The safe harbors also cover options issued or transferred between members of an affiliated group.

A facts and circumstances test applies in determining whether an option is reasonably likely to be exercised. The regulation also provides safe harbor rules, which generally apply if the option exercise price is close to the stock's value. If one of the safe harbors applies, the option is not treated as exercised, and the group retains its affiliated status.

Reg. § 1.1504-4(e) takes a broad approach to determining the elimination of federal income tax liability. It provides for examining the tax consequences to all involved parties. Using a deduction that otherwise would not be utilized or deferring gain recognition are examples of elimination of federal income tax liability. If allowing affiliated status would not change the group's income tax liability, there is little or no abuse potential. In this case, treating the options as exercised would be of little consequence. The regulations contain several examples that illustrate application of these rules.

2. Ineligible Corporations

The following corporations cannot be part of an affiliated group: corporations exempt from tax under § 501; insurance companies taxed under § 801; foreign corporations; corporations that have a § 936 possession tax credit election in effect; regulated investment companies and real estate investment trusts; DISCs as defined in § 992; and S corporations. I.R.C. § 1504(b). Those corporations are subject to their own tax regimes.

Section 1504(d) permits domestic corporations to treat certain foreign corporations as domestic corporations. The domestic corporation can elect to do so if the foreign corporation meets three requirements. First, the domestic parent must own or control 100% of the foreign corporation's capital stock (except directors' qualifying shares). Second, the foreign corporation must be organized under the laws of a contiguous country (Mexico or Canada). Third, the foreign corporation must be organized solely to comply with the other country's laws regarding title and operation of property.

The IRS narrowly construes § 1504(d), allowing only elections that are made solely for purposes of ownership and operation of property. In one ruling, it held that the provision's purposes were not met when a domestic corporation formed a Canadian corporation solely for purposes of applying for a Canadian government grant program. Rev. Rul. 71-523, 1971-2 C.B. 326. The North American Free Trade Agreement and other changes in Mexican and Canadian law may affect the application of § 1504(d). For example, in 1996 Mexico removed many restrictions on foreigners owning real estate in Mexico. In 2001, the IRS declared obsolete a 1970 ruling that permitted consolidated returns to include Mexican corporations that were incorporated to hold real estate in Mexico. Rev. Rul. 70-379, 1970-2 C.B. 179, *obsoleted by* Rev. Rul. 2001-39, 2001-2 C.B. 125. Changes in Canadian banking laws permitting foreign banks to function directly in Canada led to Notice 2000-7, 2000-1 C.B. 419. That notice limited the application of § 1504(d) to domestic corporations that incorporated a group member in Canada to engage in the banking business in Canada. Section 1504(d) relief is unnecessary if domestic corporations can engage in activities directly in the foreign country.

3. Reconsolidation Following Disaffiliation

Section 1504(a)(3)(A) provides that a corporation included or required to be included in a consolidated return that ceases to be a group member must wait until the 61st month beginning after the year in which it ceased to be a group member before rejoining that group. The same rule applies to its joining another group headed by the same common parent or a successor of that common parent. This rule limits taxpayers' ability to enter and leave groups simply to exploit the use of tax losses or other benefits of the group. Section 1504(a)(3)(B) lets taxpayers rejoin a group sooner if they receive a waiver from the IRS.

4. Good Faith Affiliation and Disaffiliation

The IRS will generally not challenge a group's affiliation if it is based on a good faith determination that the affiliation rules were met. It will also pardon inadvertent disaffiliation resulting from such activities as issuing stock to non-group members, redemptions from group members, and recapitalizations. Notice 2004-37, 2004-1 C.B. 947.

E. Consolidated Returns

1. Overview

Section 1501 gives affiliated groups of corporations the privilege of filing a consolidated income tax return. Each corporation that was a group member at any time during the year must consent to the election. That consent is required only for the first return. New members must be included on the consolidated return in subsequent years; their consent is not required.

This section also addresses the treatment of any corporation that is part of the group for only a portion of the year. The consolidated return includes that corporation's income only for the part of the year during which it was a group member.

Section 1502 authorizes consolidated return regulations covering periods before, during, and after the affiliation period. It states the congressional purpose of having a clear reflection of income tax liability and preventing the avoidance of that liability.

Corporations filing consolidated returns engage in the same transactions that standalone corporations engage in. Consolidated corporations must consider both the rules applicable to standalone corporations and consolidated corporations in determining how to report a transaction. For example, if a corporation that is included in a consolidated return engages in a reorganization, it must satisfy the rules governing reorganizations. Consolidated return rules, such as those dealing with intercompany transactions and basis adjustments, will also apply to the transaction.

2. Deciding to File Consolidated Returns

Consolidated returns have several advantages. Advantages relate to sharing profits and losses on a single tax return. If one member's profits can be reduced by another member's losses, the profitable member's taxable income is reduced. Group members may avoid paying taxes on gains from transactions within the group. They can also receive tax-free dividend distributions from other group members.

Consolidated returns also have several disadvantages. Group members may have fewer options for using accounting methods and periods because of a need to conform to the group's methods and periods. Loss deduction limitations and loss deferral rules apply to group members. In addition, the election is binding, it is nearly impossible to deconsolidate, and the consolidated return regulations are complex. Consolidated returns are likely to involve large groups of corporations that conduct diverse businesses. Directors of a small group may decide that the benefits of filing consolidated returns do not outweigh the costs of tracking the complex regulations involved. Simplification might not be achieved by substituting a single consolidated return for several separate returns.

3. Procedure for Filing Consolidated Returns

Procedurally, the corporate parent indicates that a consolidated return is being filed by checking a box on Form 1120, the U.S. Corporation Income Tax return. It attaches Form 851 to identify the common parent and each group member and provide other information about group members. Each subsidiary completes a Form 1122 to indicate its consent to being included in the consolidated return (and future consolidated returns if it remains eligible). The parent attaches the Forms 1122 to the consolidated tax return.

All group members must consent to the filing of a consolidated return. If a group member fails to sign Form 1122, it may still be considered part of the group based on the facts and circumstances. Relevant factors include whether its income and deductions were included in the consolidated return, whether it filed a separate return for that taxable year, and whether it was included in the Form 851 affiliation schedule. Generally, if a group member fails to consent to the filing of a consolidated return, each corporation's tax liability is determined on a separate basis unless the IRS is satisfied that the failure was due to a mistake of law or fact or was due to inadvertence. Reg. § 1.1502-75(b)(3). Section 1501 provides that the making of a consolidated return is treated as consent to make such a return.

4. Deconsolidating

After corporations elect to file consolidated returns, their decision is difficult to undo. The election is, in many ways, a permanent one. Reg. § 1.1502-75(a)(2) provides that a group that filed or was required to file a consolidated return for the immediately preceding year must file a consolidated return for the current year unless it has made an election to discontinue filing under Reg. § 1.1502-75(c).

Reg. § 1.1502-75(c)(1) authorizes the IRS, for good cause shown, to grant permission to discontinue filing a consolidated return. It lists factors that might result in the IRS granting permission to deconsolidate. These include substantial adverse changes in the law affecting the group's tax liability, changes in law or circumstances, including changes that do not affect federal income tax liability, and changes in the law that result in a substantial reduction of the consolidated net operating loss.

Tax savings are not good cause. For example, in Rev. Rul. 74-378, 1974-2 C.B. 287, it held that saving on taxes imposed by a state on out-of-state subsidiaries was not good cause. Rev. Rul. 74-91, 1974-1 C.B. 252, held similarly in the context of achieving international tax savings. The revenue ruling stated that events, activities, and economic conditions affecting individual members of a group are not considered material insofar as the interrelationships of the group members are concerned. Such circumstances, including shifting from a consolidated return basis to a separate return basis to achieve temporary tax reductions or advantages, are not good cause.

There are other, but limited, methods for achieving deconsolidation. For example, a corporation that no longer meets the 80% ownership threshold necessary for affiliation becomes a disaffiliated member and is not eligible for inclusion on the consolidated return. This may be the only method available to most taxpayers.

5. Group Remaining in Existence

The life of a consolidated group is not static. New members join the group, and other members leave. The group remains in existence for a tax year if the common parent remains as the group's parent and at least one subsidiary that was affiliated with it at the end of the prior year remains affiliated with it at the beginning of the current year. Reg. § 1.1502-75(d). This rule applies whether or not one or more subsidiaries ceased to be subsidiaries at any time after the group was formed.

> **Example 14-8.** Parent Corporation acquired 100% of the stock of Subsidiary Corporation 1 on January 1, Year 1. Parent and Subsidiary 1 filed a consolidated return for that calendar year. On May 1, Year 2, Parent acquired 100% of the stock of Subsidiary Corporation 2, and on July 1, Year 2, Parent sold the stock of Subsidiary 1. The group (consisting originally of Parent and Subsidiary 1) remains in existence in Year 2. Parent has remained as the common parent and at least one

subsidiary (now Subsidiary 2) remains affiliated with it. Although Parent no longer owns the stock of Subsidiary 1, it and Parent were still affiliated on January 1, Year 2.

In some instances, even the disappearance of the group's common parent does not cause deconsolidation. Reg. § 1.1502-75(d)(2)(i) treats the group as remaining in existence if the parent engages in an F reorganization, which is a mere change in form rather than one in substance. A group's existence can also continue even if the parent disappears. The other group members must become the owners of substantially all the former parent's assets, there must remain one or more chains of includible corporations, and the new common parent must have been a group member before the original common parent ceased to exist. Reg. § 1.1502-75(d)(2)(ii).

Reg. § 1.1502-75(d)(3) provides rules relating to the merger of two or more groups. If Group A's parent merges with and into Group B's parent, the regulations provide that the larger group is treated as the survivor group. In determining size, the regulations look to the percentage of stock received by the shareholders of the merged group.

Example 14-9. Consolidated Group A merged with Consolidated Group B. The shareholders of Group A received more than 50% of the stock of the parent of Group B. Group A is treated as surviving and must continue filing its consolidated returns with the parent of Group B as its new common parent. The members of former Group B become part of the reconstituted group.

The regulations are designed to preserve the filing of consolidated returns in almost all situations. Allowing taxpayers to deconsolidate and reconsolidate at will could lead to abuses in the computation of corporate tax liability. Reg. § 1.1502-75(e) provides that the failure to include an affiliated member in the group's consolidated return does not invalidate the consolidated return to the extent a consolidated return is required. The taxes, if any, paid on a separate basis are treated as paid on a consolidated basis. Similarly, Reg. § 1.1502-75(f) provides that including a corporation that is not a member of the group in the consolidated return does not invalidate that return. Instead, the tax liability of the nonmember corporation is computed as if it had filed a separate return.

F. Computing Consolidated Taxable Income

Computing the group's taxable income is challenging. Some of the consolidated return regulations take a single entity approach (items are calculated on a separate corporation basis). Others take an aggregate approach (items are calculated on an aggregate basis). The general rules for calculating consolidated taxable income are found in Reg. §§ 1.1502-11 and 1.1502-12. Their complexity is increased by the impact of other provisions.

After calculating the group's consolidated tax liability, the group's parent normally pays the tax owed on behalf of the group. Reg. § 1.1502-6(a) makes each group member severally liable for the entire tax owed by the group. Reg. § 1.1502-6(c) provides that agreements between group members or any other person do not reduce the tax liability imposed by the section. Reg. § 1.1502-6(b) lets the IRS limit the potential liability of a group member that has been sold before the assessment of a deficiency against the group. If the IRS believes that the recovery of the deficiency will not be jeopardized, it can decide to collect from the former member only the amount attributable to it.

1. Intercompany Transactions

a. Overview

The intercompany transaction rules are an important aspect of consolidated returns. The regulations contain specific rules for specific transactions. When encountering an intercompany transaction, you should first determine whether a specific rule is applicable. If no specific rule is applicable, use the regulation's general rules to determine the outcome. This section provides a short overview of those rules.

Reg. § 1.1502-13(a)(1) provides that the purpose of the intercompany transaction rules is to clearly reflect the group's taxable income. The rules operate to prevent transactions between group members from "creating, accelerating, avoiding, or deferring consolidated taxable income (or consolidated tax liability)." Reg. § 1.1502-13(a)(2) is especially important. It provides that group members "are treated as separate entities for some purposes but as divisions of a single corporation for other purposes." When one group member sells to another, this regulation affects the buyer and seller corporations. It treats the two corporations as separate entities with respect to the amount and location of the intercompany and corresponding items. It treats them as divisions of a single entity with respect to timing, character, source, and attributes. Generally, the selling member maintains an account for gain realized on a sale within the group. It defers recognizing that gain until the property is sold outside the group.

Reg. § 1.1502-13(b)(1)(i) defines an intercompany transaction as "a transaction between corporations that are members of the same consolidated group immediately after the transaction." Examples include sales or exchanges of property, performance of services, licensing of technology, rental of property, and distributions of money or other property. Virtually every economic transaction between group members is an intercompany transaction and is subject to the intercompany rules. The technical rules that apply are the Reg. § 1.1502-13(c) matching rule and the Reg. § 1.1502-13(d) acceleration rule.

b. Matching and Acceleration Rules

The matching rule ensures that gains or losses are appropriately assigned to group members. The regulations use several formulas to achieve this result. These formulas involve intercompany items, corresponding items, and recomputed corresponding items. If one group member sells to another, the seller's income, gain, deduction, and loss attributable to the transaction are the intercompany items. The buyer's income, gain, deduction, and loss are the corresponding items. The recomputed corresponding items reflect the amounts that would be reported if the two corporations were parts of a single entity rather than separate corporations.

> **Example 14-10.** Buyer Corporation and Seller Corporation are members of a consolidated group. In Year 1, Seller sold land to Buyer for $100. Seller's basis for the land was $70. Buyer later sold the land to a nonmember for $110. Seller and Buyer each held the land for investment and each held it for more than one year. The intercompany item is Seller's $30 gain on the sale to Buyer. The corresponding item is Buyer's $10 gain on the property, and the recomputed corresponding item is the $40 gain on the sale to the nonmember. When the land left the group, the group recognized a $40 long-term capital gain, allocable $30 to Seller and $10 to Buyer. Reg. § 1.1502-13(c)(7)(ii) Example 1.

The acceleration rule applies when treating the corporations as divisions of a single entity is no longer achievable. Generally, this occurs when one of those corporations leaves the group or is otherwise no longer affiliated with it. In that situation, the acceleration rules cause the group to recognize income and treat the deferred intercompany transaction as a sale or exchange to a nonmember.

> **Example 14-11.** Assume that Seller left the consolidated group before Buyer sold the land to a nonmember. Because the land was not sold to a nonmember before Seller was deconsolidated, the intercompany item is $30, the corresponding item is $0 and the recomputed corresponding item is $0. Because Seller was sold, the matching rule is no longer applicable. Seller was required to take its intercompany gain into account immediately before becoming a nonmember. Seller's de-

parture from the group caused the group to recognize the $30 gain on the land sale.

Several of the intercompany transaction rules apply to particular situations. These include rules for intercompany debt, transactions involving member stock, boot in intercompany transactions, and intercompany to non-intercompany status shifts. When faced with a transaction involving group members, study the specific rules in addition to considering the general concepts applied to intercompany transactions. The regulations' preambles include explanations of these provisions.

Reg. § 1.1502-13(h) provides anti-avoidance rules. This section is reminiscent of § 269, as it provides that if a transaction is structured with a principal purpose to avoid the purposes of the intercompany transaction regulations, then adjustments must be made to carry out those purposes.

2. Basis Investment Adjustment Rules

The Reg. § 1.1502-32 basis investment adjustment rules reflect an underlying concept: to prevent economic distortions, a subsidiary's outside (stock) basis should be adjusted to reflect changes in its inside (money or other property) basis. These rules ensure that the basis one group member has in another member's stock reflects that member's fluctuating investment.

Example 14-12. Parent Corporation transferred $100 to Subsidiary Corporation, a newly created corporation, in exchange for all the Subsidiary stock. The two corporations elected to file a consolidated return. Parent's original basis for its Subsidiary stock was $100. During the first year of consolidation, Subsidiary earned $100, which was included in the group's consolidated taxable income. Parent then sold the Subsidiary stock for its $200 value. Unless Parent could adjust its basis for the Subsidiary stock to include the $100 Subsidiary income reported on the consolidated return, Parent would recognize a $100 gain on its sale of Subsidiary stock and Subsidiary's income would have been taxed twice. Parent could avoid double taxation by having Subsidiary distribute a $100 dividend, which would reduce Subsidiary's stock value and eliminate Parent's gain. Section 243 would give Parent a 100% dividends received deduction. The basis investment adjustment rules give the same result without requiring Subsidiary to distribute assets. Parent could increase its basis for its Subsidiary stock to $200 to reflect Subsidiary's income. Parent would then recognize no gain on its sale of Subsidiary stock.

The basis investment adjustment rules also work in reverse. Parent would reduce its basis for Subsidiary if Subsidiary recognized a loss. Otherwise, Parent could receive a double deduction.

Before 1994, the basis investment adjustment rules were keyed to the subsidiary's E&P. The current regulations de-link subsidiary basis adjustments from E&P because the prior linkage did not produce the desired results. The current regulations provide for adjusting the basis for the subsidiary stock with respect to four items: (1) taxable income or loss; (2) tax-exempt income; (3) noncapital, nondeductible expenses; and (4) distributions with respect to the subsidiary's stock. Reg. § 1.1502-32(b)(2). When a parent corporation receives a tax benefit attributable to its ownership of subsidiary stock, its basis should generally be decreased. Noncapital, nondeductible expenses represent a decline in the subsidiary's wealth. The regulations decrease the parent corporation's basis by the amount of these disallowed expenses. A similar rule applies to tax-exempt income. When a subsidiary receives tax-exempt income, the basis of the subsidiary stock should generally be increased.

> **Example 14-13.** Parent Corporation created Subsidiary Corporation with a $100 investment. Subsidiary earned $100 in tax-exempt income, which increased its value to $200. Parent can increase its basis for Subsidiary stock to $200; if it did not do so, it could end up being taxed on Subsidiary's tax-exempt income.

Section 243 provides a 100% deduction for dividends received from an affiliated subsidiary. A distribution that reduces the subsidiary's wealth increases the parent's wealth. The parent's basis for the subsidiary stock is decreased to reflect this nontaxable accession of wealth. Without this adjustment, the parent would report less gain or more loss when it sold the subsidiary's stock.

> **Example 14-14.** Parent Corporation formed Subsidiary Corporation with a $100 investment. Subsidiary earned $100 in the year of its formation, which resulted in Parent's basis increasing to $200. Subsidiary then distributed $100 to Parent (nontaxable under § 243). Parent must decrease its basis for the Subsidiary stock to $100, as it has effectively received that amount tax-free. Otherwise, Parent would be able to recognize a noneconomic loss of $100 when it sells its Subsidiary stock.

3. Loss Disallowance Regulations

Former Reg. § 1.1502-20 was promulgated to prevent the duplicate loss deduction. It prevented a parent from deducting a loss when it deconsolidated a subsidiary. These rules were attacked as arbitrary and capricious, not reflective of § 1502 and, more important, as providing rules that are more punitive for corporations filing consolidated returns. After part of these rules were invalidated in *Rite Aid Corp. v. United States*, 255 F.3d 1357 (Fed. Cir. 2001), Congress responded by amending § 1502 in 2004. Its last sentence now reads: "In carrying out the preceding sentence [adopting regulations to clearly reflect income], the Secretary may prescribe rules that are different from the provisions of chapter 1 that would apply if such corporations filed separate returns." Reg. § 1.1502-35, issued in 2006 and amended several times (most recently in 2010), is designed to prevent a group from claiming more than one tax benefit from a single economic loss. Reg. § 1.1502-36, issued in 2008, is designed to prevent reducing a group's consolidated taxable income through the creation and recognition of a noneconomic loss on stock in a subsidiary. It is also designed to prevent group members from obtaining more than one tax benefit from a single economic loss.

Checkpoints

- A controlled group can be a parent-subsidiary controlled group, a brother-sister controlled group, a combined group, or an insurance group.
- The controlled group is treated as one corporation for certain tax benefits. For example, group members cannot separately benefit from the § 11 graduated tax rates.
- An affiliated group is a group of corporations whose stock is owned directly or indirectly by a common parent. Group members must own at least 80% of the voting power and stock value of each group member other than the common parent.
- An affiliated group of corporations can elect to file a consolidated return for all the members of the group.
- Once an election is made to consolidate, it is difficult to deconsolidate the group. The group remains in existence even though members enter or exit.
- The tax liability of the consolidated group is several. Liability is computed as the sum of each group member's separate liability, adjusted for certain consolidated items listed in the regulations.
- Transactions between group members are treated under the intercompany transaction rules. Generally, transactions between group members are ignored until the property or the member leaves the group. The basis investment adjustment rule ensures that the basis one member has in another's stock reflects fluctuations in its investment.

Chapter 15

S Corporations and Their Shareholders

Roadmap

- S corporation status
- S corporation income, loss, deduction, and credits
- Taxation of S corporation shareholders
- Shareholder's basis for stock and debt
- Distributions if corporation has E&P
- Redemptions, liquidations, and reorganizations

A. Chapter Overview

This chapter covers the requirements for being an S corporation. These include limits on the number and types of shareholders and a requirement that there be only one class of outstanding stock. It also addresses the computation of corporate income or loss, taxes imposed at the corporate level, shareholder treatment of undistributed corporate income, shareholder treatment of corporate losses, shareholder treatment of distributions, and shareholder basis for stock and debt. If an S corporation has E&P from prior existence as a C corporation, or because a C corporation merged into it, the shareholder's tax consequences are affected by those E&P.

B. S Corporation Status

1. Definition

A corporation is an S corporation if it is a small business corporation and has an election in effect. I.R.C. § 1361(a)(1). To be a small business corporation for purposes of S corporation status, the entity must be a domestic corporation that is not an ineligible corporation. It must also meet requirements related to its shareholders and its outstanding stock.

2. Domestic Corporation

A domestic corporation is a business entity that is created or organized in the United States or under the laws of the United States or of any state and that is classified as a corporation for purposes of federal taxation. I.R.C. § 7701(a)(4); Reg. § 301.7701-5(a). An unincorporated entity is included if it is classified as an association taxable as a corporation by Reg. § 301.7701-2. Reg. § 1.1361-1(c). An LLC or a limited liability partnership that makes an S corporation election is treated as having elected to be taxed as a corporation. Reg. § 301.7701-3(c)(1)(v)(C).

An entity may be domestic even if created or organized in another country if it is also created or organized under the laws of the United States or a state. Reg. § 301.7701-5(a). This book ignores such entities.

3. Ineligible Corporations

The Code makes four categories of corporation ineligible for small business corporation status. I.R.C. § 1361(b)(2). The first ineligible corporation is any financial institution that uses the reserve method of accounting for debts. A financial institution that instead uses the specific charge-off method of accounting for bad debts is not an ineligible corporation. The second ineligible corporation is any insurance company taxed under Subchapter L. The third ineligible corporation is any corporation that is allowed a tax credit for income from Puerto Rico and from U.S. possessions. The possessions credit was phased out beginning in 1995. The fourth ineligible corporation is any Domestic International Sales Corporation (DISC) or former DISC. A former DISC is any corporation that was treated as a DISC in a previous tax year and has undistributed previously taxed income or accumulated DISC income. I.R.C. § 992(a)(3). A fifth ineligible corporation, the taxable mortgage pool, is listed in the regulations. Reg. § 301.7701(i)-4(c)(1).

4. Making and Terminating an S Election

a. Election

A corporation that qualifies for S status becomes an S corporation by electing that status. It makes the S election by filing a completed Form 2553, Election by a Small Business Corporation. Reg. § 1.1362-6(a)(2)(i). Every shareholder at the time of the election must consent to the election. I.R.C. § 1362(a)(2). Shareholders added later do not have to consent. If the corporation elects S status without obtaining all necessary consents, it may qualify for relief if it can establish the election was made inadvertently. I.R.C. § 1362(f).

The corporation makes the election for any taxable year either during the preceding taxable year or before the 16th day of the third month of the taxable year. I.R.C. § 1362(b)(1); Reg. § 1.1362-6(a)(2)(ii)(A). An election made after this time is effective for the next taxable year. I.R.C. § 1362(b)(3).

> **Example 15-1.** For a calendar-year corporation to have S corporation status for 2017, it had to file its election by March 15, 2017. An election filed after March 15, 2017, would be effective for 2018.

Although an election made during the first two and one-half months of the current year is normally effective for that year, § 1362(b)(2) postpones the election's effect until the next year. It applies if the corporation failed to meet the requirements for S status on any day that year before the election was made. It also applies if any person owning stock before the election was made that year did not consent to the election.

b. Termination

The S election continues in effect until it is terminated. A termination is accomplished by: (1) revocation, (2) generating passive investment income under certain circumstances, or (3) ceasing to be a small business corporation. I.R.C. § 1362(d)

If a termination takes effect during a taxable year, the year is an S termination year. I.R.C. § 1362(e)(4). The termination creates two short taxable years, the S short year and the C short year. I.R.C. § 1362(e)(1). The corporation computes income allocable to the S short year, using computations discussed in Section C. Any remaining items are assigned to the C short year. The corporation allocates items attributable to the S short year on a pro rata basis (per-share, per-day). Two exceptions automatically apply to the pro rata allocation rules: (1) § 338 applied to the termination; or (2) there was a sale or exchange of more than 50% of the corporation's stock during the S termination year. I.R.C. § 1362(e)(6)(C)–(D). A third exception applies if the corporation elects to account for all items in accordance with its normal accounting procedures. I.R.C. § 1362(e)(3). Every person who held shares at any time during the S short year must consent to that election, as must every person who held shares on the first day of the C short year.

1. Revocation

Shareholders holding more than one-half of all the stock must consent to a voluntary revocation of the S election. It does not matter whether the stock has voting rights. I.R.C. § 1362(d)(1)(B); Reg. § 1.1362-2(a)(1). A revocation made during the first two and one-half months of the taxable year is effective retroactively to the first day of that taxable year. A revocation made later is effective on the first day of the following taxable year. The corporation can instead specify the date on which the revocation becomes effective. I.R.C. § 1362(d)(1)(C)–(D). The corporation must file the notice of revocation. Reg. § 1.1362-6(a)(3)(i).

> **Example 15-2.** ABC S Corporation has 1,000 shares of common stock outstanding. Arlene owns all 500 shares of the voting stock and Bill owns all 500 shares of the nonvoting stock. A revocation would be effective only if both Arlene and Bill consent. Neither shareholder can effectively consent alone because neither owns more than one-half of the ABC stock.

2. Excess Passive Investment Income

An S election is terminated if two conditions exist: (1) the S corporation has accumulated E&P at the close of each of three consecutive taxable years; and (2) more than 25% of its gross receipts for each of those taxable years is passive investment income. I.R.C. § 1362(d)(3)(A)(i). Because it has no E&P unless it acquires a C corporation's E&P, this rule does not apply to a corporation that has S status from its beginning and never acquired a C corporation by merger.

> **Example 15-3.** DEF Corporation was a C corporation in Year 1 and ended the year with E&P. DEF made an S election effective for Year 2. In Years 4, 5, and 7, DEF had excess passive investment income. Its election does not terminate because it did not did not have passive investment income for three consecutive years in which it was an S corporation. The fact that it had accumulated E&P in each of three consecutive years does not matter; termination requires meeting both conditions.

3. Ceasing to Be a Small Business Corporation

A corporation's failure to satisfy any of the qualification requirements causes the S election to terminate. Those requirements involve limits on the number of shareholders, the types of eligible shareholders, and the classes of outstanding stock.

c. Election After a Termination

Not surprisingly, corporations cannot elect S status for years in which the election gives tax advantages, terminate that status when it does not, and then immediately elect again the next year. A corporation that has had its election terminated generally cannot reelect S status for five taxable years after the termination year. I.R.C. § 1362(g). The IRS can waive the five-year requirement. Reg. § 1.1362-5(a). Waiver will generally occur if there has been more than a 50% change in the corporation's ownership since the termination date. It will otherwise ordinarily be denied unless the corporation establishes that the event causing termination was not reasonably within its control or the control of shareholders having a substantial interest and was not part of a plan on the part of the corporation or those shareholders to terminate the election.

d. Inadvertent Elections and Terminations

The IRS can waive the effects of certain inadvertent invalid elections or inadvertent terminations. I.R.C. § 1362(f). It makes the determination as to whether the invalid election or termination was inadvertent. I.R.C. § 1362(f)(2); Reg. § 1.1362-4(b). The corporation requests this determination through a ruling request. Reg. § 1.1362-4(c).

The IRS can waive an inadvertent election or termination. The corporation must take steps to acquire the necessary consents (election) or requalify itself as a small business corporation (termination) within a reasonable period after discovery of the circumstances that resulted in an ineffective election or in a termination. The corporation and each shareholder during the non-S-status period must agree to make any IRS-specified adjustments. I.R.C. § 1362(f)(3)–(4).

5. Permissible Number of Shareholders

The term "small business" for purposes of S corporation status focuses on the number of shareholders, not on the corporation's assets or gross receipts. The starting point is § 1361(b)(1)(A), which limits the corporation to 100 shareholders. The number of owners, rather than the form of ownership, governs. For example, two persons who own a single share of stock as joint tenants with right of survivorship count as two shareholders unless the family rule described below applies to them. Reg. § 1.1361-1(e). A corporation may have more than 100 separate shareholders during the taxable year so long as there are no more than 100 at any time.

Example 15-4. GHI S Corporation had 100 unrelated shareholders on January 1 of this year. On March 1, one of its shareholders sold her stock to an individual who was not previously a shareholder. Although 101 individuals owned GHI stock during the year, the corporation never had more than 100 shareholders at any time that year.

The 100-shareholder limit is modified by § 1361(c)(1)(A), which treats spouses (and their estates) and all members of a family (and their estates) as one shareholder rather than as separate shareholders. The definition of family members includes individuals who are related by lineal descent, adoption, or marriage; it can even include foster family relationships. I.R.C. § 1361(c)(1)(B)–(C).

Family members include a common ancestor, lineal descendants of that common ancestor, and any spouse (or former spouse) of the common ancestor or a lineal descendant. Adopted children are treated as though they are lineal descendants if they are legally adopted, lawfully placed with an individual for adoption, or eligible foster children.

There are limits on the number of generations a family can include for purposes of this rule. An individual cannot be a common ancestor if, on the applicable date, she was more than six generations removed from the youngest generation of shareholders who would otherwise be considered family members. The applicable date is the latest of: (1) the date the S corporation election was made, (2) the earliest date that a family member holds stock in the S corporation, or (3) October 22, 2004. I.R.C. § 1361(c)(1)(B)(iii). A spouse (or former spouse) is treated as being of the same generation as the individual to whom such spouse is (or was) married.

The regulations treat the first date as the election's effective date, not its signing date. They apply the second date to the individual who would be considered the common ancestor. I.R.C. § 1361(c)(1)(B); Reg. § 1.1361-1(e)(3).

Example 15-5. JKL S Corporation has five equal shareholders. Amanda is unrelated to Bill, Carla, David, and Edna. Bill is married to Carla. David is their birth child, and Edna is their adopted child. Bill, Carla, David, and Edna are family members and are treated as one shareholder. JKL thus has two shareholders for purposes of the 100-shareholder limit rule.

Example 15-6. All the MNO S Corporation stock is owned by 100 married couples. During the year, one couple divorced and each ex-spouse retained shares of the corporation's stock. The corporation still has only 100 shareholders for purposes of § 1361(c)(1). Because a former spouse can be a family member, the divorced spouses are treated as one shareholder.

Example 15-7. All the PQR S Corporation stock was owned by eight lineal generations of a single family when the S election became effective. Members of seven generations are treated as one shareholder (ancestor and six additional generations). Unless the excluded generation has more than 99 members, GHI does not have more than 100 shareholders.

Example 15-8. Assume that the PQR stock was owned by George, his five children, 10 grandchildren, 20 great-grandchildren, 40 great-great-grandchildren, 80 great-great-great-grandchildren, 160 great-great-great-great-grandchildren, and 320 great-great-great-great-great-grandchildren. The 320 members of the youngest generation would prevent PQR from qualifying for S corporation status if only George could be the common ancestor. We could instead treat each of his five children as a common ancestor of his or her own family. PQR would then have only six shareholders—George and the five family groups of which his children were the common ancestors.

The six-generation rule is applied on the applicable date described above. The regulations provide that lower-generation descendants can be treated as part of the family if they acquire stock after that date. Reg. § 1.1361-1(e)(3)(i). The ability to add lower-generation members is important as older generation family members die or otherwise dispose of their stock.

A family can also include the estate or trust of a deceased family member, and it can include family members who own their stock indirectly through an ESBT, a QSST, voting trusts, certain other trusts, and even disregarded entities. Reg. § 1.1361-1(e)(3)(ii).

6. Permissible Types of Shareholders

a. Individuals

Any individual may be a shareholder if he is a citizen or resident of the United States. A nonresident alien cannot be a shareholder. I.R.C. § 1361(b)(1)(C). The individual's age does not matter. Stock can be held in a UTMA custodianship account for a minor; the minor is the shareholder in that situation.

Foreign trusts are specifically excluded as shareholders even if the trust is otherwise qualified. I.R.C. § 1361(c)(2)(A)(flush language); Reg. § 1.1361-1(h)(2).

b. Estates

A decedent's estate may be an S corporation shareholder. I.R.C. § 1361(b)(1)(B). A prolonged delay of the administration of an estate may cause the IRS to assert that the estate is a testamentary trust. *Old Virginia Brick Co. v. Commissioner*, 367 F.2d 276 (4th Cir. 1966).

The estate of an individual in bankruptcy is an eligible shareholder. I.R.C. § 1361(c)(3). After the bankruptcy proceeding ends, the stock may end up owned by an individual or by an entity. If an ineligible shareholder receives the stock, the corporation's S corporation status may terminate.

c. Grantor Trusts

An individual may transfer property into a revocable inter vivos trust, retaining the power to revoke the trust or retaining the right to trust income. These trusts are often used as tools for avoiding state-law probate administration when the transferor (who may be referred to as the grantor or the settlor) dies. For purposes of the federal income tax, the transferor is usually treated as the owner of trust income under the grantor trust rules. The trust's income is taxed to him, even if he does not receive it, rather than to the trust itself or to those beneficiaries who receive the income. In appropriate circumstances, someone other than the transferor may be treated as the grantor for purposes of the income tax. For example, if another person has the power to vest the trust corpus in herself, and needs no one else's consent, she is treated as the owner of that portion of the trust. I.R.C. § 678(a)(1).

The grantor trust provisions are generally covered in estate planning or trust income tax courses. For purposes of this chapter, a trust that is treated as owned by an individual who is a citizen or a resident of the United States is a permissible shareholder. I.R.C. § 1361(c)(2)(A)(i).

A grantor trust can continue as an S corporation shareholder for two years following the deemed owner's death. I.R.C. § 1361(c)(2)(A)(ii). If the terms of the trust name a new owner of the trust, the new owner is the shareholder, not the first owner's estate. Reg. § 1.1361-1(k)(1) Example 2(iii).

d. Trusts Receiving Stock Pursuant to a Will

A trust that receives stock pursuant to a will's terms may be a shareholder for up to two years. The two-year period begins on the day the stock is transferred to the trust. I.R.C. § 1361(c)(2)(A)(iii); Reg. § 1.1361-1(h)(1)(iv). If the trust otherwise qualifies as a QSST, the current income beneficiary can file a QSST election. Reg. § 1.1361-1(j)(6).

e. Voting Trusts

A trust created primarily to vote the shares transferred to it is a permissible shareholder. I.R.C. § 1361(c)(2)(A)(iv). Each beneficiary is considered a shareholder for purposes of the 100-shareholder limit. I.R.C. § 1361(c)(2)(B) (iv). Family members continue to qualify for treatment as a single shareholder. To qualify as a voting trust, the written agreement must: (1) grant voting rights to one or more trustees; (2) require current distribution of dividends; (3) provide that upon its termination stock will be distributed to the beneficial owners; and (4) terminate upon the happening of an event or date. Reg. § 1.1361-1(h)(1)(v).

f. Electing Small Business Trusts

An Electing Small Business Trust (ESBT) may own shares in an S corporation. I.R.C. § 1361(c)(2)(A)(v). These trusts have three requirements: (1) all beneficiaries are individuals, estates, or certain tax-exempt organizations; (2) no interest in the trust was acquired by purchase; and (3) the trustee made a timely election. I.R.C. § 1361(e)(1)(A). Although the election procedures generally mirror those described below for a QSST, a QSST cannot be an ESBT. I.R.C. § 1361(e)(1)(B)(i).

For purposes of determining the beneficiaries of an ESBT, each "potential current beneficiary" is treated as a shareholder for purposes of the 100-shareholder limit. I.R.C. § 1361(c)(2)(B)(v). Any person who is entitled to receive a distribution of principal or income is a potential current beneficiary. Any person who may, in the trustee's discretion, receive such a distribution is also a potential current beneficiary. A person who holds only a remainder or reversionary interest in the trust is not a potential current beneficiary. Reg. § 1.1361-1(m)(4)(i). If there is no potential current beneficiary, the trust is treated as the shareholder.

> **Example 15-9.** STU Corporation has 91 shareholders. Ninety of them are unrelated individuals. The 91st is a small business trust that names the settlor's 15 closest friends, none of whom is related to the settlor or each other, as discretionary beneficiaries. Because the trust has 15 potential current beneficiaries, STU is treated as having 105 shareholders and cannot be an S corporation.

g. Qualified Subchapter S Trusts

Commonly used trusts that can qualify as Qualified Subchapter S Trusts (QSST) include marital deduction trusts and trusts for minors. These trusts are often established for probate-avoidance or estate planning purposes. To qualify as a QSST, a trust must satisfy six requirements:

- The trust beneficiary must elect to treat the portion of the trust that owns the S corporation stock as a grantor trust for income tax purposes. I.R.C. § 1361(d)(1); Reg. § 1.1361-1(h)(1)(iii). The beneficiary effectively is the owner of the stock and thus the shareholder. She is taxed on her allocable share of the corporation's income and deductions.

- There can be only one income beneficiary of the trust while the current income beneficiary is alive. I.R.C. § 1361(d)(3)(A)(i). No one may have a special power to appoint trust income or corpus to anyone other than the current income beneficiary. Reg. § 1.1361-1(j)(2)(iii).
- If trust corpus is distributed during the life of the current income beneficiary, it may be distributed only to that beneficiary. I.R.C. § 1361(d)(3)(A)(ii).
- The current income beneficiary's income interest in the trust must terminate on the earlier of her death or the termination of the trust. I.R.C. § 1361(d)(3)(A)(iii). The trust can terminate on an earlier event specified in the trust document.
- If the trust terminates during the current beneficiary's life, it must distribute all its assets to her. I.R.C. § 1361(d)(3)(A)(iv).
- All trust income must be distributed (or be required to be distributed) currently to a single individual who is a citizen or resident of the United States. I.R.C. § 1361(d)(3)(B). If the trust requires a distribution, the trustee's failure to distribute income does not disqualify the trust as a QSST.

The income beneficiary must make a QSST election by filing a statement with the IRS service center with which the corporation files its income tax return. Reg. § 1.1361-1(j)(6).

h. Other Eligible Entities

Certain charitable organizations and qualified retirement plan trusts organized pursuant to § 401(a) may be S corporation shareholders. I.R.C. § 1361(b)(1)(B), (c)(6). Although a retirement plan trust may have numerous beneficiaries, the trust itself is the shareholder.

> **Example 15-10.** Five retirement plan trusts own all the VWX Corporation shares. Each retirement trust has 25 employee-beneficiaries. Although there are 125 beneficiaries, VWX is treated as having only five shareholders and can qualify as an S corporation.

7. One Class of Stock

An S corporation cannot have more than one class of stock. I.R.C. § 1361(b)(1)(D). We disregard differences in voting rights in determining if a corporation has more than one class of stock. I.R.C. § 1361(c)(4). All outstanding shares must confer identical rights to distribution and liquidation proceeds. Reg. § 1.1361-1(l)(1).

The governing provisions determine whether the shares have identical rights. The governing provisions include the corporate charter, articles of incorporation, bylaws, state law, and any other binding agreements relating to distribution and liquidation proceeds. Reg. § 1.1361-1(l)(2)(i).

> **Example 15-11.** The bylaws of YZ Corporation require that any person who is issued stock in exchange for property other than money must waive all rights to receive distributions until the shareholders who contributed money have received distributions equal to their contributions. This bylaw provision makes distribution and liquidation rights non-identical for all outstanding shares of stock. YZ is treated as having more than one class of stock.

a. Buy-Sell and Redemption Agreements

In determining whether shares of stock confer identical rights, we disregard certain agreements. These include agreements to purchase or redeem shares upon death, disability, divorce, or employment termination. Reg. § 1.1361-1(l)(2)(iii)(B). We also disregard forfeiture provisions that cause a share of stock to be substantially nonvested under § 83.

We usually disregard buy-sell agreements, agreements restricting stock transferability, and redemption agreements in determining whether a corporation's outstanding shares of stock confer identical distribution and liquidation rights. We do not disregard an agreement if: (1) a principal purpose of the agreement is to circumvent the one class of stock requirement; and (2) the agreement establishes a purchase or redemption price that is significantly greater than or below the stock's value at the time the agreement is made. Reg. § 1.1361-1(l)(2)(iii)(A).

The regulations do not provide any standards for determining whether the agreement had, as a principal purpose, circumvention of the one class of stock requirement. The regulations do provide a safe harbor for the second limitation. A purchase price is not considered significantly more or less than the stock's value if the price is book value or a price between fair market value and book value. Reg. § 1.1361-1(l)(2)(iii)(A)(flush language). Two safe harbors are provided for determining book value. The IRS will respect a determination of book value made in accordance with Generally Accepted Accounting Principles (including permitted optional adjustments) or a determination used for any substantial nontax purpose. Reg. § 1.1361-1(l)(2)(iii)(C).

Example 15-12. ABC S Corporation had two equal original shareholders, Carol and Don. A buy-sell agreement provided that no shareholder could transfer stock to an ineligible shareholder without first offering the other shareholder or the corporation the right to purchase the stock. The agreement was not limited to repurchase upon a certain event and called for the stock to be purchased at book value. Two years after the agreement was made, ABC purchased Carol's stock for its $15/share book value when its fair market value was $20/share. We ignore the agreement because the purchase price, when the agreement was made, was book value. Thus, ABC did not have a second class of stock.

b. Varying Interests

Distributions are often made immediately after the end of the taxable year, when the amount of the previous year's income is known. A shareholder who disposed of her stock during the previous year or in the current year but prior to the distribution is still entitled to receive a distribution based on the previous year's allocation. An agreement that provides that distribution in one tax year will be made on the basis of the shareholder's varying interests during the immediately preceding year does not alter the rights to liquidation proceeds and distributions. Reg. § 1.1361-1(l)(2)(iv).

Example 15-13. DEF S Corporation had two equal shareholders, Evelyn and Frank. On July 1, Year 1, Evelyn sold one-half of her stock to Greta. DEF had $100,000 of income for the year. DEF's income is allocated on a daily pro rata basis so that Evelyn reported $37,500, Frank reported $50,000, and Greta reported $12,500. On March 16, Year 2, DEF distributed $20,000. Frank received $10,000, Evelyn received $7,500 and Greta received $2,500. Although Evelyn was then a 25% shareholder but received 37.5% of the distribution, no second class of stock was created. Her distribution reflected her proportionate interest in the immediately preceding year.

c. Restricted Stock

A corporation may give service providers rights to stock that is subject to a substantial risk of forfeiture. The rights do not ripen into absolute ownership until the service provider has worked for a specified number of years, the corporation has met certain earnings targets, or some other condition has been met. While it is subject to a substantial risk of forfeiture, such stock generally is not treated as outstanding stock for purposes of determining whether a corporation has more than one class of stock. However, if the service provider elects under § 83(b) to include the forfeitable stock in gross income in the year of receipt, we take that stock into account in determining whether the corporation has a second class of stock. Reg. § 1.1361-1(b)(3). Even though it remains forfeitable, the stock is not treated as a second class of stock if it confers distribution and liquidation rights that are identical to the rights conferred by the other outstanding shares. Reg. § 1.1361-1(l)(3).

d. Debt Instruments

Although an entity may be funded solely through equity interests, that is unlikely to be the case. Entities routinely borrow money on both a short-term and a long-term basis. The first situation, often involving accounts payable to other entities with which it does business, generally has no effect on the borrower's qualification as an S corporation. The second situation, involving long-term debt, usually evidenced by a security, can cause problems if the debt instrument has both debt and equity characteristics. For example, a long-term bond that can be converted into shares of the corporation's stock has both debt and equity characteristics. Perhaps it might be treated as an impermissible second class of stock.

The Code and regulations provide a safe harbor for straight debt. An instrument qualifies if there is a written unconditional promise to pay a sum certain in money. Payment must be due on demand or at a specified date. The interest rate (and payment of interest) must not be contingent on profits, the borrower's discretion, or similar factors. The instrument cannot be convertible into stock or any other equity interest. The creditor must be an individual who is not a nonresident alien, an estate, a trust that is eligible to be a shareholder, or a person that is actively and regularly engaged in the business of lending money. The mere fact that a debt is subordinated to other corporate debt does not convert it into a second class of stock. I.R.C. § 1361(c)(5); Reg. § 1.1361-1(l)(5). Reg. § 1.1361-1(l)(4) addresses situations not governed by Reg. § 1.1361-1(l)(5). For example, it provides for treating a non-stock instrument as a second class of stock if it is treated as equity under general principles of federal tax law and it was issued for one of two purposes: (1) circumventing the rights to distribution or liquidation proceeds conferred on the outstanding stock; or (2) circumventing the limitation on eligible shareholders.

C. S Corporation Income, Loss, Deductions, and Credits

1. Introduction

The S corporation and its shareholders are linked for purposes of federal income tax. Unlike a C corporation, an S corporation is generally exempt from federal income tax, alternative minimum tax, accumulated earnings tax, and the tax on undistributed personal holding company income. I.R.C. § 1363. Despite the exemption, the S corporation must report its income, loss, deductions, and credits to the IRS, using Form 1120S, and to its shareholders. Its shareholders report their respective share of those items on their own tax returns. I.R.C. § 1366(a).

2. Computation of Corporation's Taxable Income

a. In General

The S corporation computes its taxable income to determine the amount that passes through to its shareholders. Section 1363(b) provides for computing tax as an individual would, but with four exceptions.

An initial difference is in how the corporation classifies items of income, loss, deduction, or credit. Items are either part of nonseparately computed income or loss, or they are separately stated items. Nonseparately computed income or loss is the difference between the S corporation's gross income and deductions. It does not include items of income, loss, deduction, or credit whose separate treatment could affect any shareholder differently from any other shareholder. I.R.C. § 1366(a)(2). Nonseparately computed income or loss passes through as net income or net loss. Shareholders do not report its components as separate items on their tax returns.

Separately stated items are items of income (including tax-exempt income), loss, deduction, or credit that could affect the tax liability of any shareholder differently from any other shareholder on their separate tax returns. I.R.C. § 1366(a)(1)(A). Separately stated items do not affect the computation of the corporation's nonseparately computed income or loss. The corporation instead reports them as separate items to its shareholders. I.R.C. § 1363(b)(1).

The second difference relates to items the corporation cannot deduct. Section 1363(b)(2) refers to those items listed in § 703(a)(2), a partnership provision. It lists six items: the deduction for personal exemptions; the deduction for foreign taxes; the deduction for charitable contributions; the net operating loss deduction; the deductions provided individuals by § 212 through § 223; and the depletion deduction for oil and gas wells. Although not included in that list, the standard deduction is also unavailable. The corporation reports nondeductible items to its shareholders as separately stated items.

The third difference relates to the § 248 deduction for organizational expenses. S corporations deduct that expense in the same manner as C corporations. I.R.C. § 1363(b)(3). The fourth difference relates to the § 291 corporate preference provisions. These apply to S corporations only if they were C corporations in any of the three preceding taxable years. I.R.C. § 1363(b)(4).

b. Separately Stated Items

The corporation separately reports items of income that could affect shareholders differently. Reg. § 1.1366-1(a)(2) lists capital gains (both long-term and short-term); § 1231 gains; passive activity portfolio income (which includes dividends); gains from wagering transactions; portfolio income; tax-exempt income; and any other items listed in guidance issued by the IRS. Although neither the corporation nor its shareholders is taxed on interest from state and local government obligations, these amounts do increase the shareholders' basis for their S corporation stock. In addition, tax-exempt interest might affect the taxation of a shareholder's Social Security benefit. I.R.C. § 86(b)(2). The regulation treats only permanently excludible income as tax-exempt income for this purpose. Income excluded by either § 101 (life insurance proceeds) or § 103 (interest on state or local obligations) is a separately stated item. Income excluded by § 108 (debt discharge) or § 109 (improvements made by a tenant) is not.

Section 1366(a)(1) does not list separately stated deductions or losses. Its flush language indicates that it includes two items listed in § 702(a) — charitable contributions and taxes paid to foreign countries. The regulations provide more information about separately stated items. Reg. § 1.1366-1(a)(2) lists capital losses (both short-term and long-term); § 1231 losses; charitable contributions; taxes paid to foreign countries; losses from wagering transactions; soil and water conservation expenditures; § 179 expenses; medical expenses; deductions provided individuals by § 212 through § 223; any itemized deduction subject to limitation by either § 67 or § 68; expenses related to portfolio income; adjustments and tax preferences for purposes of the alternative minimum tax; and any other items listed in guidance issued by the IRS. Forms and instructions constitute guidance for this purpose.

The § 34 credit related to certain uses of gasoline is not a separately stated item. Other credits are separately stated items.

Example 15-14. ABC S Corporation, which has five equal shareholders, had sales revenue of $1 million, cost of goods sold of $400,000, and other operating expenses of $250,000 for the year. ABC also donated $15,000 to charity. ABC reported $70,000 of nonseparately stated taxable income and $3,000 of charitable contributions to each of its five shareholders. Because charitable contributions are subject to shareholder-level deduction limits, ABC would report the charitable gift separately even if it had only one shareholder.

c. Attributes Reported for Corporate Items

The character and other attributes of separately stated items is generally determined at the corporate level. I.R.C. § 1366(b). Limited anti-abuse exceptions apply to avoid converting ordinary income into capital gain or avoiding capital loss limitations. Reg. § 1.1366-1(b)(1)–(3). Character includes such attributes as short-term and long-term capital gain and loss status, type of capital gain and loss (e.g., whether the property sold was a collectible), and percentage limitations associated with the donee of a charitable gift.

Example 15-15. If ABC also realized a gain from selling a capital asset, each shareholder's pro rata share of that gain is characterized as a capital gain. This is the outcome even if a shareholder happens to be a dealer in that type of property. ABC will report whether the gain was short-term or long-term. If the gain was long-term, ABC will indicate whether the property sold was a collectible or had unrecaptured § 1250 gain.

d. Elections

As a rule, the corporation rather than its shareholders makes any elections regarding the computation of its income or deductions. Shareholders individually make any elections concerning deductions related to mining exploration expenditures and taxes paid to a foreign country. I.R.C. § 1363(c).

e. Fringe Benefits

S corporations may provide their employees with fringe benefits, just as other corporations and unincorporated businesses do. Limitations apply if the S corporation has employee-owners. In addition to any limits found within specific fringe benefit provisions, 2-percent shareholders are subject to the partnership fringe benefit rules. These rules are less generous than those applied to C corporations. A shareholder is a 2-percent shareholder if she owns more than 2% of the corporation's outstanding stock or if she owns stock possessing more than 2% of the voting power. Her ownership includes both actual and constructive ownership, using the § 318 attribution rules. I.R.C. § 1372.

f. Income and Deductions of Qualified Subchapter S Subsidiaries

Although other corporations cannot own S corporation shares, an S corporation may have a "qualified Subchapter S subsidiary" (QSSS or QSub). A QSub is a domestic corporation that satisfies three requirements. First, it is not otherwise ineligible to be an S corporation. Second, it is 100% owned by an S corporation parent. Third, the S corporation elects to treat it as a QSub. I.R.C. § 1361(b)(3)(B).

If a QSub election is in effect, the QSub is disregarded as a separate entity for income tax purposes. Its assets, liabilities, income, deductions, and credits are treated as those of the parent S corporation. I.R.C. § 1361(b)(3)(A); Reg. § 1.1361-4. As a result, intercompany transactions between the parent and the subsidiary are ignored. Although the QSub is disregarded for federal income tax purposes, it remains a separate corporation for state law purposes. Thus, it may still participate in various reorganizations as either the target or acquiring corporation.

When the S corporation elects to treat an existing corporation as a QSub, the subsidiary is treated as having liquidated in a tax-free § 332 liquidation immediately before the election is effective. If an S corporation makes a qualified stock purchase of a target corporation, it may make a § 338 election. If it does, the QSub election is not effective before the day after the acquisition date. The deemed liquidation occurs immediately after the deemed asset purchase. Reg. § 1.1361-4(b)(4).

3. Built-In Gain Tax

When a C corporation liquidates or distributes appreciated property to shareholders, both the corporation and its shareholders are taxed unless § 332 applies. I.R.C. §§ 311(b), 336(a). Because an S corporation itself is not taxed, C corporation shareholders would have an incentive to convert the entity to an S corporation before liquidating it, thus avoiding the corporate-level tax on the gain. The § 1374 tax on built-in gain is designed to prevent this result. The regulations provide computation rules and numerous examples.

A corporation that has been an S corporation throughout its existence is generally not subject to this tax. I.R.C. § 1374(c)(1). However, if an S corporation acquires a C corporation in a reorganization, it would be subject to the built-in gain tax on assets for which it used the C corporation's basis. I.R.C. § 1374(d)(8); Reg. § 1.1374-8(a). Only the assets of the C corporation are considered for this purpose. The corporation can avoid the tax by realizing the gain after the five-year recognition period expires. I.R.C. § 1374(d)(7). The beginning of that period is affected by whether the assets were acquired before the corporation made its S election or were acquired when it was already an S corporation.

Example 15-16. On January 1, 2016, DEF Corporation converted from C corporation to S corporation status. The basis of its assets was unchanged. Any net built-in gain on those assets will not be subject to tax after December 31, 2020, the end of the five-year period.

Example 15-17. GHI S Corporation has always had an S election in effect. This year GHI was the surviving corporation in a tax-free merger with a C corporation. GHI's basis for the assets it received is the same as the C corporation's basis for those assets. GHI's net built-in gain on the assets acquired from the C corporation is subject to the built-in gain tax for a 5-year period beginning on the date of the merger.

The S corporation treats the tax as a loss sustained during the year the tax is imposed. The character of the loss is determined by allocating the loss proportionately among the recognized built-in gains that gave rise to the tax. I.R.C. § 1366(f)(2).

4. Tax on Passive Investment Income

Section 1375(a) imposes a tax on an S corporation in any year in which it has accumulated E&P and more than 25% of its gross receipts are from passive investment income. The tax is imposed on the excess net passive income.

An S corporation can have accumulated E&P because: (1) it was initially a C corporation and had accumulated E&P when it made the S election; (2) it accumulated E&P during a period between two valid S elections; or (3) it acquired E&P from a C corporation in a reorganization.

The gross receipts that constitute passive investment income are those derived from royalties, rents, dividends, interest, and annuities. Section 1375(b)(3) refers to the definition used in § 1362(d)(3) for determining passive investment income and gross receipts.

The tax is imposed on *excess net* passive income, not on passive investment income. We obtain net passive income by reducing the corporation's passive investment income by the deductions that are directly connected with producing that income. I.R.C. § 1375(b)(2). If the corporation does not have net passive income, it cannot have excess net passive income. No tax will be imposed even if its passive investment income exceeds 25% of its gross receipts. When computing gross receipts for this purpose, we take gross receipts from the sale or exchange of stock or securities into account only to the extent of gains; we count gross receipts from the disposition of other capital assets only to the extent of capital gain net income. I.R.C. § 1362(d)(3)(B).

> **Example 15-18.** JKL S Corporation had gross receipts of $50,000, of which $20,000 was attributable to rental income. Because JKL provided no significant services to tenants, its rental income is passive investment income. JKL had $22,500 of expenses attributable to the rental income. Although its $20,000 rental receipts exceeded 25% of its $50,000 gross receipts, JKL had no *net* passive income. It was not subject to the § 1375 tax for that year.

To compute excess net passive income, we first subtract 25% of gross receipts from the corporation's passive investment income. We then determine what percentage that amount is of its passive investment income. Finally, we multiply that percentage by the corporation's net passive income. Section 1375(b)(1)(A) expresses this as a ratio. Excess net passive income is the amount that bears the same ratio to net passive income as passive investment income in excess of 25% of gross receipts bears to passive investment income.

> **Example 15-19.** MNO S Corporation had $140,000 of gross receipts, of which $100,000 was passive investment income. MNO had $20,000 of expenses attributable to its passive investment income. MNO's net passive income was $80,000. Its excess net passive income was $52,000, computed using the above formula. We subtract 25% of MNO's gross receipts (25% * $140,000=$35,000) from its $100,000 passive investment income. We divide that $65,000 difference by MNO's $100,000 passive investment income. We multiply that percentage by MNO's net passive investment income (65% * $80,000) and get excess net passive income of $52,000. Expressed as a ratio, the formula for excess net passive income ($x) would be: ($100,000—(.25 * $140,000))/$100,000=$x/$80,000.

One limitation applies. Excess net passive income cannot exceed the amount of the corporation's taxable income for the taxable year, modified as provided in § 1375(b)(1)(B). If MNO Corporation's taxable income for the year had been only $40,000, its excess net passive income would have been limited to $40,000.

We calculate the tax owed on the excess net passive income by multiplying the highest current corporate tax rate by the excess net passive income. I.R.C. § 1375(a).

Example 15-20. A 35% tax rate applies to MNO's $52,000 excess net passive income, using rates in effect at the end of 2016. The tax on $52,000 is $18,200. If MNO's taxable income had been only $40,000, its excess net passive income would have been limited to that amount, and the tax would have been only $14,000.

The corporation reduces each item of passive investment income proportionally by this tax. It passes those items through to its shareholders. I.R.C. § 1366(f)(3).

Example 15-21. PQR S Corporation converted to S status two years ago. This year PQR had gross receipts (and taxable income) consisting of $30,000 of dividends and $50,000 of rents. All $80,000 was passive investment income, which resulted in a tax of $21,000 on the excess passive investment income of $60,000. The tax was allocated 5/8 to rent and 3/8 to dividends. PQR passed through $36,875 of rent ($50,000—$13,125) and $22,125 of dividends ($30,000—$7,875) to its shareholders.

In certain instances, the IRS can waive the tax on excess passive investment income. I.R.C. § 1375(d). The corporation must establish that it determined in good faith that it had no accumulated E&P at the close of a tax year, and, during a reasonable period after it was determined that it did, in fact, have accumulated E&P at the close of that tax year, it distributed those E&P.

5. Passive Investment Income and Termination of S Status

As discussed in Section B, a corporation's S status terminates if it has excess passive investment income for three consecutive taxable years in which it also has accumulated E&P. It has excess net passive income if passive investment income exceeds 25% of its gross receipts for the year.

Note the difference between the conditions leading to termination and the conditions leading to imposition of the tax on excess net passive income. Termination occurs if there is excess passive investment income and accumulated E&P in three consecutive years. The § 1375 tax applies if the S corporation has both excess net passive income and accumulated E&P in any year.

D. Taxation of S Corporation Shareholders

1. Introduction

The taxation of S corporation shareholders is somewhat like that of partners in partnerships. The entity's income, deductions, losses, and credits pass through to the shareholders, who report them on their tax returns even if the entity makes no distributions. The character of these items passes through as well. The items pass through either as separately stated or nonseparately computed amounts.

2. Pass-Through Items

a. Nonseparately Computed Income or Loss Items

Nonseparately computed income or loss is the difference between the S corporation's gross income and deductions other than items whose separate treatment could affect any shareholder differently from another shareholder. I.R.C. § 1366(a)(2). Nonseparately computed income or loss passes through as net income or net loss. If, for any reason, the amount of a shareholder's gross income must be determined, the shareholder uses her share of the corporation's gross income, not her share of its net income or loss. I.R.C. § 1366(c).

b. Separately Stated Items

Items must be separately stated if they could affect any shareholder's tax liability differently. This rule applies to income, gain, deduction, loss, or credit items. I.R.C. § 1366(a)(1). In determining whether an item could affect a shareholder differently, we focus on whether the item could do so in theory, not on whether it actually does so.

The character of each separately stated item also passes through, and most ceilings and limits on various deductions apply at the shareholder level. I.R.C. § 1366(b); Reg. § 1.1366-1(a)(2).

1. Capital Gains and Losses

Long-term capital gains enjoy preferential treatment, while capital losses are subject to deduction limitations. I.R.C. §§ 1(h), 1211. Because multiple rates can apply to net capital gains, each category of short-term and long-term capital gains passes through separately. Reg. § 1.1366-1(a)(2)(i).

Although C corporations cannot deduct a net capital loss, that rule does not apply to S corporations. The S corporation passes capital losses through as separately stated items. Each shareholder remains subject to the § 1211(b) limit on the deduction for capital losses for any taxable year. Generally, an individual shareholder may deduct capital losses equal to capital gains plus $3,000. He combines the passed-through gains and losses with his separate capital gains and losses to determine if the limit applies. He carries any unused capital loss forward to other taxable years. I.R.C. § 1212(b).

> **Example 15-22.** S Corporation realizes $5,000 of capital gain and $3,000 of capital loss, both of which pass through to Abner, its sole shareholder. Abner individually realizes $2,000 of capital gain and $8,000 of capital loss. He reports $7,000 of capital gains as gross income and can deduct $10,000 of capital loss in computing adjusted gross income. He carries his remaining $1,000 capital loss forward as a possible future deduction. The loss retains its character as short-term or long-term.

2. *Section 1231 Gains and Losses*

An S corporation's § 1231 gains and losses pass through to shareholders to be aggregated with their individual § 1231 gains and losses. Reg. § 1.1366-1(a)(2)(ii).

3. *Charitable Contributions*

Because the limits on the charitable contributions deduction apply at the shareholder level, corporate contributions pass through separately to each shareholder. Each shareholder takes a pro rata share of the contributions and aggregates it with his own charitable contributions to determine if he is subject to the ceiling on the deduction.

When the corporation reports contributions to its shareholders, it indicates whether contributions in property were of capital gain property and whether contributions of capital gain property qualify for the 30% or the 20% of contribution base limits found in § 170(b).

4. *Tax-Exempt Interest*

Tax-exempt interest passes through to shareholders. Reg. § 1.1366-1(a)(2)(viii). It retains its character as tax-exempt interest and is therefore not taxable to the shareholder. It does, however, affect the potential taxability of the shareholder's Social Security benefits. I.R.C. § 86. The tax consequences of those benefits reflect a modified AGI that includes tax-exempt interest.

Expenses related to the production of tax-exempt income also pass through to shareholders. Because these expenses are attributable to producing tax-exempt income, the shareholders cannot deduct them. I.R.C. § 265.

5. *Foreign Taxes*

Each shareholder separately decides whether to claim passed-through foreign taxes as deductions or credits on her personal tax return. I.R.C. §§ 164, 901.

6. Section 179 Deduction

Instead of depreciating the property, taxpayers can take an immediate deduction for the cost of trade or business property covered by § 179. Most qualifying property is depreciable tangible personal property, but this section can also apply to computer software and qualified real property. I.R.C. § 179(d)(1), (f). The deduction has a dollar limit, which is subject to an annual inflation adjustment. I.R.C. § 179(b)(1), (6). The maximum deduction was $510,000 for 2017. Rev. Proc. 2016-55, 2016-45 I.R.B. 707. The dollar limit is applied at the corporate level and again at the shareholder level. I.R.C. § 179(d)(8). Because a shareholder must reduce his basis for his S corporation stock by the deduction passed through to him, he uses his corporate-level deduction ahead of any separate individual deduction for which he might have qualified. I.R.C. § 1367(a)(2)(B).

> **Example 15-23.** During 2017, XYZ S Corporation purchased $600,000 of § 179 property and elected immediate expensing. The maximum deduction in 2017 was $510,000. XYZ reported a $170,000 deduction to each of its three equal shareholders, Anne, Bob, and Carol. Anne operated another business as a sole proprietor; she individually purchased $420,000 of § 179 property in 2017. Anne deducted the $170,000 that the corporation passed through to her before she deducted any of the amount she individually spent, because her basis for her stock would be decreased even if she didn't deduct the corporate item. Because Anne deducted $170,000 that XYZ passed through to her, she could immediately deduct only $340,000 of the $420,000 she spent for her other business.

The § 179 limitation may become irrelevant if Congress amends the Code to allow unlimited immediate expensing.

7. Credits

Except for the special credit for certain uses of gasoline, special fuels, and lubricating oil allowed under § 34, credits pass through separately. Each shareholder takes the passed-through credits into account in determining the amount she can claim on her own tax return.

3. Allocating Income and Loss

a. General Rule

The corporation's income, deductions, losses, and credits are allocated on a daily pro rata basis. Both the separately stated items and nonseparately computed income or loss are allocated equally to each day of the taxable year. Each day's portion is allocated on a pro rata basis among the shares outstanding on that day. I.R.C. § 1377(a).

> **Example 15-24.** ABC S Corporation began the year with two equal shareholders, Carla and Devin. On August 31, Edna bought Devin's stock. That year ABC realized a $3,650 capital loss (assigned $10/day) and had $18,250 of nonseparately computed income (assigned $50/day). Under the per-share, per-day allocation rule, Carla was assigned $1,825 of capital loss and $9,125 of net income. Devin was assigned $1,210 of capital loss ($10 * 242 days * 50%) and $6,050 of net income ($50 * 242 days * 50%). Edna was assigned $615 of capital loss ($10 * 123 days * 50%) and $3,075 of net income ($50 * 123 days * 50%).

b. Election to Close the Books

An election to close the books can be made if there is a complete termination of a shareholder's interest. I.R.C. § 1377(a)(2)(A). Closing the books has the effect of allocating all items to two different periods.

The election requires that the corporation and all affected shareholders agree. The shareholder whose interest is terminated is an affected shareholder. Anyone to whom he transfers his stock is also an affected shareholder. If the terminating shareholder transfers any of his shares to the corporation itself, all shareholders are affected shareholders. I.R.C. § 1377(a)(2)(B); Reg. § 1.1377-1(b)(1)–(2).

> **Example 15-25.** DEF S Corporation began the year with two equal shareholders, Fred and Genevieve. On August 31, Harry bought Genevieve's DEF stock. DEF had a $7,300 operating loss through August 31; it operated at a $54,750 profit for the remainder of that year. It had no separately stated items. DEF, Genevieve, and Harry elected to close DEF's books on August 31. Under the per-share, per-day allocation rule, Fred reported $3,650 of net loss for the first part of the year and $27,375 net income for the remainder of the year. Genevieve reported $3,650 of net loss for the part of the year in which she owned DEF stock. Harry reported $27,375 of net income for the part of the year in which he owned DEF stock.

c. Termination of S Election

The termination of the S election results in two short taxable years—an S short year and a C short year. The corporation allocates items of income, loss, deduction, and credit on a per-share, per-day basis for the entire S termination year. I.R.C. § 1362(e)(2)(A). It passes the amounts attributable to the S termination year through to the shareholders. The corporation is subject to Subchapter C for the second short year on the income allocated to that period, computed on an annualized basis. That income is subject to tax using the corporate tax rates. I.R.C. § 1362(e)(5)(A).

d. Election Under Regulation Section 1.1368-1(g)

The corporation may elect to have two taxable years when one of the three events described in Reg. § 1.1368-1(g) occurs. The regulation applies if any shareholder disposes of 20% or more of the corporation's stock in any 30-day period during the taxable year. It does not matter if the shareholder disposed of the stock in a single transaction or multiple transactions. It also applies if the corporation redeemed 20% or more of its shares in any 30-day period from a single shareholder in a redemption treated as an exchange by § 302(a) or § 303(a). Finally, it applies if the corporation issues an amount of stock equal to at least 25% of its outstanding stock to one or more new shareholders. All shareholders who held stock during the taxable year must consent to the election.

If a disposition results in a complete termination of a shareholder's interest, § 1377 applies instead of Reg. § 1.1368-1(g). Reg. § 1.1368-1(g)(2)(iv).

4. Limits on Loss Deductions

All corporate income is passed through to, and reported by, shareholders. Deductions for expenses and losses, on the other hand, cannot exceed the shareholder's adjusted basis for her stock and debt. I.R.C. § 1366(d)(1). The shareholder applies any passed-through loss against stock basis before she applies it against debt basis. She makes basis adjustments for income and distributions before using any losses to offset basis. Reg. § 1.1366-2(a)(4)(i).

Other limits may be relevant. Even if the shareholder has basis, her loss deductions may be subject to the § 465 at-risk rules and the § 469 passive activity provisions.

E. Shareholder's Basis for Stock and Debt

1. Investment in the Corporation

a. Initial Stock and Debt Basis

A shareholder's original basis for stock or debt is determined in the same manner as the basis of stock or debt in a C corporation. She may have acquired the stock or debt through purchase, gift, inheritance, or transfer from a spouse or former spouse incident to a divorce. She may also have acquired it in exchange for property in a transaction governed by § 351 or in a § 355 divisive transaction, in which case Code sections based on those provisions governed her basis.

b. Additional Investment

A shareholder who makes additional investments, through direct purchases from the corporation or from another shareholder, increases her basis by the amount she pays. Basis rules for gifts, and other non-purchase events, apply if she acquires her shares other than by purchase.

c. Corporate Debt

Instead of loaning funds to the corporation, a shareholder might instead guarantee the corporation's debt to a third party. If the corporation repays the third party, the shareholder will not be called upon to indirectly increase his investment by paying the corporation's debt. Courts have held that guaranteeing corporate debt does not increase a shareholder's basis. *Estate of Bean v. Commissioner*, 268 F.3d 553 (8th Cir. 2001); *Sleiman v. Commissioner*, 187 F.3d 1352 (11th Cir. 1999). These decisions look for an economic outlay by the taxpayer.

Another scenario involves a shareholder borrowing money directly and loaning it to the corporation. In that situation, he has made a direct investment even if he is likely to be repaid when the debt comes due.

Hitchins v. Commissioner, 103 T.C. 711 (1994), represents another attempt to increase the shareholder's basis. The shareholder controlled both an S corporation and a C corporation. The C corporation was indebted to the shareholder. The S corporation assumed that debt, but the C corporation remained liable. The shareholder was not allowed to increase his basis for his S corporation stock or for the corporation's indebtedness to him. The court reiterated a requirement from earlier decisions. The taxpayer could not increase basis without making an economic outlay in the corporation that sustained the loss. It also noted that the shareholder could have increased his basis had he structured the transaction differently. He could have had the C corporation transfer the S corporation's note payable in satisfaction of the C corporation's debt.

If a shareholder is forced to satisfy any of a debt he guaranteed, his basis increases. The IRS has also ruled that his basis increases if he substitutes his personal note for the corporate debt and the lender relieves the corporation of liability. Rev. Rul. 75-144, 1975-1 C.B. 277. The *Hitchins* decision distinguished Rev. Rul. 75-144 based on the different facts involved in the loan transactions. In *Phillips v. Commissioner*, T.C. Memo. 2017-61, the taxpayer guaranteed a bank loan to the corporation, but the lender did not release the corporation from liability. When it defaulted, the bank obtained a judgment against her. Although she had not paid that debt, she argued that her basis for her stock or corporate indebtedness to her should be increased. The court denied the basis increase because the judgments against her did not constitute an economic outlay.

2. Pass-Through of Corporation's Income, Deductions, and Losses

a. Effect on Stock Basis

Separately stated income items and nonseparately computed income increase the shareholder's basis for his stock. To ensure its permanent exclusion, even tax-exempt income increases his basis. If he did not increase his basis, he would have to recognize the tax-exempt income when he disposed of his stock in a taxable transaction. Separately stated deductions and losses and nonseparately computed loss decrease the shareholder's basis. it. Basis is also decreased by any tax-free distributions under § 1368 and by nondeductible expenses that are not properly chargeable to capital account. Corporate depletion deductions also affect basis. I.R.C. § 1367(a). Additional information and ordering rules for basis increases and reductions are covered later in this section. That discussion includes the effect of distributions.

> **Example 15-26.** Jack received all the stock in GHI S Corporation from Irene as a gift at the end of Year 1. Irene's $10,000 basis for the stock became Jack's initial basis. In Year 2, GHI received tax-exempt interest of $20,000. It had no other income or deductions. The tax-exempt interest passed through to Jack as a separately stated item and increased his basis to $30,000. Jack sold his GHI stock for $30,000 at the end of Year 2. He realized no gain on the sale. If the tax-exempt interest had not increased his basis, Jack would have realized and recognized a $20,000 gain. That would have effectively caused the tax-exempt interest to be taxed.

Because a shareholder can deduct these items only to the extent of his basis, passed-through items cannot create negative basis. When he acquires basis, he can deduct the excess loss, after which his basis is decreased to reflect the loss deduction.

b. *Effect on Debt Basis*

If the shareholder is also a creditor, passed-through income and deductions can affect her basis for debt instruments she owns. The shareholder offsets losses and other deductions against basis for debt only if she has a zero basis for her stock. As with stock, she cannot reduce her basis for debt below zero. I.R.C. § 1367(b)(2)(A).

The reduction applies only to the basis of debt held at the end of the taxable year; the shareholder does not reduce the basis of debt that has been satisfied or forgiven during the taxable year. Reg. § 1.1367-2(b)(1). If she holds more than one corporate debt, she reduces her basis for each debt by the proportion that each debt's basis bears to her bases for all corporate debt.

> **Example 15-27.** Nina owns all the shares of MNO S Corporation, for which her basis is $3,000. Nina had initially loaned MNO $15,000 (Debt 1), for which her basis is currently $6,000. She later loaned MNO $20,000 (Debt 2), for which her basis is currently $14,000. MNO incurred a net loss of $18,000 this year and made no loan repayments to Nina on either loan. Nina can deduct the entire loss but she must reduce her basis for her shares and for the debt. Nina reduces her basis for the MNO stock from $3,000 to zero. She reduces her basis for the two debts by the remaining $15,000 loss; the reduction is in proportion to her basis for each debt. Nina's basis for Debt 1 is reduced by $4,500 ($15,000 * $6,000/$20,000) to $1,500. Nina's basis for Debt 2 is reduced by $10,500 ($15,000 * $14,000/$20,000) to $3,500.

If a shareholder's basis for debt was decreased in a prior year, any net increase in a later year restores his basis for the debt before it increases his basis for his stock. I.R.C. § 1367(b)(2)(B). Net increase is not the same as net income. An S corporation's net income does not include separately stated items. Its net increase is the net of the increases that could be made to stock basis under § 1367(a)(1) and decreases that could be made under § 1367(a)(2). Reg. § 1.1367-2(c)(1). This computation does include separately stated items.

The shareholder can restore only the basis of debt he held on the first day of the taxable year in which the net increase occurs. Reg. § 1.1367-2(c)(1). No matter how much basis was decreased, the shareholder cannot restore his basis for debt above the outstanding balance of the debt determined as of the first day of the taxable year in which the net increase occurs.

If the shareholder held multiple corporate debts on the first day of the corporation's taxable year, any net increase first restores the reduction of basis for any debt repaid, in whole or in part, in that taxable year to offset any gain that would otherwise be realized on the repayment. Reg. § 1.1367-2(c)(2). The remaining net increase restores each outstanding debt in proportion to the amount that the basis of each outstanding debt has been reduced and not restored. If the corporate note is a capital asset in the creditor-shareholder's hands, he has a capital gain to the extent that any amount repaid exceeds his adjusted basis for the debt.

If the corporation repays a debt before its basis is restored, the shareholder reports gross income.

> **Example 15-28.** Pam owned all 50 shares of stock in STU S Corporation; her basis was zero. Pam made three loans to STU. The loan amounts were $5,000 (Debt 1), $10,000 (Debt 2), and $15,000 (Debt 3). In Year 1, STU passed through a loss of $12,000, which reduced the basis of each debt in proportion to their aggregate bases. Pam thus reduced her basis for Debt 1 by $2,000 ($12,000 * $5,000/$30,000) to $3,000. She reduced her basis for Debt 2 by $4,000 ($12,000 * $10,000/$30,000) to $6,000. She reduced her basis for Debt 3 by $6,000 ($12,000 * $15,000/$30,000) to $9,000. Although STU did not have a net increase for Year 2, it fully repaid Debt 1 on October 1. The repayment exceeded Pam's basis for Debt 1 by $2,000.

> **Example 15-29.** STU instead had a net increase of $7,000 for Year 2. Pam would first restore her basis for Debt 1 by $2,000 immediately before the repayment. As a result, her basis for Debt 1 at the time of repayment would be $5,000 and she would report no gain. She would then allocate the remaining $5,000 net increase to the other two debts in proportion to the amount that each debt had been reduced previously. Pam would increase her basis for Debt 2 by $2,000 ($5,000 * $4,000/$10,000) to $8,000. She would increase her basis for Debt 3 by $3,000 ($5,000 * $6,000/$10,000) to $12,000.

3. Distributions

If an S corporation has no accumulated E&P, the rules are straightforward. To the extent that the shareholder has basis, the distribution is tax-free. I.R.C. § 1368(b)(1). The shareholder's basis is reduced but not below zero. I.R.C. § 1367(a)(2)(A). Any excess amount is treated as gain from a sale or exchange. I.R.C. § 1368(b)(2). If the shareholder holds the stock as a capital asset, the gain is capital gain.

Example 15-30. GHI S Corporation has no E&P. It made a $100 distribution to Tim, its sole shareholder. After the pass-through of income, loss, and deductions for the year, Tim had a $70 basis for his stock. The distribution decreased Tim's basis to zero. Tim also had a $30 capital gain.

The shareholder cannot avoid reporting a gain by reducing his basis for corporate debt to offset a distribution that exceeds his stock basis. Section 1368(b)(1) does not provide for treating distributions as tax-free reductions of his basis for debt.

Example 15-31. JKL S Corporation has no E&P. At the start of the year, Ursula, its sole shareholder, had a basis for her stock of $80. She also held a JKL note, for which she had a basis of $140. The corporation reported no pass-through items that year but did distribute $100 to Ursula. The distribution decreased Ursula's stock basis to zero. Ursula also had a $20 capital gain. Her basis for the debt did not change.

Although a distribution does not decrease the shareholder's basis for corporate debt, she must take the distribution into account in determining whether there is a net increase for debt basis restoration purposes. If the distribution exceeds the net increase, she does not restore the debt's basis. If the distribution is less than the net increase, she restores the debt's basis to the extent of the difference. Reg. § 1.1367-2(e) Examples 4 & 5.

Example 15-32. Keith owns all the shares of VWX S Corporation; his basis is zero. On July 1, Year 1, he loaned VWX $20,000. VWX had a net loss of $6,000 for Year 1; that loss reduced his basis for the debt to $14,000. VWX distributed $10,000 to him in Year 2. The sum of the items increasing basis under § 1367(a)(1) was $8,000 for Year 2; VWX had no items of loss or deduction that would decrease basis. There was no net increase because the $10,000 distribution exceeded the $8,000 increase. As a result, Keith's basis for the debt remained $14,000. His basis for the stock increased to $8,000 to reflect VWX's income and then decreased to zero because of the distribution. He reported a gain of $2,000, which is the amount by which the distribution exceeded his basis for the stock.

Example 15-33. The sum of VWX's items increasing basis was instead $14,000. In that situation, there was a net increase of $4,000 ($14,000—$10,000). Keith's basis for the debt increased to $18,000. His basis for the stock remained zero.

If an S corporation distributes property other than money, the amount distributed is the amount of money plus the fair market value of the other property distributed. The rules regarding the shareholder's tax consequences are the same as if only money was distributed.

If the corporation distributes appreciated property, it recognizes gain and the gain passes through to the shareholders as though the corporation had sold the property and distributed the proceeds. I.R.C. § 311(b). An exception applies to distributions in tax-free reorganizations. I.R.C. § 361(a). If the property distributed is worth less than the corporation's basis, the corporation cannot recognize loss. I.R.C. § 311(a). The shareholder's basis for the distributed property, whether it is gain or loss property, is fair market value. I.R.C. § 301(d).

4. Ordering Rules if Shareholder Owns No Corporate Debt

If a shareholder does not own corporate debt, determining how income, deductions, and distributions affect stock basis is relatively simple. Section 1367 divides items into those that increase basis and those that decrease it.

Three items increase basis. I.R.C. § 1367(a)(1)(A)–(C). These items are the separately stated items of income; nonseparately computed income; and the excess of depletion deductions over the basis of property subject to depletion. Reg. § 1.1367-1(b)(1) indicates that this does not apply to depletion attributable to oil and gas property.

Five items decrease basis. I.R.C. § 1367(a)(2)(A)–(E). The first is any distribution described in § 1368. Those are distributions by a corporation that had no E&P. The second is any separately stated item of loss or deduction. The third is nonseparately computed loss. The fourth is any noncapital, nondeductible expense. The fifth is any oil and gas depletion allowance to the extent the deduction does not exceed the shareholder's proportionate share of the mineral property's adjusted basis.

Reg. § 1.1367-1(f) provides the ordering rules used in adjusting stock basis. The three basis increases come first. They are followed by the basis decreases in an order that differs slightly from the Code section listing and that combines some items. As a result, there are three categories of decrease in the ordering regulation. The first item is any distribution by a corporation that had no E&P. The second decrease is for noncapital, nondeductible expenses and the decrease for oil and gas depletion. The third decrease is for separately stated items of loss or deduction and nonseparately computed loss.

The adjustments are generally made at the close of the corporation's taxable year. They are made immediately before the shareholder disposes of his stock if the disposition occurs before year-end. If there is an election to close the corporation's year because a shareholder's interest terminated or a disposition described in Reg. § 1.1368-1(g)(2) occurred, adjustments are made at the end of the day on which the termination or disposition occurred. Reg. § 1.1367-1(d).

A shareholder can instead elect the ordering rules provided in Reg. § 1.1367-1(g). If he does so, he cannot return to the normal ordering rules without obtaining IRS permission. The elective ordering moves the fourth item above to be the second item.

F. Distributions if Corporation Has E&P

An S corporation may have E&P because it was previously a C corporation. It may also have E&P acquired from a C corporation in a reorganization. If the corporation has E&P, we determine the shareholder's tax consequences by considering its accumulated adjustments account (AAA) and its E&P.

1. Accumulated Adjustments Account

The accumulated adjustments account is a corporate-level account used in computing a shareholder's tax consequences from receiving a distribution. The corporation's AAA is particularly important because it allows the shareholder to offset distributions against basis instead of reporting them as taxable distributions of corporate E&P.

The AAA is computed the same way as the shareholder's basis for the S corporation stock, but with three major exceptions. I.R.C. § 1368(e)(1)(A). First, tax-exempt income and the expenses associated with that income do not increase or decrease the AAA even though they affect the shareholder's basis for his stock. Second, pass-through items do not reduce stock basis below zero, but the AAA can carry a deficit attributable to those items. Third, the AAA is not adjusted for federal taxes attributable to any year in which the corporation was a C corporation. Reg. § 1.1368-2(a)(1)–(3).

The AAA generally is adjusted at year-end before the tax effect of distributions is determined. If an election is made under § 1377(a)(2) or Reg. § 1.1368-1(g)(2), and the corporation treats the year as if it consisted of two taxable years, the adjustments are allocated between the two years. Reg. § 1.1368-2(e).

2. Tax Consequences of Distributions

Unless an S corporation elects otherwise, distributions are not treated as dividends to the extent of the corporation's AAA. I.R.C. § 1368(b)(1), (c)(1).

Example 15-34. MNO S Corporation has an AAA of $42 and accumulated E&P of $45. Vance, its sole shareholder, has a basis for his MNO stock of $24. If MNO distributes $22 to him, Vance reports a $22 tax-free recovery of basis even though MNO has E&P because MNO's AAA exceeded the $22 distribution. MNO's E&P account remains at $45; its AAA is reduced to $20. Vance's basis for his stock is reduced to $2.

If the amount distributed from the AAA exceeds the shareholder's stock basis, the excess is treated as gain from the sale or exchange of property, just as it would be if there were no E&P. I.R.C. § 1368(b)(2), (c)(1). Any distribution in excess of AAA is treated as a dividend to the extent of E&P. I.R.C. § 1368(c)(2).

Example 15-35. If MNO instead distributed $41 to Vance, he reports a $24 tax-free recovery of basis and a $17 gain from the sale or exchange of stock because the $42 AAA exceeded the $41 distribution. MNO's E&P account remains at $45; its AAA is reduced to $1. Vance's basis for his stock is reduced to zero.

Example 15-36. If MNO instead distributed $62 to Vance, he reports a $24 tax-free recovery of basis and an $18 gain from the sale or exchange of stock. Those amounts equaled the $42 AAA. He also reports a $20 dividend because MNO had at least that much E&P. MNO's E&P account is reduced to $25; its AAA is reduced to zero. Vance's basis for his stock is reduced to zero.

A distribution that exceeds E&P is treated as a distribution by an S corporation with no E&P: the excess first reduces any remaining stock basis and is then treated as gain from the sale or exchange of property. I.R.C. § 1368(c)(3).

Example 15-37. If MNO instead distributed $100 to Vance, he reports a $24 tax-free recovery of basis and an $18 gain from the sale or exchange of stock. Those amounts equaled the $42 AAA. Vance reports a $45 dividend because MNO had that much E&P. The remaining $13 he received would have reduced his stock basis if he still had any basis. Because he did not, he reports that $13 as gain from the sale or exchange of stock. MNO's E&P account, its AAA, and Vance's basis for his stock are all reduced to zero by this distribution. Vance's total reported gain is $31.

Example 15-38. If Vance's basis in Example 15-37 had instead been $51, he reports a $42 tax-free recovery of basis. That amount equaled the $42 AAA. Vance reports a $45 dividend because MNO had that much E&P. Of the remaining $13 he received, $9 is a tax-free recovery of basis and $4 is gain from the sale or exchange of stock. MNO's E&P account, its AAA, and Vance's basis for his stock are all reduced to zero by this distribution.

3. Timing of Distributions

Adjustments to the AAA and to the shareholder's basis are made at year-end. They are not affected during the year by account distributions made before year-end. If the corporation had negative income for the year, we determine the AAA at year-end for purposes of determining the treatment of distributions, without regard to the negative amount. I.R.C. § 1368(e)(1)(C); Reg. § 1.1368-1(e).

Example 15-39. PQR S Corporation's sole shareholder Wilma had an adjusted basis of zero for her shares at the beginning of the year. PQR had an AAA of zero and accumulated E&P of $40. On August 1, PQR distributed $70. On that date, it had net income of $80. By December 31, however, PQR's net income for the entire year was only $50. That amount passed through to Wilma to report on her tax return. She increased her adjusted basis to $50; PQR increased its AAA to $50. Wilma received only $50 of the distribution tax-free; the remaining $20 was a dividend. For the year as a whole, she reported total income of $70 (pass-through income and dividend income). Her stock basis was reduced back to zero.

Example 15-40. The results would be different if PQR had net income of $50 on August 1 and net income for the full year of $80. The $80 net income passed through to Wilma to report on her tax return. She increased her adjusted basis to $80; PQR increased its AAA to $80. Wilma received all $70 of the distribution tax-free. For the year as a whole, she reported total income of $80 (all pass-through). Her stock basis ended at $10.

4. Accelerating Dividends

The corporation's shareholders may want to eliminate the E&P and avoid the termination rules and the passive investment income tax discussed earlier in this chapter. The corporation can do so by electing to bypass the AAA. I.R.C. § 1368(e)(3). In that case, any distribution comes first from accumulated E&P. Distributions to shareholders are taxed in the following order: (1) the distribution is a dividend to the extent of accumulated E&P. I.R.C. § 1368(c)(2); (2) any excess over E&P is a tax-free recovery of stock basis to the extent of the AAA. I.R.C. § 1368(c)(1); and (3) any amount that exceeds stock basis or the AAA is treated as gain. I.R.C. § 1368(b)(2), (c)(3). The corporation reduces its AAA only by the portion of the distribution that exceeds the balance in the E&P account and is attributable to the AAA.

Example 15-41. STU S Corporation had accumulated E&P of $100 and an AAA of $50. Sally, its sole shareholder, had a basis for her stock of $50. STU distributed $150 to Sally this year. If an election to accelerate dividend treatment is in effect, the amount distributed is treated as a dividend to the extent of the $100 of E&P. The additional $50 distributed decreased Sally's basis for her stock and STU's AAA by $50 to zero.

Example 15-42. VWX S Corporation distributed $150 to Tim, its sole shareholder. VWX had E&P of $100 and an AAA of $40. Tim had a basis of $40 for his stock. If an election to accelerate dividend treatment is in effect, the amount distributed is treated as a dividend to the extent of the $100 of E&P. The additional $50 distributed reduced Tim's basis for his stock to zero; Tim also reported a $10 gain. VWX's AAA account was reduced to zero.

The election to distribute dividends is not as disadvantageous with respect to double taxation as under prior law because qualified dividends receive preferential rate treatment under § 1(h)(11). Unless the § 1411 tax on net investment income tax applies, the maximum tax rate is 20% and can be as low as 0%. Even if it does apply, the maximum rate is currently only 23.8%.

5. Post-Termination Distributions

An S corporation may completely cease operations when its S status terminates. Alternatively, it may continue operating as a C corporation. If it continues operations, the former S corporation can continue to make tax-free distributions from its AAA if it meets two conditions. The distribution must be in money, and it must be made during the post-termination transition period. Property distributions cannot be made tax-free during a post-termination transition period. If all shareholders consent, the corporation can elect to have distributions applied against earnings before applying them against its AAA. I.R.C. § 1371(e).

The post-termination transition period begins the day after the end of the S corporation's final taxable year as an S corporation. It ends the later of one year after its starting date or the due date plus extensions for filing the tax return for its last year as an S corporation. I.R.C. § 1377(b)(1)(A). Ignoring extensions, the return is due by the 15th day of the third month after the close of its taxable year. I.R.C. § 6072(b). The post-termination transition period also includes the 120-day period of any determination pursuant to an audit that is after the S election terminates. The audit must result in an adjustment of an item of income, loss, or deduction that arose during the S period. That period is the corporation's most recent continuous period as an S corporation. Finally, it includes the 120-day period beginning on the date of a determination that the S election had terminated for a previous taxable year.

G. Redemptions, Liquidations, and Reorganizations

S corporations are not limited to making regular distributions to shareholders. They may also redeem stock from a shareholder. They may make liquidating distributions. They may be parties to reorganizations. Section 1371(a) provides that Subchapter C rules apply to S corporations unless a provision provides otherwise or those rules are inconsistent with the provisions of Subchapter S. Section 1371(c) provides for adjusting the corporation's E&P for various types of distributions.

Because S corporations are pass-through entities and differ in other respects from C corporations, many Subchapter C rules do not apply or apply differently to S corporations. The discussion in this section provides only an overview of redemptions, liquidations, and reorganizations in the S corporation context. Distributions are illustrated by numerous examples in the regulations interpreting § 1368.

1. Redemptions

If an S corporation makes a redemption distribution, the tax consequences are, to some extent, the same as those discussed in Chapter 6. The redemption may qualify as a sale or exchange because it meets the § 302 or § 303 requirements for that status. If it fails to qualify, it may be treated as a dividend distribution if the corporation had E&P.

If the redemption qualifies for treatment as a sale or exchange, and the corporation had E&P, it reduces its E&P account by the redeemed stock's ratable share of E&P. I.R.C. § 312(n)(7). It reduces its AAA account by the redeemed stock's ratable share of that account. Distributions that would be treated as dividends reduce the AAA account before it is reduced for redemption distributions. Reg. § 1.1368-2(d).

If the redemption is not treated as a sale or exchange, the shareholder's tax consequences vary based on whether the corporation had any E&P. If the corporation does not have E&P, the distribution is first applied to the shareholder's basis for her stock. Any amount exceeding basis is treated as gain from the sale or exchange of stock. I.R.C. § 1368(b). If the corporation has E&P, the distribution takes into account the AAA before treating the distribution as a dividend from the E&P account. As was described in Section F, the shareholder reports gain once he has recovered basis. I.R.C. § 1368(c).

2. Liquidations and Deemed Sales

If an S corporation liquidates, its shareholders use § 331 to report gain or loss. I.R.C. § 1371(a). The corporation computes recognized gain or loss under § 336. The loss limitation rules discussed in Chapter 11 apply to S corporations. The shareholders take a fair market value basis for any property they receive. I.R.C. § 334(a).

Because S corporations are pass-through entities, shareholders report their share of corporate gains and losses in addition to their share of corporate operating items. Their tax consequences (income, deduction, and stock basis) are affected by the corporation's gain and loss attributable to the liquidation.

An S corporation can be a target for purposes of a § 338(h)(10) election. Reg. § 1.338(h)(10)-1(b)(4). The S corporation shareholders and the corporation that purchases the S corporation's stock must join in the election. Even shareholders who do not sell their stock must join in the election. Reg. § 1.338(h)(10)-1(c)(3). After the election is made, the S corporation is treated as if it sold and then repurchased its assets, its shareholders report their pro rata share of gain or loss on the deemed sales and adjust their stock basis accordingly. They are treated as having received the S corporation's assets in a liquidating distribution, which might result in their reporting gain or loss. They do not recognize gain or loss on selling their stock to the acquiring corporation. A shareholder who does not sell his stock has his basis adjusted to the stock's fair market value. Reg. § 1.338(h)(10)-1(d)(3)–(5).

The sellers of shares in an S corporation can also be treated as sellers for purposes of § 336(e). Shareholders of an S corporation can make a § 336(e) election when there is a qualified disposition of the S corporation's stock within a 12-month period. The regulations govern their tax computations, which take into account the target's recognized gains and losses on the deemed disposition of its assets and the corporation's results of operations. The regulations also discuss S corporations as new targets and as old targets. Reg. § 1.336-2(b)(1)(iii). An S corporation target loses its S corporation eligibility if any of the acquiring shareholders is an ineligible shareholder or if there are more than the permitted number of shareholders after the purchase. If the target qualifies for S corporation status after the purchase, it must make a new election. Reg. § 1.336-2(b)(1)(ii).

3. Reorganizations

The requirements for maintaining the S election may make it difficult for an S corporation to reorganize and maintain its election. If it is the acquired corporation, it can maintain its status only if it qualifies as a QSub of an acquiring corporation that is itself an S corporation. If it is the acquiring corporation, it cannot transfer its stock to any person who could not be an S corporation shareholder. If an S corporation acquires the assets of another S corporation in a reorganization or liquidation that is covered by the § 381 attribute carryover rules, and either or both corporations have AAA accounts, those accounts are combined. Reg. § 1.1368-2(d)(2). If an S corporation transfers part of its assets in a D reorganization to which § 355 applies, its AAA is allocated between itself and the controlled corporation in a manner that resembles the E&P allocation provided by § 312(h) and its regulations. Reg. § 1.1368-2(d)(3).

Checkpoints

- An S corporation can have no more than 100 shareholders. Family members can be treated as a single shareholder. A retirement trust is treated as one shareholder.
- An S corporation generally can have only individuals as shareholders. Only certain types of trusts and estates can be shareholders.
- A nonresident alien cannot be an S corporation shareholder.
- An S corporation can have only one class of stock outstanding.
- S corporation status is elective.
- Generally, all items of income and deduction pass through to the shareholders of an S corporation. The shareholders report passed-through income on their tax returns even if they do not receive distributions.

- Items pass through on a per-share, per-day basis.
- Items are passed through as nonseparately computed amounts and as separately stated items. An item is separately stated if it could affect tax consequences at the shareholder level differently.
- A shareholder is limited in the losses that he can take to the sum of his basis for his S corporation stock and his basis for any debt the corporation owes him.
- S corporations do not generally pay tax on their taxable income. They may be subject to the built-in gain tax and excess passive investment income tax.
- To the extent that the shareholder has basis for stock or debt, distributions are generally tax-free unless the corporation has E&P. Distributions that exceed a shareholder's basis are treated as gains from a sale or exchange and are probably taxed as capital gains.
- S corporations do not have E&P unless they have a C corporation history. If the corporation has E&P, shareholders' treatment of distributions is affected by the corporation's accumulated adjustments account (AAA), its E&P, and their basis for their stock.

Mastering Corporate Tax Checklist

Chapter 1 · Introduction

- ❑ Business owners can select from several forms, including sole proprietorship, various forms of partnership, C corporation, S corporation, and limited liability company.
- ❑ The check-the-box regulations allow some unincorporated entities to decide whether to be taxed as a corporation or to instead be treated as a partnership or a disregarded entity.
- ❑ Because dividends paid by a C corporation are not deductible, both the corporation and its shareholders are taxed on distributed corporate profits.
- ❑ Transactions that follow statutory language may be ignored if a court finds they do not comport with congressional purpose. Doctrines such as substance over form, business purpose, step transaction, and economic substance may be invoked.
- ❑ Personal service corporations and their employee-owners may lose tax benefits when they are formed or used for the principal purpose of avoiding or evading tax on their employee-owners. The IRS can reallocate income, deductions, and credits between the corporation and the employee-owners.
- ❑ Transactions between related persons may be scrutinized more closely than other transactions. The definition of "related person" is not the same in all contexts.
- ❑ Some Code sections apply even though the Code sections governing the transactions do not directly refer to them. Sections 267(a)(1) and 1239 are examples of such provisions.
- ❑ Different Code sections may define a term in the same way, or they may define it differently.

Chapter 2 · Taxation of C Corporations

- ❑ Many of the rules governing individuals apply, often with modifications, to C corporations. The tax rates applied to C corporations are different from those applied to individuals.

- ❑ In some instances, C corporations are subject to different rules based on their gross receipts, ownership concentration, or status as a personal service corporation.
- ❑ The accumulated earnings tax and personal holding company tax apply to C corporations.
- ❑ A corporation's E&P account reflects its ability to pay taxable dividends. The E&P computation adds some items that are excluded from gross income and subtracts some items that are not deductible in computing taxable income.

Chapter 3 · Funding Corporations

- ❑ A corporation can issue both debt and equity to finance its capital needs.
- ❑ Debt generally involves a fixed obligation to repay and bears interest. Creditors' rights are superior to those of shareholders.
- ❑ The corporation can deduct interest payments. It cannot deduct dividend payments.
- ❑ The distinction between stock and indebtedness is blurred when a corporation issues debt that can be converted into stock or issues debt that is held only by shareholders.
- ❑ Section 385 lists factors the IRS can consider in issuing regulations categorizing an interest in the corporation as stock or indebtedness.
- ❑ A corporation and the holders of a hybrid interest are generally bound by its classification. The government is not bound.

Chapter 4 · Transfers to a Corporation

- ❑ No gain or loss is recognized on the transfer of property solely for stock of a corporation if the transferor(s) control(s) the corporation immediately after the transfer within the meaning of § 368(c).
- ❑ The shareholder's basis and holding period for the property transferred generally carry over to the stock she receives. The corporation generally takes the shareholder's basis and holding period for the property transferred to it.
- ❑ The shareholder recognizes gain, but not loss, if he also receives boot.
- ❑ With exceptions for tax avoidance and liabilities exceeding basis, the shareholder does not treat debt assumption as boot for purposes of gain recognition.
- ❑ Section 362(e) might limit the corporation's basis when it receives property that has a built-in loss.

Chapter 5 · Dividend Distributions

- ❑ A dividend is a distribution of property to a shareholder, made with respect to his stock, out of the corporation's E&P.
- ❑ The corporation has taxable gain if it distributes appreciated property. It cannot deduct a loss if it distributes loss property.
- ❑ A dividend distribution reduces the corporation's E&P, but not below zero. Distributions can offset both current and accumulated E&P.
- ❑ The shareholder has gross income from dividends if the corporation has sufficient E&P.
- ❑ The shareholder reduces his stock basis by distributions that exceed E&P. If basis is reduced to zero, the shareholder reports gain even if he does not sell the stock.
- ❑ Stock in the distributing corporation is generally not property. The shareholder reports no gross income and allocates the basis of the original shares between those shares and the new shares.
- ❑ Some distributions of stock or stock rights are treated as distributions of property and are taxable. The distributions covered by § 305(b) can be used to change shareholders' relative interests in the corporation's E&P or assets. Examples include letting shareholders elect to receive stock or money or distributing stock to some shareholders and money to others. In those situations, the shareholder's basis for the new stock is its fair market value.
- ❑ Current E&P are allocated to distributions pro rata. Accumulated E&P are allocated to distributions only if current E&P are insufficient.

Chapter 6 · Redemption Distributions

- ❑ A redemption involves a corporation acquiring its own stock in exchange for property.
- ❑ Redemptions can be treated as exchanges if the shareholder's stock ownership is sufficiently reduced or eliminated or if other statutory events occur.
- ❑ In determining whether a redemption is treated as a sale, we consider the shareholder's actual and constructive stock ownership.
- ❑ Section 302 redemptions qualify as exchanges if they are not essentially equivalent to a dividend, are substantially disproportionate, are a complete termination of a shareholder's interest, or are a partial liquidation.
- ❑ Section 303 redemptions qualify as exchanges if stock included in the decedent's gross estate meets certain tests based on value, death-related expenses, and time periods.

- ❑ Section 304 applies if stock in one corporation is acquired by a related corporation and the shareholder has more than a 50% ownership interest in both corporations or if the corporations have a parent-subsidiary relationship. Redemptions can satisfy the requirements of § 302 or § 303 even if they are done through a related corporation.
- ❑ When § 306 applies, sales and redemptions of preferred stock may be treated as dividends instead of as exchanges. It applies if the distribution and disposition of preferred stock provide a means for the shareholder to convert ordinary income into capital gain without losing rights to future corporate growth.
- ❑ If a redemption is not treated as an exchange, it is treated as a dividend (assuming adequate E&P). The shareholder's basis for the redeemed stock may be reallocated to his remaining shares or to a related person.
- ❑ Redemptions offer a means for transferring control in a marital dissolution or for accomplishing other ownership shifts. The tax consequences are affected by whether the remaining (or new) shareholders were primarily and unconditionally obligated to acquire the redeemed shares.

Chapter 7 · Introduction to Reorganizations

- ❑ A transaction cannot qualify as a reorganization unless it satisfies the requirements of § 368 and its regulations.
- ❑ The regulations may require business purpose, continuity of interest, and continuity of business enterprise. Doctrines such as step transaction may apply.

Chapter 8 · Acquisitive Reorganizations

- ❑ The A reorganization is a statutory merger or consolidation. The B reorganization is an exchange of voting stock of the acquiring corporation solely for stock of the target corporation. The C reorganization is an exchange of assets solely for voting stock (but up to 20% boot is permitted). The acquisitive D and G reorganizations involve an exchange of assets for stock.
- ❑ The substantially all requirement applies to triangular A, to C, and to acquisitive D reorganizations. An IRS ruling position generally required that 90% of the target's net assets or 70% of its gross assets be acquired.
- ❑ A control requirement applies to B, C, and acquisitive D reorganizations. For B and C reorganizations, control means ownership of stock possessing at least 80% of the total combined voting power of all classes

of stock entitled to vote and at least 80% of the total number of shares of all other classes of stock. For acquisitive D reorganization, the control requirement is lowered to 50% of voting power or stock value.

- ❑ In C and acquisitive D and G reorganizations, the acquired corporation must distribute the assets received in the transaction as well as its other assets. Generally, only one corporation survives.
- ❑ Assets acquired in A, B, C, and G reorganizations can be dropped down to a subsidiary corporation of the acquiring corporation. Administrative provisions permit drop-down of assets in D reorganizations and push-up of assets.
- ❑ The target's shareholders recognize no gain or loss on exchanging their stock solely for stock. Its securities holders recognize no gain or loss on exchanging their securities for stock or securities so long as the principal amount of securities they receive does not exceed the principal amount of the securities they exchange. Basis and holding period carry over.
- ❑ The target recognizes no gain or loss on exchanging its assets for stock or securities. If it receives other property, it does not recognize gain or loss if it distributes that property. If it retains that property, it recognizes gain but not loss.
- ❑ The target's basis and other tax attributes carry over to the acquiring corporation in an acquisitive reorganization other than a B reorganization. The target retains its basis and other attributes following a B reorganization.

Chapter 9 · E and F Reorganizations

- ❑ An E reorganization involves a change in the corporation's ownership structure. None of its assets are acquired; and it does not acquire assets of another corporation.
- ❑ An F reorganization involves no change in ownership structure. The ownership structure after the F reorganization must be identical to that of the prior corporation. One or more shareholders may receive money without preventing the transaction from being an F reorganization.
- ❑ E and F reorganizations are not subject to the continuity of interest and continuity of business enterprise requirements.
- ❑ Shareholders recognize no gain or loss if they receive only stock in exchange for the stock they relinquish. Nonqualified preferred stock may not qualify unless it is received in exchange for nonquali-

fied preferred stock or there is a recapitalization of a family-owned corporation.

Chapter 10 · Divisive Reorganizations; Section 355

- ❑ Spin-offs, split-offs, and split-ups are the major types of § 355 transactions.
- ❑ So long as 80% or more of the stock of a controlled corporation is distributed and the other § 355 requirements are met, the transaction qualifies for nonrecognition.
- ❑ Limits on the application of § 355 are designed to prevent taxpayers from using it as a device for avoiding shareholder-level tax on undistributed E&P. The regulations list both device and nondevice factors.
- ❑ A § 355 transaction that is undertaken for a corporate business purpose will likely qualify for nonrecognition. A corporate business purpose can coexist with a shareholder business purpose so long as the transaction is motivated by the corporate business purpose.
- ❑ Either continuing shareholders or former shareholders of the distributing corporation must continue to hold an interest in the controlled corporation. The continuity of business enterprise requirement is subsumed into the active trade or business requirement.
- ❑ Both distributing and controlled corporations must be engaged in an active trade or business.
- ❑ Section 355 will not apply to the distributing corporation if 50% or more of the stock of the distributing or controlled corporation was acquired by purchase within the five-year period ending on the distribution date.
- ❑ If a transaction qualifies under § 355, no gain or loss will be recognized, the basis of the stock received will generally mirror the basis of the stock exchanged in the transaction, and the shareholder will retain whatever holding period she had in the exchanged stock.
- ❑ If a D/355 transaction occurs, the distributing corporation must meet the requirements of both § 355 and § 368(a)(1)(D).

Chapter 11 · Liquidations

- ❑ In a § 332 liquidation, the subsidiary recognizes no gain or loss on distributions to the corporate parent. It recognizes gain (but not loss) on distributions to minority shareholders.
- ❑ The parent corporation recognizes no gain or loss and takes a carryover basis for any property received in the distribution. It also takes over the subsidiary's holding period for the property and assumes the subsidiary's E&P account.

- ❑ The parent corporation must own at least 80% of the subsidiary's voting power and stock value on the date the liquidation plan is adopted and until it receives the final liquidating distribution.
- ❑ If § 332 does not apply, the liquidating corporation recognizes gain or loss on distributions to shareholders in complete liquidation.
- ❑ Section 336(d) may disallow or limit the corporation's loss on certain distributions to related persons or on sales, exchanges, or distributions of property transferred to it for the purpose of generating a loss.
- ❑ The shareholders recognize gain or loss, which is generally capital rather than ordinary. Their basis for property received in the liquidation is its fair market value at distribution. Their holding period does not include the corporation's holding period for the property.

Chapter 12 · Carryover of Tax Attributes

- ❑ Section 381 generally provides that certain tax attributes carry over in § 332 liquidations and certain nondivisive reorganizations.
- ❑ The taxable year of the transferor or distributor corporation ends on the date of the transfer or distribution.
- ❑ The acquiring corporation cannot carry back any NOLs of the acquired corporation.
- ❑ Section 382 severely limits the use of the NOLs of a loss corporation after an ownership change.
- ❑ An ownership change occurs when one or more 5-percent shareholders increase their interest in the corporation by more than 50 percentage points.
- ❑ Section 383 applies the § 382 limitations to certain excess credits, capital losses, and foreign tax credits.
- ❑ Section 384 imposes limitations when a gain corporation is acquired.

Chapter 13 · Taxable Acquisitions: Sections 338, 336(e), and 1060

- ❑ The § 338 election is available only if a qualified stock purchase is made. That requires a purchase of 80% or more of the stock of the target corporation within a 12-month period.
- ❑ The target corporation is treated as having sold its assets and then repurchased them.
- ❑ Gain or loss on the deemed sale is the difference between the aggregate deemed sale price (ADSP) and the target's basis for the assets. The basis of the assets deemed purchased is the adjusted grossed-up basis (AGUB) in the assets.

- ❑ The § 338(g) election is made by the purchasing corporation. The § 338(h)(10) election is made by both the purchasing corporation and the selling group.
- ❑ A § 336(e) election is available to a corporation that sells, exchanges, or distributes its stock in a target corporation that it controlled. If it makes the election, the target is treated as selling its assets to an unrelated purchaser and then repurchasing those assets at fair market value.
- ❑ The regulations for § 336(e) reflect much of the rules, with language based on disposition rather than on purchase, used in § 338.
- ❑ Section 1060 applies certain allocation rules of § 338 to a purchase that is an applicable asset acquisition (generally a trade or business).

Chapter 14 · Controlled and Affiliated Corporations; Consolidated Returns

- ❑ A controlled group can be a parent-subsidiary controlled group, a brother-sister controlled group, a combined group, or an insurance group.
- ❑ The controlled group is treated as one corporation for certain tax benefits. For example, group members cannot separately benefit from the § 11 graduated tax rates.
- ❑ An affiliated group is a group of corporations whose stock is owned directly or indirectly by a common parent. Group members must own at least 80% of the voting power and stock value of each group member other than the common parent.
- ❑ An affiliated group of corporations can elect to file a consolidated return for all the members of the group.
- ❑ Once an election is made to consolidate, it is difficult to deconsolidate the group.
- ❑ Group tax liability is computed as the sum of each group member's separate liability, adjusted for certain consolidated items listed in the regulations.
- ❑ Generally, transactions between group members are ignored until the property or the member leaves the group. The basis investment adjustment rule ensures that the basis one member has in another's stock reflects fluctuations in its investment.

Chapter 15 · S Corporations and Their Shareholders

- ❑ An S corporation can have no more than 100 shareholders. Family members can be treated as a single shareholder. A retirement trust is treated as one shareholder.

- ❑ An S corporation generally can have only individuals as shareholders. Only certain types of trusts and estates can be shareholders.
- ❑ An S corporation can have only one class of stock outstanding.
- ❑ Generally, all items of income and deduction pass through to the shareholders of an S corporation. The shareholders report these items on their tax returns even if they do not receive distributions.
- ❑ A shareholder is limited in the losses that he can take to the sum of his basis for his S corporation stock and his basis for any debt the corporation owes him.
- ❑ S corporations do not generally pay tax on their taxable income. They may be subject to the built-in gain tax and excess passive investment income tax.
- ❑ To the extent that the shareholder has basis for stock or debt, distributions are generally tax-free unless the corporation has E&P. Distributions that exceed a shareholder's basis are treated as gains from a sale or exchange and are probably taxed as capital gains.
- ❑ S corporations do not have E&P unless they have a C corporation history.

Table of Internal Revenue Code Sections

Table of Regulations

Treasury Regulations

Proposed Treasury Regulations

Temporary Treasury Regulations

Table of IRS Rulings

Table of Cases

Index